Penguin Education

Economics of Retailing

Edited by K. A. Tucker
and B. S. Yamey

Penguin Modern Economics Readings

General Editor

B. J. McCormick

Advisory Board

K. J. W. Alexander
R. W. Clower
G. R. Fisher
P. Robson
J. Spraos
H. Townsend

Economics of Retailing

Selected Readings

Edited by K. A. Tucker and B. S. Yamey

Penguin Education

Penguin Education
A Division of Penguin Books Ltd,
Harmondsworth, Middlesex, England
Penguin Books Inc, 7110 Ambassador Road,
Baltimore, Md 21207, USA
Penguin Books Australia Ltd,
Ringwood, Victoria, Australia

First published 1973
This selection copyright © K. A. Tucker and B. S. Yamey, 1973
Introduction and notes copyright © K. A. Tucker and B. S. Yamey, 1973
Copyright acknowledgement for items in this volume will be found on page 361

Made and printed in Great Britain by
Richard Clay (The Chaucer Press) Ltd,
Bungay, Suffolk
Set in Monotype Times

Contents

Introduction

Everyone knows about retailing. By its nature, retailing is ubiquitous, in rich and poor countries alike. Children, students and housewives who do not participate in the economic system as producers of goods or services for monetary reward nevertheless have frequent and numerous contacts with retailing firms and their activities. Retailing is also visible. Much of its activities takes place in public, often even in the public highway. Changes in the structure of retailing take place for all to see. Large retail units replace small ones; and new forms of retailing replace old. Changes in the location of retail activities take place before one's eyes. In one shopping centre dress shops and shoe shops edge out grocery shops and fishmongers. Elsewhere brand-new shopping complexes on the periphery of cities, towns and suburbs are set up, and in some places the old-established city centres – which had for decades been the hub of retailing activity – seem on the point of decline and decay.

One might have thought that retailing, being so widely experienced, would have been exploited in text-books on general economics or on more specialized branches such as price theory to provide examples to illustrate economic phenomena or processes. Indeed, some discussion of aspects of retailing is to be found in the works of Adam Smith, John Stuart Mill, Alfred Marshall and Knut Wicksell. But in contemporary general text-books references to retailing are rare. Alchian and Allen's *University Economics* has one reference to retailing, where retailers are included among those who are engaged in 'information-economizing activity'. Perhaps it is even more surprising that retailing or retailers do not appear in the indexes of either Chamberlin's *The Theory of Monopolistic Competition* or Robinson's *The Economics of Imperfect Competition* – though 'red-haired men', 'railways' and 'rolling-mill' appear in the index of the latter.

The fact is that in much of the ostensibly relevant branches of economic theory and analysis the favoured treatment abstracts from the presence of intermediaries, such as retailers, between the production and the consumption of goods and services: the treatment is as if the producer sold to the consumer. This type of abstraction might be wholly desirable within the context of the specific purposes to be served by the theory or analysis. Indeed, some of the more specialized studies or analyses of retailing itself, including some of the readings in the present volume, are fitted into the limiting analytical framework which predominates in economic theory.

The retailer is viewed as the producer of retail services which are bought (together with the goods themselves) by consumers, who in the process 'consume' the retail services. Another abstraction in much of economic analysis is to assume that the product of the 'producer' is homogeneous and standardized. This treatment is sometimes followed in more specialized analyses of retailing. The 'product' of retailing – the retail service – is assumed to be a standardized item or bundle of items, for which a uniform price (margin) is charged by the retailer. Some of our selections adopt this approach; and they gain more in additional analytical insight than they lose in their apparent lack of realistic detail.

Other papers included in this volume demonstrate that the treatment just referred to is inappropriate for the examination of certain important phenomena and problems in retailing. Thus the consideration of retailing in isolation as a separate activity is misleading when applied to such matters as the pricing and marketing policies of manufacturers, notably of branded and otherwise differentiated goods. Much that is of interest in the retail field, both to business firms and to those concerned with issues of public policy, concerns the forays of manufacturers into retailing, either by ownership or by long-term contractual arrangements. And retailing is a fascinating field of applied study as well because of the relative ease with which the individual consumer – or sometimes collectivities of consumers – can do for himself some of the things which previously had been done for him by retailers.

The shifting of activities between the retailing sector and the household sector has not been in a single direction, while the determinants of the decisions of consumers at a particular period of time or in a particular economic environment are highly complex. Their analysis in a specific setting is a rewarding exercise in applied economics, involving an appraisal of consumer preferences, the effects of consumer incomes and wealth, working habits and opportunities for paid labour, technological opportunities for substitution between labour and capital in the provision of services, and so on. At the same time such shifts between activities in the retailing and the household sectors greatly complicate investigations into such topics as inter-temporal or international differences in the 'size', output or efficiency of the retailing sector. The formidable complexities present a challenge to economists. The challenge will not, however, be met as long as there prevails a preference among economists for the avoidance of complexities and for making rather cavalier use of available statistics.

The treatment of the output of a retailer as being that of a standardized service has been mentioned above as a second kind of abstraction. Again, however, much that is of interest in the economics of retailing is left out by this treatment. Typically, different producers and consumers make different use of services supplied by a particular retailer (and, of course, different retailers make available different combinations of services). To take some obvious examples, some households want credit, and others do not; some buy in large quantities at a time, others in small; some regularly buy a large proportion of the available range of goods, others concentrate on a small sub-set of the range; and yet others make sporadic visits and selective purchases. The range of services offered by a retailer is one of the variables he can deploy in the process of competition. On the other hand, difficulties arising from organizational constraints or from the costs of making the necessary discriminations in pricing make it likely that established categories of retailers or types of retail operation tend to become progressively less able to meet the special requirements of some producers or consumers, or new requirements reflecting changes in tastes, needs or technologies. The establishment of new types of retail operation is a major form in which competitive forces assert themselves in the market-place. Both historical changes in the structure of retailing and contemporary changes in retailing methods can be explained to a large extent in terms of the complexities which are generally (and often usefully in some contexts) assumed away in the standard analytical approach.

The applied economist can also find in retailing a fruitful field for the study of the impact and implications of a variety of measures of public policy. The range of intervention is indeed wide. The location of new retailing centres or premises is often controlled by local authorities. Shop opening hours are rarely left to the free play of the market. Safety regulations affect certain kinds of retailing, such as that of petrol. Restrictive agreements either among retailers or between manufacturers and retailers are prohibited in some countries and not in others; and the relevant law differs. Advertising by retailers may or may not be controlled. Certain pricing practices may or may not be regulated; and so on. Moreover, sometimes the number of retailers is subject to official limitation for a variety of reasons, and sometimes in disregard of Adam Smith's well known pronouncement:

The prejudices of some political writers against shopkeepers and tradesmen are altogether without foundation. So far is it from being necessary, either to tax them, or to restrict their numbers, that they can never be multiplied so as to hurt the public, though they may so as to hurt one another.

There does not appear to us to be a special 'economic theory' of retailing or even a need for such a theory. Nevertheless, it is useful to talk of a branch of applied economics which can be called the economics of retailing. Within this branch there are phenomena, processes, problems and issues of a kind familiar to the general applied economist who is skilled in the use of the standard tools of the trade. But, as we have suggested, there are within this branch of applied economics other subjects of study which call for special-purpose tools and more distinctive methods of approach – which may, however, prove to be of utility in other branches of applied economics. Our selection of readings covers both these classes of subject-matter while at the same time it deals with major problems and issues of specific interest within the field of retailing.

The readings in Part One of this volume are concerned with pricing policies and the behaviour of retail prices. Several short extracts from the works of early authors are included both because they are of interest in the development of the subject and also because they clearly expose the nature of some of the main phenomena to be explained. Some of the readings also illustrate in some detail the more general points made in this introduction about features which are present in retailing to a particularly marked degree.

Some of the readings in Part Two also bear on these general points, while their main emphasis is on competition and concentration in retailing. (The distinction between Parts One and Two is unavoidably blurred.) Inevitably they are concerned to some degree with the relevance of analytical models of market structure and pricing, and with the efficiency of the retailing system.

The readings in Part Three are concerned with cost functions in retailing, the structure of costs, and differences in costs among different sizes of firms or units. They have a bearing on the question of the efficiency of resource use in retailing. Studies in this general field are seriously affected by changes and differences in the composition and quality of retail services, and also by possible measurement biases in the available data.

Some of the real-world complexities which bedevil work on subjects falling within the scope of Part Three are of obvious importance to the organization and conduct of retail operations in such matters as range of commodities to be handled, services to be supplied, and pricing policies to be introduced and implemented.

The four articles in Part Four are concerned specifically with the determination of the optimal combination of major features of retail operation under the control of the individual retailer acting within the constraints of competition, factor prices, technology and consumer preferences and opportunities.

The concluding Part Five is headed 'Other Aspects' and has three papers. The first two deal with pricing arrangements – the first with an aspect of resale price maintenance as a marketing strategy available (where permitted by law) to manufacturers, and the second with trading stamps, one pricing technique available to retailers. Both these arrangements have attracted a good deal of public attention. The third paper analyses aspects of trading, including retailing, in a less developed country, Nigeria. It examines features of the economic environment which help to explain phenomena which are also to be found in other less developed countries and, indeed, were present in earlier periods in the now developed countries.

The rapid changes in the structure of retailing, in retailing practices, and in legislation affecting retailing in Britain and the United States may give a somewhat dated air to certain examples presented in some of the less recent Readings. Since the reader should have no difficulty in adjusting his perspective, we have not attempted to provide editorial guidance in the form of annotations.

Because there is no special economic theory or analysis more or less uniquely necessary for the study of the economics of retailing, and because the economics of retailing is best viewed as a branch of applied economics, it follows that several of the other volumes of Penguin Readings include papers of close interest to readers of the present volume. From the point of view of economic analysis the relevance of *Price Theory* and *The Theory of the Firm* is apparent. *The Economics of Industrial Structure* is relevant not only inasmuch as retailing is an 'industry' but also because of the importance of vertical relationships between manufacturers of goods and their distributors. At the other end of the producer–consumer spectrum, the relevance of *Consumer Behaviour* needs no stressing. Studies in *Urban Economics* consider some of the environmental determinants and constraints which affect the location and nature of retailing activity. Finally, several of the papers in *Monopoly and Competition* refer more or less specifically to matters of interest to the student of the economics of retailing.

References
ALCHIAN, A. A., and ALLEN, W. R. (1967), *University Economics*, 2nd edn, Wadsworth.
CHAMBERLIN, E. H. (1933), *The Theory of Monopolistic Competition*, Harvard University Press.
ROBINSON, J. (1936), *The Economics of Imperfect Competition* Macmillan.

Part One
Retail Prices and Pricing Policies

Readings 1, 2 and 3 are the views of three famous economists – Mill, Marshall and Wicksell – on the determinants of retail prices, including influences such as custom, consumer preferences as well as consumer ignorance, and the nature of retailing costs. Each author is concerned to see to what extent the analysis of retail prices could be accommodated within his theory of prices.

Turning from the past to the present, Holton (Reading 4) analyses the pricing policies and practices of large-scale retailers in terms of price discrimination to maximize profits, taking into account inter-relationships in demand as well as features of retailing costs. Jung (Reading 5) explains differences in the retail prices paid for automobiles in terms of the bargaining strategies of buyers and the extent of information disclosed by retailers. Cassady (Reading 6) shows the importance of the actions of suppliers in certain types of intensely competitive situations in retail markets.

1 J. S. Mill

Retail Prices and Competition

Excerpt from J. S. Mill, *Principles of Political Economy with Some of their Applications to Social Philosophy*, 1848, new edn Routledge & Kegan Paul, 1912, pp. 246–7 and 440–41.

There is no proposition which meets us in the field of political economy oftener than this – that there cannot be two prices in the same market. Such undoubtedly is the natural effect of unimpeded competion; yet every one knows that there are, almost always,[1] two prices in the same market. Not only are there in every large town, and in almost every trade, cheap shops and dear shops, but the same shop often sells the same article at different prices to different customers: and, as a general rule, each retailer adapts his scale of prices to the class of customers whom he expects. The wholesale trade, in the great articles of commerce, is really under the dominion of competition. There, the buyers as well as sellers are traders or manufacturers, and their purchases are not influenced by indolence or vulgar finery, nor depend on the smaller motives of personal convenience, but are business transactions. In the wholesale markets therefore it is true, as a general proposition, that there are not two prices at one time for the same thing: there is at each time and place a market price, which can be quoted in a price-current. But retail price, the price paid by the actual consumer, seems to feel very slowly and imperfectly the effect of competition; and when competition does exist, it often, instead of lowering prices, merely divides the gains of the high price among a greater number of dealers. Hence it is that, of the price paid by the consumer, so large a proportion is absorbed by the gains of retailers; and any one who inquires into the amount which reaches the hands of those who made the things he buys, will often be astonished at its smallness. When indeed the market, being that of a great city, holds out a sufficient inducement to large capitalists to engage in retail operations, it is generally found a better speculation to attract a large business by underselling others, than merely to divide the field of employment with them. This influence of competition is making itself felt more and more through the principal branches of retail trade in the large towns; and the rapidity and cheapness of transport, by making consumers less dependent on the dealers in their immediate neighbourhood, are tending to assimilate more and more the whole country to a large town: but hitherto

1. Substituted in the 3rd edn (1852) for the original 'very often'.

[1848] it is only in the great centres of business that retail transactions have been chiefly, or even much, determined, by competition. Elsewhere it rather acts, when it acts at all, as an occasional disturbing influence; the habitual regulator is custom, modified from time to time by notions existing in the minds of purchasers and sellers of some kind of equity or justice.

In many trades the terms on which business is done are a matter of positive arrangement among the trade, who use the means they always possess of making the situation of any member of the body, who departs from its fixed customs, inconvenient or disagreeable. It is well known that the bookselling trade was, until lately, one of these, and that notwithstanding the active spirit of rivalry in the trade, competition did not produce its natural effect in breaking down the trade rules.[2] All professional remuneration is regulated by custom. The fees of physicians, surgeons, and barristers, the charges of attorneys, are nearly invariable. Not certainly for want of abundant competition in those professions, but because the competition operates by diminishing each competitor's chance of fees, not by lowering the fees themselves.

Since custom stands its ground against competition to so considerable an extent, even where, from the multitude of competitors and the general energy in the pursuit of gain, the spirit of competition is strongest, we may be sure that this is much more the case where people are content with smaller gains, and estimate their pecuniary interest at a lower rate when balanced against their ease or their pleasure. I believe it will often be found, in Continental Europe, that prices and charges, of some or of all sorts, are much higher in some places than in others not far distant, without its being possible to assign any other cause than that it has always been so: the customers are used to it, and acquiesce in it. An enterprising competitor, with sufficient capital, might force down the charges, and make his fortune during the process; but there are no enterprising competitors; those who have capital prefer to leave it where it is, or to make less profit by it in a more quiet way. [. . .]

[. . .] Before commencing the inquiry into the laws of value and price, I have one further observation to make. I must give warning, once for all, that the cases I contemplate are those in which values and prices are determined by competition alone. In so far only as they are thus determined can they be reduced to any assignable law. The buyers must be supposed as studious to buy cheap, as the sellers to sell dear. The values and prices, therefore, to which our conclusions apply, are mercantile values and prices; such prices as are quoted in price-currents; prices in the wholesale markets, in which buying as well as selling is a matter of business; in which the

2. Until the 4th edn (1857) the text ran: 'the bookselling trade is one of these . . . competition does not produce' etc.

buyers take pains to know, and generally do know, the lowest price at which an article of a given quality can be obtained; and in which, therefore, the axiom is true, that there cannot be for the same article, of the same quality, two prices in the same market. Our propositions will be true in a much more qualified sense of retail prices; the prices paid in shops for articles of personal consumption. For such things there often are not merely two, but many prices, in different shops, or even in the same shop; habit and accident having as much to do in the matter as general causes. Purchases for private use, even by people in business, are not always made on business principles: the feelings which come into play in the operation of getting, and in that of spending their income, are often extremely different. Either from indolence, or carelessness, or because people think it fine to pay and ask no questions, three-fourths of those who can afford it give much higher prices than necessary for the things they consume; while the poor often do the same for ignorance and defect of judgment, want of time for searching and making inquiry, and not infrequently from coercion, open or disguised. For these reasons, retail prices do not follow with all the regularity which might be expected the action of the causes which determine wholesale prices. The influence of those causes is ultimately felt in the retail markets, and is the real source of such variations in retail prices as are of a general and permanent character. But there is no regular or exact correspondence. Shoes of equally good quality are sold in different shops at prices which differ considerably; and the price of leather may fall without causing the richer class of buyers to pay less for shoes. Nevertheless, shoes do sometimes fall in price; and when they do, the cause is always some such general circumstance as the cheapening of leather: and when leather is cheapened, even if no difference shows itself in shops frequented by rich people, the artizan and the labourer generally get their shoes cheaper, and there is a visible diminution in the contract prices at which shoes are delivered for the supply of a workhouse or of a regiment. In all reasoning about prices, the proviso must be understood, 'supposing all parties to take care of their own interest.' Inattention to these distinctions has led to improper applications of the abstract principles of political economy, and still oftener to an undue discrediting of those principles, through their being compared with a different sort of facts from those which they contemplate, or which can fairly be expected to accord with them. [. . .]

2 A. Marshall

Retail Prices

A. Marshall, 'Retail Prices', from an undated MS, in A. C. Pigou (ed.), *Memorials of Alfred Marshall*, Macmillan, 1925, pp. 353–7.

A retail dealer when once he has established a good connection has always had a partial and limited local monopoly. If he has used it ill, he has lost it sooner or later. But, so long as he has retained it, he has not been under the necessity of adjusting his charge for each particular service to the cost of that service. His prices may be arbitrary to an extent that is impossible in the case of middlemen or ordinary producers who supply business customers. For a business customer will scrutinize the charge for each individual thing; and, if that charge is above its true cost, he will find someone prepared to supply it at its true cost: if he fails to do this, he is likely to fail in business altogether; since a small percentage on the things which he buys may affect his net profits by a large percentage. But the private consumer has often better things to do with his time than to give it to discovering the cheapest market for each class of purchases; and, not being a good judge of quality, his judgment is often mistaken when he does try. The retailer, knowing this, is apt to adapt his charges not to the cost of the services rendered, but to what the consumer will bear: he is apt to charge highly in those branches of his business in which his clientele cannot form a good judgment for themselves or are unlikely to trouble themselves to buy in the cheapest market.

For instance the customer seldom knows when the wholesale price of a thing has fallen, and will probably expect to be supplied at his old price; so the retailer, unless for some special reason, is slow to follow a fall in wholesale prices. There may indeed be a special reason to the contrary. He may seize the opportunity of using that commodity as a decoy to attract customers: he may put down its price so low that it no longer pays its share of the general expenses of his establishment, and advertise the price prominently. Or some rival may have done just that and compelled him to follow suit. Sooner or later something of this kind is certain to happen. The longer retailers generally have delayed to follow a fall in wholesale prices, the more striking is the effect which an ambitious firm can attain by prominent offers of large quantities of the commodity at a very low price: and for a long time to come the remaining retailers may find themselves partly crowded out. The fear then that a long delay to lower the price may be disastrous to them partly overcomes their unwillingness to move, even before the general public has learnt that they ought to move. But the unwillingness is strong; the gain to be got by selling at the old price to contented customers is clear; the danger may not seem pressing; the wholesale price may perhaps rise again and a hasty movement may need to be soon retraced. Again, every change is an evil in itself: it does not press only on old-fashioned tradesmen; but is sometimes specially troublesome to progressive retailers, who bring out expensively priced catalogues at intervals, and encourage customers to send orders in writing which can be filled up with great economy of labour in the warehouse without touching the open shop. When therefore the retailer thinks it no longer safe to ignore a fall in wholesale price, he often prefers giving a rather better quality at the old price, to formally lowering his price. He thus pleases his customers, does not bruit about the fact that wholesale prices have fallen, does not disturb his price list; and yet he puts as great a difficulty in the way of a rival, aiming a sensational stroke, as if he had lowered his price.

Lastly the retailer's working expenses are not affected by wholesale price. If that falls by say a quarter, he has made the full corresponding reduction in retail price when he has deducted a quarter of the old wholesale price, a quarter of the insurance against risk that the commodity would depreciate before sale, and rather less than a quarter of his own net profits. Hence the retail price cannot be expected to fall in the same ratio as the wholesale price, unless there has been meanwhile a reduction in the proportion which the retailer's working expenses bear to his turnover. And, though such a reduction may be in progress and in fact has been in constant progress for many years, it would not except by accident make a perceptible advance during a rapid fluctuation of wholesale prices. These seem to be the chief causes of the well-known fact that retail prices seldom fluctuate downwards as far and as fast as the corresponding wholesale prices.

Retail prices are rather quicker to follow upward than downward movements of wholesale prices for several reasons. When, as often happens, there is an understanding among retailers in the same trade as to prices, a rise in the wholesale market is more likely than a fall to stimulate prompt common action; and trade etiquette is apt to condemn as aggressive the action of a retailer who refuses to go with the others, on the ground that he has laid in a large stock before the rise in price. And even where there is no such understanding, the retailer stands to gain something in hand by promptly following a rise, just as he does by delaying to follow a fall.

But on the other hand the customer who is jolted out of his habit, finding the price raised against him, is apt to be set on the inquiry whether he cannot do better elsewhere. So the retailer prefers keeping the price nominally fixed, but supplying a rather inferior quality. And as in the case of falling prices a temporary change, which may need soon to be reversed, is inconvenient; and in any case the rise in retail price corresponding to a rise in wholesale price ought not to be in equal proportion, because working expenses are not affected by the change.

Thus then a fall in wholesale prices tends to raise, a rise in wholesale prices tends to lower, the qualities of the goods retailed under the same name. The real retail price, that is the price account being taken of quality, falls a good deal more slowly than the wholesale price; and it rises rather more slowly. Fluctuations of the nominal price are smaller and slower than those of real retail price, which again are smaller and slower than those of wholesale price. When, as before 1873, prices were generally rising, adulteration was rampant in almost all classes of goods. The following period of almost steadily falling prices saw a general dwindling of the area covered by adulteration. About 1873 'woollen' goods were largely made of cotton: twenty years later cotton was seldom found except in fabrics where it served some useful purpose; or again, in fancy dress materials, the fashion for which had extended downwards to strata which demanded cheap stuffs for occasional wear during the short life of the fashion. Of course there are numerous exceptions: the progress of chemical and mechanical science is always bringing cheaper substitutes, which are more taking or will really answer the purchasers' purposes better than the earlier substitutes: and they will make their way in spite of a fall in the price of the genuine commodity. But this does not impair the truth of the broad proposition that a rise in price increases and a fall in price diminishes the inclination of retailers to offer inferior goods to their customers, rather than to tempt them with better goods than they have bought before.

It stands to reason that retail prices follow wholesale prices the less closely the larger the elements of partial monopoly and of expenses of working that enter into them; and therefore, other things being equal, the smaller the quantities in which they are retailed. The retail price of milk scarcely fluctuates at all: a fall of 50 per cent in the price of tea is not likely to be reflected in the charge made for a cup of afternoon tea at a fashionable hotel. Railway companies, the largest of retail dealers, do not revise their list of passenger fares to meet a fluctuation in the price of coal; unless they had nearly decided on that course on other grounds, and the rise in the price of coal serves to precipitate their action, as a heavy shower of rain may bring down a rock that is already almost on the move.

Again in commodities such as beer and tobacco, which are sold by the quart or ounce for a few pence, a small variation in nominal price is not possible. So small alterations in wholesale price (or in cost, for the retailer is often an agent of the producer), including those due to taxation, work themselves out in changes of quality, unless it happens that a change in nominal price had already been impending. Things which are not sold by measure, but by name, are altered quickly in quantity; and, since selling by name is the rule in backward districts, retail prices in them are often astonishingly sensitive.[1]

Further, there must always be a good many movements of retail price which stand in no relation to changes in the wholesale trade, or are even in opposite directions. They are like snow flakes which rise as they fly past a house in a strong wind, not because gravitation is in abeyance, but because it is overborne by the force of wind eddies. Thus, when fashion changes, average retail prices of dress stuffs may fall while wholesale prices are rising; because in the former goods that are going out preponderate and in the latter goods that are coming in. When a harvest of high quality is followed by one in which much of the grain was spoilt, old flour will be worth more than new; and retailers may be raising the prices of their remaining stocks, while wholesale prices show a decline. Again, an individual retailer may move the price of a certain commodity apparently at random, when he or a neighbouring rival begins or ceases to make it a catch article; or when the stock he has laid in turns out to be in bad condition and must be cleared out at a sacrifice; and so on. But all cases of this kind put together cover a very small part of the transactions of life: and, it would not have been worth while to call attention to them at all, were it not that they have furnished sensational material to writers who have argued that retail prices generally are arbitrary and scarcely at all subject to economic law.

1. For instance, in 1878, when the taxes on salt were readjusted throughout India, being raised in the southern half and lowered in the northern, it was expected by many that the rule of custom and the smallness of retail purchases would prevent the raiyat from feeling the change for a long time to come. But the result was opposite. Salt was retailed by the pinch. And from the day when the new rule came into operation, the pinch was increased in size in the northern, and diminished in the southern half.

3 J. G. K. Wicksell

Pricing in Retail Trades

J. G. K. Wicksell, 'Pricing in retail trades', excerpt from J. G. K. Wicksell, *Lectures on Political Economy*, Routledge & Kegan Paul, 1934, vol. 1, pp. 86–8 (trans. by E. Classen of the original of 1901).

Retail prices are frequently regarded as exceptions both to the law of costs and generally to every rational process of price formation, which is all the more remarkable since these prices are the only ones which are of direct interest to the consumer and which are directly influenced by consumption. Yet the laws of retail prices are perhaps not so difficult to ascertain and do not seem, in the main, to depend on any other factors than those which we have already treated, except that they are more complex and more difficult to unravel. To a considerable extent, the apparent divergence of retail prices from the law of costs and from wholesale prices is to be regarded as an example of the phenomenon of *joint supply* – which we have just considered. Unlike the wholesaler, whose general costs for his whole business constitute only a small part of his annual turnover, the retailer's general costs for premises, heating, lighting, advertisement, wages for his assistants and for his own labour, etc., are very considerable. The first item in particular assumes large proportions since, for the convenience of his customers and for purposes of advertisement he must seek to acquire business premises which are as central as possible. What proportion of these general costs shall be apportioned to each parcel of goods, over and above the purchase or wholesale price, cannot be determined *a priori*, but depends upon a number of variable circumstances. It is of great importance in this connection that certain kinds of goods require much more *expert knowledge* for their valuation than others; the latter, such as sugar, flour, etc., the quality of which anybody can easily judge, yield, if I am not mistaken, a comparatively small profit. With the former goods, on the other hand, the buyer, if he is not exceptional in possessing such knowledge, will, in order not to be sold inferior goods, deal with a seller in whom he has confidence. The service which the retailer thus renders him is that of an expert buyer, and the customer quite reasonably has to pay him a relatively higher price.

The desire for stable retail prices must also be taken into account. For many customers it is of great importance to be able to determine their household expenses well in advance. Retailers, who usually have a fixed circle of customers, therefore endeavour to afford this advantage of approximately fixed prices, which they calculate so that the profit and loss of good and bad times to some extent cancel out. Naturally, greater and more permanent variations in wholesale prices are ultimately reflected in retail prices – though, as a rule, later and in a modified form – just as a thermometer buried deep in the ground responds slowly to changes of temperature on the surface.[1]

In conclusion, we should not forget that practically every retailer possesses, within his immediate circle, what we may call an actual sales *monopoly*, even if, as we shall soon see, it is based only on the ignorance and lack of organization of the buyers. He cannot, of course, like a true monopolist, raise prices at will – only in places remote from trade centres can a considerable local rise in prices occur – but if he maintains the same prices and qualities as his competitors, he can almost always count upon his immediate neighbourhood for customers. The result is not infrequently an *excess of retailers*, apparently for the convenience, but really to *the injury, of the consumers*. If, for example, two shops of the same kind are situated at different ends of the same street, it would be natural that their respective markets would meet in the middle of the street. Now if a new shop of the same kind is opened in the middle of the street each of the others will, sooner or later, lose some of its customers to the new shop, since the people living round the middle of the street believe that if they get the same goods at the same price they are saving time and trouble by making their purchases at the nearest shop. In this, however, they are mistaken, for the original shops which have now lost some of their customers without being able to reduce their overhead expenses to a corresponding degree, will gradually be compelled to raise their prices – and the same applies to the new competitors who have been obliged from the beginning to content themselves with a smaller turnover. This should

1. In an essay in *Ekon. Tidskrift*, October 1908, and also in his work, *Den ekonomiska fördelningen och Kriserna*, Brock has sought to prove that the above conception of the relation between retail and wholesale prices is not correct. Retail prices, in his view, show a strong tendency to follow wholesale prices *upwards*, but very little tendency to follow them *downwards*. The statistics (from America) on which Brock bases this assertion would seem to show merely that of recent years retail prices have, on the whole, risen as compared with wholesale prices; a fact which, owing to the great relative increase of retailers, is in itself probable and is quite in accordance with what we are about to say. As a general doctrine, Brock's view (and that of Lexio and others) is clearly absurd; it would imply that retail prices would diverge more and more from wholesale prices at each cyclical fluctuation – which would lead to absurd consequences. Obviously, we do not attribute any altruistic motives to retailers when we speak of their endeavour to keep prices as steady as possible for their customers' convenience. It is well understood that it is in the interest of every business man to satisfy his customers.

explain the observation which is said to have been made on the abolition of the *octroi* – the tax on the entry of goods into a town, common on the continent – that the expected reduction in prices never took place, though the number of retailers considerably increased. The correct remedy, unless one of the competitors (such as a great store) manages to overshadow all the others, is clearly the formation of some form of organization among buyers. But so long as such an association does not exist – and between persons in different positions in life and without more intimate bonds it is extremely difficult to establish – the anomaly must remain that competition may sometimes raise prices instead of always lowering them, as one would expect.

4 R. H. Holton

Price Discrimination in Supermarkets

R. H. Holton, 'Price discrimination at retail: the supermarket case', *Journal of Industrial Economics*, vol. 6, 1957, pp. 13–32.

In spite of the quite extensive study of business firms' pricing practices over the past twenty-five years, the application of the theory of the firm to the retailing case has been left at an unnecessarily primitive stage.[1] For the most part the published discussions of the competitive equilibrium in retailing posit single-product firms, an assumption which can be viewed as unrealistic.[2] This paper is an attempt to establish a more adequate theoretical framework for explaining the price and product policies of retail firms. Primarily because empirical support for the thesis expounded here is most accessible in food retailing, the supporting evidence will be mostly in reference to supermarkets, but the conclusions would seem to be equally significant for other types of retailing.

Although it may be granted immediately that retail firms are almost always multi-product firms, there is evidence of some confusion over the nature of the product. Several writers have noted that the output of retailing consists not of the goods sold to customers but really of the services of storage, selling, wrapping, delivery, credit extension and so forth.[3] But this kind of statement makes retailing appear more unique than it really is. By the same logic we must admit that the automobile manufacturer's out-

1. Part of the explanation of this situation lies in the economists' general lack of interest in the distributive sector. Perhaps this is partially due to the fact that so many of the problems in the area become analytically messy when we must abandon one of our most venerable assumptions, namely that consumer tastes and preferences are given. And there may be a feeling among economists that the whole field of marketing is not quite honorable because marketing men so frequently create value by changing consumer indifference maps for their own benefit rather than by producing goods to sell into a world of given indifference functions.

2. See Aubert-Krier (1954, pp. 281–300); Hall (1949), especially chapter 3; Smithies (1939, pp. 215–21); and Lewis (1945) [Reading 7]. Due (1941, pp. 380–97), is an exception but the full implication of the multi-product nature of the firm was not worked out. Several authors have written on price policies of retail firms, using the multi-product assumption, but none of these have advanced their discussions to a formal solution of the price-product equilibrium of the retail firm. See Alt (1949a, pp. 92–110); Knauth (1949, pp. 1–12); Walker (1950, pp. 529–37).

3. See Hall and Knapp (1955, p. 312) [Reading 15]; and Stigler (1947, pp. 15, 16).

put consists not of automobiles but rather of the services of milling, stamping, shaping, machining, assembling, painting, storing and so on. For purposes of measuring value added in the industry it is these services which are relevant. But in a discussion of pricing policy, on the other hand, one must focus on the unit of sale. The grocer expresses his prices as so much per pound of coffee, and so much per pound of beef rather than as so much per dollar of credit extended or per pound-mile of delivery service. In the following discussion, then, the product being priced is understood to be the unit of sale.

The central thesis of this paper can be stated briefly. Given a multi-product retail firm, profits are maximized only if a type of price discrimination is practiced. The reason for this is that retailers' cost structures are much more like those of public utilities than has generally been recognized and profit maximization under conditions of high fixed costs and common costs is essentially a matter of operating as close to capacity as possible and setting prices so as to take into account the elasticities of the various demands which the producer faces. But the public utility analogy provides only a starting point for the analysis of retail pricing. Like some utilities (railroads, for instance, which can bid for traffic of differing demand elasticities) retailers are typically free to add or delete product lines. But many types of retailers and especially supermarkets are free to manipulate their product lines and prices in order to take into account not only the various demand elasticities but also the inter-related demands. Because of the much-advertised convenience of 'one-stop shopping' the cross elasticities of demand are negative among countless combinations of goods in the supermarket. Profit-maximizing pricing must take these cross elasticities into account.

There is considerable evidence that supermarket operators do indeed establish prices with not only price elasticities but cross elasticities in mind. The staple foods, for which the demand functions *faced by the individual store* are quite elastic, probably carry very low margins over direct cost whereas the non-staples, for which the demand functions faced by the individual store are more inelastic, are probably priced so as to make a much more substantial contribution to overhead and profit. Thus the buyer of the coffee on the 'special' list is being favored while the consumer whose tastes run to caviar and canned onion soup is being discriminated against.

The material which follows first deals with the probable nature of the cost functions for the supermarket retailer. Then the theory of the price and product equilibrium of the firm, given differing demand elasticities among the products sold, interrelated demand functions and the option of adding products, is discussed. The empirical evidence that the theory is an explanation of actual practice is reviewed and finally some of the implications of the theory are set forth.

A number of writers have commented on the fact that retailing costs other than wholesale cost of the merchandise are fixed in the short run.[4] Occupancy costs and other overhead expenses are fixed and even the labor cost is in large measure a fixed cost. Advertising costs and promotion costs in general are neither fixed nor variable but rather discretionary.

The unique nature of labor costs in retailing has seldom been sufficiently stressed in the few discussions of the equilibrium of the retail firm. In the case of the manufacturing concern, an increase in the work force plus the other requisite inputs leads to an easily predictable increase in output in the short run. In the case of the retailer, however, merely increasing the number of clerks in the store will not necessarily increase the number of customers or the monthly sales. This reinforces the strength of the comparison of the retail firm with certain public utilities. The retail store's wage bill is, to a considerable extent, a capacity cost. Just as electricity cannot be stored, neither can the service component of the retail goods be stored. The explanations about the merchandise, the initial recording of the sale, the wrapping of the goods and the transfer of the merchandise from the clerk to the customer can only be accomplished at the time of sale. Thus the retail firm must stand ready to serve its clientele largely *at times which please the clientele*. Because of the lack of symmetry between the public's favored shopping hours and conventional working hours and because demand can only be predicted with moderate accuracy, the retail firm typically faces the problem of excess capacity in its work force during part of the day or part of the week.

Many retailers, especially the firms with larger stores, have been able to reduce substantially this excess capacity problem. In some cases retailers encourage mail orders since this type of sale can be handled, within certain limits, at the pleasure of the retailer rather than at the pleasure of the customer, i.e. in off-peak hours. Part-time help can be hired for peak hours. Some versatile 'floating' sales personnel in larger stores can be dispatched to those departments where clerks are taxed, and so on. Nevertheless, the point seems clear that although the work force capacity can be more readily and accurately adjusted to output levels than, say, the plant capacity of the power utility, this adjustment is surely considerably less complete than in the case of the manufacturer.

If the retailer is essentially a high fixed cost enterprise particularly sensitive to sales volume, we would expect to find price discrimination

4. See Due (1941, pp. 384–5); and Smith (1948, p. 26); and Hawkins (1940, p. 384).

practiced just as it is practiced among public utilities. But in the super-market case the possibility of discriminating among customers buying the same product is limited since the markets cannot be completely insulated from one another. Canned soup cannot be sold at one price to some customers and at another price to others because resale is too simple. Yet in spite of the ease of resale, types of price discrimination are found in the supermarkets. Off peak load pricing is common. Since far more than 50 per cent of their sales occur during the last three days of the week, many stores offer free glassware, dishes or kitchenware with purchases of, say, five dollars or more on Mondays, Tuesdays and Wednesdays. Bloc pricing also has its parallel in multiple unit pricing (e.g., one can for fifteen cents, three for forty-three cents).[5] The trading stamp practice now causing such an uproar in US supermarkets is also an illustration of price discrimination. With each dollar's worth of goods bought, the customer is given a certain number of stamps which can be accumulated and used as currency in the purchase of all sorts of appliances, toys, etc., from the trading stamp company which sold the stamps to the retailer in the first instance. This is a type of volume discount since a considerable number of stamps must be acquired before one has a sufficient number to redeem.

Though the public utility analogy is a suggestive heuristic device for studying the pricing policies of retail firms, we must move well beyond the analogy in order to construct a more realistic model. The first step in this direction consists of recognizing, as several writers have done, that price discrimination can be extended to cover the case of the multi-product firm selling several products at different percentage mark-ups over cost (either full cost or direct cost).[6] Profit maximization, then, requires that the multi-product firm set its prices so as to receive a greater contribution to overhead and profit from its products which face a less elastic demand than from its products sold in markets where the demand is more elastic.

In an article on price discrimination and the multi-product firm, Clemens (1950–51) has developed an approach which nearly fits the supermarket case. He has not dealt, however, with the interrelated demand aspect and consequently his model is but a first approximation to a solution of the problem with which we are concerned here. We will first review Clemens's model as it applies to the supermarket.

Let us posit the retail firm in the large numbers case selling a single product. The Chamberlinian tangency solution follows with its proof of excess capacity. But if it is simple for the single-product firm to become a

5. Bliss (1951), pp. 381–3, has discussed some extensions of this pricing policy.
6. See Ralph Cassady, Jr (1946, pp. 9–11); Watkins (1934, p. 352); Clemens (1950–51, p. 2).

multi-product firm, as it is in retailing, we must drop the single-product assumption, for the retailer will cast about for another product which can be sold to utilize the excess capacity. Here Clemens introduces the assumption that the marginal cost function is not affected by the choice of the alternative products, i.e. it matters not whether output is increased by adding product B or product C, the marginal cost is the same in both instances. Thus in Figure 1 there is but a single marginal cost function shown. In order to increase profit by the greatest possible amount, the retailer will add those products for which marginal revenue exceeds marginal cost by the greatest amounts. It follows that the firm will adjust prices, and hence output, so that the marginal revenues will be equated to each other and to marginal cost paralleling Robinson's model.

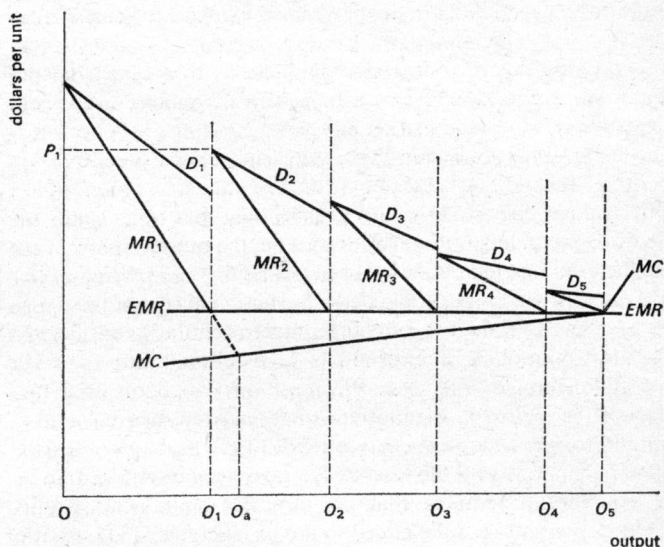

Figure 1

The nature of Clemens's equilibrium is shown in Figure 1. Given the marginal cost function MC, the retailer will first invade the product market for which the demand is least elastic. If he were to remain a single-product retailer, he would expand output of the initial product to O_a where marginal cost and marginal revenue are equated. But if he can enter the market for the second product, it is clear that profits can be increased if he were to divert some of his capacity from the first product to the second since at any price lower than OP_1 the marginal profit on the first product is less than the marginal profit on the first units of the second product. Similarly the retailer will proceed to invade all those product markets in which marginal revenue exceeds marginal cost, so adjusting prices as to equate to marginal cost the marginal revenues for all items handled. In Figure 1 *EMR* is the line formed by the points of equal marginal revenue.

Given this equilibrium of the multi-product firm, price discrimination is practiced in the sense that various percentages of profit are earned on the several products. Clemens points out that price discrimination of this sort is essentially the same as price discrimination among identical goods (or services) sold in markets of differing demand elasticities. The firm reaches several markets by producing several products or several variations of the same product. In order to be in long-run equilibrium, then, the firm must have invaded all the product markets in which the price exceeds the marginal cost.

Clemens proceeds to spell out various limitations to product diversification, but we do not need to review them here. We can move on to adapt Clemens's analysis to the supermarket case.

We can immediately free ourselves of Clemens's assumption that the marginal cost function is unaffected by the product mix. A more widely applicable version of his model would assume only that at any time the marginal cost of expanding output (by expanding the output of *any* of the several products) can be identified – it need not be the *same* marginal cost for each product. In the multi-product case the marginal cost of increasing the output of a given product is, of course, more accurately considered a function of the output of all other products. So we should drop the single marginal cost function of Figure 1. We must then abandon Clemens's formulation of the short-run equilibrium (marginal revenues equated to each other and to 'the' marginal cost) in favor of the more general statement that marginal profits for the various products must be equated. In the long run, equilibrium requires that all products on which marginal revenue exceeds marginal cost be added to the product line, and output of each expanded to the point where marginal profits are all zero.

This model differs from the familiar Robinsonian model primarily in that it substitutes the multi-product assumption for the single-product, multi-market assumption, and it assumes that the number of products is variable.

The same model can be derived from Brems's multi-product case by dropping the criteria (characteristics), other than price, which he includes as variables.[7] Brems's analysis runs in terms of the marginal cost of

7. Brems (1951, especially chapter 7).

increasing revenue, rather than output. Revenue can be increased not only by altering the price but also by altering the various characteristics of the product or by increasing the number of products. For any given increase in revenue there exists a least-cost change in criteria (including price) for achieving that increase in revenue. By increasing revenue from zero by a succession of least-cost steps, a minimum total cost function, with revenue as the independent variable, can be constructed. Equilibrium can then be described in terms of the total cost and total revenue functions. If the criteria other than price are taken as data in the Brems model, profit maximization in both Brems and our adapted Clemens model results in price discrimination (in the broader sense) if the products face demand functions of different elasticities.

Even without specific evidence on the question, one would expect this brand of price discrimination to be practiced in the supermarket. The fact that supermarkets handle a multitude of products is enough to indicate that the opportunity to discriminate exists, for surely the hundreds of price elasticities are not identical.[8] For any given firm the demand functions for the staples are probably considerably more elastic than the demand functions for the non-staples. The term 'staple' in this context implies that the good is one bought frequently and in considerable quantity by the housewife. She will surely be more aware of price differences on such items than on the items which are bought less frequently. Since all supermarkets carry staples, price comparisons are relatively simple to make. Price comparisons on non-staples, on the other hand, are less likely not only because the housewife buys any given non-staple less frequently but also because the money spent on any single non-staple is too small relative to the total food budget to warrant price-consciousness with respect to that item.

There is ample evidence that supermarket operators are well aware of the opportunity to practice price discrimination. One text on retailing notes:

Seldom is it feasible to apply a uniform mark-up percentage throughout the store. Variance in turnover rates, *competition*, legal regulations, controls by suppliers, customary prices, *traffic-building sales promotions, customers' concepts of value*, and differences in markdowns and shrinkage are among the factors that make it necessary or advisable to deviate from the 'average' mark-up requirement. (Italics mine.)[9]

8. One study of a supposedly typical supermarket chain revealed that 2983 different items were stocked at the time of the study. See Mueller (1956, p. 341). It has been said that a 'well stocked' supermarket by the end of 1955 was carrying about 5000 items (*Facts in Grocery Distribution*, 1956 edn, p. 6).

9. Brown and Davidson (1943, p. 320).

And later:

Demand curves facing the individual merchant are not synonymous with the general demand curves for the products he handles. For example, the over-all market demand for such items as soap and cigarettes is not particularly sensitive to price changes. The sales potential on these items is strongly elastic, however, as far as *any one retailer* is concerned. Of course, this is not true for all products. The merchant learns through experience just where demand is quite sensitive to price changes *in his particular store*, and where it is not.[10]

In partial support of this point, one chain has reported margins of only 5·8 per cent on cigarettes, 6·2 per cent on sugar, 8·4 per cent on soap and 9·8 per cent on baby foods in spite of the store-wide margin of 17·9 per cent of sales.[11] This evidence is grossly unsatisfactory, of course, since we do not know the marginal selling costs (i.e. marginal cost less invoice cost) of handling these items, but the deviation from the average margin is striking even though inconclusive.

The well-known phenomenon of the 'loss leader' is clearly an application of price discrimination.[12] And in some areas, at least, coffee especially is a favorite item on which to take a low profit margin at all times since it is a conspicuous staple.[13] The margin sacrificed on the loss leader is, of course, a promotion expense incurred to boost the sales of other products of the store. Price discrimination incurred for this reason is discussed later.

The attempt to practice price discrimination must account in large measure for the multiplication of product lines which has characterized US food retailing especially in the last five to ten years. The proliferation of items has indeed been impressive, as Table 1 shows. This expansion of items handled has been caused in part by the manufacturers' development of new products such as cake mixes, frozen foods and so on. There is little doubt, however, that these new products have been welcomed by the retailers because they afford some opportunities for price discrimination since many of them are bought by high-income consumers who are less sensitive than others to the prices charged, or by the middle-income consumers who are equally insensitive to the price because of the infrequency of the type of purchase.

10. Brown and Davidson (1943, p. 321).

11. *Facts in Grocery Distribution* (1956 edn, p. 18).

12. See Federal Trade Commission (1933, pp. 17–29); Adelman (1948, p. 113); Smith (1948, p. 32); and Phillips (1941, pp. 381–3).

13. For example, during the rise in coffee prices in 1954 one supermarket operator was quoted as saying '. . . we are holding down our coffee prices strictly so as to increase our stores' overall sales volume'. See *Supermarket Merchandising* (1954a, p. 88). In the same article it is stated that in Detroit, supermarket operators frequently 'football' coffee (make a price leader of it) and at the time were selling coffee at an average of ten cents under cost, cost being about one dollar a pound.

But the multiplication of items handled has not been due solely to the addition of new food products. Increasingly supermarkets have been adding non-food items such as 'health and beauty aids', houseware, paper products and, in some cases, staple clothing items. The common explanation for this expansion of product lines is that the retail margins on food have been narrowing, forcing the operators to find goods which carry better margins to add to the existing lines.[14] It is interesting that in the case study of chain store margins mentioned earlier the highest margin, over thirty-three per cent, was on pet supplies.[15]

Table 1 **Number of items by product groups**

	1928	1950	1954
Frozen foods	—	121	149
Dairy	44	158	185
Beverages	26	133	194
Soaps and detergents	37	65	95
Household supplies	51	175	377
Paper products	—	52	75
Canned vegetables	42	166	185
Canned fruits	24	94	139
Flour and mixes	17	84	110
Drugs and toiletries	—	185	300
Candy, gum, nuts	34	190	191
Soups	4	43	67
Baby foods	—	108	183
Cereals	17	60	92
Canned meats	7	44	57

Source: Mueller (1956, p. 340). Although Mueller does not give the source of these data, the 1928 data are clearly from *Merchandising Characteristics of Grocery Store Commodities* (1932, pp. 32–4). Although most of the Louisville survey covered twenty-six stores, the 1928 data of the above table are based on but one store, selected as 'representative' of a great many retail grocery stores throughout the country.

If we are correct in our hypothesis that the development of more non-staple foods and the addition of non-food lines has made it possible to discriminate in favor of the staples, we would expect to find that over the years the margins on the staples relative to the margins on non-staples would have fallen as the ratio of non-staples sales volume to staples sales volume has risen. Again, data on margins on specific items seem to be so

14. See, for example, *Supermarket Merchandising* (1953, p. 46).
15. *Facts in Grocery Distribution* (1956, p. 18). As mentioned above, the size of this margin is inconclusive evidence of price discrimination since the marginal cost of handling this particular product is not known.

scarce that we cannot be fully satisfied that this has happened. But the available evidence, unsatisfactory though it is, does point in this direction. In Table 2 some margins reported in 1928 by twenty-six stores in Louisville are compared with 1954 margins in a Cleveland study of chain store margins. In this comparison we can only hope that these two groups of stores, presumably modal for the Midwest, are sufficiently representative so that at least the major changes in margins can be considered significant. Of the twenty-six classes of items for which margins are available for both years, the five classes registering the greatest decline were cigarettes, sugar, soap, canned and powdered milk, and soup. The five classes registering the least

Table 2 **Margins as a per cent of sales for twenty-six grocery product groups, for twenty-six Louisville stores in 1928 and 5 units of a Cleveland chain in 1954**

Product group	Louisville, 1928	Cleveland, 1954	1954 as % of 1928
Cigarettes	23·7	5·8	24·4
Sugar	22·4	6·2	27·6
Soaps	23·3	8·4	36·0
Canned and powdered milk	19·5	8·5	43·5
Soups	24·9	11·6	44·1
Beverages	22·7	10·4	45·8
Baking supplies	24·9	11·8	47·3
Canned meats	26·2	13·3	50·7
Canned fish	26·2	14·1	53·8
Cereals	24·5	13·3	54·2
Salad dressings, oil	26·0	16·0	61·5
Canned fruit	26·9	18·1	67·2
Macaroni and spaghetti	29·4	19·9	67·6
Canned vegetables	28·8	20·8	72·2
Dried foods	26·8	19·7	73·5
Candy, gum and nuts	32·1	24·1	75·0
Dried fruits	27·8	21·0	75·5
Jams, jellies and spreads	28·3	21·4	75·6
Flour and flour mixes	16·9	12·9	76·3
Condiments	29·9	24·2	80·9
Spices and extracts	33·0	26·9	81·5
Syrups	24·1	20·3	84·2
Household supplies	31·0	28·4	91·6
Paper products	25·6	23·9	93·3
Drugs and toiletries	29·0	27·7	95·5
Crackers and cookies	24·4	23·5	96·3

Source: 1928 data are from *Merchandising Characteristics of Grocery Store Commodities* (1932, pp. 32–4). 1954 data are from *The Progressive Grocer* (January 1955, pp. 57–63).

decline were syrups, paper products, drugs and toiletries, and crackers and cookies. The first group are quite clearly staples, the latter non-staples. Thus the hypothesis is substantiated in so far as these data are acceptable.

The above review of the evidence suggests that price discrimination is practiced not only to take advantage of differences in demand elasticities. In large part the supermarket operators are recognizing that demand for their various products is interrelated, the cross elasticity of demand being negative among product lines.[16] The 'traffic-builder' item is clearly one which is presumed to have a large negative cross elasticity of demand with other goods handled. Any item which is priced to 'get people into the store' is successful only if it has a large negative cross elasticity. It is true that the items which can be substituted for the specially priced items will suffer since they have high *positive* cross elasticities with the 'specials', but the increased volume on the complementary goods is expected to more than compensate for the loss in volume on the competing goods.

Relatively low margins on staples and relatively high margins on non-staples, therefore, may be found not only because the differences in the demand elasticities make it possible to practice price discrimination but also because the demand for the non-staples is complementary to the demand for the staples.

The equilibrium of the firm under conditions of interrelated demand has been discussed by Coase and his solution can be extended to the super-market case.[17] He suggests that in the two-product case the marginal cost function for product A be lowered by the marginal profits received from product B as a result of increased sales of A, the price of B remaining fixed. Similarly the marginal cost function for product B could be lowered by the marginal profits on A. He notes that the marginal profits earned on product A will not necessarily bear any clear relationship to the sales of B. But in the supermarket case, the nature of the costs and complementarity would seem to permit of some fairly definite statements. First, it is probably not incorrect to consider the marginal cost of handling any particular product as constant in the short run.[18] Secondly, the ratio of A sales to B sales, in physical units, may well be stable and independent of the quantity of B sold. This would be the case if lowering the price on B attracts a larger clientele, all of whom buy as many units of A, relative to B, as the original

16. Although positive within product lines, of course. The importance of interrelated demand has been stressed by Alt (1949b, pp. 441-7), but the resulting pricing policy was not discussed. See also Hawkins (1940, pp. 388-9).

17. Coase (1946, p. 278).

18. The marginal costs may fall if marginal handling costs remain constant, since inventory costs presumably would be reduced by a faster turnover.

clientele.[19] If these two conditions are met, a 'corrected' marginal cost curve (marginal cost as usually defined less marginal profits on A sales resulting from change in B sales) for B can be drawn, if the price of A is given, as in Figure 2. There MC_B is the marginal cost of handling B, marginal cost being defined in the classical manner. CMC_B represents the

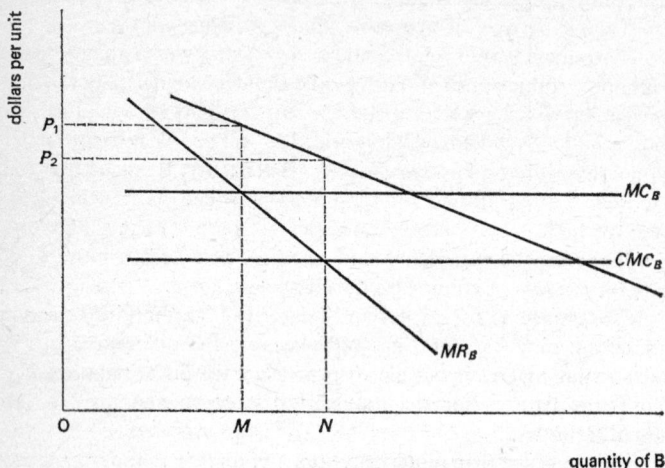

Figure 2

'corrected' marginal cost of B, i.e. marginal cost in the usual sense minus the marginal profits earned on A because of changes in the sales of B. If A and B were not complementary, the profit maximizing output of B in the short run would be OM. But due to the complementarity of demand between A and B, the profit maximizing price of B is OP_2, rather than OP_1. 'The loss leader' case is shown in Figure 3. If the complementarity is sufficiently great, CMC_B will be so far below MC_B as to yield an equilibrium price OP_2 which is below the marginal cost of B, OR. Of course, the term 'loss leader' is a misnomer. If it is successful it is more appropriately a 'profit leader'. Clearly if the complementarity is as strong as Figure 3 indicates, the entrepreneur does not maximize profits by keeping the price of B at or above MC_B.

The margin between MC_B and CMC_B will depend not only on the

19. This is a special, but common, case of complementary demand. The usual example of complementary demand involves the individual consumer buying more of product A because the price of B has fallen. In the supermarket case the lower price of B attracts trade which also buys A, even though the original clientele may not increase its purchases of A. In the latter case A and B illustrate what has been called complementarity in purchase as contrasted with complementarity in use. See Balderston (1956, p. 178).

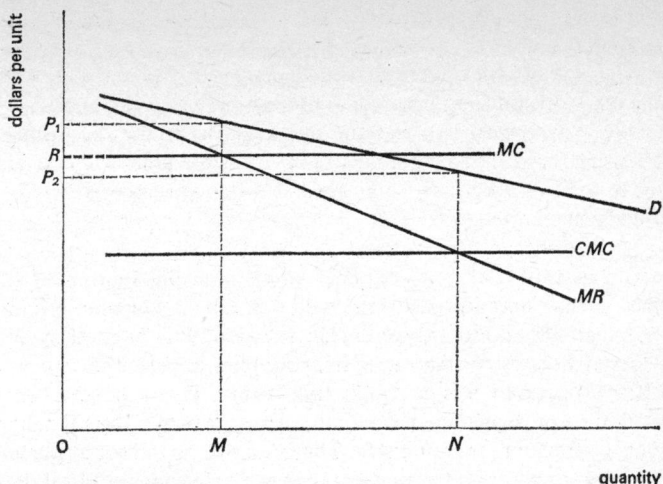

Figure 3

complementarity of A and B but also on the price of A since the greater
the price of A the greater the marginal profit on each unit of A sold. For
every price of A we will have a different CMC_B, so every price of A will
yield a different profit-maximizing price and output for B. Similarly the
profit-maximizing price and output for A will depend on the price of B.
The higher the price of A the lower the CMC_B in Figure 2 if the demand
for A is perfectly inelastic with respect to price. This follows from the
higher marginal profits on A at the higher prices. Therefore, the greater
the price of A the lower the equilibrium price of B. This is the typical joint
product case. If the demand for A is less than perfectly inelastic, a rise in
the price of A reduces the ratio of units of A sold to units of B sold, given
the price of B. Therefore, a rise in the price of A lowers the CMC_B in
Figure 2 less than if the demand for A were perfectly inelastic. It follows
then that the more price elastic the demand for A, the greater (algebraically) the slope of the function showing the profit-maximizing price of
B (as the dependent variable) given the price of A (the independent variable). And given the price elasticity of demand for A, the slope of this
function is greater (algebraically) the greater the elasticity of demand for B.
If the demand for A is sufficiently price elastic, CMC_B may move *toward*
MC_B with a rise in the price of A, depending on the magnitude of the
marginal cost of handling A.[20]

20. The greater the marginal cost of handling A, the lower the marginal profits on A,
given the price of A. If the marginal profit is relatively small, a given price change in A
will be less likely to raise the CMC_B than if the marginal profit on A is large.

Thus the equilibrium price of B may rise with increases in the price of A, whereas the equilibrium price of B would fall with increases in the price of A if the demand for A were sufficiently inelastic.

Given the profit-maximizing price for B corresponding to each possible price of A, we can proceed by the same method to compute the profit-maximizing price for A corresponding to each possible price for B. The intersection of the two functions would represent the two prices at which profits would be maximized.

If the equilibrium of the firm requires price discrimination among product lines, certain questions as to the nature of the market equilibrium arise. If the supermarket discriminates against certain types of goods, why don't the specialty shops concentrating in those lines undersell the supermarkets? If the supermarket is discriminating against these products, they must be carrying a price yielding more than full cost whereas the specialty shop need charge no more than full cost. There are two possible answers to this. Perhaps the specialist is charging less than the supermarket. But if the item in question is low-priced and/or unimportant in the family budget, the demand for it in any given supermarket is relatively inelastic because of the complementary demand. In other words the supermarket enjoys a spatial monopoly on that item *once the consumer is in the store*. The other possible answer is that the supermarket charges less than the specialist, even while discriminating against the product, because the supermarket's full cost of handling the product may be below the full cost in the specialist's shop. Remembering that the supermarket is a self-service store while the specialist shop is a clerk-service store and that food store margins are lower than the margins of the specialist shops subject to raiding by supermarkets, we can see that this relationship between costs is a distinct possibility. Therefore, we need not expect the specialist necessarily to be able to price below the supermarket.

This view of the price-product equilibrium in retailing differs substantially from that put forward by Due.[21] He argues that the retailer prices all his goods at an estimated full cost rather than marginal cost. Because of the joint cost problem, at any one time retailers may be tempted to raid other retailers' trade by offering a particular item at something less than full cost but more than marginal cost. As reciprocal raiding continues, prices will be cut so as to force some operators out of business. The reduction in the number of competing firms will permit prices to rise once more, but then the raiding will be resumed and the cycle repeated. Retailers understand the nature of this cycle and consequently avoid marginal cost pricing, preferring to price all goods at an estimated full cost. Due fails to

21. Due (1941, pp. 390).

reconcile this with the variable margins which are actually applied in practice.

Due, then, would anticipate that the high margin items handled by the supermarkets would be raided by the competition, thereby forcing the supermarkets to eliminate price discrimination. Here one must distinguish between two types of potential raiders, the specialist shop handling the item against which the supermarket is discriminating and the competing supermarkets. The limited opportunity for retaliation afforded the specialist has already been commented on. Since the supermarket will discriminate only against products which are of limited importance in the family budget, the specialist shop has a difficult time attracting customers away from the supermarket unless the specialist can offer a price advantage or an advantage in the form of wider selection sufficient to compensate the housewife for the time and cost of travel to the specialist shop.[22] Thus the margin must be rather large compared with the price of the item. The raiding by competing supermarkets will be limited in part by the fact that the price differential must compensate the shopper for the bother of going to the competing store for the subject of the raid. It will also be limited, however, by the fact that the raiding supermarket cannot shift its margins to the staples since the latter are more important than the non-staples in attracting trade.

Supermarket raiding on other supermarkets is found to be of a limited variety, then. Retaliation does not take the form of retaliation on the identical item which the competition is featuring, as Due implies, for this is price competition of the clearest sort and anathema to the oligopolist. Consequently, retaliation will take the form of price cuts in *other* items. As part of the retaliatory strategy the 'specials' are shifted, of course, in order to make it even more difficult for the consumer to engage in really satisfactory price comparisons.

Both theory and evidence, then, point to the existence of extensive price discrimination in the supermarkets. Indeed, we would expect it in many types of retailing, but we will remain with the supermarket case as the clearest example.

A number of conclusions follow from all this.

1. Low-income people may have higher real incomes if they live in well-to-do towns than if they live in poor towns. If a store handles primarily staples, the price of staples must cover full cost; if, on the other hand, the store were to handle, in addition, many luxury items selling to less price-conscious customers, the staples can be charged narrower margins while the goods with the less elastic demand make more substantial contributions

22. See Baumol and Ide (1956, p. 95) [Reading 19].

to overhead and profits. This is simply an extension of a rather ancient notion. The physician in private practise can minister to a larger number of charity patients if he has some wealthy patients than if he has none. Similarly in the low-income areas of the world the low-income consumers must pay full cost whereas in the high-income areas they are more likely to enjoy the benefits of price discrimination working in their favor.

2. This view of retail pricing policy sheds light on a well-known complaint of farmers in the United States to the effect that while food retail margins fell in the United States prior to World War II because of the introduction of the chains, they have not fallen since then, indicating, presumably, that food retailers have not increased their efficiency in the last decade. The retailers respond that their store-wide margins have remained stable, but that this has been due to the addition of new lines of foods and non-foods, lines which typically carry higher margins than the more familiar products. Although satisfactory retail margin data on specific staples are not available for past years, the theory of price discrimination extended and adapted to the supermarket case would seem to support the retailers in this debate. New lines added are commonly items bought less frequently than staples and yet low enough in cost so as not to arouse price shopping tendencies – in other words, the new lines typically face rather inelastic demand curves. Hence, they can subsidize the more competitive lines.

3. The income redistribution effect of the variety of price discrimination discussed here is likely to prove sensitive to cyclical variations in personal income. Since the income elasticity of demand for the non-staples is greater than the income elasticity of demand for the staples, a drop in personal income will reduce the sales of the non-staples relative to the staples and will thus necessitate shifting margins back toward the staple items.

4. But the effect of a decline in personal income will be two-fold. Not only will the demand functions for any single store's non-staples fall off to the left; they will also become more elastic with the return to greater price consciousness. The complementarity between the demand for the staples and for the non-staples will be weakened as the decline in income shifts the consumer's marginal rate of substitution of time and money so as to encourage more serious price shopping. This is to say that the spatial monopoly which the supermarket has for any single non-staple in so far as customers *already in the store* are concerned, is weakened by falling personal incomes. It is worth recalling that the supermarket in the United States was a child of the depression and that the price appeal was considered much more effective than it would have been during the period of high income in the late 1920s.

5. Finally, this exercise points to some conclusions as to the future of product diversification in supermarkets. It has been pointed out that the supermarkets are entering increasingly the fields which historically have been handled by other types of stores, primarily drug stores and hardware stores but more recently clothing stores as well. Just where is this likely to stop? Can we seriously consider the possibility of the supermarket developing to the point where it will become simply a department store with food as one of the departments?

If the analysis of this paper is correct, new lines are added by supermarket operators because they offer opportunities to extend the practise of price discrimination. (This presumes that supermarkets have no great advantages over the specialists.) To qualify for admission to the product mix, then, a candidate item must have a relatively inelastic demand. It is this requirement which seems to be of overwhelming importance in influencing the choice of new lines. The candidate good should be one in which the supermarket enjoys a partial monopoly not necessarily because of product differentiation with respect to the product defined in the narrowest sense as the physical item which the buyer carries off, but rather because of the spatial monopoly with respect to the people who have come to the store primarily to buy other goods.

It seems, then, that the most likely candidate goods would be convenience goods, rather than shopping goods. Convenience goods have been defined as 'those articles that consumers wish to purchase with a minimum of effort . . . such purchases usually involve a small unit price'.[23] It might be stressed that consumers will spend a minimum of effort in seeking out and purchasing a convenience good generally *because* the unit price is low. Price variations among alternative sellers on low-priced goods would have to be larger, percentage-wise, to compensate the consumer for the time and effort spent in seeking out the seller with the lowest offering price. It has been noted that one of the reasons some manufacturers prefer to operate under resale price maintenance contracts with retailers is that by thus eliminating price variations on the good among retailers, it takes on some of the characteristics of a convenience good.[24] And indeed it is well known that fair traded items are particularly attractive to supermarket operators when they are considering expanding their product lines.

Convenience goods might be more satisfactorily defined as those goods for which the price and quality differences among alternative sellers are small in absolute terms relative to the consumer's appraisal of the searching costs. Shopping goods, on the other hand, can be defined as those goods on which the price and quality differences among alternative sellers

23. Maynard and Beckman (1952, p. 32).
24. Corey (1952, p. 51).

are large in absolute terms relative to the consumer's appraisal of the searching costs.[25] It is important for our purposes to note that what may be a convenience good for one consumer may be a shopping good for another, as the sensitivity to price differences is probably greater for low-income than for high-income consumers. Given that the marginal utility of money is greater for low-income people than for high-income people, low-income people will consider as shopping goods many items which high-income people will view as convenience goods.

Because possible price differences among alternative sellers are less, relative to searching costs, in the case of convenience than in the case of shopping goods, the complementarity of demand between convenience goods and standard food lines will be considerably higher than the complementarity between shopping goods and standard food lines. The supermarket operator does not have that little bit of monopoly power over the customer in the case of the shopping good. This is true in part because the customer feels that by incurring the searching costs necessary to become informed as to the alternative goods and prices available in other stores, he may make a considerable saving. In addition, the shopping good is bought less frequently than the convenience good and generally the demand for a shopping good is not felt as urgently by the customer as the demand for a convenience good. Consequently, the customer loses little by postponing the purchase a few days. But such a postponement means that the customer gets outside the store and thus the store loses the spatial advantage it enjoyed when the customer was in the store.

It cannot be concluded that supermarkets will not eventually enter into merchandising of what are *now* considered by most people to be shopping goods. As incomes increase, more and more goods shift from the shopping goods category to the convenience goods category if the marginal utility of money is lower at the higher incomes. Under such circumstances the supermarkets may be able to add non-food lines such as minor appliances and clothing and thus extend their spatial monopoly.[26] This argument is supported by the experience of the supermarkets in recent years in the

25. This definition is consistent with Maynard and Beckman's description (Maynard and Beckman, 1952, p. 33).

26. Baumol and Ide (1956) [Reading 19], establish an intriguing model for the determination of the optimum variety in retail operations. Commenting on the large number of items stocked by supermarkets, they express doubt that any great further increase in number of items stocked is to be expected unless the values of some of their coefficients change. But one of their coefficients includes the opportunity cost of the shopping trip. This can be defined, if I interpret the authors correctly, to include the savings foregone by not bothering to compare prices. Thus to the extent that the rise in incomes operates to reduce the subjective appraisal of this opportunity cost, the conclusion here is consistent with the Baumol and Ide article.

United States. While the consensus at one recent conference was that appliances and women's apparel are not successful in supermarkets,[27] one supermarket in a high-income town has reported that its appliances are doing well, with customers picking up minor appliances sometimes right at the check-out counter.[28] Thus these appliances have become virtually convenience goods with these high-income customers. Until incomes rise, it would seem, supermarkets cannot enter the field of shopping goods with any advantage stemming from complementary demand over the established outlets for such goods. This does not rule out, of course, the possibility that some supermarkets may successfully enter the shopping goods field. But to be successful they will have to rely on lower costs, better merchandising and careful pricing rather than complementary demand.[29]

27. See *Supermarket News* (1957, p. 21). This article reports that limited lines of baby clothes are reasonably successful, supporting the above point about convenience goods.

28. *Supermarket Merchandising* (1954b, p. 3131).

29. [In Reading 20 J. P. Cairns questions whether elasticity of demand is as decisive for a retailer's decisions on additions to his range of products as is suggested in the present Reading. R. H. Holton comments briefly at the end of Reading 20 (p. 319). Eds.]

References

ADELMAN, M. A. (1948), *The Dominant Firm with Special Reference to the A & P Tea Company*, unpublished Ph.D. Thesis, Harvard University.

ALT, R. M. (1949a), 'The internal organization of the firm and price formation; an illustrative case', *Q. J. Econ.*, vol. 63.

ALT, R. M. (1949b), 'Competition among types of retailers in selling the same commodity', *J. Marketing*, vol. 14.

AUBERT-KRIER, J. (1954), 'Monopolistic and imperfect competition in retail trade', in E. H. Chamberlin (ed.), *Monopoly and Competition and their Regulation*, Macmillan.

BALDERSTON, F. E. (1956), 'Assortment choice in wholesale and retail marketing', *J. Marketing*, vol. 21.

BAUMOL, W. J., and IDE, E. A. (1956), 'Variety in retailing', *manag. Sci.*, vol. 3, pp. 93–101.

BLISS, J. A. (1951), 'Retail prices patterned after utility rates', *J. Marketing*, vol. 15.

BREMS, H. (1951), *Product Equilibrium under Monopolistic Competition*, Harvard University Press.

BROWN, P. L., and DAVIDSON, W. R. (1943), *Retailing Principles and Practices*, Ronald Press.

CASSADY, R., Jr (1946), 'Some economic aspects of price discrimination under non-perfect market conditions', *J. Marketing*, vol. 11.

CLEMENS, E. W. (1950–51), 'Price discrimination and the multi-product firm', *Rev. econ. Stud.*, vol. 19.

COASE, R. H. (1946), 'Monopoly pricing with interrelated costs and demands', *Economica*, n.s., vol. 13.

COREY, E. R. (1952), 'Fair trade pricing, a reappraisal', *Harvard bus. Rev.*, September–October.

DUE, J. F. (1941), 'A theory of retail price discrimination', *S. econ. J.*, vol. 7.

FACTS IN GROCERY DISTRIBUTION (1956), published by *The Progressive Grocer*.

FEDERAL TRADE COMMISSION (1933), *Chain-Store Price Policies*, Senate Document no. 85, 73rd Congress, 2nd Session.

HALL, M. (1949), *Distributive Trading*, Hutchinson.

HALL, M., and KNAPP, J. (1955), 'Gross margins and efficiency measurement in retail trade', *Oxford econ. Papers*, vol. 7.

HAWKINS, E. R. (1940), 'Marketing and the theory of monopolistic competition', *J. Marketing*, vol. 11.

KNAUTH, O. (1949), 'Considerations in the setting of retail prices', *J. Marketing*, vol. 14.

LEWIS, W. A. (1945), 'Competition in retail trade', *Economica*, vol. 12.

MAYNARD, H. H., and BECKMAN, T. N. (1952), *Principles of Marketing*, 5th edn, Ronald Press.

MERCHANDISING CHARACTERISTICS OF GROCERY STORE COMMODITIES (1932), Louisville Grocery Survey Part 3A, Distribution Cost Studies, no. 11, US Department of Commerce.

MUELLER, R. W. (1956), 'Retail distribution of food in the US', *J. farm Econ.*, vol. 38.

PHILLIPS, C. F. (1941), 'Price policies of food chains', *Harvard bus. Rev.*, vol. 19.

SMITH, H. (1948), *Retail Distribution*, 2nd edn, Oxford University Press.

SMITHIES, A. (1939), 'The theory of value applied to retail selling', *Rev. econ. Stud.*, vol. 6.

STIGLER, G. J. (1947), *Trends in Output and Employment*, National Bureau of Economic Research, cited in Hall and Knapp (1955).

Supermarket Merchandising (1953), 'Mayfair leaps into non-foods', April.

Supermarket Merchandising (1954a), 'Caution on coffee, operators decide', March.

Supermarket Merchandising (1954b), 'You ought to sell appliances', May.

Supermarket News (1957), 'No trend in non-foods buying method', 11 March.

The Progressive Grocer (1955), 'Sales and margins by product groups, foodtown stores, Cleveland, Ohio'.

WALKER, Q. F. (1950), 'Some principles of department store pricing', *J. Marketing*, vol. 14.

WATKINS, M. W. (1934), 'Price discrimination', *Encyclopaedia of the Social Sciences*, vol. 12.

5 A. F. Jung

Price Variations among Automobile Dealers

A. F. Jung, 'Price variations among automobile dealers in Chicago, Illinois',
Journal of Business, vol. 32, 1959, pp. 315–26.

The prices at which new automobiles can be purchased at dealers has been a subject of considerable controversy. There has existed a widespread feeling that car prices have been cloaked in considerable mystery and that systematic advantage has been taken of consumers who were not in a position to protect themselves. Last year Congress passed legislation that dealt with automobile pricing at the dealer level by requiring that the list or retail price suggested by the manufacturer be prominently displayed on each new car until sold.

However, in spite of congressional inquiries and voluminous writings about the automobile industry, there has been very little reliable empirical evidence available concerning price variations at the dealer level. Information of this type has almost certainly been obtained by the manufacturers, but the findings have never been made public.

The commonly held attitude that consumers might be charged widely varying prices for the same product implies that competition is not very keen and that there is substantial ignorance of prices by consumers. The present study of Chicago dealers was designed to determine the existence of any variations in retail automobile prices among dealers and to ascertain if each customer received the same quotation from a given dealer or if different prices were quoted to supposedly sophisticated 'hard-bargaining' customers than to less-knowing types. An attempt was also made to quantify the possible effect of bargaining in lowering the originally quoted price. The selling effort of the sales force was measured in terms of whether dealer salesmen were trying to 'sell' cars or were merely engaging in price quotations.

The study of all Ford and Chevrolet automobile dealers in Chicago, Illinois, was conducted during a ten-day period in February, 1959. It was found that some dealers do offer lower prices than others and that lower prices can be obtained by shopping around. However, there was little evidence that individual dealers varied prices in any systematic fashion in order to take advantage of unsophisticated customers who were ignorant of actual market quotations. Three different persons using three different buying approaches visited every Ford and Chevrolet dealer in Chicago, and, on the average, they found that there were no large differences in prices quoted. However, bargaining, using a standardized approach, was found to be effective in lowering car prices by more than $50·00 on average. The study also found that there was not much difference in the prices quoted by large 'volume' dealers and by smaller dealers in Chicago. The level of selling effort on the part of auto salesmen was quite low and consisted primarily of quoting prices, with little attempt to sell on features, dealer, service, or any other factors.

Method of investigation

This study consisted in shopping new-car dealers to find out at what price they would sell a new car. It was hypothesized that the type of approach used by an individual in purchasing a new car might have a substantial effect on the price obtained. A buyer who showed complete familiarity with cars and indicated some knowledge of the automobile business might receive a much lower price than someone who had never purchased a car before or who seemed naïve to dealer salesmen. This has been a widely held attitude which the study was designed to test.

Three shoppers using three different approaches priced identical dealers to ascertain if there were systematic differences in prices that were related to these approaches. The three approaches tried to cover a wide range of approaches used by car purchasers. One shopper posed as a person who had just completed the prescribed course at an automobile-driving instruction school, had just received a driver's license, and was anxious to buy a car from the specific dealer contacted. The second interviewer used what might be termed an 'average shopping approach'. This person was interested in price, indicating that other dealers would be contacted. The third interviewer, the author, posed as the person well versed in car-buying procedures and an individual who would shop extensively to save money on his forthcoming car purchase. These approaches will be referred to in this report as the soft, medium, and hard approaches, respectively.[1] Needless to say, for each approach every call was stated to be the first stop on the shopping tour, because it was felt that giving previous price quotations might bias a dealer's salesman.

Standardized bargaining, if it can be called that, was used only after the third (hard) approach. A short while after a price had been quoted by a salesman, the interviewer would simply state that the price was more than he would pay and that he was interested in paying X dollars.[2] In every

1. For a more complete description of each approach see Appendix A.
2. X dollars equalled $2250 for a Chevrolet and $2300 for a Ford. It was felt that these prices would be fairly close to dealer cost, not be too unreasonable a price to suggest, and yet a price at which the dealer would refuse to sell the car.

instance the salesman retorted that this suggested price could not be met.[3] Then the interviewer simply asked how low a price the salesman could offer. The price received at this point was the one recorded. No attempt was made to secure a lower price. Bargaining was not employed with the other approaches. The car would always be purchased for cash[4] and without a car taken in trade.[5] At every dealer the shopper obtained the salesman's card.

Sample

All dealers in new Ford and Chevrolet cars within the city limits of Chicago were contacted. This represents a sample of all factory-authorized new-car dealers in Chicago, Illinois. It was felt that a more thorough study of two makes was preferable to a sampling of all makes. These two makes were chosen because Ford and Chevrolet have captured about half the Chicago market in recent years.

Previous experience had indicated that pricing one model at each dealer would provide the information desired. A popular model was selected so that it would be easy for the dealer to get it if it was not already in stock. A four-door sedan (not a hardtop) in the medium-price line of each brand seemed best to meet the requirements. The final selections were the Ford Fairlane 500 and the Chevrolet Bel-Air four-door sedans. The following equipment was included for every car priced: eight-cylinder engine (lowest horsepower V8), automatic transmission (Fordomatic and Powerglide), fresh-air heater, radio (lowest priced model), and windshield washers.[6] Any solid color was suitable. The same car was priced by all shoppers at all Ford and Chevrolet dealers.

All dealers were advised that, even though the prospective purchaser was anxious to consummate the deal at once, it did not matter if it took a couple of weeks to get the car, equipped as desired.[7] The shopping contacts were completed satisfactorily without arousing suspicion.[8] In only one case did a

3. Most salesmen stated that this was an impossible price, considerably below dealer cost.

4. Since dealers may receive a commission on credit terms and can often procure a sizable commission on the insurance which usually goes with a credit deal, it was felt that some dealers might offer different prices for cash and credit transactions.

5. If the consumer has an automobile which he wishes to trade in, additional advantages may be gained by shopping because all dealers may not appraise a used car at the same price. The wholesale value put on a used car by a dealer thus becomes an additional factor in considering the net price of a new car.

6. For a more complete description of the cars involved see Appendix A.

7. Every dealer did not have a car of this type in stock, so the interviewer would wait for delivery rather than take a different model or a car with different equipment on it.

8. The author believes that in all shopping contacts the dealer would actually have sold the car for the price which was quoted.

dealer salesman refuse to quote a price.[9] No dealer questioned the desirability of this car, although in sixteen Ford contacts (out of ninety) salesmen tried to switch interviewers to the Galaxie model.[10] The thirty Ford dealers and twenty-eight Chevrolet dealers (174 buying interviews) were contacted by the three prospective purchasers within a ten-day period, 6 February to 15 February 1959.

Results

The findings indicate that there is a great price variability among Ford and Chevrolet dealers (see Tables 1 and 2). Each dealer willingly offered a discount from the factory-suggested list price to all three shoppers. The factory-suggested list price was approximately $3034 for Ford and $2969 for Chevrolet.[11] Some dealers quoted list prices slightly different from the above.[12] It seems that the new federal law that requires posting of suggested prices on the car has eliminated 'price-packing'.[13] For the last several years differences in list price as high as $200 were prevalent in the Chicago area.

Discounts ranged from $159 to $539 for Ford and from $239 to $569 for Chevrolet; the average discount for Ford was $444 (14·6 per cent) and for Chevrolet $472 (15·9 per cent). Chevrolet dealers offered a significantly higher discount than Ford dealers did.[14]

Only one dealer quoted the same price to all three shoppers, and in only eight cases did a dealer quote the same price to two of the three shoppers. Evidently dealer salesmen reacted to the shoppers in many different ways, but much of this variability is evidently random, as is explained in detail in a following paragraph. Further inspection of what happened when two or all three shoppers had visited a dealer on the same day revealed no instances of two shoppers receiving the same price. Moreover, since all buying contacts were completed between Friday, 6 February 1959, and Sunday, 15 February 1959, there seems little likelihood that dealers would change their pricing policies several times within this short period.

9. One salesman refused to give a price to the interviewer using the hard approach until other price quotations were procured.

10. Some salesmen stated that the Fairlane 500 was difficult to obtain and that Ford would soon discontinue its production.

11. The fact that Chevrolet had a lower list price on the model priced than Ford did should not be misconstrued as meaning that the author believes that a lower-priced Chevrolet is equal to a higher-priced Ford. Lower prices on the average for Chevrolet have undoubtedly been obtained because of the lower initial list price.

12. No dealer varied more than $10·00.

13. Price-packing is the practise of quoting a price above the list price in order to offer a greater discount or to overvalue a trade-in.

14. The t-test: $x/\sigma = 5·3$ – considerably below the 1 per cent level.

Table 1 **Prices quoted by Ford dealers classified by approaches: Ford prices***

Ford dealer	Soft approach	Medium approach	Hard approach		Mean price
1	$651	$725	$575		$650
2	725	650	725		700
3	550	490	500		513
4	514	825	450		596
5	573	550	425		516
6	532	573	523		543
7	715	545	555		605
8	650	500	485		545
9	550	498	500		516
10	587	495	625		569
11	536	550	575		554
12	532	675	700		636
13	550	550	570		557
14	650	600	575		608
15	550	610	615		592
16	648	561	683		631
17	634	519	595		583
18	596	570	578		581
19	650	550	665		622
20	550	583	550		561
21	730	500	530		587
22	535	575	500		537
23	545	685	550		593
24	595	600	592		596
25	875	650	700		742
26	610	525	600		578
27	586	550	600		579
28	621	673	578		624
29	600	540	550		563
30	650	596	650		632
Mean	$2610	$2584	$2577	Grand mean	$2590
Standard deviation	77	75	72		
Median	2596	2566	2575	Grand median	2575
Range	2514–2875	2490–2825	2425–2725		

* $2000 has been subtracted from all prices except means etc.

Table 2 Prices quoted by Chevrolet dealers classified by approaches: Chevrolet prices*

Chevrolet dealer	Soft approach	Medium approach	Hard approach	Mean price
1	$495	$467	$475	$479
2	426	415	464	435
3	445	400	457	434
4	444	480	562	495
5	477	550	400	476
6	525	495	495	505
7	450	464	440	451
8	585	550	500	545
9	600	562	575	579
10	540	514	538	531
11	550	500	551	534
12	590	500	482	524
13	525	529	530	528
14	560	488	505	518
15	600	514	460	525
16	490	510	444	481
17	498	525	550	524
18	484	529	481	498
19	550	500	525	525
20	500	500	470	490
21	569	500	600	556
22	550	600	500	550
23	400	400	400	400
24	431	410	433	425
25	467	440	470	459
26	450	500	450	467
27	485	492	485	487
28	491	676	†	†
Mean	$2507	$2494	$2490	Grand mean $2497
Standard deviation	56	49	51	
Median	2498	2500	2482	Grand median 2498
Range	2400–2600	2400–2600	2400–2600	

* $2000 has been subtracted from all prices except means etc.

† This dealer did not quote a price for the hard approach. His prices for the first two approaches have been eliminated from all computations.

It has been widely held that the approach used by a prospective car buyer would have a substantial effect on the price quoted to him. However, the results of this study far from substantiate this belief. In the case of both Ford and Chevrolet the medium approach averaged a slightly lower price than the soft and the hard approach slightly lower than the medium or the soft (see Tables 1 and 2).

Table 3 **Analysis of variance of Ford prices by approaches**

Source of variation	Sum of squares	Degrees of freedom	Mean square	F	Level of significance
Dealers	227,457	29	7843	1·65	0·05 (approx.)
Approaches	17,603	2	8802	1·86	Between 0·10 and 0·30
Interaction	338⎱ 275,051	1⎱ 58	338⎱ 4742		
Residual	274,713⎰	57⎰	4820⎰		
Total	520,111	89			

Tukey test for interaction: 338/4820 = 0·07; approximate level of significance about 0·80.

Note: The estimated variance components, thinking of the main effects as random, are: Dealers, estimated variance = 1034; estimated standard deviation = 32·2. Approaches, estimated variance = 135·3; estimated standard deviation = 11·6. Residual, estimated variance = 4742; estimated standard deviation = 68·9.

Statistical evaluation indicates that the differences in prices obtained with the different buying approaches are not significant at the 95 per cent level of confidence (see Tables 3 and 4). There is approximately one chance in five that the differences obtained were the result of random variation. In any case the average difference in price quotation to the unknowing unsophisticated buyer (soft approach) was only slightly more than to the knowledgeable shopping buyer (hard approach). The soft approach obtained an average price only slightly more than one per cent above that of the hard approach in the case of Ford dealers ($2610 versus $2577) and less than one per cent higher in the case of Chevrolet dealers ($2507 versus

Table 4 **Analysis of variance of Chevrolet prices by approaches**

Source of variation	Sum of squares	Degrees of freedom	Mean square	F	Level of significance
Dealers	151,162	26	5814	4·67	< 0·0005
Approaches	4068	2	2034	1·64	Between 0·10 and 0·30
Interaction	2567⎱ 64,713	1⎱ 52	2567⎱ 1244		
Residual	62,146⎰	51⎰	1219⎰		
Total	219,943	80			

Tukey test for interaction: 2567/1219 = 2·12; level of significance between 0·10 and 0·20.

Note: The estimated variance components, thinking of the main effects as random, are: Dealers, estimated variance = 1523; estimated standard deviation = 39·0. Approaches, estimated variance = 29·3; estimated standard deviation = 5·4. Residual, estimated variance = 1244; estimated standard deviation = 35·0.

$2490). The residual or unexplained variance of Ford price quotations appears to be significantly greater than for Chevrolet.[15]

The prices that were obtained when two or three interviewers saw the same salesman can be seen in Table 5. In eighteen out of twenty-two cases, the harder approach received a lower price. The sign test shows that this is significant.[16]

There are definite price differences among dealers of Ford and among

Table 5 **Price variation for different shoppers by the same salesman**

Dealer	Soft approach ($)	Medium approach ($)	Hard approach ($)
Ford dealers*			
3	550		500
4	514		450
5	573	550	
6		573	523
7		545	555
14	650	600	575
17	634		595
18	596	570	
20	550		550
23	545		550
29		540	550
30	650		650
Chevrolet dealers*			
7	450		440
8		550	500
10	540		538
14	560	488	
16		510	444
18	484		481
19	550	500	
20	500	500	
21	569		600
22	550		500
23	400	400	
27		492	485

* $2000 has been subtracted from all prices.

15. No reliable explanation of this difference is presently available. The difference in pattern may be related to the fact that Chevrolet dealers were generally offering larger discounts from list price, which may reflect greater need to reduce price in order to obtain sales than was the case for Ford outlets. Such need to rely on price may have made for greater uniformity in price quotations by Chevrolet salesmen.

16. Significance level: $a = 0.004$.

dealers of Chevrolets, as can be seen in Tables 1 and 2. This lends credence to the belief that it pays to shop at different dealers for an automobile. In trying to establish how many dealers one should see, the value of one's time and endurance must be considered. Below are presented the expected savings that can be gained by shopping at additional dealers based on the results of this study. By viewing the average expected savings, each person can determine how many dealers it would pay him to see (see Table 6).[17] This is all based on the first price quoted by a dealer and in no way allows for bargaining for a lower price.

Table 6 **Average savings to be expected from shopping additional dealers**

| | Ford | | Chevrolet | |
No. of dealers shopped	Total savings ($)	Marginal savings ($)	Total savings ($)	Marginal savings ($)
1	0	0	0	0
2	42·92	42·92	29·55	29·55
3	64·38	21·46	44·33	14·78
4	78·31	13·93	53·92	9·59
5	88·50	10·19	60·94	7·02
6	96·42	7·92	66·39	5·45
7	102·89	6·47	70·84	4·45
8	108·37	5·48	74·62	3·78

Significantly lower prices for both Ford and Chevrolet were gained by the use of standardized bargaining (see Table 7). The author believes that additional savings could have been obtained at almost every dealer by a continuation of the bargaining process. He feels that after seeing several dealers, time is probably more profitably spent in bargaining than in additional shopping.

If we compare the dealers who quoted above average prices for the hard approach with those who quoted prices below the average, we find that above-average dealers offered a higher amount of discount after standardized bargaining than did those who quoted lower initial prices (see Table 8).

17. The price to be expected equals the grand mean plus random-dealer effect plus residual effect. The variance of price expected equals the standard deviation of random-dealer effect squared plus the standard deviation of random-residual effect squared. The standard deviation of price expected equals the square root of the variance of price. The standard deviation for Ford was $76·1 and for Chevrolet $52·4. The savings were then computed from a table of mean values of the order statistics. This table is from Dixon and Massey (1957, p. 407).

Table 7 Price advantage gained at Ford and Chevrolet dealers by standardized bargaining*

Dealer	Ford dealers			Chevrolet dealers		
	Price for hard approach	Price after standardized bargaining	Savings from standardized bargaining	Price for hard approach	Price after standardized bargaining	Savings from standardized bargaining
1	$575	$540	$ 35	$475	$450	$ 25
2	725	625	100	464	400	64
3	500	450	50	457	400	57
4	450	425	25	562	500	62
5	425	400	25	400	375	25
6	523	500	23	495	445	50
7	555	525	30	440	420	20
8	485	485	0	500	450	50
9	500	500	0	575	515	60
10	625	550	75	538	463	75
11	575	520	55	551	478	73
12	700	475	225	482	422	60
13	570	530	40	530	480	50
14	575	500	75	505	450	55
15	615	540	75	460	400	60
16	683	560	123	444	425	19
17	595	515	80	550	500	50
18	578	520	58	481	440	41
19	665	515	150	525	450	75
20	550	500	50	470	420	50
21	530	500	30	600	500	100
22	500	475	25	500	450	50
23	550	500	50	400	350	50
24	592	542	50	443	400	43
25	700	575	125	470	375	95
26	600	550	50	450	425	25
27	600	525	75	485	395	90
28	578	525	53			
29	550	500	50			
30	650	550	100			
Mean	$2577	$2514	$63	$2490	$2436	$54
Median	2575	2518	50	2482	2440	50
Range	2425–2725	2400–2625	0–225	2400–2600	2350–2515	19–100

* $2000 has been subtracted from all prices except means etc.

Table 8 Average price reduction resulting from standardized bargaining

	Dealers who quoted above average prices for the hard approach ($)	Dealers who quoted below average prices for the hard approach ($)
Ford dealers	94·00	33·00
Chevrolet dealers	63·00	48·00

Table 9 Relation of sales volume to price quoted

1958 sales volume (in cars)*	Ford			Chevrolet	
	No. of dealers		Average price ($)	No. of dealers	Average price ($)
Under 500	12		2574	7	2505
500–999	12		2615	9	2515
Over 1000	6		2575	11	2476
Total	30	Grand mean	2590	27	Grand mean 2497

*Passenger cars only; fleet sales are not included.

Large-volume Ford and Chevrolet dealers[18] did offer lower than average prices to the consumer, but the difference is much smaller than might be expected (see Table 9). Especially noteworthy are the prices offered by the small-volume dealers. The results of this study indicate that many of the claims about 'terrific savings' offered by dealers (mostly large-volume dealers) in advertising media do not appear to be substantiated in fact.

Car dealers who have gone into business within the last seven years do not appear to offer lower or higher prices than the 'old-timers' (see Table 10). A check was also made to see whether there was any relation between the income of a particular neighbourhood and the prices offered by dealers located there. None was noted.

A secondary purpose of the study was to gain some insight into the character of automobile selling. Automobile manufacturers spend huge sums of money each year trying to convince consumers to visit one of their dealers and purchase a new car. Because of the high unit price of an automobile and the large advertising expenditure to invite consumers to visit dealers, it would seem reasonable to expect a dealer to spend some time

Table 10 Relation of years in business to prices quoted

Years in business	Ford			Chevrolet	
	No. of dealers		Average price ($)	No. of dealers	Average price ($)
7 or less	16		2593	6	2482
8–17	5		2584	5	2538
18 or more	9		2589	16	2490
Total	30	Grand mean	2590	27	Grand mean 2497

18. The 1958 sales volume of the largest-volume Ford dealer was greater than the combined volume of the fifteen Chicago Ford dealers with the least sales volume. For Chevrolet, the sales volume of the largest-volume was greater than the combined volume of the twelve lowest-volume Chevrolet dealers.

selling the qualities of his product and service anytime a prospect walks into his showroom.

The evidence in Table 11 seems to indicate that dealer salesmen are not doing much selling. More effort was expended on customers using the soft or medium approach than the hard approach. Even in these cases the salesmen did only about one-third of the things that could induce a sale. Perhaps salesmen feel that anyone entering the showroom has already been sold on brand and is only interested in price. In most cases the salesman failed to point out the advantages of buying a car from the specific dealer he represented. Even though price may be the most important consideration in the minds of many consumers when purchasing a car, other factors such as excellence of the service department, reliability, willingness to help the consumer if real trouble develops with his new car, etc., can go a long way in limiting the consumer's price interest.

Although over 60 per cent of all salesmen recorded the prospect's address and/or his phone number, only about 20 per cent thought it desirable to follow up the prospect with either a phone call or by mail.[19]

It appears that the Ford salesmen were doing a slightly better job of trying to sell customers than were the Chevrolet salesmen. An interesting aside is that the interviewers found only a few instances in which they felt the salesman was trying to take advantage of them. These findings may be influenced by the relative popularity of these two makes in early 1959 and the relative ease of selling these on features or on price.

It should be noted that the attempt to gain some information about the level of automobile selling played only a minor role in the study. The factors considered in a cursory way by the shoppers are only a few of the points upon which the sales ability of a sales force might be judged.

Summary and conclusions

It seems that approximately the same price will be quoted to an individual regardless of the approach used by the potential customers. The new car market in the city of Chicago, and presumably in other major metropolitan areas, appears to be sufficiently competitive to deter any systematic exploitation of the uninformed buyer. However, the wide variations in price obtained in these shopping interviews indicate that the consumer can benefit from visiting more than one dealer. Further, the shopper who is willing to bargain can obtain his automobile for a significantly lower price.

Automobile dealers in Chicago appear to be efficient agencies of distribution. The average mark-up at Ford dealers was approximately 9·7 per cent using the grand mean of all prices obtained before bargaining and

19. Only eight pieces of literature were received by mail. All the dealers that mailed them had previously followed up by telephone.

Table 11 Tabulation of questions concerning the actions of dealer salesmen as reported by the shopping interviewers by number of yes answers

Question	Ford dealers					Chevrolet dealers				
	Soft approach	Medium approach	Hard approach	Total	Percentage*	Soft approach	Medium approach	Hard approach	Total	Percentage*
Did the salesman offer a demonstration ride?	14	9	1	24	26·7	8	7	3	18	21·4
Did the salesman offer any literature?	10	8	3	21	23·3	6	5	3	14	16·7
Did the salesman try to sell you additional accessories?	8	14	9	31	34·4	9	7	5	21	25·0
Did the salesman mention any reasons for buying his make of car?	6	9	8	23	25·6	7	10	6	23	27·4
Did the salesman mention any reasons for buying the car from the dealer he represented?	10	13	8	31	34·4	8	12	5	25	29·8
Did the salesman take your address and/or phone number?	25	18	16	59	65·6	20	17	12	49	58·3
Did the salesman contact you after you left the showroom?††	13	7	4	24	26·7	6	4	2	12	14·3
Do you feel the salesman tried to take advantage of you?	4	4	2	10	11·1	4	3	2	9	10·7

* Based on 90 Ford contacts and 84 Chevrolet contacts.
†† All interviewers kept a record of all follow-up telephone calls and mail received. No salesman later contacted an interviewer in person.

6·9 per cent after bargaining.[20] For Chevrolet dealers the average mark-up approximated 8·3 per cent before bargaining and 6·0 per cent after bargaining. Since most consumers undoubtedly engage in some form of bargaining when purchasing a car, the mark-ups of 6·9 per cent for Ford and 6·0 per cent for Chevrolet would seem to approach the true mark-up. Very few marketing institutions serving the ultimate consumer offer their merchandise at lower prices (percentage-wise) over cost.

The automobile salesman has been pictured by many as an unscrupulous individual, taking unfair advantage of as many consumers as possible. The shoppers participating in this study found few instances in which this general belief held true, although salesmen were given many opportunities for 'foul play', especially in the soft approach. The absence of price-packing and package-pricing[21] tends to indicate that automobile salesmen of today have abandoned certain practises prevalent in the recent past.

Appendix A

Car-shopping instructions

Each interviewer received about eight hours of personal instruction regarding how to shop for the Ford and the Chevrolet. This helped to keep written instructions to a minimum. Training in the particular approach to be used required the most time. In essence, the three approaches were as follows.

The soft approach. This interviewer had never purchased a car before and knew little about them. She had just finished a course in driving instructions and had obtained a driver's license recently.[22] She did not intend to shop, and, if given a fair price, she would sign up at once. Upon receiving the price, she merely stated that it sounded fair and then broke the bad news about having to talk it over with her sister.

The medium approach. This person showed some familiarity with cars, having bought them before, and could definitely be classed as a shopper. Price was an important consideration but not the only one. This person had a fairly good idea about the type of car desired but was still open to suggestions.

The hard approach. In this approach the interviewer tried to show complete familiarity with automobile shopping and could be considered a hardened

20. Based on an approximate cost of $2340 for the Ford priced in this study and $2290 for the Chevrolet.
21. The practise of quoting one total price for the car and additional equipment and a practical refusal to itemize the accessories.
22. These facts were actually true about the person who used this approach.

shopper. He knew definitely what he wanted and made his shopping familiarity known by the comments he made.[23] He attempted to show that price was his only consideration. After the initial price was received, standardized bargaining was employed.

The shoppers were schooled orally in how to appear as a person definitely interested in a new car and how to deal with possible questions that a salesman might ask. Needless to say, every call was stated to be the interviewer's first stop. This simplified the answer to questions about previous price quotations. The interviewers were always cooperative and many times were taken to see the dealer's selection of new cars. In the first two approaches the shoppers selected the desired car with the help of the salesman.

Each interviewer was given instructions (listed below) about the type of car being shopped.

Chevrolet

There are three models being sold – the Biscayne (the least-expensive model), the Bel-Air (the medium-priced), and the Impala (the most expensive). We are always interested in the Bel-Air, four-door sedan (not a hardtop). It lists for about $2490. Chevrolet has a six-cylinder engine and several eight-cylinder engines. We are always interested in the regular V8. This is the lowest priced and lowest horsepower V8 and does not have four-barrel carburetion. It is called a 'Turbo-Fire V8' and has 185 h.p. It lists around $118. We always want automatic transmission called 'Powerglide'. There is another automatic transmission available with four-barrel carburetion called 'Turboglide', but we do not want this. Powerglide costs about $199·10. Be sure to include a radio – the manual radio. Chevrolet also makes a more expensive push-button radio, but we want the cheaper one. This costs about $63·00. The heater we desire is the fresh-air heater; this is the more expensive and is called 'Air-Flow', or 'Deluxe'. This lists for approximately $80·00. The only other accessory desired is the windshield washer. Chevrolet has two models; we prefer the model with two-speed electric wipers. It lists for about $16·00. In summary, we desired a Chevrolet Bel-Air, four-door sedan (not a hardtop), V8 engine, Powerglide, manual radio, air-flow heater, and two-speed windshield washer.

Ford

Ford is currently selling four models – the Custom 300 (the lowest-priced model), the Fairlane (between lowest and medium), the Fairlane 500

---

23. A typical comment when questioned about what he intended to trade was: 'I'm going to sell my car myself, since I know you fellows can only give me the whole-sale price.'

(medium-priced), and the Galaxie (the highest-priced). We are always interested in the Fairlane 500, four-door sedan (not a hardtop). It is called a 'Town Sedan'. It lists for about $2580. Ford has a six-cylinder engine and several eight-cylinder engines. We are always interested in the regular V8 engine (200 h.p.). This is the lowest priced and does not have four-barrel carburetion. It is called the 'Thunderbird 292 V8'. It lists around $118. We always desire automatic transmission called 'Ford-o-matic'. Another automatic transmission (more expensive) is made for four-barrel carburetion; it is called 'Cruise-o-matic'. Ford-o-matic costs about $189·50. The radio we want is the cheaper radio. It has push buttons and is called the 'Console Range' radio. We do not care to have the more expensive one with 'Signal Seek'. This Console Range radio lists for $58·50. Please include the more expensive fresh-air heater called 'Magic-Aire'. This lists for about $74·50. Ford makes only one windshield washer, and we want it. It costs about $13·70. In summary, we desire a Ford Fairlane 500, four-door Town Sedan (not a hardtop), V8 engine, Ford-o-Matic, Console Range radio, MagicAire heater, and windshield washer.

In twelve of the 174 contacts salesmen insisted strongly on an additional accessory or two. Being cooperative in these twelve cases, the would-be purchasers graciously accepted these strong recommendations.[24] The additional accessories were removed from all prices in this report by deducting their approximate cost to the dealer from the price quoted. No Chevrolet salesman tried to switch the shoppers from the Bel-Air, but sixteen Ford salesmen strongly urged the purchase of the Galaxie model for about $50 more. This was easily side-stepped by stating dislike for the 'squared' look of the Galaxie. The author believes that the participating shoppers did an excellent job in performing their roles as prospective car purchasers.

24. These extra accessories were low-priced accessories, such as undercoating, padded dash, outside mirror, etc.

References

DIXON, W. J., and MASSEY, F. J., Jr (1957), *Introduction to Statistical Analysis*, 2nd edn, McGraw-Hill.

6 R. Cassady, Jr

Retail Price Wars in Gasoline Distribution

R. Cassady, Jr, 'Retail price wars in gasoline distribution', excerpts from R. Cassady, Jr, *Price Making and Price Behavior in the Petroleum Industry*, Oxford University Press and Yale University Press, Petroleum Monograph Series, 1954, chapter 15, pp. 262–80. A case study of a price war (pp. 270–74) and a footnote on proposed legislation in New Jersey (p. 279) have been omitted here.

In certain industries from time to time intensive price disturbances develop out of the competitive struggle for markets. Often in such situations prices spiral downward without regard to costs. These intensive disturbances – designated price wars – are perhaps more common in gasoline distribution than in any other distributive trade.[1] The fact that price wars are prevalent in this field is prima-facie evidence of the existence of intensive rivalry. This chapter will examine the nature of price wars and attempt to find out why they exist; try to determine how the impact of such disturbances is borne, the results that can be expected from price wars, and the ways by which they are terminated.

1. There is some difference of opinion as to whether price wars occur in connection with the sale of other types of petroleum products. According to one well-informed jobber association official, price wars develop in the sale of burning oils also. Such wars are not as obvious as they are in gasoline distribution, he states, because of the absence of point-of-sale price signs and probably are not as prevalent or as intensive either. When there is an oversupply of heating oil, as when the weather has been exceptionally warm and stocks have begun to back up, the price cutter aggressively seeks custom and publicizes special offerings. He will use the telephone and direct-by-mail and other types of advertising in an attempt to raid his competitors' business.

While most domestic consumers have contracts with suppliers, competitors' activities are difficult to police; consequently the price cutter will sell considerable amounts of product in a short time on the basis of a price inducement. In addition to discounts on product prices such sellers often offer free burner service and burner parts, etc. According to this informant price wars develop even in residual fuel. When there is an oversupply there will be intensive competition, which is designed not only to take business from rivals within the industry but also to attract custom from sellers of competitive fuels such as coal and gas .

Other industry people equally well-informed state that price wars such as those found in gasoline distribution do not exist in connection with the sale of other types of petroleum products. The difference of opinion may be in part a matter of semantics. The question is, what does one mean by a price war? The fact seems to be that while intensive price competition develops in the sale of other petroleum products such as home heating oils and residual fuels just as in gasoline distribution, the open type of downward spiralling raids and counter-raids are not prevalent .

Adjusting prices to those of price-cutting rivals

It should be kept in mind that the large bulk of retail gasoline outlets are operated by dealers rather than by supplier companies themselves. In the abstract at least such dealers are independent businessmen and therefore have complete control over their own retail policies. Actually, however, some degree of influence is exerted by suppliers if only because successful operations depend on the maintenance of clean stations, good service, etc.

Influence of suppliers

Among other policies in which the supplier has an important stake is that relating to retail pricing. The company's product may be well and favorably known and the stations through which the product is sold might be well located and well kept but the prices may be out of line. This means, of course, that sales will be affected. Companies have different ideas about the degree of control that should be exerted over the retail outlets in the matter of the retail price to be charged. Differing attitudes may be classified as follows:

1. Complete hands-off policy. The only suppliers who would be apt to follow such a policy would be independent operators and especially those selling on a rebrand basis.

2. Absolute control over price charged. Few if any suppliers exert absolute control over retail prices although in some areas, as has been mentioned, some sellers have 'fair-traded' the product.[2]

3. Counselling of dealers by suppliers on pricing matters. Dealers are free to act as they please under such a policy but are given the benefit of the broad pricing experience of suppliers.[3]

As was implied above, the major companies particularly exert some degree of control over pricing matters. The counselling of dealers by suppliers in pricing matters appears to be the most common policy of major sellers and, as one supplier has put it, 'We consider that it is our obligation to advise our dealers in respect to good business practises and we feel free to make suggestions in connection with the gasoline prices that he posts'. Suppliers, majors particularly, strive to avoid open price cutting with its almost inevitable depressing effect on the price level; they

2. Usually such contracts fix only the minimum price below which the retail vendor may not go in selling his product and have nothing to do with the maximum price.

3. Some sellers may exert a firmer control, however, in the matter of the use of promotional price signs. That is, they may merely advise a retailer not to cut prices at this time (say) but may well order him to take any signs down. This is because of the intensifying effect of such signs on the spread of price cutting.

also aim to avoid the attempt by retailers to keep prices at non-competitive levels with a resulting loss of volume.[4]

The reliance by suppliers on counselling for control of prices is in general quite effective. This is due in part at least to the fact that the type of individual who becomes a major company dealer is not likely to be aggressively independent. The fact that the dealer is operating under a cancelable lease may have some bearing also, but in this writer's judgment this is a minor point.[5] The exertion of control over retail dealers by petroleum suppliers results in a substantial degree of (but not complete) price uniformity in normal times (although it makes for an absence of uniformity when intensive disturbances prevail). That is to say, price cutting during normal times will be discouraged while price cutting for the purpose of meeting the cuts of competitors will be encouraged.

Reaction to price cutting by rivals

The decision as to whether to exert some degree of control over retail gasoline prices is only one phase of a supplier's retail price policy. Another aspect is how a supplier should react to price cutters' activities. From the supplier point of view, this involves decisions as to:

1. The sellers to whose prices adjustments should be made.
2. The promptness with which adjustments should be made in response to reductions by price cutters.
3. The precise amount of such adjustments in retail prices.
4. The area over which the adjustments are to be made.

Each company must decide how aggressively competitive it wishes to be. Companies differ greatly in these matters. While no major seller can very well take the offensive aggressively in retail pricing matters (since others would be forced to meet him and thus neutralize the action), some are conservatively defensive and others are aggressively defensive. Actually

---

4. As a top executive of one large integrated company has said: 'It is difficult to be categorical about what form such advice might take in any given situation but, generally speaking, we would feel that a dealer cannot consistently post a price above that posted by the retailer of a major branded gasoline situated in the same market or general area. In respect to the extent to which we would be forced to meet the low prices posted by an unbranded competitor, it is even more difficult to make a definite statement. Generally speaking, it has been our experience that, if the unbranded dealer in the same market posts a price more than 2c a gallon below the price that our dealer posts . . ., he will over a period of time take business from that dealer.'

5. One reason for this is that you cannot very well force dealers to operate effectively; they must be taught to do so. Moreover, the attempt to force ostensibly independent operators to act according to the dictates of a supplier may well have some antitrust implications.

any one of a number of different types of policy may be followed by suppliers:

1. The retail dealer may be advised (perhaps encouraged) to meet promptly within a cent (say) or possibly on the nose any reduction made even by an obscure seller. The stress here is on the price cut and not on the effect of the cut.[6]
2. The retail dealer may be counselled to observe results of any price reductions by major company dealers and to make prompt adjustments where and in the amount necessary to avoid loss of business.[7]
3. The retail dealer may be advised to make adjustments only in the light of the impact of competition on his business and not until after the impact has definitely been established.[8]

Any supplier policy which is designed to share the function of retail price making usually provides a system of subsidies to assist dealers in meeting the reductions of aggressive price cutters. That is, the supplier assumes part of the burden of a price reduction accompanying an intensive price disturbance. Such subsidies (which are actually temporary reductions in the dealer tank wagon price) vary considerably among companies in terms of the amount and basis of payment and the area within which aid is provided.[9]

6. As was mentioned earlier, this aggressively defensive type of policy is not generally followed by suppliers. However, some companies come close to operating in this manner in particular market situations which seem to call for aggressive action, and one company especially appears to operate in this manner fairly frequently. One other company which had lost position in many of its markets during and immediately following the war period also found it necessary to be unusually alert competitively in order to recover its lost position.

7. One company which acts in a rather conservative manner in this regard (it moves slowly in a price-cutting situation) in one instance actually computed the value of merchandise premiums offered by dealers competing with its outlets and adjusted its price to within 1·5c of the competitive dealer's prices *after* allowing for the value of the premium.

8. The top executive of one very alert major company says: 'Adjustments are only made in the light of impact of the competition on our business. We have found that there is no formula providing a fixed margin of so much per gallon that will apply generally. . . . Therefore, we only act when our business is affected. Politically, we must let a bad situation get 'ripe' before we move. We find it best to let conditions spell out their own remedy. We are apt to confer with our dealers more frequently under pressure, asking them what they believe ought to be done, not with the idea of any agreements, but rather to find out when industry opinion is in tune with a market move. We act in our own interests but we can do so best when our moves are so belated that everyone agrees that something should be done.'

Another company operating in an entirely different area has a similar policy but expresses it differently. This firm will not make adjustments in its prices as a result of independent price cutting only but will wait for a move by other majors before acting.

9. One large company official states: 'In determining the amount of assistance we

It should be obvious that a major company's retail price policy may have a substantial effect on independent competition. Price cutting, of course, is almost mandatory for successful independent operation. If a major seller meets each price cut immediately and on the nose, independent competition is unable to gain a foothold or even if it does it cannot survive. Most (if not all) major sellers, realizing this fact, adopt a live-and-let-live policy; that is, they aim toward a price differential which protects their dealers from raids by price cutters but at the same time does not draw heavily from independent competitors. Some aggressive price competitors are extremely cognizant of the importance of the size of the retail price differential also and attempt to keep it within bounds.[10]

Causes of price wars in gasoline distribution

Some areas seem to be more susceptible to price wars than others. There are numerous market areas in the United States which seem to be particularly vulnerable to acute price disturbances in gasoline distribution at the retail level. Among these are Los Angeles, Chicago, St Louis, Kansas City, Milwaukee, to name only a few. The reasons for this vary with the community. It may be that the city is a refining center with attendant supplies of gasoline for sale at lowest price quotations at the rack (Los Angeles is an example of this), or that low-cost methods of transportation are available which make possible 'importing' supplies from refining centers at a price which will justify undercutting the market (Chicago).

It may be, on the other hand, that the key factor in the situation is an aggressive merchant who happens to be in that area or who decides to enter the market. In the early 1920s in Sioux City, Iowa, a community of approximately 80,000 population, the distribution of gasoline was in the hands of several large companies, one or two secondary marketers, a strong local company which jobbed products under its own brand, and a handful of smaller jobbers, some of whom handled recognized national brands and others who marketed under private brands. An individual doing business under what shall be designated the X oil company reportedly arrived in Sioux City, secured a piece of property on one of the

---

will give them [dealers], we try to go no farther than necessary to enable them to have the minimum margin that they require and still post a price that will enable them to defend their position in competition with the stations who are cutting the price.' The top official of one major concern states: 'Geographically, adjustments must cover a natural marketing area. Counties are generally natural marketing areas where people can center their shopping. Likewise cities and villages. The test is, what area can we delineate which will disturb surrounding areas least?'

10. In fact, one leading independent seller (in a powder-keg market) polices other similarly situated sellers in order to preserve differentials of not over 2c between major and nonmajor brands.

main streets which had railroad siding facilities, erected a portable steel building, and advertised gasoline to the public at a retail price several cents below the price prevailing in other stations in the city. It was strictly a cash operation; no service was given, not even air service.

The diversion of volume from long-existing operations was reported to be phenomenal. When other companies reduced their own retail gasoline prices and a temporary slowing of volume transference occurred, the X company made a further reduction. Finally, several leading marketers met X company prices. Presently a large billboard was erected at the X location advising the public that the station was temporarily closed because the railroad had sidetracked gasoline intended for the station. A few days later the station reopened and for several months the price war raged. Eventually, according to reports, several local jobbers organized a company which shall be called the Y oil company. A competing station of the same type was constructed in the vicinity of the X station. For some time it was operated on the policy of remaining open when X was open, closing when X closed, and always selling at the same prices. Eventually the X station was discontinued, and it was reported that the proprietor moved to Omaha, engaged in the same type of program in that community, and at the psychological time sold the business to a group of local companies which closed it.

One does not have to look far to find the basic causes of price wars in gasoline distribution. The intensive price disturbances which occur in this trade from time to time are largely a function of the supply of product, and, it will be recalled, the supply of the product is not easily controlled.

Approaching the problem in more specific terms, gasoline price wars develop out of:

1. Surplus gasoline in storage at refineries, including low-grade, recycled motor fuel which moves into some markets occasionally.[11] This surplus product may be a) an oversupply of the commodity for the whole industry (or at least the segment serving the particular market in which prices are weak),[12] or b) an excess supply of the product by some one seller, possibly because he has just entered the market and has not yet sufficient product acceptance for his refinery output.[13]

11. A condensate from which a natural gasoline and L.P.G. are distilled. Its principal detrimental characteristic is that it has a very erratic boiling range. This would be classified as a 'poor product', for the reason mentioned.

12. It should be noted that when storage tanks are full the product must move out into the market. Supplies in storage, therefore, may have a depressing effect on market prices.

13. Oversupply of this type may be almost as effective in depressing prices as if a general oversupply existed, because often the particular seller must find a market for his product promptly and hence may have to make heavy concessions to buyers.

2. Low laid-down cost of gasoline at the tank car level. Some markets, as a result of Mississippi or Ohio River barge operations or the Great Lakes Pipeline, or refineries located in close proximity, are particularly vulnerable to the unloading of low-cost supplies with a resulting commodity availability at lower-than-market prices.[14]

3. New-type, cut-price operators at the retail level, including trackside stations[15] and more recently self-serve stations.[16] The entrance of such functionaries into a market, or an attempt by them to increase gallonage and market position in an area which they already occupy, results in a siphoning of volume from rival stations and subsequent retaliatory action by those affected.

These, note, are basic causes of price wars in gasoline distribution; but this does not necessarily mean that because one or more of these conditions exist a price war would result. A general surplus of gasoline in one area might be disposed of in another market where gasoline is not in oversupply. An oversupply of gasoline by some one company might be, and often is, disposed of by sale to other refiners or by some sort of trading arrangement. Those importing gasoline into an area by some low-cost method of transportation might use restraint in their pricing. The operators of new-type gasoline dispensaries might elect to run their organizations on

14. As rail transportation of gasoline declined and was replaced by pipeline and barge movement on the Mississippi and Ohio rivers, it became easier to move surplus supplies of so-called 'distress' gasoline through terminals sometimes owned and operated by high-volume, low-cost operators. When such supplies are in abundance, an existing cut-price operator may decide that it is worth while to build additional volume, even temporarily, by means of the price-reduction technique. Such a move will result in other cut-price competitors following suit. Then the branded operators feel it necessary to protect their volume by at least a partial reduction in their prices. Eventually the oversupply situation is corrected and the prices of all sellers advance.

15. Beginning in the 1920s all over the Middle West, reportedly, the 'trackage' type of low-cost operator (who bought in tank car lots and accepted delivery into large tanks from a tank car spotted on a spur track) expanded in numbers until in practically all large centers of population operators of that type existed. Often a periodic price war occurred which was directly attributable to the scramble for volume among low-price stations competing with each other, and even, perhaps, among the conventional stations having to protect themselves against inroads on volume caused by such competitors.

16. In April, 1949, a gasoline price war took place in Denver, Colorado, which involved the cut-rate stations but did not involve the dealers of the major companies. It is interesting in this connection that the newspaper story report on this skirmish stated 'leaders in the price cutting said privately Saturday that all competing companies may hoist the white flag within the next few days, and that they have been 'talking it over'' among themselves' (*The Denver Post*, 24 April 1949). One spokesman said he thought 'they will reach the agreement stage Sunday'. Another said, 'As soon as one moves his prices back the rest will follow.'

a live-and-let-live basis. Actually in time, however, these forces will tend toward intensive price-competitive conditions. This is particularly true if more than one of these conditions exist in combination, e.g., new-type distributive outlets and excess supplies of product.

The nature of gasoline price wars

[. . .] In their early stages price wars appear to be, and indeed possibly are, the mere exercising of normal or near-normal price competitive tactics. That is, vendors are attempting to wrest business from other sellers or to protect their business from the inroads of competitors and in the process are relying heavily on price as a competitive tool. As in real war, however, when aggressive forces are on the move (due in part to a need or fancied need for 'more room'), an action by one leads to counteraction by another. Submarine warfare (unilateral in the early stages) results first in secrecy of departure of ships and then zigzag tactics; this may be followed by the equipping of merchant vessels with antisubmarine weapons. These tactics, note, are merely defensive. But continued (and possibly increasingly intensive) action by the aggressor eventually calls for all-out offensive action by those affected.

So in price wars, raids by aggressive price competitors result first in the use of non-price-competitive devices and the offering of higher quality service by some vendors,[17] then indirect[18] or selective[19] price appeals may be made to retain customers. At the same time moderate open-price adjustments on the principal product are made by some dealers. Later more and more dealers reduce prices on the principal item and price cutting becomes more drastic. The final stage (not always reached) is when countermeasures are taken by the initiators of the reduction, which in turn may be undercut by defensive competitors, until the level of prices has been reduced to a point where it is considerably below total (and even in some instances below direct) costs. [. . .]

Several concluding statements should be made concerning the present nature of price wars in gasoline distribution:

1. Price wars in this day usually (if not always) originate at the retail level

17. Non-price-competitive devices are those which rely on persuasion to attract custom. This may be in the form of advertising, point-of-sale or display, or by personal contact with potential customers, as in establishing friendly relations at the time of sale or house-to-house soliciting.

18. Price concessions on items other than gasoline.

19. Discriminatory discounts to regular customers, to those who complain about prices, or to others. Many stations cater particularly to commercial trade. Sometimes, reportedly, they post a cut price, but usually the signs read 'discounts to trucks' or simply 'trucks'. In other instances two or three colored electric lights are displayed which indicate the number of cents off the posted price for trucks.

and except for subsidy arrangements made by suppliers are confined to that level.

2. There is little if any evidence that major companies start price wars in the sense that they initiate price decreases at the retail level, although major company gasoline often is sold in the stations which touch off the 'fireworks'.

3. Unlike the situation which obtained in the old Standard Oil trust days, modern gasoline price wars are not the result of local price cutting by suppliers for the purpose of eliminating rivals but are, rather, the result of attempts by new factors to enter a market or expand operations, or simply of any supplier to unload excess supplies of product.

Impact and possible results of price wars

Industry spokesmen to the contrary, price wars may actually achieve certain competitive results. In any case one may not necessarily be able to avoid such disturbances simply because they are destructive. It should be emphasized that competition is rugged and impersonal and is not presumed to be easy.

It appears from the evidence that gasoline price wars usually are not planned; rather, the participants become involved in them during the heat of everyday rivalry. That is, in striving for patronage, the tactics of one group (such as certain independent sellers) may be especially successful; consequently competitors may make moves designed to prevent further inroads on their custom or even to recapture what has been lost. Such sellers may possibly cut price secretly at first. Finally the participants may find themselves in the midst of a vicious struggle which no vendor really wanted and from which no individual seller can withdraw until the heat of battle subsides.

Assuming the existence of competition, however, the participants very possibly would be forced to make the same decisions again with the full realization that they are running a risk of becoming involved in another price war. Sellers must assume a calculated risk of becoming involved in intensive price disturbances if they are to compete vigorously to gain or maintain a position in the market.

The impact of price wars is felt by all functionaries concerned – suppliers, wholesale distributors, and retail dealers. Assuming no help is provided by the supplier, the retail vendor probably is hardest hit by a price war because:

1. His margin is greatly reduced if not actually eliminated during an 'engagement'.
2. His whole business is affected.
3. He is not usually well resourced.

R. Cassady 71

The wholesale distributor, if an independent, is next hardest hit, assuming no aid is given by the supplier. Suppliers – those distributing the product over a wide area at least – are not usually as seriously hurt, if only because of the fact that a relatively small proportion of their business is affected.

Actually, as has been seen, some aid usually is forthcoming from suppliers in the form of margin guarantees, although such guarantees may be considerably short of the normal margin earned in the absence of price war conditions. Hence neither the retail dealer nor the wholesale distributor suffers as much as he might otherwise. This is another way of saying that the burden is shifted to some extent from marketers to suppliers. Needless to say, however, price wars mean losses for all concerned except, of course, the ultimate consumer.

In view of the costs of price wars it might be well to look at the results which might be expected from them. Considering the matter in the abstract only for the moment, price wars may have three types of results:

1. The price war might have the effect of correcting or modifying whatever maladjustments or other factors gave rise to the war – the existence of surplus merchandise, the use of hyperaggressive competitive tactics by certain sellers, etc. – and thus competitive conditions would be restored to normal. As a result no further price disturbance would be likely to occur, at least for a time. Under such conditions the sharing of the market by those competing in it might return to that existing before the war or it might continue as adjusted by price war conditions.

2. The price war might have little effect in altering basic factors underlying the disturbed market conditions, but fundamental changes might occur in the psychology of one or both of the participants or groups of participants so that attitudes of competitors would be altered. This change in attitude might apply to a) those well established in the market who now may have decided that they will be satisfied with a smaller share of the market, or b) the invaders who may now accept a live-and-let-live philosophy and henceforth be less aggressive in their competitive activities. Under such conditions the cessation of hostilities may, of course, be temporary or may have a considerable degree of permanence, depending to some extent upon the attitude of the group making the concessions and on supply and demand conditions.

3. The price war might have little or no effect except that both sides would have suffered losses during the period of the war. Assuming surplus supplies were the cause, excess supplies might still overhang the market; assuming aggressive competitors precipitated the war, they may still be determined to strive aggressively for a larger share of the market, given the oppor-

tunity. Any armistice under such conditions is merely a breathing spell (possibly even designed for tactical purposes), with a resumption of hostilities a certainty in the future.

Termination of price wars

Price wars usually do not continue indefinitely but normally come to an end in time. It is interesting to consider the various methods of termination which might manifest themselves in the market place.[20]

It would, of course, be possible for a price war to peter out from sheer exhaustion on the part of the participants. It would, for example, be possible that the end would be self-generating in that the individual responsible for its initiation would consider himself beaten and decide to capitulate; thus the contending parties would move back to pre-price-war levels. Generally it is very difficult to see how any single retail vendor could make a move which would have any material ameliorative effect on the situation; and obviously it would tend to ruin the seller making the move upward unless others could be expected to follow immediately.[21]

There is no question but that some new crystallizing force is usually needed to bring about the termination of a price war. These forces may be of any one of several types:

1. The price leader or some other strong factor in the market with a chain of service stations might announce an increase in prices in its outlets in the hope that this will lead toward a restoration of normal prices.

2. The price leader or some other strong factor in the market might raise tank wagon prices or abandon an existing dealer subsidy plan in the hope, perhaps, that other suppliers would follow suit and that dealers would then have to increase prices.

3. The leader or some other strong factor in the market might let it be known that his company would be receptive toward a solution of a certain type and would move in a certain way if 'proper' action were taken by the individual competitor or group of competitors concerned.

4. The leader or some other strong factor in the market might announce his intention of meeting cut-raters on the nose[22] if they continue to sell at a price lower than the usually acceptable (typically $2 \cdot 0c$) differential.[23]

20. One prominent oil jobber seems to feel that the best way to end them is never to start them. See Bero (1952).

21. Or alternatively, unless the initiator of the increase were to retreat promptly.

22. This would have a ruinous effect on such sellers. Such a threat was reported by a large terminal operator in the St Louis area as having been made by a strong major supply factor in that area some time ago. This threat reportedly had the desired effect.

23. Although this varies from market to market.

5. The leader or some other strong factor might cut off supplies of one or more of the aggressive price competitors[24] as a disciplinary measure (with the hope that this would bring price cutters to terms).

6. Representatives of the contending forces might actually get together and come to some agreement concerning a solution.[25]

While any one of the forces mentioned may be successful in bringing a price war to a conclusion, no solution will have any degree of permanency if the condition causing the price war still persists. That is, if large supplies still overhang the market the price situation will be extremely acute; likewise if ambitious aggressive price competitors remain in the market, assuming no change has taken place in the psychology of the contending party or parties.

While price wars are painful to participants they are manifestations of vigorous competitive conditions and should not be condemned by public, authorities, unless the device is used by powerful sellers to eliminate competitors. Attempts to outlaw them by some drastic legislative scheme would be a step toward the abandonment of competition, which in the author's judgment would be tragic.

There are in certain states, as has been mentioned, cost-floor laws which prohibit selling below a seller's cost if the intent is to destroy competition. The use of this type of legislation probably could not do much harm and might possibly do some good[26] if

1. Sellers fully understand their rights with respect to the use of their own costs as evidence in this type of law.

2. 'Costs' can be properly interpreted to include variations arising out of volume operations.

3. Assurance could be had of an absence of concerted action by sellers. It would not appear that these laws so operate at present.

24. In the price skirmish in the Denver, Colorado, market area in April, 1949, mentioned earlier, one company spokesman said that there had been an instance of a cut-rate company being 'cut off at its gas source entirely until it changed its prices', although the firm mentioned denied it (*The Denver Post*, 26 April 1949).

25. This is not too likely if it requires supplier company participation or even acquiescence (although by no means impossible) because of the danger of involvement with the Department of Justice. It is more likely if individual dealers or groups only are involved. . . .

26. Professor E. T. Grether of the University of California, Berkeley, has an interesting hypothesis on the possible results of price-floor legislation – that since deep-price cutting is prohibited, price cutters will make moderate reductions on a wide line of items. That is, instead of practicing deep cutting on only one or two items of a line for loss-leader purposes, there would be moderate reductions on the whole offering perhaps.

More drastic suggestions have been made in some quarters. It has been suggested that the service station trade be controlled by a governmental board which would, in the manner of public utility regulation, set the prices to be charged by retail vendors. This type of setup is used in some states in the barber trade and in beauty parlor and cleaning and dyeing operations. The scheme has been evaluated and condemned elsewhere by this author, on the ground that it practically eliminates price competition, tends to vitiate progress in methods of distribution, and is not in the public interest (Brown and Cassady, 1947). It would be this author's conclusion that the aggressive price competitor should not be restricted in his activities. It is out of such rivalry that low prices of superior product-services and a strong and healthy industry develop.

References

BERO, J. L. (1952), 'Hold that line, Mr Oil man', an address before the convention of the North West Petroleum Association (pamphlet).
BROWN, W. F., and CASSADY, R., Jr (1947), 'Guild pricing in the service trades', *Q. J. Econ.*, vol. 61, pp. 311–38.
The Denver Post (1949), 24 and 26 April.

Part Two
Competition and Concentration

The spatial features of the market are central to any analysis of competition in retailing. Lewis (Reading 7) develops a theory to derive the optimal number and size of retail units, proceeding from initial assumptions about retailing costs, customer density and location, transport costs, and amounts purchased. His paper also ranges widely over the economics of retail trade practices and regulation.

Hood and Yamey (Reading 8) present a critical examination of attempts to use the theory of imperfect competition to explain competition in retailing. The same authors (Reading 9) describe the development of middle-class consumer cooperative retailing in Britain in the second half of the nineteenth century. It is a case-study of innovation in retailing and its impact on competition and prices, and an extended illustration of points made by Wicksell [Reading 3]. Metcalf (Reading 10) looks at an aspect of the contemporary retailing scene – the extent of concentration in the retail grocery trade.

7 W. A. Lewis

Competition in Retail Trade

W. A. Lewis, 'Competition in retail trade', *Economica*, n.s., vol. 12, 1945, pp. 202–34.

The prejudices of some political writers against shopkeepers and tradesmen are altogether without foundation. So far from it being necessary either to tax them or to reduce their number, they can never be multiplied so as to hurt the public though they may be so as to hurt one another. The quantity of grocery goods, for example, which can be sold in a particular town, is limited by the demand of that town, and its neighbourhood. The capital, therefore, which can be employed in the grocery trade, cannot exceed what is sufficient to purchase that quantity. If this capital is divided between two different grocers, their competition will tend to make both of them sell cheaper than if it was in the hands of one only; and if it were divided among twenty, their competition would be just so much the greater and the chance of their combining together, in order to raise the price, just so much the less. Their competition might, perhaps, ruin some of themselves; but to take care of this is the business of the parties concerned, and may be safely left to their own discretion.

Thus spake the old master in 1776 (Smith, pp. 341–2). His conclusion has never been widely accepted. Retailers have always claimed that competition hurts the public no less than themselves and sought public support for their elaborate efforts to restrain it. Even the classical writers were unsure.[1] Modern economists feel more confident to tackle the problem, using as tools the newly shaped theory of monopolistic competition, but a combined knowledge of theory and of the structure of retailing is all too rare and attempts at a synthesis all too infrequent. A further venture does not therefore seem superfluous. Neither is the moment untimely. In November 1941, the Board of Trade made an Order prohibiting any person from opening a new retail business in this country except under licence. This was purely a wartime measure, and the President of the Board pledged himself to withdraw it after the war. But its enactment raised some hopes that permanent restrictions would follow, and recent fortunes at the polls have helped to revive these hopes. Meanwhile, some town planning authorities are already using, or planning to use, their powers in such a way as drastically to reduce the number of shops. This article may, perhaps, help to clarify the issues involved.

1. Cf. the extracts from the classical economists gathered together in Smith (1937, chapter 4).

The procedure adopted is to analyse first the effects of competition in prices and in services. The third section deals with certain special forms of competition which have been denounced as unfair, and the fourth section tries to reach conclusions on the main issues in the debate.

The number, size and location of shops

1. In the contemporary approach, the earliest doubts of the effectiveness of competition in retailing are associated with the name of Hotelling. In a stimulating article (1929) he argued, on certain special assumptions, that the effect of competition would be to cause sellers to cluster together, instead of dispersing at equal distances, and showed that this undesirable result in location causes transport costs to be excessive. Various writers interested themselves in the problem, but the outstanding advance is the contribution of Lerner and Singer eight years later, in an article (1937) which generalizes Hotelling's case, and is the most convenient starting point.[2]

The basic assumption is that the customers are strung out at equal distances along a road. Then, on the further assumptions

(a) that no two shops can be on the same spot;
(b) that each end of the road is a cul-de-sac;
(c) that each customer pays his own transport costs;
(d) that the number of shops is given;
(e) that the price is fixed;
(f) that there are no economies of scale;

Lerner and Singer show that in equilibrium (i) there cannot be more than two shops together, and (ii) there must be two shops together at each end of the road. They also imply that each shop must have the same number of customers, unless there is an odd number of shops, when one may have more than the others; but this is not so. The third condition of equilibrium is only that no shop may have less customers than half the number between any two other shops, or less than the shops at the end. Shops may be equidistant, but need not be, and as in any case the end shops must be paired, transport costs must be above the ideal.

Removing some of these assumptions brings the equilibrium conditions nearer to the ideal. Assumption (a) makes a negligible difference. Removing assumption (b) destroys conclusion (ii); if the road connects, say, two big market centres, the first shop at either end of the road may stand alone. As for assumption (c), Lerner and Singer themselves reach the important

2. From the bibliography included in the latest edition of Chamberlin (1933), a number of articles bearing on this subject seem to have appeared in American journals since 1939. On account of the war these journals have not yet arrived at the Library of the London School of Economics, and I have not been able to consult them.

conclusion that if transport costs are paid not by the customers but by the sellers, shops will be located at equal distances from each other, which is the ideal situation.

2. To advance the analysis beyond the Lerner–Singer stage it is necessary to remove the remaining assumptions. If the number of shops is not given, and prices are not fixed, and there are no economies of scale, the number of shops will be as great as the number of customers. This odd conclusion brings into the open the odd assumption underlying the whole analysis that transport cost from wholesaler to retailer can be neglected, but not transport cost from retailer to customer, an assumption which becomes the more unreasonable the greater the ratio of shops to customers. Nevertheless, the conclusion serves to remind us that the convenience of customers requires that there should be as many shops as possible, each small, and that it is only economies of scale which prevent this. The assumption of constant costs is incompatible with equilibrium in retailing, given dispersal of customers. For if a reduction in the size of shops will not increase costs, it will pay some seller to insert himself between two existing shops.

Should shops, then, be of 'optimum' size, meaning the minimum size consistent with minimum average cost, or should they be smaller, and if so, how much smaller? If we can assume that the inconvenience of not having a shop nearby can be translated into monetary terms as a function of the distance of the shop, the problem is capable of precise solution.

Let us assume:

(a) that all shops have the same costs;
(b) that there are no prime costs, but only an overhead, so that the average cost curve is a rectangular hyperbola (marginal costs are assumed away only for convenience of exposition; what matters is the assumption of falling average cost);
(c) that the customers are strung out along a road on either side of each shop, one customer for each unit of distance;
(d) that each customer buys one unit (money value) of merchandise;
(e) that the inconvenience of distance can be expressed as one unit of money per unit of distance, paid by the customer.

Then the following diagram shows the position.

AC is a rectangular hyperbola, representing the average cost curve of any shop, varying with the number of its customers (and therefore sales). *MTC* is the curve of marginal transport costs; the first two customers, one on either side, incur one unit each, the next two customers incur two units each, and so on; the curve can thus be drawn for simplicity as a straight line with a slope of 0·5. Total transport cost is the area lying beneath it, and average transport cost per customer will be a line with a slope of 0·25.

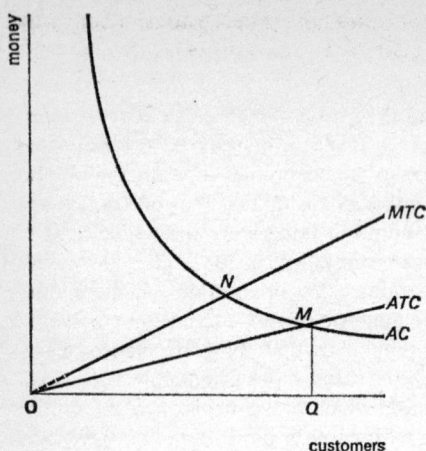

Figure 1

The ideal number of shops (or number of customers per shop) is such that, given the total number of customers to be served, the sum of shop costs and transport costs is at its minimum. This condition is fulfilled when for each shop the sum of average shop costs and average transport costs is minimized. Since for each new customer the former falls and the latter rises, the condition is fulfilled when the negative slope of AC equals the positive slope of ATC. AC being a rectangular hyperbola and ATC a straight line from the origin, this will be at the point where they meet. M gives us the ideal size of shop. It cannot correspond with the point where average shop cost would be minimized; since ATC is rising and AC is falling, the minimum point of $ATC + AC$ must be to the left of the minimum point of AC. In other words, it is desirable that shops should be of less than 'optimum' size.

Will competition bring about the right size? If there is free entry, and if there cannot be abnormal profits, the price charged by each shop (its gross margin) must lie somewhere along AC. If a shop reduces its price by one unit it will attract two customers, one on either side, who transfer their custom from its rivals. It pays therefore to lower the price by one unit if getting two more customers will reduce AC by more than one unit. Its equilibrium is therefore at the point N where the slope of MTC equals the slope of AC.[3] Thus shops will not cut their prices low enough to bring the right size. In competition, there will be too many shops, each too small.

3. N corresponds to Chamberlin's 'ideal adjustment' and to R in Figure 15 of his *Theory of Monopolistic Competition*, p. 92. The slope of MTC here corresponds to the slope of dd^1 in that diagram.

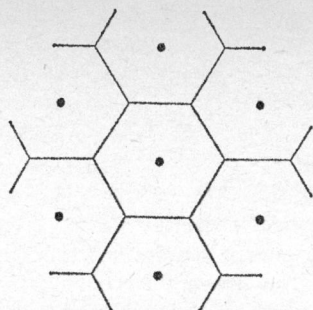

Figure 2

The result can be generalized by assuming that consumers do not live along a road, but are distributed over an area, one in each unit of space. It remains desirable that shops should be equidistant, and this condition can only be fulfilled if each is at the centre of a hexagon. How many shops there should be, and what should be the size of each, is then determined if we know how large the hexagon should be. Retaining our previous assumptions, the solution is as follows. If we write r for the length of the radius of the inscribed circle, the length of each side will be $1 \cdot 15r$. The number of customers equals the area of the hexagon, $3 \cdot 46r^2$. Writing a for the overhead costs of each shop, average cost per customer,

$$AC = \frac{a}{3 \cdot 46r^2}.$$

To calculate transport costs we first divide the hexagon into its twelve right-angled triangles. In each, taking the customers living along the base, the nearest lives at distance r and the furthest at distance $1 \cdot 15r$. The sum[4] of the distances for the base customers is $0 \cdot 61r^2$, and the total transport cost for the hexagon is twelve times the integral of this, i.e., $2 \cdot 41r^3$. This divided by the number of customers gives average transport cost per customer,

$$ATC = 0 \cdot 70r.$$

The ideal number of shops is given by the condition that the slopes of AC and ATC must be the same. Differentiating gives

$$\frac{a}{1 \cdot 73r^3} = 0 \cdot 70,$$

thus $r = 0 \cdot 93a^{\frac{1}{3}}$.

Now, in competition a shop will cut its price by one unit so long as the

4. I am indebted to Professor R. G. D. Allen for the formula.

resulting increase of customers reduces AC by more than one unit. Equilibrium therefore results when

$$\frac{a}{1 \cdot 73r^3} = 1,$$

thus $r = 0 \cdot 83a^{\frac{1}{3}}$.

This analysis brings out the relevant points. The number of shops depends on the extent of the economies of scale, the density of population (determining the number of customers per unit of distance), and the inconvenience or cost of distant shopping. The greater the economies of scale, and the less the cost of transport, the fewer shops there will and should be. The denser the population, the larger shops will be, and this is worth noting since many people believe that the decentralization of urban populations which has occurred since 1920 is one of the principal factors explaining the increase in the numbers engaged in distribution in this country (for example, Ford, 1936). In any case, given the dispersion of customers, the ideal size of shop is less than the 'optimum'; and, given competition, the actual size will be less than the ideal.[5]

3. Several qualifications are needed before we can derive from this anything like a complete picture.

First, the analysis has so far assumed that there is price competition, and that each shop cuts prices without taking the reaction of its competitors into account. This does not require that the price of every one of the hundreds of commodities it sells should be keenly competitive; it is enough that average gross margins for any class of trade must be adjusted to the level set by competition, and if this is so, the effect on size is the same. But even this is not a complete picture. To begin with, retail prices in certain trades – cigarettes, patent medicines, some groceries, milk, coal, confectionery, books, periodicals, stationery, lamps, cycles, petrol, motors and motor accessories – are maintained by elaborate arrangements between manufacturers, wholesalers and retailers, which impose heavy penalties for price cutting. The assumption that retailers are free to compete in prices however holds good in other trades – some groceries, fish, meat, fruit and vegetables, flowers, furniture, most hardware, drapery, footwear, clothes, pottery and others – and to these the analysis applies, subject to further qualifications.

5. The above example assumed that goods are transported as the crow flies. More realistic assumptions do not upset the argument unless immensely complicated routes have to be used. For example, if we assume that main roads run direct from shop to shop, and that side roads are perpendicular to these main roads at intervals of one unit, total transport cost becomes $2 \cdot 98r^3$; the optimum number of shops will be given by the equation $r = 0 \cdot 88a^{\frac{1}{3}}$, and the competitive number remains at $r = 0 \cdot 83a^{\frac{1}{3}}$.

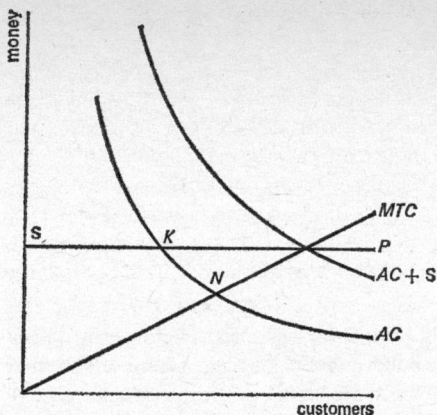

Figure 3

When prices are fixed the number of shops is a direct function of the level at which they are fixed. In terms of Figure 3 (which is constructed on the same cost assumptions as Figure 1), equilibrium is given by the point K at which the horizontal price line SP cuts AC. So long as shops are larger than this they will be making profits; new entrants will then be attracted, reducing the share of each in the trade, until abnormal profits vanish. As the price is usually too high under these schemes (for reasons we shall examine later) the number of shops will be excessive. At this point, however, it will pay any one shop to compete by offering better service. If all shops do this, as they must in competition, all make losses unless their number contracts, and in competition it will contract up to the point where the new cost curve (including the additional services) has the same slope as MTC. If, as in Figure 3, the extra services take the form of an addition to overhead costs, shops will be larger than they would be if there were competition in price but not in service, but prices will be higher. If they take the form of an addition to marginal costs, shops may be larger or smaller, high or rising marginal costs making for smaller shops.

Shops may, of course, compete neither in prices nor in service, even though prices are not maintained. If each shopkeeper takes into account the fact that if he cuts prices or offers more service his rivals will follow, shops will be still smaller and more numerous. The limit to their smallness will be set by the elasticity of demand in the market as a whole, i.e., by Q in Chamberlin's Figure 15 (1933, p. 92); in our diagram where elasticity is assumed to be zero it would be one shop for each customer. It is most unlikely in practice that this movement towards the upper limit will get very far. It is certainly unlikely in the United States of America, where aggressive competition is the rule, with chains, supermarkets and independents at each other's throats. Competition is not so keen in this country, but competition between the cooperatives, the multiples and the independents is nevertheless keen enough in non-price-maintained trades to keep the size of shops near to N. In the price-maintained trades price competition is ruled out; service competition tends to check the decrease in shop size, but it is not always very strong and, given the fall in wholesale prices which had been occurring steadily after 1920, it was possible for more and more redundant shops to establish themselves on an ever widening gross margin.

4. The second qualification concerns transport costs. The conclusion that in competition there must be too many shops depends on the assumption that customers pay transport costs. If the shop pays transport costs, it will take on an extra customer so long as the price exceeds the cost of transporting to him (marginal selling cost being on our assumptions zero). But since (Figure 1) MTC equals the price $(AC+ATC)$ at the point where $AC+ATC$ is at its minimum, it follows that the point of equilibrium for the shop paying transport costs is the same as the ideal equilibrium, represented by the output OQ. There will be too many shops if customers pay their own transport costs, but the ideal number of shops if there is free delivery.

The reason for this is that free delivery is a form of price discrimination (in this case perfect discrimination), and, if average costs are falling, discrimination usually brings output nearer to the ideal. The discrimination arises because the nearest customers pay a price in excess of AC plus the cost of transporting to them, and the furthest pay the same price which is much below AC plus the cost of transporting to them (indeed the furthest customer contributes nothing towards AC); in a sense the nearer subsidize the further. The same sort of result would be attained by any other form of discrimination, and is not the result of competition in service as such. If all the customers get as much service as they pay for, the result is merely to lift the average cost curve; shops may be larger, but the gap between the ideal and the competitive equilibrium is not diminished. However, there are also forms of service other than delivery which involve discrimination, e.g., credit and subsidized restaurants in department stores. Whenever a service is paid for by some who do not use it, and used by some *who would buy elsewhere but for this service*, the effect is to bring the competitive equilibrium nearer to the ideal equilibrium.

We must also note precisely what transport cost means in this context. MTC is a measure of all the inconvenience associated with buying at a distant shop. It is not the same as what it would cost the shop in money to deliver one's purchases. A customer who shops in the centre of the town may be quite capable of carrying home a pair of shoes without much extra trouble or inconvenience, and if asked to pay an extra sum equal to what delivery would cost the shop, might prefer to carry for himself. When therefore one concludes that shops will be larger and of optimum size if they offer free delivery but not otherwise, one concludes too much. If the firm's transport costs exceed the value of the real convenience conferred on the customer, the shop will not reach optimum size even if there is free delivery, and may indeed be smaller than it would be without free delivery if the disparity is great.

5. The third qualification is to remove the assumption of zero elasticity of demand. It will be more profitable for the shopkeeper to lower his price if he can count on selling more to his existing customers as well as on attracting other people's customers, so an elasticity exceeding zero will bring the competitive number of shops nearer to the ideal number, or even below it. There may be no 'excess capacity' if elasticity is large enough. Of the many modifications elasticity introduces into the results, this is the important one.

6. Next we must consider the assumption that there cannot be abnormal profits in equilibrium. This rests on two further assumptions. The first is that customers have no irrational preferences for shops, so that if two shops differ in nothing but their average price levels, customers will always buy from the cheaper. There has been some attempt to explain retailing, using as a large element in the analysis the irrationality, ignorance and inertia of customers.[6] While it is impossible to deny that these factors have some importance, it is impossible to agree to any significant importance in view of the rapid changes constantly taking place in the structure of retailing, as reflected in the relative strengths of independents, multiples, department stores, street markets, and the cooperative societies. Any shopkeeper who used the irrationality, ignorance, or inertia of his customers as major elements in his policy would soon find himself in Carey Street.

The other assumption necessary to keep prices equal to average cost is that continuous variability in the number of customers per shop is possible in each locality. This cannot be taken for granted. In the suburbs a new shop sets up between two other shops, and its impact is borne more heavily by the sales of these shops than it is by the sales of other shops. At any given moment, therefore, with a given number of shops, it may be that if a new shop could be introduced in such a way as to take trade away equally from all shops (i.e., if all the shops were re-located at shorter

6. See especially Smith (1937, chapter 5).

intervals and one added), the new shop could remain permanently, but that since it would in fact be limited to sharing in the trade of two or three others, the shop will not be established. Certain consequences flow. First, profits may be abnormal without new shops being established, because there is more than enough for two but not enough for three; the corollary is that shops may be larger and fewer than the true competitive equilibrium. On the other hand, if too many shops come into existence, there is less likelihood of price or service competition, because in a small market sellers are more likely to take account of each other's reactions; and the entry of a new shop results simply in higher prices. There is, however, a check on this. Suburban shops compete not only with each other but also with shops in the large shopping centres, which are more aggressive. This fact makes possible continuous variability; it prevents suburban shop-keepers from exploiting a local monopoly, and keeps down the number of shops.

7. The fifth qualification is now to take full account of the existence of these large shopping centres.

From the analytical point of view, the difference is that we remove the assumptions that the customers are strung out evenly, one in each spot, and that transport costs are involved. For at a shopping centre there are thousands of persons who find themselves there for reasons other than shopping, and who, once there, can shop without counting transport cost. If we remove the assumption of transport costs, and assume large enough numbers of customers, it follows that in a large shopping centre shops should be of 'optimum' size, meaning that average cost is at a minimum. The customer in Oxford Street takes real feminine pleasure in shopping; she moves around comparing prices and qualities, consulting her friends, and taking hours (or days) to make up her mind. It would be too much to claim that elasticity of demand is infinite for each shop, especially in the naïve sense that a small shaving of price immediately expands sales; but it is not too much to say that, in trades where the customer shops around, shops with cheap prices will sooner or later bankrupt those which try to sell similar qualities with similar service at a higher price level in the same centre. In the long run, therefore, shops in large shopping centres must approximate to optimum size.

This conclusion at once explains two common phenomena. First that shops in the centre are usually larger than those in the suburbs, and secondly that their prices are in consequence frequently lower[7]; and it

7. Differences in rent complicate the issue. Higher rents may or may not outweigh larger turnover. For department stores of equal size, rent is decisive in the United States; see Burnham (1940, p. 455). It does not seem to be so decisive in England, but the evidence is not so clear; see Plant and Fowler (1939). For some theoretical discussion, see Chamberlin (1933), Appendix C.

reinforces the point that the suburban shop has only a precarious local monopoly. At the same time it raises another question. Since there is usually more than one shop of each kind in a large shopping centre, an 'approximate long run infinite elasticity of demand' is consistent only with the assumption that the economies of scale are fairly easily exhausted. Otherwise there would be only one shop of each kind. How true is this?

The evidence is scanty, contradictory, and difficult to assess. It is quite clear that a medium-sized shop has lower costs than a very small one-man shop, if similar factors are similarly remunerated. But, of course, this is not always so. The small man who converts his parlour into a shop where he or his family serve part-time may have very low transfer costs, and be able to carry on indefinitely with low gross margins. To return, however, it is clear that where transfer earnings are similar the medium-sized shop has lower costs than the smallest shops. For example, Colin Clark's analysis (1940, p. 334) of the grocery trade of a number of stores controlled by a large cooperative society revealed the following situation:

Average turnover (£ per week)	Costs (including interest but excluding profit) as percentage of turnover
100–200	13·21
200–300	11·51
300–400	11·13
400–500	10·50
500 upwards	10·08

A similar picture is suggested by Cadbury Brothers as applying to confectionery shops (*Industrial Record, 1919–39*, p. 49).

It is in comparing the medium and the large shop that the evidence is inconclusive. The authors of a careful American survey (Twentieth Century Fund, 1939, p. 145) conclude that, apart from the high cost of the one-man business, there is 'no convincing evidence of a general tendency for costs to decrease progressively as store size increases', and proceed to quote exceptions. Everything depends on the nature of the trade. The principal economy of large shopkeeping is the economy of having specialist buyers purchasing in large quantities. The more the goods can be standardized the greater is this economy. It is therefore small in the millinery business, but large in the Woolworth type of trade. The classes of shop which most multiply themselves in central shopping centres, those selling women's wear and household goods, are the classes in which standardization tends to be least, and the advantages of scale small. The shops selling standardized goods are seldom found in great numbers even in the largest shopping centres, because it is more convenient for them to be widely distributed through the suburbs. They secure the economies of large buying through concentrating several shops under one management rather than by having a large turnover per shop; but the number of customers congregating in the centre may be sufficient to support two or three or more in any trade, each of more or less 'optimum' size.

The department store fits with difficulty into the pattern of this argument. In a large shopping centre there is usually more than one. Yet the evidence is clear that there are substantial economies of scale, both in the United States[8] and in this country.[9] It is true that the American evidence shows the medium-sized department store having lowest costs, but this is because delivery and publicity expenses are higher for the largest stores, and these expenses are not relevant if we are considering merely competition between two stores in the same centre, with nearly infinite long-run cross elasticities. The large department store should be able to drive all others out of its centre simply by cutting prices. Why, also, does it not drive out the specialist shops?

The latter is easier to answer. It must be remembered that even the largest department store is really only a collection of several small or medium-sized shops under one roof. A large department store may be able to buy more cheaply than a small one. But the shoe department of a large department store is not necessarily bigger than an independent shoe shop, and not necessarily able to buy more cheaply. Indeed, department stores are keenly conscious of the competition of the specialist shops. This is one reason why the multiple shop idea has spread over into the department store field, and why some of these multiple department stores have now adopted central buying. But the main strength of the department store is not price competition, but the fact that it offers the opportunity to buy everything under one roof, plus delivery, credit, and various amenities, and on these it concentrates its appeal. It is really doing a different class of trade from the specialist shop, and not strictly comparable.

This also yields the clue to competition between department stores themselves. The price competition is real, and governed also by the need to compete with specialist shops both at the centre and in the suburbs, which may be able to offer lower prices because they offer also less service. But because service is so important, price competition is not decisive. No two department stores have quite the same atmosphere, or give quite the same service, and the larger would not necessarily bankrupt the smaller by cutting its prices five per cent. Moreover, even if it could, the struggle would

8. Cf. Burnham (1938, p. 211).
9. Cf. Plant and Fowler (1939).

be long and costly. Prudence, and the small number of department stores, demand that while price competition should be real, it should be 'based on costs', within the limits of what competition by specialist shops allows. In effect, the department store trade is rather special, and though it has close substitutes, is sufficiently limited for the oligopolistic phenomenon of 'excess capacity' to prevail even in the shopping centre.

Moreover, in trying to analyse the existing situation, we must not treat it as if it were in 'equilibrium'. The department store in the 1930s was going through an awkward phase. When first it appeared, in the second half of the nineteenth century, it was a pioneer of modern methods of retailing, and its wide success was largely due to outdistancing its rivals in this respect. By the 1920s its rivals had caught up with it, and were giving it a stiff fight, and it is doubtful whether it continued to expand relatively to other forms of retail trade. It has been forced to review its policies, to decentralize internal management, to consider central buying with other stores, and to rely more and more on service. As costs of service have risen, the policy of relying on service has itself been brought into question, since some competitors, unhampered by the high costs of free delivery, rest rooms, subsidized cafes, credit, and the rest, have pushed the price feature in their 'cash and carry' policy. Most of the department stores in the United States and many in this country were losing money during the 1930s. It would be unwise to prophesy what policies they will be pursuing in the 1950s.

8. We have thus two different types of analysis to apply to retailing, one assuming that the customers are dispersed and find a dispersal of shops convenient (with an excessive number[10] of small shops as the result), and the other assuming that the customers are concentrated in shopping centres (with the right number of shops, of optimum size). Both, of course, apply; moreover to some extent they apply to quite different classes of trade. Here the American distinction between 'convenience' and 'shopping' goods is useful. The former are articles purchased regularly and preferably from the nearest shop. The customer knows from daily experience just what he wants: there is no 'shopping around', and the shops tend to be spread evenly over the whole area – beef, fish, cigarettes, groceries, beer, medicines and the like tend to be bought at the nearest outlet. With shopping goods, on the other hand, the customer wishes to compare prices and qualities before she makes up her mind – hats, curtains, dresses, even stockings – and the shops selling these things tend to congregate in shopping centres. The division is not watertight; some convenience goods shops of more or less optimum size are to be found in shopping centres, in competition with the suburban shops; while it is possible to find shops selling shopping

10. Unless elasticity of demand is large enough to bridge the gap.

goods in isolation in the suburbs, e.g., the ubiquitous draper. Department stores are in both classes of trade.

One further point is needed to complete the picture. So far we have spoken as if shops are to be found either clustered together in a central area, or spread over the suburbs in lonely isolation. A little observation shows that nearly all shops are in a centre of some kind. Nevertheless the distinction between the central and the suburban shopping centres remains. The shops which are found together in the suburban shopping area tend to be shops selling different classes of goods. These shops are not in close competition with each other, except in the sense in which all shops are competing for the consumers' incomes, and the fact that these different shops stand together does not invalidate the analysis. The theory of the optimum number of suburban shops becomes instead a theory of the optimum number of suburban shopping centres. Account must, however, be taken of the fact that these centres vary in size. This is due to the fact that the desirable frequency of shops varies in different trades, with the importance of overhead costs, the convenience of nearness, and the percentage of the population consuming the particular commodity. We should expect to find a large number of small centres, and smaller numbers of larger ones. Precisely where each centre is and which centres are large, are determined more by geographical considerations – the layout of streets, the junctions of main roads, the flow of traffic, and so on – than by the differential calculus, but overhead cost, density and convenience, the factors included in our calculations, are plainly not irrelevant. Ranging shopping centres in order of size, from the smallest to the largest, we should find that some suburban centres have sufficient trade to support several shops of one kind, each of optimum size, while in other trades there may be only one shop, of less than optimum size, and in others no shop at all. From the point of view of the trades in the first category this is a central shopping centre, because it is large enough to support more than one shop of optimum size, while from the point of view of the trades in the other categories it is a suburban shopping centre because it is not large enough. As the size of centres increases, so does the number of trades in which shops can be of optimum size, and to which this is a central shopping centre, until we reach the largest centres, with their department stores straining to reach the optimum.

9. We may now return to the end of section 6, where we began to take account of the effect of the existence of central shopping centres on shops in the suburbs. The first effect is a tendency for shops to be both smaller and at greater distances than they would be from each other, because the density of buying population in the suburbs is reduced. On the other hand, suburban shopkeepers, having to face the competition of central shopping

areas, are less likely to try to exploit local monopoly positions, and this increase in competitiveness is a factor on the side of lower prices and fewer and larger shops. The extent of price competition, however, varies. In price-maintained convenience goods trades – and nearly all such trades are price-maintained – the suburban shopkeeper faces only competition in service, which, at a distance, may not be very effective. In such trades it is certain that there will be too many shops. In the shopping goods trades the position is different; the suburban shops are faced with both price and service competition from shops of optimum size at the centre, and are compelled to keep their prices as low as is consistent with the fact that they themselves cannot attain to optimum size. (This is one of the reasons why price maintenance is unlikely to spread over into such trades.)

10. We may conclude by summarizing:

(a) Suburban shops should be of less than optimum size; if there is free entry into retailing they will be smaller and more numerous than they should be, unless elasticity of demand is large enough to bridge the gap; and if there is price maintenance they will be still smaller and more numerous, with perhaps too much service;

(b) Free delivery and other discriminatory services tend to bring shops nearer the ideal size and number;

(c) In central shopping centres shops will be of optimum size, and shops selling shopping goods will tend to cluster together here; department stores are an exception in that they are probably too numerous and too small.

Competition in service

1. Retailing is not a homogeneous 'commodity'; it varies widely in quality, and correspondingly in cost. We must now examine the contention that the effect of competition is an excess of the more expensive forms, as well as the reverse contention, that competition causes the quality of the service to deteriorate.

It is useful to begin by distinguishing the features which make for expense. One is the very existence of service. 'Help yourself' shops exist in the United States, and show the lowest margins of all. Then there is the speed with which service is effected – how long the customer has to wait before an assistant attends to him. Speedy service is particularly costly because the flow of customers into the shop is irregular. If the shop tried to keep enough assistants to be able to deal with the largest number of customers ever likely to be in the shop, most of these would be idle for much of the time, sales per assistant low and operating costs high. In retailing as in transport, costs would be much reduced if customers could distribute themselves evenly throughout the day and (though this is not so important) throughout the year. Next comes the quality of the assistants. In some trades the customer relies on the shopkeeper for information of the comparative qualities of the merchandise, and shop assistants have to be specialists trained in its qualities and uses. This means not only a more expensive kind of assistant, but also a smaller average number of customers per assistant than in, for example, the Woolworth type of trade. Another important service is performed when the shop offers the customer a wide choice of styles, colours, sizes or makes from which to suit his requirements. Some shops, especially department stores, add to this the right to return the purchase if on going home the customer changes her mind – American department stores report that one day's sales in eight are returned (Twentieth Century Fund, 1939, p. 308) – and find this a heavy burden. Lifts, escalators, rest rooms, credit, free delivery, information – the list becomes too long for elaboration.

Account must also be taken of forms of retailing which do not involve the customer in going to the shop. Orders by telephone or by mail are convenient if the customer knows just what he wants, and this form of business has low operating costs. Or the shop may go to the customer, in the form of the travelling van or the door-to-door salesman. Here operating costs are usually high.

2. In order to arrive at the conclusion that competition leads to an excess of the more expensive forms of retailing, in substitution for the less expensive, it is necessary to establish one of two propositions – either that customers get what they want, but should not be allowed to get it; or that they get what they do not want, through market imperfection. The first proposition has its adherents; they admit that the customer prefers good service even when there is a real choice open to him of less expensive forms, but they contend that this is a luxury he should not be allowed. In wartime we have all accepted this view in the United Kingdom, in order to release resources for other purposes. In peacetime too, 'productive' output would be greater if 'distributive' activity were curtailed, and in a planned economy a planning authority which attached little value to convenience in shopping relatively to increased outputs of other utilities would undoubtedly take steps to restrict the more expensive forms of retailing. In this country, however, where women exercise the vote, such restrictions are unlikely. To a busy woman – and with the decline of domestic service and the increased entry of women into jobs and professions nearly all women will be busy women – good shopping facilities are essential; if she can get served without waiting, see at once a wide range from which to choose, and obtain delivery, she can get back rapidly to her duties; to reduce such facilities would mean that the public spent more time in

shopping, and some of what was gained in distribution costs would be lost in other ways.

It is more important to examine the proposition that some who would prefer less service and lower prices are deprived of it. This depends on market imperfection. In a large shopping centre where all kinds of shops are competing it is highly unlikely. There are shops with much service and high prices, and shops with less service and lower prices, and the customers are free to sort themselves out. In 1931 one of America's leading authorities on retailing (McNair, 1931, p. 39) wrote:

To judge from what is happening in the department store field and from what is happening in the chain store field, it is a fair generalization that types of distributive enterprise tend to develop through three stages. They start off very largely on a price basis – as chain stores did for instance, they catch the attention of the consumer by distributing merchandise at low prices because of a low overhead. That is the first stage. The next stage is the 'trading up' of the quality of the merchandise handled. We can see chain stores going through that stage today. After they have traded up the quality of the merchandise handled, and some of the price advantage has been lost in the process, distributive enterprises develop into a third stage, characterized by competition in services of all kinds, for instance in allowing customers to return merchandise; by high costs of doing business; by largely competitive advertising; and by an increase in the ratio of the fixed investment to the total investment. Department stores to-day are in that stage.

This would seem to support the view that the public inevitably prefers better services to low prices, but events have not justified this conclusion. The department stores, having reached the third stage, have found themselves losing so much to cheaper rivals (including the 'supermarket', which was just making its appearance when the passage was written) that they have greatly extended their 'bargain basements', and some of them are beginning to urge on the fraternity that delivery and similar services should be charged for separately, so that the stores can retain some of the custom they have been losing to cheaper rivals. The tendency to higher costs, if it exists, is only like an escalator in the sense that as fast as some move up others come in at the bottom; the better simile would be a cycle, since the fourth stage brings lower costs than the third. The fact that the public is free to choose between the cheaper and the more expensive acts as a check preventing too much service from being offered.

The practice of 'price lining' may seem to support the opposite view. If prices tend to stick around certain figures, e.g., the eleven pence three-farthingses, increased efficiency would seem to lead not to lower prices but to better quality at the same price. This, however, is an illusion, since this better quality now sold cheaply was formerly sold at some higher price level. Price lining prevents prices from being continuously variable, but it does not prevent them from falling.

However, we cannot apply the same analysis to shops situated not in central but in local markets. There the element of local monopoly means that the customer has not an effective choice between several shops offering different degrees of service. Here there may well be too much service, especially in price-maintained trades, in the sense that some customers are getting more than they want. In non-price-maintained trades the competitive incentive is not so much to offer service as such, if the shop is able to offer different customers different degrees of service, as to offer types of service which involve price discrimination in favour of marginal customers, and which tend therefore to bring the shop nearer to the ideal size. Is this desirable, or does it mean that there is too much service? There are two sides to the argument. Clearly there is too much service in the sense that the marginal customers are getting more than they pay for: they are being subsidized. On the other hand, since the shop will have more customers, shops will be larger, fewer in number, and less costly. It is the old argument for price discrimination in new form.

If the services offered are real, and performed at minimum cost, we can say that there will not be too much service even in imperfect competition, provided that the imperfection is not due to any significant extent to 'irrational' elements. The three services which most merit analysis in this light are information, a range of styles, and delivery.

3. Information is a real service. We are all conscious of the wastes involved in competitive advertising, and tend to dismiss all publicity expenditure as wasteful. That it is not necessarily so has long been emphasized in economic literature.[11] For a market to be perfect all the buyers and all the sellers must know what is available and at what prices. Publicity expenditure which serves this purpose is really useful. Advertising is wasteful only when it is unnecessary because buyers and sellers already know the facts, or when it is false or misleading. Now, while much advertising by manufacturers is wasteful for these reasons, this is not usually the case with retailers' advertisements. Actually, only a very small proportion of retailers think it worth while to advertise, this itself being a tribute to the fact that the retail market is not as imperfect as some writers have suggested. And perusal of the advertisements published by retailers will show that while the element of reputation building is not absent, they tend to concentrate on straightforward information about particular lines which are on offer. It seems therefore legitimate to conclude that in retailing such publicity expenditure as there is performs for the most part a valuable service.

We cannot, however, dismiss manufacturers' advertisements as irrelevant to competition in retailing, for they are not. Since there is competition,

11. E.g., Braithwaite (1928).

every retailer is subject to pressures requiring him to stock as wide a range as his customers are likely to want to choose from, and this is indeed a factor on which manufacturers strongly rely in spending money on advertisements. This, therefore, brings us straight to the second problem, the range of goods retailers carry.

4. If in each commodity demand concentrated on one or two styles, economies of scale could be exploited, and prices would be lower. This is the basic case for the 'utility' scheme in wartime England. The first question is therefore why the market itself does not provide for getting these economies. To some extent it does. If a retailer finds that by concentrating all his efforts on a single style he can buy and sell more cheaply, he has an incentive to do so. The Woolworth type of business, which is one of the most successful forms of retailing, is based on this principle; the multiple shops, the department stores, and many independents also work on this basis to a larger extent than is generally recognized by those who advocate that the 'utility' scheme should be made permanent. Broadly speaking, standardization is the basis of large-scale retailing, and one of the reasons why in so many lines of production the retailer dominates the manufacturer.[12] In small-scale retailing, the retailer is not able to give large orders in standard designs, but relies rather on the wholesaler to do this. The wholesaler is to the small retailer as the centralized buying department is to the multiple shop, and if wholesalers were as efficient as the buyers of large-scale retailing, the whole pattern of retailing would be different. When Schumacher (1944) suggests virtually a state monopoly of wholesaling as the simplest way to control both production and distribution, he certainly puts his finger on the central weakness in the distributive chain (whatever the merits of the particular proposal). More efficient wholesaling would deprive the larger retailers of their principal advantage over the small, and would promote greater standardization of manufactures.

But, whatever the desire of large retail buyers or wholesalers to standardize, two other forces act as a check. One is the creation of 'consumer insistence' by manufacturers' advertisements. The case made for such advertising is varied. (a) Some useful commodities, e.g., the typewriter, would never have reached the public as quickly without it. This is undoubtedly true; some advertising performs the useful function of information. But this does not apply to all the £80,000,000 to £100,000,000 a year spent on advertising in this country.[13] (b) Advertising frequently leads not to an increase but to a reduction in the number of styles, and to

12. Nearly all the important groups of multiple shops in this country are manufacturer chains, in contradistinction to the United States.
13. This is the estimate made by Bishop (1944), chapter 3.

savings in production cost, by persuading the public to concentrate most of its purchases on one or two well advertised brands. This also is true. But the opposite is also frequently true; and if from the £100,000,000 we must subtract something for the cases where economies of scale are secured, if we are to have the true cost of advertising, we must also add something for the cases where consumer insistence hinders standardization. Bishop also advances two other ingenious arguments. (c) Advertising makes people want things they cannot afford; it therefore increases the propensity to consume and consequently increases employment. The argument might be impressive if there were not less costly ways of maintaining employment, but as there are, economists cannot be expected to take the argument seriously. (d) The press is always subsidized; where proprietors cannot get revenue from advertisers they sell themselves to political parties or the government, and in the long run subsidy by advertisement is far more healthy for the public. This may be true. But there are alternatives. If the government decided to prohibit advertising in the press, and if the press must be subsidized, let the government undertake to pay a subsidy varying only with circulation; e.g., to pay newspaper proprietors 1d. for each copy sold, on the understanding that there shall be no advertisements. Provided the subsidy were open to all on these terms, the press would remain independent and free to criticize. It would in fact be much freer than it is today, when the political and other views of large advertisers have to be borne in mind.

Some reformers are content to try to control the impact of advertising. There are some who advocate strict legal controls, penalizing misrepresentation, as the Federal Trade Commission seeks to do in the United States.[14] Others hope that in this country, as in the United States, independent testing agencies will grow up, private- or State-maintained, to inform the consumer of the true merits of different brands. Or even that the press will allow manufacturers to speak plainly in their advertisements about the inferiority of their rivals' products.[15] To the present writer none of this seems sufficiently fundamental. What is of value in the case for manufacturers' advertisement is that it supplies information, and that it sometimes concentrates demand on a few styles. But both these services could be supplied equally by retailers, at less cost, and more impartially, especially if greater steps, voluntary or compulsory, were taken to promote standardization, and more so still if something like Chamberlin's advocacy of trade mark infringement proved practicable (1933, Appendix E). It should not be on the manufacturer's strident claims that the public has to rely for information. The retailer, usually a better judge of merchandise

14. For a discussion of American attitudes and practices see Reid (1938), part 6.
15. Cf. the discussion by Plant (1938).

than the consumer, is better able to decide which brand is worth buying in large quantities, and pushing. In the view of the present writer, while branding should be retained to facilitate identification, manufacturers should be allowed to advertise only in trade journals for circulation amongst wholesalers and retailers, and not in the ordinary press. In this country we have already banned advertisement from the wireless, will, it is to be hoped, ban it from the sky, and are always talking about banning it from the hoardings. To ban it from the ordinary press would not be as revolutionary as it sounds, and would also greatly increase the perfection of the market, and reduce waste.

There remains, however, a further check on retailers which prevents them from carrying as small a range of styles as they might otherwise desire. It is the desire of their customers to be able to choose from as wide a range as possible, and indeed, in some cases, notably women's wear, the desire to have something different from what other people will have. In some cases, in a large shopping centre, this does not matter. If there are enough people who prefer cheapness and standardization to variety, some retailers will be able to concentrate on mass lines, and to secure for such consumers all the economies of scale. But in other trades it may remain the case that if all customers were compelled to accept the standard brand, costs would be lower than they could be without such compulsion. Should such compulsion be exercised? This is clearly a question for the philosopher rather than for the economist.

5. We come, thirdly, to delivery costs. That the several vans of different shops should be delivering in the same road has long seemed a conspicuous source of waste. The waste, however, such as it is, consists not in the fact of delivery, but in the inefficiency with which delivery is organized. If shop-keepers would use, not their own delivery vans but the services offered by public transport contractors, costs would be reduced, as each contractor could deliver on behalf of several different shops. Competition between the shops would not be affected by this any more than competition between manufacturers is affected by common use of the railway system or the post office. That they do not use public transport facilities is due principally to the fact that the convenience of delivering for oneself (plus the slight advertisement value of having one's own vans) outweighs what would be saved. This applies equally to pooled delivery services, such as have been enforced in wartime. Moreover, there is reason to believe that the extent of possible savings is grossly exaggerated. The case most quoted in England is milk delivery. Yet an independent investigator, who made a careful survey in Battersea, concluded (Booker, 1939):

To limit the number of distributors to a maximum of four in any road would cause such a small increase in the sales of these four as to have an almost negligible effect upon costs. To limit the number to two in this area would increase the sales of the two largest distributors by 66 per cent, but one is not convinced that even to limit it to one distributor would materially reduce the large distributor's costs. With the largest distributor only a small portion of the roundsman's time is taken in covering the actual length of road; most is taken in going from door to door, in bringing the customer to the door and engaging her in conversation. In one respect only does it seem probable that giving a particular area completely to one milkman would materially reduce costs, and that is in preventing people from buying from two or more distributors. In this area 11 per cent of the families bought from two or more distributors; in Oxford Dr Murray found nearly 15 per cent dealt with two dairymen. This seems a complete waste, and probably its abolition would reduce distributive costs by 10 per cent, say at least 1d. per gallon.

The principal cause of waste in milk distribution, of course, is the fact that the authorities have maintained the minimum retail price at a level allowing a margin so grossly in excess of the costs of large and efficient distributors that an altogether excessive number of firms is able to exist, and also an excessive amount of service.[16]

6. Finally we must consider the proposition that competition causes service to deteriorate. The shopkeeper, it is said, pressed by competition, and unable to make both ends meet, is driven to reduce the quality of the product and the service, and to misrepresentation and fraud.

To say that the quality will deteriorate is only another way of saying that the price will rise in competition, and we have already examined the conditions in which this is possible. In a really competitive market a shopkeeper may offer less value for the same money, but this will usually be on his way out. If consumers are unable at the time of making a purchase to distinguish between good and bad quality, a retailer may pass off bad as good, but the consumer will discover the difference on using the article, and retailers who do this will lose goodwill and disappear. It remains possible that there are articles whose quality the consumer cannot distinguish even in the course of use, and which he buys relying solely on the retailer's advice, or on high price as a guarantee of quality. Much is made of this by some writers, quoting quality tests which show low correlation between quality and price. The range of articles to which this applies cannot be very great, and would be smaller still if some teaching on how to use the market were supplied to the consumer through the press, the wireless, films, women's institutes, guilds, unions, and other media for adult education.

16. The facts are given in two official papers: *Report by the Food Council to the President of the Board of Trade on Costs and Profits of Retail Milk Distribution in Great Britain* (1937) and *Report of a Committee appointed to examine Costs of Milk Distribution* (1940).

That competition may stimulate fraud cannot be questioned. In some countries the primitive view prevails that every act of sale is a battle of wits, and even the strictest laws prohibiting adulteration or controlling weights and measures or the like cannot entirely outlaw sharp practice. Honesty is the best policy only where shopkeepers are competing in honesty; not where they are competing in dishonesty. Fortunately in this country the competitive forces work in the right direction. Especially is this so where the shopkeeper depends on the regular support of a loyal clientele, and cannot afford to lose their goodwill. It is less so where the customer will buy from any seller infrequently – perhaps only once – as in buying durable goods or buying in the course of a journey. Here the shopkeeper may be tempted to follow too literally the biblical injunction to take in the stranger. If he does this consistently he will probably sooner or later get a bad name and disappear; but he may get away with it, if done infrequently, or may be replaced merely by someone else who follows the same policy. The best safeguard for the public is to learn to shop around making enquiries before committing oneself to the purchase of an expensive durable good.

7. We may now summarize the conclusions of this section as follows:

(a) In large shopping centres it is unlikely that more service is provided than is wanted; competition between different forms of retailing tends to prevent such waste.

(b) In smaller suburban centres some customers may receive some service which they would rather not have; others, through price discrimination receive more service than they are willing to pay for, but the effect of this is to make shops nearer ideal size.

(c) All forms of retailing might have lower costs but for manufacturers' advertisements to the public, and but for the public's desire for variety of styles. How far these should be controlled, however, raises issues independent of the degree of competition in retailing.

(d) Service may deteriorate as a result of competition, but this is not likely in this country.

Unfair competition

1. In this section we are concerned with arguments that certain forms of competition are unfair and distort the distributive process. The practices in question are (a) claiming the status of a retailer without fulfilling all the functions; (b) 'poaching' in one trade by retailers in another (e.g., grocers selling patent medicines); (c) direct sales to the public at 'wholesale' prices; (d) 'special' prices to large traders; (e) gift coupons and trading stamps; and (f) sales to cooperative societies.

2. We can begin with two points common to all these problems. The first

is that the retailer's criterion of what is fair is not the economist's. The retailer characterizes as unfair almost anything which upsets his expectations, especially if it does so by diverting trade to a different form of retailing. The economist cannot condemn a practice solely on these grounds.

Secondly, underlying most of these cases is the belief that distortion of the 'normal' channels of distribution raises costs. Coupon trading is a good example of this. If chocolate manufacturers give away cameras in redemption of coupons, the retailers of cameras claim that this reduces the sales of cameras through existing outlets, and therefore increases costs. All the forms of 'unfair competition' listed above would be attacked on this ground, among others.

For this line of argument to be valid, four propositions must be established. First, that the new form of retailing does diminish the business done by the old. Secondly, that when the business done by the old diminishes, the effect is an increase in its costs, i.e., that the number of shops does not diminish *pari passu*, the remaining shops having the same average turnover as before. Thirdly, that the costs of the new form exceed the marginal costs of the old. And fourthly, that the difference in costs is not justified to the consumer by difference in service or other convenience.

It is not always accepted that the new form of retailing diminishes the business done by the old. For example, some supporters of gift coupons claim that the persons who get cameras through this medium would for the most part not be willing to buy cameras, and that having got the cameras they buy films from photographic dealers and have them developed, so that the trade of the ordinary dealer is not reduced but increased. It is always possible in some cases that the extension of a new cheap form of retailing may so expand demand that even the older and more expensive forms of retailing also benefit (just as publication in the Penguin series sometimes increases sales of the expensive edition of a book), but there must also be many cases in which the net effect is that the turnover of the older forms is reduced.

If this is the case, the effect will be different in large shopping centres and in small. The large shopping centre being defined, for any given commodity, as one where the number of customers is large enough to support several shops each of optimum size, the effect will be simply that one or more of these shops is put out of business, the others keeping the same size, costs and prices. In the smaller centres, however, the effect is different. Unless the new form replaces the old form altogether, its effect is to detach some customers lying within the area of each shop. This is a reduction in the density of the buying population, which, as we have already seen, results in smaller shops and higher costs.

When this is the case, some customers are benefiting from the new form of competition at the expense of others who pay higher prices. If it were possible for all customers to transfer to the new form, the public would not be harmed by this. For example, if it could be shown that the effect of the spread of cooperatives was not simply to bankrupt some private traders, but rather to raise the prices paid by non-cooperators, no economist would justify restrictions on cooperatives on this ground, since it is open to all customers to join cooperatives. But the case is different with coupon trading; we cannot advise all persons who want cameras to get them through eating chocolates. Where the cheaper form of distribution is not open to all, the problem is more difficult.

The key to the solution is total costs. If the sum of the costs of the total sales under new and old systems is less than it would cost to distribute the same output through the old system exclusively, the new form is justified. This will be the case so long as the costs (prime plus fixed) of the new form of retailing are less than the marginal costs of the old. But the new form will not be justified even if its average cost (and price) is less than the average cost (and price) of the old if it is not also less than the marginal cost of the old. In these conditions a case can be made for prohibiting the new form of retailing. The problem arises only because some retailers who have falling average costs cannot discriminate in favour of the type of customer to whom the new form of retailing makes its restricted appeal. If they could discriminate they could prevent the new form from establishing itself by quoting prices, based on marginal cost, less than the new form could support. As they cannot discriminate, the new form emerges, and social costs are increased.

To complete the argument it must be shown that the customers who would patronize the new form would gain only to the extent of the lower price; that there is no special convenience or service attached to the new form, such as would justify higher social costs; in a word, that the two forms of retailing are nearly perfect substitutes. Thus the suburban shopkeeper cannot argue that the cheap shops in the centre should be closed even if he could show that their average costs exceed his marginal costs, for shopping in the suburbs is not an exact substitute for shopping in the centre, and many people who live in the suburbs would find it more convenient to shop in the centre even if prices were the same. Nor, to turn the argument round, can the cheaper forms of retailing apply a similar argument for eliminating the more expensive; the two are not exact substitutes. For the argument to be applicable it must be shown that the price is the only practical difference from the consumer's point of view.

It seems a revolutionary conclusion that costs can sometimes be reduced by eliminating the 'cheaper' forms of retailing, but as we shall see, the practical significance of the conclusion is very limited. Let us now take each form of 'unfair' competition in turn.

3. A number of retail trade associations in this country have agreed with manufacturers or wholesalers that a person should not receive retailer's discounts on his purchases unless he has or is prepared to have a regular shop, open at the usual hours, carrying certain minimum stocks, and perhaps offering after-sales or other usual services. This 'fair trading' policy, as it is called, is found, for example, in the bookselling, photographic and motor car trades.[17] This sort of policy is aimed partly at the small part-time retailer, who keeps a parlour shop, partly at 'poaching' in one trade by members of another, and partly at direct sales to the public at wholesale prices. It thus covers the first three cases on our list.

It is most unlikely that this restriction could be justified on the ground that the average costs of those excluded exceed the marginal costs of those that remain. The real costs of the man with the parlour shop are low, because his transfer costs and rent are low. So also are the costs of the 'poacher', who enters the extra trade usually because he has already under-utilized premises and staff for his own trade. From the point of view of real costs, one can say broadly that the more 'poaching' there is the better, since this gives the average shop in each district a larger total trade and lower costs (the limit to 'poaching' is set by the advantages of specialization). And as for sales direct to the public at wholesale prices, this is the case least likely to fit the argument, since the consumer's cost of retailing to himself is zero (though he may have a heavier transport cost). The 'fair trading' policy cannot therefore be justified on the ground that sales through these channels are uneconomic.

Neither is the justification usually attempted on these lines. First, in some trades the retailer says, in effect, 'To do my business properly I must carry a wide range of models, to offer the public a good choice; it is unfair that I should lose trade to someone who does not do the same'. It is not unfair that some shops should stock less wide ranges than others; those customers who wish to be able to consult a wide range are free to do so at the more expensive shops, while others may chose the cheaper. But the argument is more subtle. The retailer with the wide range argues that other retailers benefit from his policy; sales in the other shops are larger because there are shops displaying a wide range; in effect the retailer with the wide range is bearing part of the 'information' costs of the whole trade. The argument is unimpressive; no retailer is compelled to act in this philan-

17. The fullest survey of the facts about each of the principal retail trades is to be found in a series of articles published in the *Manchester Guardian Commercial Weekly* in the second half of 1938 and the first half of 1939. For books and motor cars the relevant dates are 24 June and 28 October 1938.

thropic way. If he really thinks that it is possible to thrive off other people's stock carrying, there is nothing to stop him from doing so. This, however, brings us to the second argument. Manufacturers frequently support the fair trading policy because they think that it is in the interest of the trade as a whole that retailers should carry a wide range of stocks; it has advertising value, and causes total sales to be greater. In discriminating against retailers who do not carry this range they are in effect paying a subsidy to others for advertising. The desirability of this rests therefore on the desirability of advertising, and in particular of advertising simply to divert demand from other commodities to the advertised. This can hardly be justified as 'information'. The public knows of the existence of the particular class of merchandise, and multiplication of the varieties within the class in order specially to catch its eye deserves no special protection. The third argument is more weighty. It is that in certain trades the retailer should have special qualifications, e.g., that in the photographic trade the public would be badly served by retailers who gave bad advice on the respective merits of cameras, or bad after-sales service. Where the commodity is purchased frequently, the public needs no such certificate of qualification; the buyer soon finds out for himself whether his grocer is to be trusted. But where the service is infrequent, some certificate would be useful; e.g., how is the householder to know whether the radio dealer round the corner can really mend a silent wireless set without at the same time doing irremediable and temporarily concealed damage inside? There is something to be said for requiring retailers in certain durable goods trades to pass some test of competence, particularly in the photographic trade, radios, and garages, as is already done for chemists; or at least for an optional test, enabling the public to distinguish between certified and uncertified. But it is a fundamental principle that such tests must be conducted independently, and not by interested parties, such as manufacturers or a retail trade association.

Lastly, sales to the public at 'wholesale' prices are opposed on the ground that it is unfair that the retailer should face such competition from the people who sell to him. This is indeed a common complaint, especially in the drapery, sports goods, cycle, meat, jewellery and outfitting trades,[18] and includes protests against sales to members of clubs at special prices. The saying that 'only saps pay retail prices' indicates how common is the practice. A manufacturer (or wholesaler) may adopt it in one of two circumstances. It may be that he is able to distribute to the consumer at a cost less than the margin the retailer claims. If the retailer's margin barely covers the retailer's costs, this means that the manufacturer is able to

18. See the relevant articles in the *Manchester Guardian Commercial Weekly*. For an American discussion see Tallman (1939, p. 339).

distribute more cheaply by direct methods of sale, and there is no case for preventing him from doing this. But it may be that the margin exceeds retailers' costs, and that the efficient retailers are prevented from reducing their prices by a resale price maintenance scheme. It would certainly be unfair of manufacturers to undersell retailers who are compelled to maintain prices, but the problem this raises is whether prices should be maintained in this way, and this is reserved for the final part of this paper.

Alternatively, the manufacturer may be discriminating, and earning a higher profit on his sales to retailers than on his sales to the public. This is unlikely to be profitable if it results in sales to the public expanding at the expense of sales to retailers – and if it does not the retailer has no ground for complaint, because the manufacturer is then substituting less for more profitable sales, unless the expansion of direct sales is much greater than the decline of sales through retailers.

A similar problem arises in connection with the allegation that large retailers flourish as a result of obtaining special prices. This problem has arisen much more acutely in the United States than it has in this country, where the multiple shops are much less aggressively competitive than their American counterparts. The role of the chain in the American distributive set-up is played in this country in a different way by the cooperative movement. Multiple, chain and cooperative owe a great part of their success to buying more cheaply than the independent shop. That there are real economies reflected in the lower prices they pay is not open to question; the large retailing organizations relieve the manufacturer of many costs he would incur if selling to small shops, and they perform the wholesaling functions for themselves more cheaply and efficiently than the wholesale firms do for the small independent shop. Nevertheless it is possible that they also get discriminatory prices, based on their great bargaining power. In the United States, where the problem has been widely debated and officially investigated, the evidence is not conclusive.[19] Three reactions may be noted. The first is the 'classification' of customers in trade categories. Here, trade associations bring pressure to bear on manufacturers to base their discounts on the trade status of the buyer rather than on quantity bought, so that the price charged for any given quantity will be different according to whether the buyer is a consumer, a retailer, or a wholesaler. This policy is clearly uneconomic from the public point of view, since it hampers the development of efficient large-scale retailing, and tends to ossify the structure of distribution and to preserve intermediaries beyond the extent justified by the services they perform. The second possible reaction is legislation against price discrimination; in the United States the Robinson-Patman Act is intended specially to protect the small

19. For a summary of the discussion see Twentieth Century Fund (1939, p. 83).

shop-keeper against discrimination. The object of such legislation is laudable; some discrimination between consumers can be defended, where average costs are falling, if it brings output nearer the ideal (especially if the discrimination is in favour of the lower income groups), but discrimination between retailers and consumers or between different classes of intermediaries is unfair in itself, as well as likely to cause an uneconomic distortion of the distributive structure. To prevent it by legislation is nevertheless a formidable task. Rather more perhaps may be hoped from the third reaction. This is for retailers to cooperate in buying, so as to secure the full economies of scale. The cooperative retail buying movement has spread very rapidly in the United States, where it has saved the small shopkeeper, but has made little progress in the United Kingdom, where small retailers prefer the protection of 'classification' and price maintenance. Cooperative buying is undoubtedly the most desirable reaction from the public point of view.

4. Retailers object to the distribution of goods through gift coupons and trading stamp schemes because it interferes with their trade. No case can be made out on the basis of real costs. The real costs of handling the goods distributed in this way seem to be rather low, as the work is done on a large scale; on the whole, the customer gets good value for his money. More interesting is the argument that the use of coupons and trading stamps increases market imperfection; customers are tied to particular commodities by coupons, or to particular retailers by trading stamps, and may have their attention diverted from the quality of the goods they are buying, or the prices charged, by the illusion of 'getting something for nothing'. Some countries have indeed prohibited or restricted coupon trading, usually in order to protect retailers, but the Board of Trade Committee which investigated the practice in 1933 concluded that the public suffers no harm, and no new evidence or arguments have since emerged to overthrow this conclusion. Coupon trading, however, is just an adjunct to non-price competition between manufacturers and to manufacturers' advertisements; and the trading stamp is primarily the product of resale price maintenance. If these sources of market imperfection were removed most of this form of trading would disappear.

5. The view that the consumers' cooperative movement is in some sense unfair still seems to persist in some quarters in this country, though recent events suggest that it does not turn many votes! To discuss the argument that the principle of cooperative trading is itself unfair would strain the reader's patience. Only special points deserve mention. One is the suggestion that the cooperative surplus is to some extent due to special prices secured from manufacturers by bargaining power. There is no

evidence of this. The exhaustive enquiry published in 1938 (Carr-Saunders, Sargant Florence and Peers, especially chapters 22 and 23) showed that the surplus arises out of the real economies of cooperative trading, especially lower publicity, rent and interest costs, but above all wholesaling economies. A second point is the insistence of some retail trade associations that where resale prices are maintained it would be unfair to allow cooperatives to pay dividends on purchases of these goods, since the dividend would represent a form of undercutting for which private traders would be penalized. There is some substance in the argument, but its final validity depends on the case for price maintenance, which we shall discuss in the last part of this paper. Finally, it is argued that it is unfair that co-operative dividends are not subject to taxation. The literature on the point is large. The opinion of the present writer is that the cooperative surplus is not comparable with the private trader's profit. That profit contains two elements, remuneration for his labour, and interest on his capital. The comparable items in cooperative trading are the salary paid to managers and the interest paid on shares; the surplus partakes of neither of these elements, but is rather a form of voluntary saving. This view is not, however, accepted universally by economists.[20]

6. We may therefore conclude as to unfair competition that the only valid and significant case is that against price discrimination between classes of buyers, in accordance with trade status; price differentiation should be based rather on the cost of handling quantities.

Limitations on competition

1. To many traders what is unfair is not just certain forms of competition, but the very fact of competition itself, whether it be competition in price, service competition, or the entry of new firms into a trade. Several retail trade associations operate schemes to enforce resale price maintenance, and many would like to imitate the newsagents in enforcing a distance limit.

2. It is not surprising that most retailers of convenience goods, operating as they must on a small scale in local markets, favour price maintenance. It seems to offer them protection from the large shops, of optimum size, in the large centres, who, correspondingly, are on the whole against price maintenance. The protection is illusory. In price maintenance the margin is set normally high enough to cover the costs of most retailers in the trade, and, if competition does not whittle profits away in more costly service, either more retailers are attracted, or 'poaching' spreads; the number of outlets increases, and turnover per outlet falls; costs per unit of sales rise; pressure is applied for a still higher margin; this attracts still

20. For discussion see Macgregor (1933), and Fay (1933).

more outlets; and the cycle continues. From the point of view of the retailer, even the highest margin will barely cover his costs, because the number of outlets, and turnover per outlet, will be adjusted to whatever the margin may be. So long, therefore, as there is free entry into a trade, directly or by 'poaching', price maintenance is no protection from competition; it is merely a costly and wasteful burden on the public. The drug trade is the stock example of what happens. Before price maintenance was adopted, the number of outlets for patent medicines more or less equalled the number of chemists; to-day, because of the attractive margins, other shops have taken up patent medicines, and outnumber the chemists in this trade by ten to one. Similarly in the tobacco trade there are twenty-three 'poachers' to every one tobacconist, and in the confectionery trade five 'poachers' to every 'legitimate' confectioner. The chemists have now been driven to bringing organized pressure to bear on manufacturers to restrict the sale of patent medicines to qualified chemists.

Surprise has been expressed that manufacturers should support price maintenance, instead of wishing their goods to be retailed as cheaply as possible. Fear of the repercussions of the 'loss leader' has some significance, but only in relation to the more fundamental explanation. The fact is that in many classes of trade sales depend more on there being many outlets than on low prices. This is the reason why the state has for centuries restricted the number of public houses, and it applies with equal force to confectionery, newspapers, books or cigarettes. Moreover, within any of these classes of trade, it may be of greater advantage to a manufacturer to have his brand available in every shop, than to have it available at a low price. These advertising considerations make manufacturers willing to fix margins high enough to encourage even the least efficient and smallest retailers to stock the brand, and to take the elaborate steps necessary to avoid a differentially low price level or loss leaders in the large central markets which would draw trade from the smaller shops and discourage them from stocking the brand. For shopping goods, which are sold mostly in large shopping centres where sales depend on keen prices rather than on wide stocking, resale prices are never likely to be fixed.

From the public's point of view resale price maintenance is doubly condemned (a) because it causes the number of shops and the amount of service to be excessive and prices to be too high; and (b) because manufacturers promote it for advertising reasons. And the fact that it does not really in the long run shelter the shopkeeper from competition simply removes any ground for sympathy, and makes the system all the more absurd. It is hardly necessary to consider two arguments which are sometimes advanced; that the public gains from price maintenance because the system tends to enforce a maximum price as well as a minimum, so that the customer cannot be defrauded; or that the public would not have 'confidence' in a commodity found selling in different shops at different prices. If it is maximum prices that benefit the public, then fix not minimum but maximum prices; and what happens to public confidence in that wide range of commodities whose retail prices are not fixed?

The case against price maintenance is beyond doubt. It is one of the major sources of waste in distribution, and the public would benefit greatly if it and the boycotts, stop lists, discrimination against cooperative societies, and other paraphernalia by which the system is enforced were made illegal.

3. The licensing of shops, however, raises more difficult problems. We have seen that, even if prices are not maintained, the number of suburban shops may be excessive. A *prima facie* case for restriction is therefore established.

Any such proposal, however, has to meet a formidable array of objections. First, many people are anxious to maintain an open door in retailing as a refuge for the small man from 'wage slavery' into 'independence'. In many quarters the small trader is regarded as the pillar of society, a view which cannot always survive closer examination of his outlook and prejudices. But, whatever the merits of the small trader, it is certainly not kind to encourage large numbers of small men to enter into retailing. By and large, the costs of small shopkeeping are high, and the rewards are correspondingly low, frequently much less than wage employment would yield. Neither is it a profession for the unskilled; the ignorance of small retailers is one of the principal reasons for their high rate of bankruptcy. In the United States it has been estimated that half the retail shops opened in any year fail within twelve months, and that the average life of a shop is only five years (TNEC, 1940, especially chapter 2). Similar information is not available for this country; thanks to price maintenance and a less aggressive atmosphere of competition the mortality rate is probably lower, but it is without doubt very high; to go into retailing is one of the easiest ways of losing the savings of a lifetime. Those who wish to keep retailing open specially to attract the small man seem therefore to be even more dangerous to the small man they may be to the public.

It is more important to consider whether restricting the number of shops really would benefit the public. At present there is some competition in prices and in service. Restriction of entry might lead merely to an increase in shopkeepers' profits and prices, and to a decline in the quality of the service. The war has taught us how quickly the quality of the service deteriorates in retailing when once the spur of competition is removed, and many members of the public would think that some excess in the number of shops is a small price to pay in order to secure the benefits of competition.

The structure of the distributive trades would also be gravely affected by restriction of entry. For the past century the efficiency of retailing has been improving largely through the expansion of large-scale retailing – coops, multiples and department stores – relatively to small-scale retailing. Large-scale retailing is able to operate on margins of anything between 30 per cent and 50 per cent less than those required by small retailers. The small retailer has, indeed, his place in the industry, especially in the sale of shopping goods, where standardization is not important, and in the sale of convenience goods in small shopping centres, and especially in building up a clientele on the basis of a high quality of personal service. This place would be even larger than it is if the efficiency of small shopkeepers could be improved, e.g., by better training facilities. A woeful ignorance of business principles is one of the chief causes of the wastefulness of small shopkeeping and the high mortality rate. For example, most small shopkeepers try to carry too wide a range of styles, brands, etc., deal with too many wholesalers and manufacturers, and offer too much service, for the limited turnover which they can secure. And the small man would be still more certain of his place if he would turn his eyes from the illusory safety of price maintenance and 'classification' to the possibilities of standardization and cooperative buying, thus challenging the large scale retailer on his own ground. There is undoubtedly room for small-scale retailing. But what case is there for measures which extend it an artificial protection by preventing the expansion of large-scale retailing, which has been the spearhead of improved efficiency in distribution? The writer is as sensitive as any, and more sensitive than most, to the values of a society in which economic power is widely dispersed through the predominance of small business. But he is highly sensitive, too, to the persistence of poverty, and the need to increase wealth by utilising as far as possible the more productive types of enterprise. To bolster up small-scale retailing beyond its proper place in the distributive structure is to condemn an important part of our economy to waste and inefficiency. It should not be forgotten that one person in seven is engaged in the distributive trades.

More probably, this issue would not arise. For restriction of entry would give the multiples an incentive to buy up more and more small shops – small shopkeeping might not be preserved, but on the contrary might disappear. Nor would the public benefit; the small retailer, protected by his licence, would refuse to sell except for a handsome price, which the multiple organization would be willing to pay, relying on the licence, and the net effect would be to raise prices against the public. Not only the multiples would play this game, but also the manufacturer. The public house is a standing example of the incentive the licensing of retail outlets gives to manufacturers to integrate forward and buy up the outlets for monopolistic purposes. Probably the principal result of restricting entry into retailing would be that multiples and manufacturers would buy up the shops, that monopoly would be greatly increased in manufacturing, and that the public would lose more in higher prices and reduced service than it loses from freedom of entry. Though there are too many shops if there is freedom of entry, merely to restrict freedom of entry would probably make the public poorer than before.

4. What causes waste in retailing is not competition but the fact that price competition is not sufficiently effective, especially in the convenience goods and suburban trades. This is due in the first instance to resale price maintenance, the abolition of which would enable the more efficient retailers to expand and to reduce prices to the consumer, and would reduce the number of shops, releasing resources for other urgent purposes.

But the number of shops might still be too large, and the average shop too small, even if price maintenance were abolished. Figure 1 shows the position. In the absence of price competition the average shop will have a size well to the left of N (in terms of Figure 3 it will be at K); price competition will increase the size to N; but the ideal size is given by M. Elasticity of demand will bring the competitive size nearer M, but not necessarily right up to it. Theoretically, the simple way to achieve the right number and size of shops is to fix a maximum gross margin QM, whereupon the number of shops will contract, and average size increase to M. But there is nothing simple about this solution in practice. There is in reality no average shop; different gross margins are appropriate in different conditions of population density and different degrees of service. The same margin cannot be fixed for every retailer. Neither is there an average commodity; even within a single class of merchandise different articles need different margins, according to the time it takes to handle them, their size, rate of turnover, and so on. It is true that margins have been elaborately controlled during the war, but no one can pretend that the hit or miss methods used in war-time would be very suitable for permanent peace-time regulation.

It may be suggested that the simplest way out is to fix a maximum margin only for one standard and popular type within each class of merchandise, in the expectation that the margins on all other types will have to correspond. This might work so long as retailers could not escape selling the selected brand. If 'utility' production is continued, this can be tried, the government allowing such low margins that only the appropriate number of shops remains in business. The retailers may be expected to fight the attempt by starting a whispering campaign against the 'utility' articles, and persuading consumers to buy only uncontrolled articles. The government would win so long as it retained power to withhold labour and raw materials from non-'utility' production, but as soon as non-'utility' lines could be freely produced, the limited price control would lose much of its effectiveness.

There is one other theoretical alternative to price fixing, which is equally impracticable, i.e., to give the cooperative societies a monopoly of retailing, or at least a monopoly of retailing convenience goods, since it is in these rather than shopping goods that there is excess capacity. If they had a monopoly of retailing, the societies would have no incentive to establish more or less than the right number of shops. The proposal is specially attractive because, whatever their shortcomings in handling shopping goods, the cooperative societies are unquestionably the cheapest distributors of convenience goods in this country, and they would be cheaper still if certain managerial and structural reforms could be effected.[21] But it is politically quite impracticable to establish any such monopoly.

5. There is in fact no practicable solution to the problem of 'excess capacity' in retailing, in the sense of reducing the gap between the competitive number and the ideal number of shops. This, however, need not daunt us, for two reasons. First because 'excess capacity' exists only where elasticity of demand is insufficient to bridge the gap, on which we have no information. And secondly because, in either case, the actual number is so far in excess of the competitive number that if we could get it down to the competitive level we should have made notable progress. The way to this level is simply to make price maintenance illegal. This is the most urgent reform needed in retailing; its repercussions would revolutionize the distributive structure.

Democrats may rejoice that one result would be a rapid expansion of the consumers' cooperative movement in many trades for which it is specially suited. Here is a movement to which more than half the families in the country belong. Freed from the trammels of price maintenance, and inspired with a sense of its mission, this movement could set prices all along the line at levels which would drive waste out of distribution. It is the pride of the movement that it protected the consumer in the days when adulteration, short weight and fraud were the bugbear of retailing. To protect him from waste would add another page to an already noble history.

21. For a discussion of needed reforms see Carr-Saunders and others (1938), especially part 4.

References

BISHOP, F. P. (1944), *The Economics of Advertising*, Hale.
BOARD OF TRADE COMMITTEE (1933), *Report of the Committee on Gift Coupons and Trading Stamps*, Cmnd 4385.
BOOKER, H. S. (1939), 'A survey of milk distribution', *Economica*, vol. 6.

BRAITHWAITE, D. (1928), 'The economic effects of advertising', *econ. J.*, vol. 38.

BURNHAM, E. A. (1938), 'The influence of size of business on department store operating results', *Harvard bus. Rev.*, vol. 16.

BURNHAM, E. A. (1940), 'The department store in its community', *Harvard bus. Rev.*, vol. 18.

CARR-SAUNDERS, A. M., FLORENCE, P. SARGANT, and PEERS, R. (1938), *Consumers' Cooperation in Great Britain*, Allen & Unwin.

CHAMBERLIN, E. H. (1933), *Theory of Monopolistic Competition*, Harvard University Press.

CLARK, C. (1940), *Conditions of Economic Progress*, Macmillan.

FAY, C. R. (1933), 'Cooperators and the State', *econ. J.*, vol. 43.

FORD, P. (1936), 'Changes in the number of shops, 1901–31', *econ. J.*, vol. 46.

HOTELLING, H. (1929), 'Stability in competition', *econ. J.*, vol. 39.

LERNER, A. P., and SINGER, H. W. (1937), 'Some notes on duopoly and spatial competition', *J. polit. Econ.*, vol. 45.

MACGREGOR, D. H. (1933), 'The taxation of cooperative dividend', *econ. J.*, vol. 43.

McNAIR, M. P. (1931), 'Trends in large scale retailing', *Harvard bus. Rev.*, vol. 10.

PLANT, A. (1938), 'The distribution of proprietary articles', in A. Plant (ed.), *Some Modern Business Problems*, Longman.

PLANT, A., and FOWLER, R. F. (1939), 'Costs of retail distribution', *Economica*, vol. 6.

REID, M. G. (1938), *Consumers and the Market*, Appleton-Century-Crofts.

SCHUMACHER, E. F. (1944), 'An essay on State control', *Agenda*, February.

SMITH, A. (1776), *The Wealth of Nations*, vol. 1, Cannan edn, pp. 341–2.

SMITH, H. (1937), *Retail Distribution*, Oxford University Press.

TALLMAN, G. B. (1939), 'When consumers buy at wholesale', *Harvard bus. Rev.*, vol. 17.

TEMPORARY NATIONAL ECONOMIC COMMITTEE (1940), *Problems of Small Business*, monograph no. 17.

TWENTIETH CENTURY FUND (1939), *Does Distribution Cost Too Much?*, New York.

8 J. Hood and B. S. Yamey

Imperfect Competition in Retail Trade

J. Hood and B. S. Yamey, 'Imperfect competition in retail trades', *Economica*, n.s., vol. 18, 1951, pp. 119–37.

In his book, *Retail Distribution*, and elsewhere (1948, 1949a and b) Henry Smith analyses the nature of competition in the distributive trades and comes to the conclusion that 'taking all the facts into account it looks as if there is something queer about competition in the retail trade, (1949a, p. 7). The 'queerness' is elucidated by him in terms of the theory of monopolistic competition with assistance from the theory of oligopolistic behaviour. Applying these theories to the facts as he observes them, the conclusions are presented that retail gross profit margins and prices tend to be rigid, and that the competitive activity that is present takes the form of the competitive supply to consumers of more (and more elaborate) retail services rather than of competitive reductions of margins and prices. From these conclusions the 'welfare' judgment is derived that competition in retailing produces a wasteful and unnecessary multiplication of shops, absorbs an unnecessarily large share of society's resources and leads to an economically unhealthy bidding up of the costs of distribution (1948, pp. 130 and 180; 1949a, p. 24).

Margaret Hall in her more recent book, *Distributive Trading*, likewise refers to the 'peculiar character of distributive markets' (1949, p. 189). Though her analysis differs from that of Smith in some respects, the similarities in approach are greater than the differences. Hall believes that 'retail trade is inherently imperfectly competitive' and that 'it is inherent in this situation that conditions of oligopoly may arise at any time' (1949, pp. 38 and 41). Hall is more cautious in stating her conclusions and in pronouncing upon the welfare aspects of competition in retailing; but the general tenor of the argument indicates that she arrives at an appraisal of the working of competition in retailing which resembles that of Smith in important respects.

The applicability of the theory of monopolistic competition to retailing is based upon the fact, which is not disputed, that *at any moment of time* a consumer about to make a retail purchase is neither willing nor able to seek out the shop at which he can obtain the merchandise he wants, together with the retail services he wants, at the lowest possible price (or more precisely, to seek out the shop at which the most preferred combination of merchandise, price and service is to be found). His choice of retail outlet for any particular purchase will in fact be based at least in part upon considerations such as the following: convenience of location, shopping habit, imperfect knowledge of alternatives, recollections of satisfactory treatment in the past, and preference for the retailer, his staff and his amenities. At any moment of time a particular retailer knows that he will not lose all his trade even if he raises his prices. He knows that an increase in his prices will not instantaneously deprive him of all sales and that a reduction in his prices will not instantaneously enlarge his business. In short, at any moment of time the demand for a particular retailer's services is not infinitely elastic, and therefore the market is not perfectly competitive.[1] Moreover, at any one place or in any one locality there cannot be a very large number of grocers, chemists or butchers. Hence, runs the argument, the retail market is really composed of a number of contiguous local oligopolies.

We do not wish to take issue with Smith or Hall on the question whether retailing is or is not a textbook example of perfect competition. We agree at once that it (or for that matter any other industry or trade) has never measured up to the exact and rigorous requirements of the model of perfect competition. The main point at issue is whether the degree and nature of the imperfections are such that it is more realistic to stress the imperfections than it is to stress the competition (particularly in its price-reducing aspect) in the study and appraisal of retail markets. 'In the field of imperfect competition, and especially in the search for workable adjustments, these matters of degree are of the essence of the problem' (Clark, 1940, p. 241).[2] We attempt to examine the usefulness of the approach and methods of analysis suggested by the theory of monopolistic competition in a study of the distributive trades, though in so doing we do not pronounce upon the general usefulness of the theory. This examination we believe to be important not only because the example of retailing seems to be tailored to fit the requirements of the theory but also because both Smith and Hall emphasize that without the developments in theory in the 1930s a realistic evaluation of retail markets is impossible. Hall writes that the assumptions underlying 'traditional economics' are 'for the purpose of the economics of distribution, bad hypotheses' which 'exclude what, for a given investigation, are the most important parts of reality' (1949, pp. 30 and 38; see also Smith, 1948, pp. 113 ff. and p. 127). Similarly we consider the relevance of the theory of oligopoly for an explanation of distributive markets which are characterized by unusually easy conditions

1. For this conclusion, see Smith (1948, p. 127), and Hall (1949, p. 36).
2. Hayek's essay (1949) contains a valuable discussion of this general problem.

of entry. Finally we look at the implications for policy of the analyses presented by Smith and Hall.

We should agree with the conclusions arrived at or suggested by Smith and Hall if they were confined to those retail trades in which resale price maintenance is prevalent and effectively enforced (thus setting minimum prices at which all competing retailers must sell to consumers). No elaborate analysis is necessary to show that resale price maintenance, with freedom of entry, tends to lead to too many shops, excess capacity, bidding up of costs and rigid profit margins and prices. And these conclusions would hold even if, apart from restrictions upon the retailer's freedom of pricing, retailing were perfectly competitive in the textbook sense. Though both Smith and Hall are clearly aware of the prevalence of resale price maintenance in Britain, it is difficult to arrive at any other conclusion than that they believe that even without resale price maintenance the inherent imperfections in retailing will in many cases produce results of the same type as those produced by price maintenance. If they did not believe this, much of their analysis would be irrelevant. Smith, discussing the abolition of price maintenance, states that 'where competition is based upon location and the provision of amenities and not on price and where the habitual percentage mark-up of the trade is strongly entrenched, it is doubtful if it [i.e., abolition of price maintenance] would make much difference' (1949b, p. 27). Both indicate that resale price maintenance 'reinforces' (Smith, 1949a, p. 8) or 'exaggerates' (Hall, 1949, p. 169) the consequences of imperfections; and both point to an analogy between behaviour with price maintenance and behaviour in imperfect markets without it (Smith, 1948, p. 180; Hall, 1949, p. 60).[3]

The desire on the part of many retailers in many trades for resale price maintenance and the fact that retailers by themselves (without the co-operation of manufacturers to enforce price maintenance) have never been successful for long in outlawing price competition among themselves suggest that there is some important omission in the new explanation of competition in retailing. If price competition in retailing were as ineffectual and as infrequent as Smith suggests, if retailers' 'private markets' were truly private, and if retailers recognized the interdependence of their actions and behaved with the restraint commonly attributed to oligopolists,

3. It is necessary to point out that in some places in Hall's book a different emphasis is suggested. Thus after describing one possible situation she notes that it 'is a very common one, and is especially characteristic of those parts of retail trade where price maintenance is imposed by manufacturers' (p. 60). Elsewhere (p. 58) she claims that her analysis is 'realistic' by referring to conclusions drawn by Cadbury Bros Ltd in a study of the pre-war confectionery trade. But the confectionery trade was (and still is) covered by resale price maintenance arrangements, although these arrangements have not always been completely effective.

it would be impossible to explain the constant efforts on the part of large groups of retailers to organize themselves and to enlist the support of manufacturers (and governments) to secure the 'stability' of protected minimum gross profit margins. The efforts of many retailers (often the majority in number) indicate more cogently than can any theoretical analysis that they are aware of the responsiveness of consumers to price differences, and that they have little faith in the security provided by 'differentiated' markets or the oligopolistic restraint exercised by their competitors. At the same time the fact that there are always some retailers who resist the introduction of price maintenance shows that some retailers believe that they are able to increase their sales and their profits by lowering profit margins.[4]

These facts provide strong grounds for rejecting an analysis which appears almost to exclude the possibility of price competition. It suggests that theoretical generalizations may have been based on the observation of situations where resale price maintenance exists. Even where such arrangements are not fully successful they may affect the behaviour of individual firms by providing a basis on which judgments as to a 'fair' margin can be made and by encouraging or inducing a habit of cooperation.

The analysis which follows attempts to bring out factors which help to explain why price competition cannot be relegated to the very minor role which it appears to play in expositions relying on the overwhelming importance of imperfections. Considered in isolation some factors may appear relatively unimportant. Taken in combination they suggest that in the absence of external restraints price competition is a most important facet of competition in retail trades.

Moreover it may be noted that sentiment in favour of price maintenance has always been strong in trades in which one would expect the factors of shopping convenience and habit (and hence the 'imperfection' of spatial differentiation) to be most important – that is in the so-called convenience goods trades such as the grocery, chemists, confectionery, tobacco and news-agency trades.[5]

4. The strength of competition and of the price consciousness of a significant number of consumers is such that resale price maintenance agreements are generally extended to prohibit indirect price cutting which would replace the more usual method of price reduction.

5. If evidence of this is necessary an example from Canada may be cited. In an enquiry into the activities of the Canadian Proprietary Articles Trade Association (PATA) it was urged that 'the druggist who benefits mostly by the adoption of the principles of the PATA as far as price maintenance is concerned is the man who operates a store in the smaller cities and towns and in those portions of the larger cities most removed from the large downtown stores. It is also contended that the Association aids the smaller cities, towns and country districts as against the competition of the depart-

Monopolistic competition[6] in retail markets

It has been agreed above that *at any moment of time* the demand for a particular retailer's services is not infinitely elastic. The retailer is well aware of this; yet he may refrain from taking advantage of the opportunity to set his prices where, at the particular moment of time, his profits are maximized. He realizes that at any particular moment of time he has a monopoly at least in respect of some customers. But he realizes, probably more clearly, that unless his prices are competitive at any moment of time the attitude of many of his former customers may change adversely for him. Some customers do learn about or discover price differences; shopping habits are not unshakeable; and housewives are not inflexibly tied for reasons of convenience to a particular retailer or retail centre. Also, it is not necessary to postulate that *all* consumers in the long run (which here means a few weeks or months at most) are mobile in their shopping habits. As long as some change their patterns of shopping in response to differences in prices the momentary inelasticity of demand for a particular retailer's services is relatively unimportant from the point of view of his price policy. Even if only a few customers of each retailer are mobile together they may provide a profitable opportunity for any retailer who is prepared to sell at more attractive prices.

At the same time the sluggishness of the buyer in most retail markets (as contrasted with the buyer's postulated agility in perfect markets) does give each retailer some little time in which to adapt his prices, etc., to competitive changes. For this reason retail pricing is an art requiring some

---

ment stores, the chain stores, and the mail order houses.' (*Investigation into the Proprietary Articles Trade Association, Report of Commissioner* [*Combines Investigation Act*], 1927, p. 23).

The history of resale price maintenance arrangements and their prevalence in countries in which they are not checked by legislative measures provide the basic empirical evidence for our general conclusions and for much of the detailed analysis. The contents of discussions in British retail trade journals, particularly before and during the commencement and early growth of resale price maintenance practices, suggest strongly that our analysis deals with important forces influencing the nature of competition in freely competitive retail markets.

6. By 'monopolistic competition' we mean here the case of differentiated products with a large number of competing suppliers. Our argument is generally couched in terms of changes and variations in price, partly because Smith particularly stresses that price competition is weak in retailing, whereas we believe that adjustments in price are the most important manifestation and instrument of competition in retailing. We are aware that the theory of monopolistic competition embraces competitive adaptations of the product. We are aware, too, that Professor Chamberlin's definition of 'monopolistic competition' in the broad sense covers more than we have included in the more restricted meaning of the term.

skill and flair, in contradistinction to the pricing automatism postulated for perfect markets. But this difference in behaviour in perfect and retail markets does not warrant the view that it is apposite to stress the imperfections in retailing. The imperfections would be significant only if retailers aimed at maximizing their profits in successive 'short runs' irrespective of long-run repercussions (i.e., irrespective of the effects of a policy adopted in one short period upon the results of later short periods). There is no evidence to suggest that retailers in general adopt such a policy, and there is ample evidence that some retailers adopt the opposite policy of planning their prices with long-run consequences in mind, even to the extent of accepting initial losses as the price of long-run success.[7] The emphasis on 'goodwill' in retailing circles suggests that long-run considerations preponderate in the formulation of retail price (and service) policy. The conclusion is that the long-run, and not the short-run, demand is relevant for the retailer's marketing policy, and that the former is much more elastic than the latter.

The exceptions to this general conclusion illustrate their own relative unimportance and the special conditions that must be present. There is Marshall's example (1932, p. 811) of shops catering for tourists, living off a never-ending stream of short-lived customers so that the long run looks after itself. Another example is provided by the monopoly position of the retailer of chocolates etc. in a theatre or sports stadium, where the mobility of the customers is restricted and where the retailer is assured of a clientele in the long run. A further example is the 'exclusive' retailer to whom any serious enlargement of his clientele may damage his main asset and for whom high prices may provide a mark of distinction. It is significant that retailers in these exceptional circumstances are not clamorous for the protection of resale price maintenance – 'exclusive' retailers, in fact, tend to avoid price-maintained goods partly because their prices are fixed and their margins often inadequate for their type of trade.

The time lag in the response of consumers to inter-shop price differences means that the retailer who wishes to expand his sales may have to adopt a variety of methods to make his shop and prices known to potential customers. In a perfect market, of course, such dissemination of information and persuasion would be neither necessary nor profitable. The presence of 'sales promotion' activity by entrepreneurs is generally regarded as a proof or a symptom of the existence of imperfections. This interpretation is misleading; for it is the essence of competitive sales promotion activity that it widens the consumers' range of knowledge about the alternatives open to them, and in many cases provides the jolt to shake consumers out of settled habits. The sluggish responses of the consumer provoke activity on the

7. See, for example, Adelman (1949).

part of some retailers to accelerate and sharpen the responses. The result is that the demand for the individual retailer's services is more elastic than it would have been otherwise; in addition, competitive sales promotion has an 'unsettling' effect on the market by constantly undermining the bases of market fragmentation.[8]

Changes in supply in retailing

We have considered, above, dynamic change on the demand side of the retail market, which tends to reduce the importance to the retailer of the imperfections present in the market at any moment of time. Turning to changes on the supply side it is necessary to look at changes of technique in retailing and at conditions of entry into retailing.

During the past fifty to a hundred years there have been significant changes in the technique of retailing. Cooperative shops, department stores, multiples, variety chains, mail-order houses and self-service shops are obvious examples where an existing type of retail service is provided more efficiently than before, or where a new type of retail service is offered to consumers. Both Smith and Hall indicate the nature of these changes. But Smith minimizes the extent to which these changes have increased price competition in retailing. He notes the changes, but observes that 'while all these are evident and obvious examples of adaptations of technique which have been adopted in order to lessen the cost of distribution *to the retailer*, we still lack proof that, except perhaps in the case of cooperative societies, there is a direct response to the demands of the consumer expressed in terms of price elasticity' (1948, p. 179).[9] It is not easy

8. The practice of 'leader' or 'loss leader' selling may be cited as an example of sales promotion activity. Because of the sluggishness of consumers a retailer may prefer to offer large price reductions on a few special lines rather than small price reductions generalized over his entire assembly of merchandise. The former reductions may be more readily obvious to consumers than the latter. The *minimum sensibile* in respect of price differences may be quite large in some cases, and if price competition is to take place at all it may have to take the form of more dramatic but selected price cuts.

It would be seriously lacking in perspective to give too much weight to 'leader' tactics in an analysis of retailing. Its role in the history of resale price maintenance has certainly been grossly overstated.

In general there is no economic reason why the different goods sold by a retailer should carry the same percentage margin of gross profit. Once this is granted it becomes difficult to distinguish leader selling from 'genuine' price competition.

9. Hall's comment that 'owing again to the peculiar character of distributive markets, important influences have militated against the evolution of more efficient forms of organization and the evolution of more efficient techniques of purchase and sale' (1949, p. 189) is more difficult to assess because of its vagueness. We would endorse it without reservation if it meant merely that one cannot have a department store or supermarket in every hamlet of a hundred souls, or that one does not find a help-yourself dress shop in Bond Street or the Rue de la Paix.

to imagine what sort of proof is required short of the discovery of the retailers' (*ex ante*) demand and cost schedules! Here it is sufficient to point out that the introduction of changes in retailing has been accompanied by large-scale changes in the shopping habits of consumers, by the new-comers stressing the appeal of lower prices and by vigorous (though usually impotent) complaints of existing retail firms about the price cutting of the newer firms.[10] The conclusion is irresistible that the proof which Smith claims to be lacking is to be found in the record of history. Further it should be remembered that while we have mentioned changes in techniques associated with new types of retail organization, in fact there is constant experimentation in retailing which produces a large number of successful small changes.

Smith's argument that innovations may confer benefits upon the innovator and not on consumers seems relevant in one situation only: that is where:

1. The innovation is one that provides an existing service at a lower average cost.
2. The innovator's marginal costs remain unaltered for the relevant range of outputs.
3. The innovation is introduced by an established firm.

This situation appears to be a rather special and unimportant one.

A feature of innovation in retailing is that successful innovations may readily be imitated by competitors without institutional hindrances, such as are contained in the law relating to patents and trade marks, and which are important in other industries. The speed with which novel ideas (in matters such as display, advertising and pricing) in retailing are taken up by competitors is remarkable.[11] Imperfections based on differentiation in service or appeal tend to be short-lived, and are not likely to influence the innovators' price policies appreciably. The assumption of a long-term private market has little basis.

10. This argument can be considered from another viewpoint. It has often been argued that the development of cost-reducing techniques has been hindered where the innovator is prevented from reducing his selling price. Thus A. J. Sainsbury says that the development of self-service in the United States 'might have been quite different if there had been a resale price maintenance policy throughout the States similar to that in Great Britain at the present time' (1950, p. 25). See also the remarks of John Ryan (1950, p. 20).

11. The same imitativeness is found, though to a lesser extent, in the location of retail outlets. It would require a degree of shopping mobility greater than exists at present to make imitativeness with respect to location as complete as it is in other directions. If such 'imitativeness' were forced upon retailers (e.g., by building and planning restrictions) the consumers would suffer a loss of convenience and be worse off, even though competition might appear to be more 'perfect'.

Even if there were no changes in retail techniques and no changes in the preferences of consumers for different kinds of retail services, the entry of new firms into the distributive trades would be a constant disturbance to stability in gross profit margins and private markets. With few exceptions[12] entry into retailing is easy, as the new entrant requires little capital and no professional qualifications. The capital is often provided by wholesale houses in competition with one another, and the deterrents to entry are further weakened by the relatively non-specific nature of the capital resources necessary in retailing. New entrants into retailing often act upon over-optimistic estimates both of their ability as retailers and of the profit potentialities in retailing. Certainly new entry into retailing is not confined to innovators and the (profit-equilibrating) entry of firms into trades or localities in which abnormally high rates of profit are being earned.[13] Newcomers open shops even if they are aware that existing retailers are *not* making abnormal profits. They merely believe that they have something to offer consumers on such terms that they will be able to produce profits for themselves – and frequently they are mistaken.

With a more or less continuous flow of new entrants into a retail trade it does not seem useful to discuss retail prices and gross margins as they would be if the trade were in long-run equilibrium (i.e., with supply adjusted to demand and firms earning 'normal' profits) – which is the approach adopted by Smith and Hall. Our view would be appropriate even if the inflow of new retailers is matched by a somewhat delayed outflow of retailers who have failed: for then the market would proceed through successive periods of disequilibrium, each tending towards but never reaching a (probably changing) position of equilibrium. In these periods of disequilibrium gross profit margins are likely to be affected. It seems fashionable to believe that gross profit margins will be adjusted upwards to accommodate the excessively large number of retailers. It appears more plausible to us that price competition will be accentuated, if only because the newcomers have to provide some inducements to consumers to change their shopping habits and have to adopt some methods of making known their presence. The offer of attractive prices is the obvious method, except where retail prices are maintained. Compared with advertised prices and bargain offers the offer of improved services by a newcomer is a poor inducement to consumers to try a new shop. At the

12. The exceptions include cases where the issue of necessary licences is limited or where the necessary premises and equipment are expensive and specific. In consequence such exceptional trades (e.g., liquor trade, the retailing of films [exhibition], and petrol filling stations) are frequently organized along lines quite different from those in the majority of retail trades.

13. Hall (1949, pp. 35, 49 and 57) appears to confine entry to these situations.

same time the struggles for liquidity on the part of unsuccessful retailers attempting to postpone or to avoid failure, and their final exit, are likely to unsettle the market.

Oligopoly in retailing

Recognition of the fact that there is a limit to the number of shops which can be located in any one area has led both writers to rely to some considerable extent on a simple theory of oligopoly for an explanation of the apparent weakness of price competition. Hall explicitly states that 'the retail market, like all imperfect markets, readily gives rise to conditions of oligopoly (1949, p. 41), while some of Smith's most important conclusions are apparently based on the implicit assumption of the importance of the 'small group' case (1948, pp. 33 and 129).[14]

Oligopolistic interdependence, it is implied, leads in general to the following sequence of events. There will be an 'irresistible incentive to the proscription of price competition by some form of agreement among (existing) sellers, whereupon competition in terms of a variety of so-called "services" takes its place' (1949, p. 61). Although prospective entrants must take account of the fact that they will have to share the market with existing retailers,[15] not all newcomers will be deterred. Existing retailers will lose some of the economies of scale, the new entrant will be unable to expand to his most economic size. The costs of all in the locality will rise and prices will probably rise to cover the new level of costs.[16] If such entry continues a snowballing of costs and prices will result.

Much of the argument is cautiously advanced. However, the reader could hardly be blamed if he were to gain the impression of small groups of shopkeepers living in mortal fear of one another, acting in a manner best calculated to invite new competition, yet possessed of the marvellous foresight and restraint necessary to enable them independently or collectively to light upon price policies which allow an increasing number of them to live in comfort.

Possibly much of the emphasis on the oligopolistic nature of the retail market derives from the simplifying assumptions often utilized in theoretical analysis of the retail trade. Attention has been focused on competition inside small and well defined market areas. While such analysis serves to isolate certain important considerations, it cannot provide the

14. Although Smith bases much of his argument on the theory of monopolistic competition, he stresses the fear of retaliation. Much of his discussion is concerned with competition in a 'neighbourhood' or 'locality'.

15. Smith (1948, p. 25); Hall (1949, p. 35). Hall does not explicitly carry the argument further.

16. Smith (1948, p. 189) admits that 'increased overhead costs . . . can only increase prices if they lead to tacit or formal combinations or agreements'.

sole basis for a realistic explanation of situations where markets are not so strictly delimited.

The inhabitants of a particular street or village, suburb or small town are not deprived of all contact with the world outside. Even where distance appears to afford a considerable measure of protection, transport costs are gradually being reduced by the advent of different forms of retailing and by changes in social habits. The travelling shop, the mail order firm or department, and telephone shopping, all reduce the significance of distance. In any case, except for small and isolated centres of population, a large number of shoppers are able to choose from amongst several retailers with only minor differences in the degree of inconvenience to themselves. New retail firms generally locate themselves where older shops are already established; they do not place overmuch value on a unique location.

This is not to deny that the scatter of retail outlets in an inhabited area is basically affected by the nature of the goods sold and the pattern of consumers' shopping behaviour; it merely suggests that particular retailers are not to any significant degree insulated against the pressure of price reductions originating outside their immediate neighbourhood.

Perhaps we have over-emphasized this aspect of the location problem. Possibly it was the intention of these writers to concentrate attention not so much on isolated firms or on isolated groups of firms as on the interdependence between such firms and groups of firms. It is somewhat difficult to reconcile the continuous variabilty of clientele which such interdependence presupposes with the 'private markets' and 'circles of customers' which figure rather prominently in the expositions of Smith and Hall. If it is 'possible for any retailer to raise his prices above those of his neighbours to an appreciable extent before losing sufficient customers to them for the defection to outweigh the increased revenue from the remaining ones' (Smith, 1948, p. 129), there seems to be no justification for the statement that 'probably the strongest motive behind the stability of retail prices is the desire to avoid retaliation and "cut-throat competition"' (Smith, 1948, p. 33). Since we must exclude the one hypothesis or the other, let us concentrate on the 'inevitable' results of the individual retailer's recognition of the danger of retaliation. Will it in fact lead to 'a marked tendency to organize common standards between themselves' (Smith, 1948, p. 33). Should we in fact anticipate widespread tacit or formal agreements leading to the adoption of 'conventional mark-ups'?

There is little justification for the assumption that all retailers are possessed of the timidity, altruism or foresight necessary to persuade them to 'live and let live' (Hall, 1949, p. 42). There are some who choose to live dangerously or to follow their own selfish ends. Some retailers feel that price competition is the most effective method of increasing sales, even though temporary loss may result from such a policy (and it need not do so). Even if we suppose that some low-cost retailers are reluctant to initiate price cutting, can we also assume that they are confident that no other trader will lead the way? A reputation for cheapness is often very desirable. Can a firm take the risk that others may gain the credit for being the pioneers in this field? In an industry such as retailing no one seller can rely on the moral fibre of his competitors. He cannot trust his rivals to refrain from cutting prices merely because they believe that such a policy may spoil the market for others. If cost conditions enable him to follow a policy of undercutting his rivals the trader may feel obliged to put it into effect.

We can pursue the question still further. Let us assume that all retailers desire to avoid price cuts, and that they are all confident that the same attitude prevails amongst their fellows. What price policy will commend itself to the individual seller? He will follow the 'price ruling on the average for the class of goods concerned'. There is, however, little reason to suppose that there will be a well defined price which he can adopt: and this problem of choosing which price to follow will confront every firm. In any case some one retailer must take it upon himself to set the standard for the rest, and there would appear to be considerable scope for misapprehension as to his identity.

The suggested solution is that each seller will fix a price sufficient to cover the costs of doing business. Being content to obtain a reasonable profit by catering for his existing clientele he will set margins sufficient to cover the costs of carrying out his present functions. But retailers vary in size and efficiency; they offer different services to suit the tastes of different types of consumer. Overheads such as rent may vary considerably within a small area. It is unlikely that the desire not to initiate active price competition will lead intuitively to the setting of the same initial mark-up by all sellers. Even if such a result were likely it would not necessarily lead to an identity in the final price. Cost price is not an independent factor of given magnitude: it may vary according to the quantity bought, to the time of purchase and to the channels utilized, and retailers are well aware of this fact. Good buying is one of the attributes of the successful retailer and varying degrees of skill in purchasing will lead to varying cost prices. The adoption of identical percentage or absolute margins will merely accentuate the effect of this source of divergence in price. Even so the analysis has been over-simplified. It has not taken account of the fact that we are dealing with a heterogeneous collection of multi-product firms selling varying combinations both of goods and services. There still remains the inherent difficulty of cost accounting in the multi-product firm. We agree that in the conditions of perfect competition assumed in strict theory different allocations of overhead costs could not exist for any length of time: the pressure of competition would speedily eliminate them. In an industry where so many possibilities of output combinations exist it seems hardly possible that identical prices should arise independently of any pressure from competitive forces.

On the whole it seems unlikely that even with the best will in the world retailers should arrive at some quasi-agreement which automatically ensures that all prices should be the same, or even that they should for long remain in the same relationship to one another. It is difficult to see how any retailer could so order his price policy that his good intentions were obvious to all, and protestations of good faith are likely to be singularly unconvincing when his prices are manifestly below those of some of his competitors. Nor is the problem solved by suggesting that some more formal agreement will result. The factors already considered will provide ample opportunity for disagreement over uniform prices; while a formal recognition of permitted price differentials, even if it were practicable, would be in need of constant revision and in constant danger of collapse. It would appear that the adoption of uniform mark-ups or prices is not inherent in the typical market situation in retailing. Indeed we can go further and state that insuperable difficulties attend any independent attempt to maintain such a system.

One more possibility deserves consideration. Let us imagine with Professor Adelman (1948, p. 1297) that two stores in a particular locality have reached 'some empirical position of live and let live' (Hall, 1949, p. 42). 'There is a constant temptation to cut prices toward [the] low cost of additional business . . . But open price cuts are futile, for they will be matched within the hour . . . Customers are not price conscious, anyway. Better to offer additional services. . . . As both do so, costs rise, and margins and prices are raised to cover them . . . The temptation to cut prices grows, but the higher the cost structure the more disastrous this can be.' What is the probable ending to this 'parable of monopoly behaviour'? 'Some low ruffian, in search not of a reasonable but of a large profit, opens a super-market nearby, engages in strenuous price competition, and puts them both out of business. . . . This is in microcosm, the rise and decline of oligopoly heaven.'

Existing firms cannot afford to ignore the possibility that innovators will destroy their carefully preserved margins. If they become complacent or forsake price competition for competition in services then some other type of trading unit may encroach upon their market. An understanding or agreement peaceably to share the market will avail them little if 'their' market is not clearly defined and may disappear under their very noses. They may not wish to invoke price competition against one another; competition from outsiders may force them to do so.

Competition from new firms is not the only source of danger to the retailer who relies on traditional mark-ups and non-price competition. Retailers in other trades can take up items carrying remunerative rates of mark-up as profitable side lines. The flexibility in the selection of merchandise open to any one retailer (unless impeded by restrictive arrangements) is a potent contribution to price competition in retailing,[17] and the reactions of the 'bona fide' dealers to such 'dabbling' testify to the force of this kind of competition.

The truth seems to be that many retailers would welcome such a system of agreed margins or prices. In practice, however, they are unable to enjoy the benefits of such a system unless there are collective agreements introducing sanctions which have a much greater deterrent effect than the mere fear of retaliation to price competition. Resale price maintenance is not the natural outcome of an oligopolistic situation in an atomistic industry. The support for such arrangements illustrates in itself the necessity for outside aid due to the impossibility of procuring and maintaining the voluntary loyalty of all distributors.[18]

A note on welfare implications

Insistence on long-term imperfections leads Smith to conclude that, quite apart from the effects of resale price maintenance, there will be excess capacity in retailing accompanied by a wasteful bidding up of costs leading to the absorption of an unnecessarily large share of the country's resources in distribution. Hall accepts this 'waste' as part of 'the facts of life' since 'consumers are geographically dispersed and they *prefer* various types of retail service to others' (1949, p. 170).[19] We agree with Hall's attitude because we believe that consumers are competent to judge between retailers and that in the absence of resale price maintenance desired alternatives would be available on competitive terms.

17. 'Supermarkets handle glassware, magazines, toilet goods and cosmetics, nylon stockings and electric toasters. The drug stores complain that grocers sell asprins, but who took the soda fountain business away from the ice-cream parlors, the boxed candy trade away from the confectioners, and packaged stationery away from the stationers? Auto accessory stores sell radios, refrigerators, washing machines, sports jackets, work clothes, men's and boys' socks, house furnishings and electrical supplies. Filling stations sell coffee makers, razor blades and soft drinks' Lebow (1948, pp. 12–13).

18. This view is supported in the recent pamphlet on resale price maintenance published by the Fair Prices Defence Committee. Proposals for the abolition of collective resale price maintenance are viewed with alarm, since not only can retailers not agree amongst themselves as to the prices to be set, but even the cooperation of individual manufacturers is not a sufficient condition. 'It is quite impracticable, in most trades, for individual producers to operate their own systems of price maintenance . . . previous attempts have proved to be ineffective.'

19. See also p. 65. A different interpretation is suggested on pp. 70n and 168.

Smith's argument is based on different premises. He believes that there are differences in the nature and sources of imperfections and that these are significant for welfare judgments and policy decisions.[20] Thus he notes that 'consumers' preference between retailers may be rational or irrational'.[21] Once this step has been taken it is easy to conclude that at least some of the imperfections are not immutable facts, but aberrations arising, for example, out of 'the amateur status of the retail purchaser' (1948, p. 180), and that these are likely to be exploited by competing retailers, particularly if consumers are not considered to be responsive to differences in prices at different sources of supply. The result is that competition leads to the supply of 'unnecessary' services that are not 'really' desired by consumers, and would not be supplied if the market were 'perfect'. Consequently any proposals for reform should be judged by inquiring 'either what its effects will be upon the "perfection of the market", or how far it promises to reproduce the effects of a perfect market by means of some other method than that of "free consumer's choice"' (1948, p. 181). And lest any reader may wonder how a perfect market will work in retailing, criteria for proposals for reform are indicated more precisely: 'Do they promise to lower retail margins to the consumer, and do they propose to check the drift of economic resources into retailing?' (1948, p. 182). Austerity in retailing is apparently to maximize the consumer's 'genuine' satisfactions. By these criteria the reform of retailing should present no difficulty – except to the consumer. Perhaps Smith did not intend to go as far as this: but his argument tends in this direction, and it is not unlike the general tenor of the arguments of others who are concerned about the wastes of less-than-perfect competition.[22]

Summary

It is not useful to rely upon an essentially static and long-run theory of monopolistic competition to explain the economics of retailing. It is not realistic to argue in terms of long-run stability in consumers' preferences, or to assume that entry is of an equilibrating kind and that innovations are of the peculiar variety implied by Smith. The use of an over-simplified theory of oligopoly is equally unrealistic. Freedom of entry and chain linking of markets make it unwise to rely upon a mere counting of numbers.

20. Chamberlin does not provide the precedent for this line of reasoning. See his discussion on the ideal output (1933, pp. 93–4). Indeed most of our criticisms are not directed at the 'new theories' but at the particular use made of them.

21. Smith (1948, p. 127). 'This dichotomy cannot be strictly maintained on logical grounds . . . But on "common-sense" grounds the line is easy to draw, even if it is an imaginary line.'

22. For example, see the *Report of the Committee on Milk Distribution*, (1948, June), especially paragraph 178.

Tacit or formal agreements are not the simple arrangements which some theories suggest.

There may be some serious criticism of sales promotion activity in retailing. But this criticism should not be based on the charge that sales promotion is merely a symptom of market imperfection and that it strengthens market imperfection, or that it is an unnecessary cost of distribution. Any action designed to increase the perfection of the market is likely to be costly (unless the perfection is spuriously attained by denying some alternatives or potential alternatives to consumers). It is possible that the method of competitive selling activity may be more costly or less effective than other methods: but this is quite a different question.

Up to a point we agree with the view that market forces in the distributive trades may tend to a condition of 'excess capacity'. But we do not agree that this excess capacity is a feature of imperfect retail markets in equilibrium. Rather the excess capacity in retailing under competitive conditions is a consequence of the ease of entry into the distributive trades and a sign of disequilibrium. It leads to lower prices, and, in a sense, the costs of maintaining it are borne by the retailers themselves in the form of lower returns than were anticipated.[23] It appears to us that the 'excess capacity' in retailing is a safeguard of the interests of consumers in that it tends to increase competition, particularly with respect to price. It is not a burden upon consumers from which they should necessarily be liberated.

23. The 'imperfect foresight' of some new entrants is clearly incompatible with perfect competition. But this type of imperfection does not form part of Smith's and Hall's arguments.

References

ADELMAN, M. A. (1948), 'Effective competition and the antitrust laws', *Harvard law Rev.*, vol. 61.

ADELMAN, M. A. (1949), 'The A & P Case', *Q. J. Econ.*, vol. 63.

CHAMBERLIN, E. H. (1942), *The Theory of Monopolistic Competition*, 4th edn, Harvard University Press.

CLARK, J. M. (1940), 'Toward a concept of workable competition', *Amer. econ. Rev.*, vol. 30.

HALL, M. (1949), *Distributive Trading*, Hutchinson.

HAYEK, F. A. (1949), 'The meaning of competition', in *Individualism and Economic Order*, Routledge & Kegan Paul.

LEBOW, V. (1948), 'Our changing channels of distribution', *J. Marketing*, vol. 13.

MARSHALL, A. (1932), *Industry and Trade*, 3rd edn, Macmillan.

RYAN, J. (1950), *Management Implications of Self-Service Stores*, British Institute of Management.

SAINSBURY, A. J. (1950), *The Management of Multiple Shops*, British Institute of Management.

SMITH, H. (1948), *Retail Distribution*, 2nd edn, Oxford University Press.

SMITH, H. (1949a), *Wholesaling and Retailing*, tract no. 272, Fabian Society.

SMITH, H. (1949b), Article in *Store*, October, pp. 27–8.

9 J. Hood and B. S. Yamey

Middle-Class Cooperative Retailing Societies in London, 1864–1900

J. Hood and B. S. Yamey, 'The middle-class cooperative retailing societies in London, 1864–1900', *Oxford Economic Papers*, n.s., vol. 9, 1957, pp. 309–22.

Contemporary accounts suggest that in the middle of the nineteenth century middle- and upper-class shoppers in London had to pay a high price for the lavish retail services which were then customary. Retailers operated on a small scale, and each confined himself to a particular branch of trade. The typical West End shop had sufficient salespeople to handle, with ease, even the rush of business in peak periods. Long credit was given as a matter of course, and, in some branches, traders called frequently for orders which were then delivered without special charge. Douceurs to servants who shopped for their employers added to retailing costs and margins. Competition in prices was rare and leisurely, while it was widely believed that retailers combined against the public and that adulteration was common in the food trades.[1]

This picture was doubtlessly exaggerated;[2] but, in general, retailing costs were high, price competition was weak, and customers rarely had an effective choice between more and less elaborate and costly methods of retailing. Dissatisfaction with the prevailing methods and practices, and the scope for more economical and cheaper methods, are exemplified in the establishment and rapid growth of middle-class cooperative retailing enterprises in London from 1864 onwards. In this article we outline the history of the three main societies, which for a few decades dominated competition in retailing in London and farther afield.[3] They were the first

1. See, for example, articles in the *Saturday Review*, 7 March 1868 and 1 August 1874; Head (1872); and A Civil Servant (1873).

2. For example, haggling was still practised, giving rise to a form of price competition, but a costly one in terms of the use of labour in retailing. Again, in bookselling there had been periods of severe price competition; a particular instance of this, and its repercussions, are discussed briefly in Yamey (1954).

3. Our main sources of information are: journals of civil service opinion, mainly the *Civilian* and the *Civil Service Review*; *The Army and Navy Gazette*; *The Times*; financial weeklies; some quarterly and monthly reviews; retail trade journals; *Report on Cooperative Stores*, of 1879 (referred to hereafter as *Report*); a number of pamphlets; the published rules of the three societies, and their catalogues and price lists. (We are grateful to the Secretary of the Army and Navy Stores for allowing us to consult his firm's collection of catalogues issued in the nineteenth century.)

(or at least among the first) large-scale retailing undertakings in England, and they promoted the practices of cash trading, of working on low margins, of marking prices uniform to all customers, and of disregarding the traditional divisions between the various branches of retailing.[4]

The first of the middle-class societies had very humble origins. In the winter of 1864 a few clerks in the General Post Office clubbed together to buy half a chest of tea, which they divided amongst themselves, allegedly saving 9d. a lb. and being assured of its quality. This initial success led them to extend their operations to coffee, sugar, and other groceries, and in January 1865 they formed the Post Office Supply Association.[5] The committee members were unpaid, and the postal authorities allowed them to use the cellar for storing and distributing goods and the library for committee meetings; but a small subscription soon became necessary to defray expenses. Originally there were forty members, but business was increased by allowing 'friends' of these members to become customers of the Association by buying 6d. tickets; after six months the society had over 700 ticket-holding friends. Goods not handled by the Association were obtainable from traders cooperating with the Association:[6] a price list was prepared to protect customers against any imposition by these affiliated traders.

The Association progressed despite the inconvenience to shoppers of

---

It is a defect of our sources that from them little can be discovered about the people who were active in directing these large enterprises. But they nevertheless make it possible to establish the main events in their history, changes in policy, and their impact on retailing in general.

4. It would be wrong to claim that the middle-class societies were the first to introduce any of these practices. According to an essay in the *Spectator* in 1712, a London merchant, John Moreton, had avoided 'the Hazards of giving Credit' and, by 'affixing the Value of each Piece itself', also 'the most infamous Guilt of Bartering', saving so much that 'Sixteen will do as much as Twenty Shillings' (see Ueda, 1956, p. 23). By the end of the eighteenth century 'the habit of setting a price-ticket on goods was extending' (Ashton, 1955, p. 70). In Dublin in the first half of the nineteenth century there had been four 'marts', which had cut across trade demarcations, sold for cash at low, fixed prices, and operated on a large scale (Hancock, 1851).

The working-class cooperatives also sold for cash only. They may have influenced the middle-class cooperatives, though in several respects their methods were different.

5. A letter in *The Times* (10 February, 1868) suggests that another society, The Bankers' Clerks' Stores, may have been the first in the field, in 1862. We have not discovered any other reference to this society.

6. By the end of 1865 the Civil Service Supply Association, as it had then become, had fifty affiliated traders supplying jewellery, pianos, cigars, crinolines, chandeliers and photographs. At this date the society itself supplied mainly groceries, ale and stout, and eau-de-cologne.

its methods. Applications for membership were made by many civil servants outside the Post Office; in April 1865 membership was thrown open to all civil servants, and the name of the association was changed to the Civil Service Supply Association (CSSA). At first it had premises in the East Central district of London, and later also in the West End.

The object of this society[7] was to supply 'Officers of the Civil Service and their Friends . . . at the lowest possible prices'.[8] Its initial capital came from the issue of non-interest-bearing shares.[9] Only civil service officers could buy these shares; at first (until 1874) there was no limit to the number which could be issued, but each member could hold only one share. A member had the right to deal at the shops of the society and of affiliated traders, and to attend and vote at meetings.[10] Certain other persons were eligible to become ordinary customers only: at the discretion of the management civil service officers who did not desire the full privileges of membership, and friends introduced by any civil service officer, could become customers on the purchase of annual tickets of 2s. 6d. and 5s., respectively.[11] The society was directed by a committee of management of fifteen elected members who were at first paid according to the funds available.[12]

Two other important London societies were founded soon after the CSSA. The Civil Service Cooperative Society Ltd. (CSCS) was registered as a limited company in April 1866, and opened its shop in the Haymarket.[13] Its capital consisted of 1000 £5 shares bearing a maximum of 5 per cent interest. There was no limit on the individual shareholdings of its civil service members, but each shareholder had only one vote.

7. The middle-class cooperative associations are henceforth referred to as 'societies' and their establishments as 'shops', though both were often referred to as 'stores'; the latter term came to be used to refer to department stores generally.

8. Similar words appear in the rules of the two other major societies.

9. These £1 shares were payable in 2s. 6d. instalments, and in fact only 10s. was called.

10. From an early date he was also given preferential treatment in respect of delivery charges.

11. A tradition soon evolved to restrict the categories of 'friends' worthy of acceptance; in 1868 these included members of Parliament, peers, members of the clerical and legal professions, and service officers.

12. In 1879 the chairman of the committee was clerk in the department of the Accountant General of the Navy; the committee members included two principal clerks, a deputy principal, three first-class clerks, and the Queen's Warehouse Keeper and Receiver of Wrecks for the Port of London.

13. The early formation of a second civil service society can be ascribed partly to the need for a West End store for civil servants. The CSSA did not open its West End branch until April 1867. There may also have been dissatisfaction with the CSSA because it paid no interest on share capital.

Again its elected directors were civil servants, and at first they were unpaid.[14] At its inception ticket-holding by non-members also was limited to civil servants, but very soon its 2s. 6d. annual tickets were available also to peers, members of Parliament, justices of the peace, army and naval officers, and clergymen.

The third important London society was the Army and Navy Co-operative Society Ltd (A & N), which began trading in Victoria Street in 1872. Its initial capital consisted of 15,000 £1 shares, and membership was open to army and naval officers, their widows, non-commissioned officers, petty officers, the secretaries of services clubs, and canteen and mess representatives.[15] In addition annual tickets were issued at the discretion of the management (at 5s. for the first year and 2s. 6d. upon renewal) to those otherwise eligible to become shareholders, and to other persons introduced by shareholders or by those eligible to become shareholders. The articles of association did not specify any limit to the return on share capital, though in fact interest was limited to 5 per cent for many years.

In all three societies many of the shareholders were men of wide experience and high professional standing. They were competent – or thought they were competent – to judge business affairs and to talk on terms of equality with the elected management committee. They were articulate, and, as customers of the societies, they were interested in the details and results of business policies.[16] In consequence management committees were forced to justify the policies and defend the trading results at frequent ordinary meetings, and at special meetings called at the request of groups of members with grievances. Meetings were often long and noisy, and sometimes disorderly. Nevertheless, on the whole management committees seem to have been able to pursue the policies which seemed to them desirable. But there were times when shareholders refused to allow the management to act on purely business considerations,[17] and the high

14. In 1879 the committee of management included the Director General, Store Department, Office of Secretary of State for India; three principal clerks; the Governor of Pentonville Prison; and the late Collector and Chief Registrar of Shipping, Customs. The honorary directors included the late Comptroller General of Her Majesty's Customs, a late Member of Council for India, and the statistician Dr William Farr, Superintendent of Statistics, Registrar General's Office.

15. In 1879 the society had eight directors – an admiral, two generals, a major-general, a rear-admiral, a major and two captains, all of them retired.

16. At meetings there often were detailed comparisons by shareholders of relative prices and qualities in the shops of the main societies. Shareholders wrote letters to the press complaining, for example, that bacon was up to 1½d. a pound dearer at the CSSA than at the A & N.

17. For instance, in 1879 A & N shareholders defeated a move to increase share capital to enable, *inter alia*, the premises to be extended. The resulting lack of space

degree of democratic control must often have been irksome to the management.

The societies offered shoppers a new combination of low prices and reduced service. Many of the customary services were much reduced or eliminated altogether.[18] Thus no credit was given: cash trading eliminated the risk of bad debts and simplified accounting. The societies also accepted deposits from customers against future orders. The strong liquid position of the societies, strengthened by receipts from the sale of tickets and the undistributed profits which they soon accumulated, enabled them to buy for cash on favourable terms and to command the attention of the most advantageous sources of supply.

Cash prices for goods kept in stock in the shops were published in price lists which were issued free up to four times a year, and which fixed the prices of most articles for the current period.[19] Prices were known and uniform to all buyers; there was no haggling or suspicion of discrimination. The lists also set a standard by which the prices of other tradesmen could be judged. Some goods were sold only in fairly large minimum quantities, which accounted in part for the relatively low prices.[20] Other goods were subject to discounts off the list price when large quantities were taken.[21]

The CSSA did not at first carry stocks of all merchandise on offer, and in the early years groceries made up the bulk of the stock-in-trade. Patterns only were kept in some departments, and certain articles were obtained for customers if they gave full details of what was wanted.[22] Some traders, appointed by the society, were given space in its premises to sell their merchandise to members.[23] These arrangements reduced the capital required to support a given volume of business; and some of them also reduced the convenience of shopping.

forced the society to restrict the issue of new annual tickets for a period. It also led to the formation of a rival society, the Junior Army and Navy Stores (see footnote 32).

18. This was done despite the fact that the societies set out to cater for members of the middle and upper classes.

19. Prices were altered more frequently when market conditions changed as in the case of tea. Where the market was known to be subject to great fluctuations, no price was quoted in the list.

20. In 1866 the CSSA sold cigars in boxes of not less than twenty-five; lemonade, sherryade, ginger beer, etc., were sold in lots of two-dozen bottles; and 2d. packets of goods such as baking powder or black lead were sold in dozens, for about half the prices suggested by their manufacturers.

21. The CSSA list in 1866 announced that tea selling at 2s. 4d. to 3s. 9d. a pound was reduced by 1d. a pound if fifty pounds were taken at one time. The first A & N list offered the same reduction on twenty pounds.

22. In both the A & N and CSSA books, magazines and music were obtained in this way and sold at wholesale prices.

23. For example, drugs, fancy goods, stationery, hosiery, linen and carpets.

Inside the civil service shops the customer had to bestir himself with little assistance from the employees. He consulted the price list and filled in the department's invoice with details of his requirements and their prices – he made out his own bill.[24] He then went to the cashier's office to pay and to have his invoice receipted. Armed with his receipt he made his way to the counter, where he often queued for some time until his order was assembled. He then took the goods away from the counter and home from the shop. Mail orders, documented in detail and accompanied by cash, were delivered if this was asked for; customers in general had to pay an additional delivery charge.[25]

By contemporary standards shopping in the shops of the societies was highly inconvenient during their early decades. As early as 1868 there were critics who suggested that the low prices charged by the societies were inadequate recompense for the inconvenience involved, and who prophesied that the societies would soon have to change their methods. But in fact for many years to come customers were content with this new mode of trading with or without minor modification. They now knew 'what things cost, and what they ought to cost. . . . Until then people had never known how much they paid for the convenience of supply provided in the ordinary way of trade' (*The Times*, 31 January 1873).

Not all goods available through the medium of the societies had to be bought in this burdensome manner. There were 'affiliated traders' who in their own shops supplied shareholders and ticket-holders with goods which the societies found too costly or too troublesome to stock. In return for the certainty of immediate cash payments and the increase in business which might be expected from their connection with the societies, the affiliated traders offered a discount of from 5 to 30 per cent off their regular prices to the privileged customers, who in other respects were in general served in the same manner as their ordinary customers.[26] In 1866 the seventy or so traders affiliated to the CSSA sold a wide variety of goods such as wines, tobaccos, baby linen, books, boots and shoes, coal, carpets, drapery, milk and butter, meat, pianos, surgical instruments and

24. In the early years he had to make it out in duplicate to economize on store labour.
25. In London the charges were at favourable rates due to special arrangements between the societies and Carter, Paterson & Co.
26. The societies helped their members to compute the discounts by including a form of ready-reckoner in their price lists.

A few traders affiliated to the CSSA transacted business with its members during certain hours only, or had special departments for this trade. One firm of hatters did not give discounts in its Sackville Street branch.

Some of the firms listed were then, and are now still, well known: Reeves & Sons, artists' colourmen; Lincoln & Bennett, hatters; Grossmith & Sons, perfumers; J. J. Carreras, tobacconist.

also many services.[27] (Societies also had professional men as affiliates, including accountants, surgeons, solicitors, architects, surveyors, estate agents and stockbrokers.) But the variety of goods made available through affiliated traders became more limited as the societies acquired more premises and funds and extended their trade to additional departments.[28]

At first competing retailers were scornful of the business efforts of the 'notoriously incapable' civil servants, but within a year or two they became seriously alarmed. Despite the austerity of their services, the shops of the societies grew and prospered greatly. In 1868 a leading article in *The Times* suggested that 'so rapid . . . is the extension of this remarkable movement, that it threatens nothing less than a social revolution'. A less sober article in the *Saturday Review* maintained that 'middle-class people . . . are in a white heat of passion against the retailers'.

The rapid advance of the movement was doubtless a surprise to its civil service pioneers. The POSA experienced great difficulty and inconvenience in catering for its rapidly increasing trade, and it had to move to larger accommodation several times. By 1867 its original membership of forty had expanded to about 5000 customers of the CSSA, and the next year saw a doubling of this number. By 1879 its annual turnover exceeded £1 million, its identifiable customers numbered about 31,800, and it had three branches. Up to this date the growth of the CSCS was more gradual but as continuous. The A & N was perhaps the most strikingly successful. It was launched at a time when the popularity of middle-class cooperative retailing had been clearly demonstrated, and in its first year its sales exceeded £130,000. By 1879 its turnover just exceeded that of the CSSA and it had more customers.[29]

The success of the three major societies gave rise to the establishment of many others. Some aimed at catering for particular groups who wished to acquire benefits similar to those already enjoyed by civil servants and

27. Other more unusual wares were offered. A teacher of the pianoforte and examiner of pianos offered for sale copies of his 'set of Original and Brilliant Studies for Amateurs in the Form of Preludes, and Dedicated to the Civil Service Supply Association'.

28. From an early date the A & N also embarked upon the manufacture of a variety of goods.

29. Annual sales of the societies (£000)

	CSSA	CSCS	A & N
1866/7	21	15	
1869/70	345	239	
1872/3	712	394	130
1875/6	953	470	664
1878/9	1475	527	1528

members of the services, while others provided goods not supplied (or not effectively handled) by the existing societies.[30] Many more enterprises were launched to take advantage of the supposed prestige of official-sounding titles and of the magic which seemed to attach to words like 'supply association' and 'cooperative'; most of them failed very soon.[31] Only two of the large number of new London societies proved in the long run to be sufficiently important to warrant special mention. They were the New Civil Service Cooperation Ltd (NCSC) of 1874 and the Junior Army and Navy Stores (Junior A & N) of 1879, both of which were formed by people who were dissatisfied with the methods or policies of the established societies.[32]

Successful middle-class cooperation was not confined to London. The Official Cooperative Society Ltd was set up in Dublin in 1872, constituted on the same lines as the principal London societies and designed to cater for officials in the public service and other professional men. Edinburgh had its Professional and Civil Service Supply Association which arranged reciprocity with the CSCS. There were Household Stores Associations in Liverpool and Manchester.

Traders in the East End of London were largely unaffected by the growth of the societies and the success of their low price policy, for they catered for a different class of trade and had not given lavish services. Traders in the West End, however, suffered considerably, as did others much farther

30. The Army and Navy Auxiliary Cooperative Supply Ltd was formed in 1880 to supply meat, fish, vegetables, forage, furniture, boots and shoes, and the services of a house and estate agency. Some A & N shareholders had felt that these fields were too risky for the A & N to enter. The Auxiliary was established with the same board of directors as the A & N, and membership of the societies was largely overlapping. By 1890 a bridge connected the two premises; and in 1919 the A & N took over the Auxiliary. It seems that the A & N had been anxious to cooperate with the Auxiliary because a rival society, the Junior Army and Navy Provision Market, had opened in Victoria Street a little while earlier; this society had a short life.

31. In our investigations we found references to over eighty retailing organizations, the names of which included words such as 'civil service', 'crown', 'army and navy', 'services', 'cooperative', or 'supply association', or which in some other way suggested similarity with the successful innovators. The dates of the establishment of these societies were bunched in three periods, 1868–73, 1879–80 and 1890; the *Statist* referred to the last wave as the 'cooperative mania'.

32. The Junior A & N was established in Regent Street in 1879 after the A & N shareholders had refused to sanction an increase in share capital. It aimed, *inter alia*, at satisfying the needs of many members of the armed services who were unable to buy shares in the A & N.

The formation of the NCSC was directly attributable to changes in the rules of the CSSA regarding the number of shareholders and the rewards to capital (see footnote 43).

afield.[33] In 1879 a Cambridge trader pointed out that 'we have a very strong competition; we are only fifty miles from London' (*Report*, 1879, Q. 3710). An Irish trader felt that in Ireland generally competition from the London societies was more serious than competition from the Dublin society (*Report*, 1879, QQ. 4381 and 4417).

As soon as the movement had shown its strength, traders were advised from all sides to fight the societies with their own weapons. Many traders gradually followed this advice, and retail trading methods and price policies were changed drastically. The most obvious and immediate effect of competition from the societies was on the general level of retail profit margins and prices.[34] The low prices charged by the societies and affiliated traders forced increasing numbers of private retailers to lower their prices to keep their trade together, and to change their methods to make this possible. It seems that by about 1880 this effect was widespread.

Those who wished to match the low prices charged by the societies were more or less obliged to follow their method of cash trading; if they wanted to sell on credit to some of their customers they had to charge them specifically to defray the extra cost of the financial accommodation. A few traders had previously bought and sold for cash only; but very many more introduced cash discounts after competition from the societies had made itself felt, and cash trading was greatly encouraged. The practice of giving *douceurs* to servants also was dying by the end of the 1870s. In short, to quote a statement made in 1879 by one of their competitors, the societies had 'done more to set tradesmen thinking about the real principles of business than anything else which has been done during the last quarter of a century' (*Report*, 1879, Q. 3553).

The societies played a large part in bringing about other changes which have generally been credited to the ordinary department stores (that is,

33. The voluminous catalogues produced a large mail-order trade; and the A & N established depots and agencies in some provincial towns.

The societies also worked up an export trade through agencies in various European countries, and the A & N had depots in India.

34. The low level of gross margins is illustrated by the following statistics of gross margins expressed as a percentage of sales:

	CSSA	CSCS	A & N
1867/8	8·4	10·8	
1869/70	11·2	9·4	
1872/3	8·6	9·3	
1875/6	9·2	10·4	8·3
1878/9	10·3	10·8	7·5

Low prices were most obvious in the sale of proprietary goods, the selling prices of which were suggested by manufacturers and undercut by the societies.

stores not organized on cooperative lines). It is probable that their shops were the first major department stores in England. The CSSA had concentrated mainly on the sale of groceries during its first few months; but other departments were soon opened, and in 1870 one could buy at its shop 'anything from a blotting-pad to a bicycle or a billiard table – from ginger beer to *carte blanche* champagne'.[35] Intrusion by a retailer into the preserves of other trades on such a scale was not common at this time. 'Before the operation of the store system you were looked upon as a very selfish person if you embarked in a branch of trade not particularly belonging to your own.'[36] The societies were also early in having marked prices, uniform for all customers: the publication of price lists alone made this inevitable. Again, customers were free to stroll about the shop – in so far as space allowed such leisurely progression – without obligation to buy. Thus most of the attractions of department store shopping in, say, the 1890s, had been offered by the shops of the societies at an early date. The major difference was the meagreness of shopping services to customers (apart from that of the availability of a wide range of goods and of services such as clock-repairing) in the early decades of the societies. But the contrast should not be over-stated; for several of the ordinary department stores originally provided only limited services, and, as is shown in the last section, by the end of the century the societies had followed the department stores in extending their retailing services to customers.[37]

Many of the hard-hit competitors of the societies were anxious to eliminate the societies, and several attempts were made to contain their

35. The *Civilian*, 19 February, 1870. By 1881 the grocery department accounted for less than half the sales volume.

36. Evidence by C. D. Harrod, son of the founder of the shop of the same name (*Report*, 1879, Q. 3264).

37. Three major department stores were in origin roughly contemporary with the societies – Harrod's, Whiteley's, and Shoolbred's.

It is quite clear that the expansion of Harrod's from a grocery shop to a department store occurred in emulation of the model of the civil service stores, in particular the CSCS (*Report*, 1879, pp. 158 and 159). Following their example, C. D. Harrod branched out into perfumes, patent medicines, and stationery in 1868. He had always sold for cash and avoided *douceurs*. But he now issued a price list and followed cooperative pricing policies; in particular he sold proprietary articles below the manufacturers' list prices and he used the slogan 'cooperative prices' in his advertisements.

Whiteley's, founded in 1863, was perhaps even more famous than Harrod's as a department store in the nineteenth century. But though this store had a large number of departments in the late 1860s, its expansion to fields other than those closely connected with drapery followed that of the civil service societies. The yearly *Diary and Almanacs* issued by Whiteley's from 1877 give evidence of the strong competition and spirit of emulation between the societies and this store. They contain several references to comparisons between its prices and those of the societies.

activities and reduce the impact of their competition by political and other coercive action. The detailed story of these largely fruitless efforts must await another occasion. Organized retailers attempted to induce manufacturers and wholesalers to boycott the societies; but in the long run these efforts misfired. The net result of this action was to force the societies to increase their business by admitting many more ticket-holders – in spite of the opposition of many of their shareholders who wished to preserve the cooperative nature of their enterprise – so that no supplier could afford to forgo their cash orders. Similarly, the long history of political action produced little positive result. The government was unwilling to interfere with the working of competition or with the right of civil servants to form trading societies, provided this did not interfere with the performance of their official duties. The inquiry by a committee of the House of Commons in 1879, the climax of the political agitation, merely gave the societies excellent free publicity.[38]

The success of the middle-class cooperatives not only influenced retailing methods generally, but also brought about major changes in the internal financial arrangements of the societies.

The societies had set out to sell goods at the lowest practicable prices. No provision had been made for the disposal of any profits which might arise;[39] and such profits did arise. It was quite impossible to price goods

Shoolbred's were said to have been considering the policy of branching out from drapery to other fields in the middle of the nineteenth century; but it seems that their expansion into groceries, for example, was induced by the successful invasion of the drapery trade by the societies.

Data on the turnover of the ordinary department stores are scanty. In 1891 Harrod's sales were just over £½ million; at this time the annual turnover of the A & N was about £2¾ million, the CSSA's well over £1½ million, and the CSCS's and Junior A & N's about £½ million. For the year 1898, by which date the A & N's sales were exceeding £3 million per annum, Whiteley's turnover was stated to be just over £2 million. Though the A & N was almost certainly the largest department store (in terms of sales) in Britain by the turn of the century, its turnover nevertheless was far below that of two stores in Paris, Au Bon Marché (over £7 million in 1898) and Louvre (about £6 million in 1898). (The data for Whiteley's and the French stores are from Grävell, 1899, p. 8).

38. One minor result of the inquiry was that the CSSA altered the times of its committee meetings so that there should be no suspicion that they took place in office hours.

The agitation which continued until the 1890s does appear to have contributed towards some stiffening of official policy on the right of civil servants to participate in the direction of business enterprises. Following the Report of the Royal Commission set up in 1886, a Treasury minute prohibited acceptance of new directorships by civil servants; but this did not appear to affect existing directorships.

39. In the CSSA an unspecified portion of profits was to be used as a rent guarantee fund, the residue to be used to reduce prices in the next period.

with such precision that selling prices covered only wholesale costs and the expenses of retailing; and normal commercial prudence and the risk of falling markets dictated that the unavoidable margin between outlays and receipts should be on the right side.[40] Again, in periods of rising prices it was unwise to sell at prices based on the earlier wholesale levels; this would lead to a rapid depletion of stocks, aggravated by the purchases of rival retailers.[41] Finally, even though gross margins were low, the rapid expansion of sales which resulted from low prices, coupled with a very high rate of turnover, reduced expense ratios still further and thus led to the accumulation of large profits.[42]

The societies could have distributed these profits to their customers in the form of periodic rebates on purchases, as was done in the working-class cooperatives; but this practice was not adopted. According to the original rules of the two civil service societies these large surpluses could not be distributed directly to shareholders as a return on their investment, and in the case of the A & N they were not at first used in this manner. Many shareholders naturally came to regard themselves as being entitled, as owners, to these accumulations of profits, and sought to amend the rules to give effect to their claims.[43] We cannot trace here the steps by which the three cooperative societies became ordinary joint-stock companies and lost their cooperative character. In each case measures were

40. At times the societies also feared that political and similar opposition from private retailers would increase if past profits were subsequently used to reduce prices too drastically.

41. In 1870 the CSSA held down champagne prices to correspond to the prices at which it had bought its stocks. On a rising market this led to a rapid reduction of stocks, accelerated because competing dealers succeeded in buying from the CSSA.

42. In the CSCS these amounted to £75,000 in 1878; in the A & N they amounted to £91,313 in 1880, although by then its interest-bearing capital had been increased four-fold; in the CSSA accumulated profits exceeded £90,000 by 1874.

43. Not all shareholders of the CSSA were in favour of strengthening their position. Some shared with the management the feeling that the shareholders should not be placed in a better position than the ticket-holders in the disposal of the profits which accrued from their joint enterprise. It was often recalled that the influx of a large number of ticket-holders had made it easier for the society to break through the boycott attempted by organized retailer opponents, and that many civil servants became shareholders only after the success of the CSSA had become an established fact. But after 1874 these sentiments were not strong enough to resist the demand for change.

In 1874 the CSSA took the first steps in the process of transforming its shareholders into shareholders with full proprietary rights. Half the members of the CSSA's committee of management resigned in protest, and were instrumental in the formation of the New Civil Service Cooperation Ltd, which was to represent the 'true spirit of cooperation'. The NCSC had an uncertain start; a brief period of prosperity followed a reconstruction, but business slumped again, and the society was eventually taken over by the CSSA in 1906.

taken so that the accumulated profits from past trading were retained in the enterprise, as part of the share capital, while members (not ticket-holders) were gradually given rights to share in current profits, and eventually the rights of equity shareholders in an ordinary company.

The societies also widened the range from which their shareholders could be drawn, doubtless in order to improve the market for the shares. In the two civil service societies shareholding was extended from civil servants, first to relatives of civil servants and then to other servants of the State, of corporations and of municipal authorities. In 1927, when the CSSA became a public company, only half its shares were in the hands of civil servants. The A & N admitted exalted officers of the realm in 1888, and in 1904 *The Times* related that the privilege of membership had been extended to certain other 'groups comprising the flower of official life'. All restrictions were removed when a stock exchange quotation for its shares was sought in 1914.

With profit-sharing rights given to shareholders, and with the drift away from the original idea of cooperative trading, ticket-holders (that is, customers who were not shareholders) could no longer rely on their shareholding fellow customers, who were in control of the societies, to look after their interests as directly as before. However, any weakening of their position was amply made good by the increasing competition in retail markets generally, which gave them all the protection they may have wanted. A fair number of people held tickets in more than one society, and could exercise indirect control by giving their custom to the society which best served their needs – or to an ordinary shop or store. In fact, the societies did not depart from their former price policies; and the two largest were frequently named as price-cutters by the organizers of resale price maintenance in the two decades preceding the First World War.

By the 1880s the three main London societies were facing sterner competition from some of the imitation cooperative societies and from department stores and other retailers who had adopted some or all of their methods. The intensified competition was particularly acute because most of their rivals had the advantage that anyone could come into their shops without payment of a subscription; moreover, some of them gave better service than the societies. Competition between the three societies themselves also became more intense; they were serving substantially the same general body of consumers. The societies reacted to the new situation largely by improving their services to their customers and by following certain of the practices of successful competitors.

The gross margins of the societies increased steadily after 1880, although they remained low.[44] It was a consequence partly of the expansion of their business to include goods which entailed greater expense or allowed higher gross margins, and partly of the improvement of services generally, giving customers more space and amenities and better attention.[45] The granting of credit began in the 1890s, some years after Whiteley's and Harrod's had departed from the policy of selling for cash only. But to a large extent the increase in gross margins was the result of extending delivery services without separate charge, or at separate charges below cost. From an early date limited free delivery had been given as a privilege to shareholders. But after 1879 competition from newer societies who used 'free' delivery as a major attraction was becoming more severe, and the main societies followed suit or reduced delivery charges in the search for business. Indeed, by the turn of the century the societies had gradually discontinued the austere trading methods which had met with such success at their inception. But there were many other traders at this date able to cater for customers who preferred to save money by forgoing some retail services.

The societies as retailing enterprises were at a disadvantage because their original rules allowed only shareholders and privileged ticket-holders to deal at their shops, thus limiting their clientele. When competition became severe, the relevant regulations of the three main societies were progressively relaxed; additional classes of people were allowed to become ticket-holders, and subscription fees were reduced and finally abolished.[46] The CSCS abolished tickets in 1919, and the CSSA in 1927 when it became a public company. In the A & N restriction of customers was retained until the outbreak of the Second World War, although from 1922 all tickets had been issued free to acceptable customers. The two stores (the CSCS was wound up in 1931) had then to explain to the general public that their doors were open to all. All cooperative characteristics had been eliminated in consequence partly of the success of their earlier

44. Gross margins as a percentage of sales

	CSSA	CSCS	A & N
1880	9·6	9·6	7·3
1885	10·5	12·2	9·2
1890	11·0	14·3	10·5
1895	11·8	14·7	12·1
1900	12·3	15·0	14·1
1905	13·1	14·6	14·9

45. Staff was increased, ordering by telephone was introduced by the A & N in 1896, the two civil service societies sent out goods on approval by 1900, and a variety of services were offered free or at a nominal charge.

46. Both Whiteley's and Harrod's made much of the fact that their stores were open to all without charge.

methods, and partly of the increasing competition which owed so much to their own pioneering steps.

References

ASHTON, T. S. (1955), *An Economic History of England: The Eighteenth Century*, Methuen.

'A CIVIL SERVANT' (1873), *London Tradesmen and Cooperation*.

GRÄVELL, A. (1899) *Zum Kampfe gegen die Waarenhäuser*.

HANCOCK, W. N. (1851), *Is the Competition between Large and Small Shops Injurious to the Community?*, Dublin.

HEAD, J. (1872), *Retail Traders and Cooperative Stores*, London.

Report on Cooperative Stores (1879), no. 344.

UEDA, T. (1956), 'Saikaku's "Economic Man"', *Annals of the Hitotsubashi Academy*, October.

YAMEY, B. S. (1954), 'Trade conspiracies: an historical footnote', *modern law Rev.*, vol. 17.

10 D. Metcalf

Concentration in the British Retail Grocery Trade

D. Metcalf, 'Concentration in the retail grocery industry in Great Britain', *Farm Economist*, vol. 11, 1968, pp. 294–303.

Introduction

Food retailing occupies an important position in the UK economy. Its sales, currently around £6000 million annually, are larger than those of any other industry in the United Kingdom. Over a quarter of consumers' total expenditure is on food items. The food processing industry depends significantly upon food retailers for outlets for their products. In the years since the end of the Second World War the food retailing industry has been subject to change greater than most other sectors of the economy. This change has been generated by both technical and economic factors and has resulted in an upheaval of the structure of the industry. Structural change in the food retailing sector does not affect solely the firms and the employees of that sector, but also they have results that are felt right through the distribution chain because of the strategic position of food retailing therein. Thus consumers, wholesalers, processors, manufacturers and farmers are all affected by the economic results which flow from the prevailing market structure in the food retailing sector, and any changes in that structure.

The importance of the retail food and retail grocery sector in the context of total retailing is shown in Table 1. (1961 is the last year for which data from the Census of Distribution are available.) It will be seen that food retailing accounts for slightly less than half of the total number of retail establishments (48·2 per cent), over half of which are grocery outlets.

It has become customary in market structure research to use the analytical framework developed by Bain (1959) to analyse an industry, or

Table 1 **Numbers of establishments, turnover and employees in 1961, United Kingdom**

	Establishments	*Turnover (£000)*	*Employees*
Total retail	577,307	8,918,860	2,524,084
All food	278,458	4,137,405	1,048,381
Grocery	149,548	2,352,772	549,123

Source: Board of Trade (1963), Part 1, Establishment Tables, Table 1, p. 1/17.

groups of industries. Bain's work suggested that there is a link, albeit tenuous in many instances, between an industry's market structure and the resulting overall economic performance of the industry. Market structure, for this purpose, consists of those characteristics which influence strategically the nature of competition and pricing within the market or the conduct or behaviour of the firms in the industry, for example with respect to pricing policy or sales promotion strategy.

The analytical framework of market structure analysis incorporated two interrelated streams of thought regarding what determined the performance of an industry.[1] Firstly, the *theorists* provided a justification of the perfectly competitive market structure, in that it provided an optimal allocation of resources (although, of course, not necessarily optimum income distribution). The conventional theory, which concentrated on analysing the economic results which flow from perfect competition as compared with monopoly, was modified in the 1930s to take account of the intermediate market structures of monopolistic competition and oligopoly. Secondly, market structure analysis provides for the performance of an industry to depend on the *organizational* aspects of that industry, for example on the height of the barriers facing new entrants and the characteristics of the product.[2]

This paper has a more limited aim than attempting to trace through a link between the structure of the grocery retailing industry, the conduct of grocery firms and the overall industry performance. Here we are concerned with one facet of market structure – the degree of concentration – and we ignore other structural dimensions, such as the ease of entry into the industry, the degree of product differentiation, the durability of the product and the elasticity of demand for the product. The degree of concentration measures the market share of a certain number of the largest firms in the industry in terms of sales, employees, establishments or some other variable. Insofar as the market share reflects market power, the degree of concentration is indicative of the market power of the firms at the

1. For a lucid discussion of market structure analysis, with special reference to the agricultural sector, see Clodius and Mueller (1961).

2. Thus market structure research is both deterministic and sequential in that the market structure determines the conduct of the firms and the performance of the industry. However, whilst satisfactory structural characteristics may be necessary for adequate performance they may not be sufficient. For example a perfectly competitive market structure is unlikely to lead to satisfactory performance with respect to the dimension of technical progressiveness. The fact that perfect competition did not necessarily provide an ideal norm, and was anyway unobtainable, led to the formulation of the concept of 'workable competition' (Clark, 1940).

As the dimensions of performance are essentially normative (each commentator being able to choose his own) this has led to a conflict of views, one writer going so far as to suggest that only 'the better' economists be allowed to participate! (Clark, 1940). For a synthesis of these views see Sosnick (1958).

top end of the size array; for example, a monopoly has more power over setting price than a firm in a perfectly competitive industry.[3]

The degree of concentration is used here to indicate the relative importance of the larger firms at both national and regional level in both the industry as a whole and also in the self-service and supermarket sector of the industry. This particular dimension of market structure is emphasized for two reasons. First, it provides a broad picture of the structure of the industry. Second, and more important, providing the relationship between structure and conduct is accepted, then tentative predictions about firm conduct may be made. In addition to presenting these untested hypotheses, we also test certain hypotheses which have been put forward (Morgan, 1965) as to what determines the degree of concentration itself. This is relevant for policy purposes, in that an understanding of the determinants of concentration facilitates changing this structural characteristic, should policy-makers so desire.

The overall degree of concentration

Empirical investigation has shown that the degree of concentration is the most important of the strategic structural dimensions which influence the behaviour of firms and overall industry performance. To measure market concentration it is necessary to make either implicitly or explicitly certain basic assumptions about the character of the market. Defining the relevant market is difficult when the measure is used to reveal the relative importance of particular firms in both buying and selling, as in grocery retailing, where firms sell in local/regional markets and buy in larger markets. In this analysis it is assumed that firms in grocery retailing buy in the national market and sell in a regional market, and different concentration measures have been developed accordingly.

National

It must be noted that when analysing firms it is no longer possible to work in terms of employees or sales, the lack of data forcing the analysis to be carried out in terms of establishments. This implies an understatement in the degree of sales concentration, the establishments of the multiples having on average higher sales per annum than establishments of independents.[4] Reference to Table 2 indicates immediately that the

3. An alternative measure of the degree of concentration, the Lorenz curve/Gini coefficient, gives a more comprehensive measure of the entire size structure spectrum of the industry but is not used in this analysis.

4. Calculations from the 1961 Census of Distribution show that average turnover per annum of establishments belonging to organizations (other than cooperative societies) with ten or more establishments is four times as large as average turnover of establishments of organizations with one to nine establishments, being £42,200 and £10,500 respectively.

overall degree of concentration in Great Britain is low. There are only thirty organizations with over 100 establishments, of which thirteen are cooperative societies. The three organizations which control over 100 establishments, Allied Suppliers, International Tea Company and Moores Stores are in reality holding companies whose constituent firms have a

Table 2 **Concentration in grocery retailing in Great Britain 1966**

	1 No. of organizations	2 No. o, establishments	3 (2) as a percentage of total establishments
1000 establishments and over	3	5000	3·3
500–999 establishments	4	2421	1·6
100–499 establishments	23	4409	3·0

Source: Calculated from the *Grocer*, *Directory of Multiples and Cooperatives*.

considerable degree of independence in pursuing policies on both the buying and selling side. It will be seen that organizations with 100 establishments and over control only 7·9 per cent of the total number of establishments. (The thirteen cooperative societies are all in the 100–499 establishments-size class and control 1876 establishments.)

The low degree of concentration indicated implies that possibilities for interdependent action on the buying side are severely limited. This is especially so as food manufacturers tend to be more concentrated than the retailers. In the study of Evely and Little (1960), food manufacturing is intermediate in terms of the degree of concentration in the ranking of manufacturing industries, with 35 per cent of net output accounted for by the three largest units.

Regional

The regional market is assumed to represent the selling market. It is recognized that the true selling market is probably somewhat smaller than the regional one but this provides a convenient intermediate point. Figures for concentration levels by regions are presented in Table 3. It will be seen that the degree of control over total establishments by multiples and cooperative societies with ten or more outlets varies from 24·2 per cent in London and the South East to 6·8 per cent in the South West. Of the 432 organizations involved, 237 are cooperative societies, although only forty-five of these cooperative organizations are in the size ranges greater than 10–49 establishments. It will be seen that the degree of concentration at the regional level, whilst higher than national concentration, is still low compared with other sectors of the economy such as food manufacturing. Nevertheless, given that our measure understates sales concentration the evidence suggests that a limited amount of interdependent action among firms may be possible in a few areas.

If a study of the structure of an industry is to be useful for public policy purposes it is necessary to go a stage further back than merely describing the degree of concentration – we must attempt to indicate what causes it. Issues of public interest would, for example, be concerned when the authorities feel that too many resources are employed in retailing, i.e. too many shops exist, and that an increase in concentration is desirable; alternatively it may be decided that a low level of concentration is necessary to ensure that firms do not collude to the detriment of the consumer, food manufacturers or other elements in the chain of distribution. Empirical evidence suggests that the degree of concentration is related to certain variables; thus we can predict from changes in these variables what change is likely in the degree of concentration and whether it is in the direction desired. If the change is too slow or in the wrong direction then public policy tools, such as fiscal policy or location policy, may be used to help achieve the desired structure and a better industry performance. If, for example, the government felt it would be desirable to hasten the reduction in the number of small independent stores then they might use a facet of fiscal policy such as imposing the selective employment tax on the self-employed.

Empirical evidence suggests that increases in concentration are related to population and income growth (Morgan, 1965). Economic growth is associated with greater population size and density and urbanization. These demographic changes tend to lower the store/population ratio for food stores. They also create conditions favourable to the emergence of large-scale retailing. Similarly, economic growth is also accompanied by rising income, greater income equality and changing consumption patterns. Income equality is important since this favours a mass market for standardized goods in which chain-stores and other large firms can achieve economies of scale. Equalization of income under the influence of tax laws, employment opportunities and growth can therefore be expected to contribute to increasing concentration in food retailing.

It may be noted immediately from Table 3 that the two regions where multiples controlling over 100 establishments are important, London and the South East and the North West, are both regions of high population density containing large conurbations. In Table 4 regional rankings of concentration levels, population density and income levels are presented. These rankings have been subject to statistical tests but the results are inconclusive. The rankings confirm, however, the importance of the density

Table 3 Regional concentration levels in the retail grocery industry, 1966

Region and size class (by establishments)	1 No. of organizations	2 No. of establishments	3 (2) as a percentage of total establishments	Region and size class (by establishments)	1 No. of organizations	2 No. of establishments	3 (2) as a percentage of total establishments
North				**South West**			
100 & over	3	499	4·9	100 & over	—	—	—
50–99	5	373	3·6	50–99	4	311	2·9
10–49	50	684	6·7	10–49	18	421	3·9
			15·2				6·8
East & West Ridings				**Midlands**			
100 & over	4	578	3·7	100 & over	3	416	2·8
50–99	12	804	5·2	50–99	3	233	1·5
10–49	21	510	3·3	10–49	24	714	4·8
			12·2				9·1
North Midlands				**North West**			
100 & over	5	602	4·8	100 & over	11	2174	8·7
50–99	5	328	2·6	50–99	8	517	2·1
10–49	31	804	5·6	10–49	52	1279	5·1
			13·0				15·9
Eastern				**Wales**			
100 & over	1	109	1·2	100 & over	1	162	1·6
50–99	4	211	2·3	50–99	2	153	1·5
10–49	22	486	5·4	10–49	24	541	5·3
			8·9				8·4
London & South East				**Scotland**			
100 & over	13	2935	14·5	100 & over	3	434	3·1
50–99	15	1051	5·2	50–99	7	546	3·9
10–49	35	913	4·5	10–49	33	780	5·5
			24·2				12·5
South							
100 & over	1	111	1·6				
50–99	6	430	6·1				
10–49	26	662	9·4				
			17·1				

Source: Calculated from *The Grocer, Directory of Multiples and Cooperatives,* 1966; Board of Trade, 1963, Table 1, p. 2/25.

Note:

[1] Where organizations operated in more than one region their outlets were divided up according to the populations of the regions involved. Thus, in the Northern region, one of the organizations listed as having between 50–99 branches was Allied Stores, which is an organization which operates all over England and Wales, 52 of the 772 branches being designated to the Northern Region.

[2] Firms which are parts of holding companies are treated as if they operate as independent units. Thus whilst the holding company Allied Suppliers operates over all Great Britain some of its constituent firms can be placed in one individual region, e.g. Cochranes in Scotland.

[3] When calculating column 3 the latest figures available for the total number of establishments by region were for 1961. If these have since fallen or risen the resulting percentages controlled by the organizations with ten or more establishments will be under- or over-stated respectively. This is not likely, however, as the total number of establishments changes only marginally from year to year.

of population and income levels in explaining the degree of concentration at the top and bottom ends of the ranking scale. London and the South East, the South and the North West, the regions with the highest concentration of control by multiples, were also among the regions with the highest income per head (ranking first, third and fifth respectively) and population density (first, fifth and second respectively). At the other end of the scale Wales and the South West, the regions with the lowest concentration levels were also low in per capita income rankings (ninth and eighth respectively) and population density (tenth and ninth respectively).

However, these two variables do not explain all the variation in regional concentration rankings, especially for those regions in the middle of the range; we must therefore turn to other variables for a more complete explanation. It is not possible to present an exhaustive list but the historical/institutional aspect must be mentioned; this is especially important with regard to cooperative societies. Thus regions such as North Midlands, North and Scotland possibly have a higher degree of concentration than that predicted from population and income because of the entrenched position of cooperative societies in these regions owing to historical, institutional and other factors.

A further possible cause of the high concentration in London and the South East, South, North West and North is the fact that these regions

Table 4 **Regional ranking of concentration levels, per capita incomes and population density**

	1 Level of concentration	2 Per capita income	3 Population density
London & South East	1	1	1
South	2	3	5
North West	3	5	2
North	4	11	8
North Midlands	5	6	6
Scotland	6	10	11
East & West Ridings	7	6	3
Midlands	8	2	4
East	9	4	7
Wales	10	9	10
South West	11	8	9

Source:
1. Table 3.
2. Family Expenditure Survey 1963–4, *Abstract of Regional Statistics*, Table 43, no. 2, 1966.
3. *Abstract of Regional Statistics*, Table 1, 1965.

are served by large ports. The multiple organizations can obtain economies in buying, transporting and handling imported foodstuffs which provides an incentive to locate establishments in these regions.

The self-service and supermarket sector

The most dynamic feature of the grocery retailing industry over the post-war period has been the self-service and supermarket sector which now accounts for over 40 per cent of all grocery sales. The number of self-service stores increased sevenfold between 1954 (2150) and 1964 (15,680). These years have also witnessed large changes in the relative share of self-service trade, the share of the cooperatives falling from 67 to 33 per cent whilst the share of multiples doubled from 20 to 40 per cent. Whilst this gives a broad indication of the importance of the self-service sector it is more important to develop the analysis at the regional level for two reasons. First, the degree of concentration influences both competition between self-service outlets and also competition between self-service and counter-service outlets. Second, it is important to determine if the ranking of concentration by regions is similar to that for the industry as a whole. In this section the degree of concentration is measured by sales area controlled by organizations with ten or more outlets. Whilst this is not a perfect proxy for sales, it is a better indicator than number of establishments.

The regional structure of this segment of the industry is presented in Table 5. It will be seen immediately that the degree of concentration

Table 5 **Concentration in the self-service and supermarket sector of the retail grocery industry**

	1 No. o firms	2 No. of establishments	3 Total sales area	4 Sales area of firms with ten or more establishments	5 (4) as a proportion of (3)
			(sq. ft)	sq. ft	%
North	328	926	952,063	507,787	53·3
East & West Ridings	324	993	971,831	498,138	51·3
North Midlands	413	1126	1,283,299	675,837	52·7
East	471	1224	1,141,875	509,601	44·6
London & South East	930	3205	3,134,271	1,836,694	58·6
South	447	988	1,101,959	393,379	35·7
South West	341	892	829,473	418,856	50·5
Midlands	412	1206	1,155,689	600,534	52·0
North West	598	1837	1,755,253	978,847	55·8
Wales	200	600	582,506	216,497	37·2
Scotland	245	1286	1,418,802	894,614	63·1

Source: Calculated from Self-Service and Supermarket, *Annual Survey and Directory, 1965–66*.
 Note: Insofar as smaller organizations, especially independents, are not reported in the Directory, the computed concentration figures (column 5) will overstate the actual figures.

inside the self-service sector is appreciably higher than in the industry as a whole. In only one region, Wales, do organizations with ten or more establishments account for less than 40 per cent of sales area. The highest degree of concentration is in Scotland where approaching two-thirds of sales area is controlled by these organizations; this is almost certainly due to the importance of cooperative societies in that region. If it is accepted that the self-service/supermarket sector is frequently a leader in price and product policies, the fact that the multiples and cooperative societies with ten or more branches control over 40 per cent of selling space in all regions but one indicates that their selling policies would be a profitable area for further study. One *a priori* hypothesis, suggested by the fact that between 40 and 60 per cent of sales are controlled by these organizations in each region, is that this might well lead to an oligopolistic situation in several of the smaller, city level, regional sub-markets. Whether this is true and what the results of this situation would be are questions that can only be answered by city level investigation.[5]

A second reason for computing regional statistics is to compare the rankings of the degree of concentration in this more narrow sector of the retail grocery industry by region with those of the industry as a whole. With the exception of the South and Scotland a stable pattern emerges from this comparison. Four of the five regions with the highest concentration in the industry as a whole (London and the South East; North West; North; North Midlands) also have the highest concentration levels in the self-service sector. Similarly those regions with lower concentration levels in the whole industry (East and West Ridings; Midlands; East; Wales; South West) retain similar rankings in the self-service sector. This tends to confirm the importance of population density, income and historical/institutional factors in explaining regional variations.

A further interesting feature of this section of the industry is the differences in the importance of supermarkets in the self-service/supermarket sector.[6] The sales area of supermarkets as a percentage of total self-service/

5. Such a study is at present being conducted in a compact sub-market in North London, consisting of eight outlets, all but two being self-service stores and all being members of multiple organizations. We are collecting price data over a number of weeks for a sample of dry goods items, with a view to testing whether there is evidence of price leadership/following. Interviews with store managers suggest that price leadership does exist. However, it must be emphasized that price leadership does not necessarily imply exploitation of the consumer. To attempt to assess this we would need to investigate the height of prices in relation to average costs. The results of the study will be reported shortly.

6. A supermarket is defined by the *Self-Service and Supermarket Directory* as a 'store of at least 2000 sq. ft sales area, with three or more checkouts, and operated mainly on self-service, whose range of merchandise comprises all food groups, including fresh meat and fresh fruit and vegetables, plus basic household requisites.'

supermarket sales area ranges from 27 per cent in the North to 45 per cent in the South. There does not appear to be any consistent relationship between the importance of supermarkets and (say) population density but in general supermarkets account for a higher proportion of the self-service sales area in the southern half of England. This, of course, reflects the importance of supermarkets owned by independents as well as those owned by multiples. Divergencies in the importance of supermarkets between regions are probably explained by factors such as the proximity to the commercial capital; availability of large stores suitable for conversion; extent of local authority redevelopment schemes; and real estate values.

Conclusions

The analysis has shown that at the national level the retail grocery industry is one of low concentration. This implies that the constituent organizations in the industry are likely to be at a disadvantage in bargaining with food manufacturers where they *buy* in the national market, although the larger multiple grocery chains definitely use their superior market power to obtain discounts from food manufacturers. However, at the regional level the degree of concentration is significantly higher reaching a peak in London and the South East where multiples and cooperative societies with ten or more establishments account for over a quarter of the total establishments (and therefore a higher proportion of sales). This implies that where these multiples buy food products in essentially regional markets their bargaining strength *vis-a-vis* food manufacturers will be higher than in the national market.

It is difficult to predict *selling* and product policies of the retailers from the concentration levels computed in the analysis. In the third section it was shown that the degree of concentration was higher in the self-service and supermarket sector than in the industry as a whole. Given that self-service and supermarket stores are frequently prime movers in determining selling policies, then in regional sub-markets the calculated degrees of concentration indicate that interdependent action may be possible. However, all the evidence on selling policies in city-level markets indicates that firms, whilst possibly aware of their mutual interdependence, do not indulge in oligopoly agreements (for example regarding pricing policies) which would be detrimental to consumer welfare (Holdren, 1965; Morgan, 1965; Nelson and Preston, 1966). An important factor working against collusion is the relative ease of entry into the industry. Thus if firms in local markets indulged in collusion and thereby achieved higher profits this would encourage entry of new firms into the market. The height of entry barriers into an industry is thus a further dimension of market structure which influences firm behaviour and industry performance.

The analysis also showed that income levels and population density are important in explaining the degree of concentration, at least for those regions with the highest and lowest concentration. Thus, as economic growth brings rising incomes and greater population density, we may hypothesize that the degree of concentration in the industry at both national and regional level is likely to increase. The question of the desirability of increasing concentration involves value judgments. It is necessary to weigh up the benefits and costs of the resulting economic flows which constitute the performance of the industry, emphasizing the necessity for detailed micro studies in addition to an analysis of overall industry trends.

References

BAIN, J. S. (1959), *Industrial Economics*, Wiley.

BOARD OF TRADE (1963), *Report of Census of Distribution and other Services 1961*, HMSO.

CLARK, J. M. (1940), 'Towards a concept of workable competition', *Amer. econ. Rev.*, vol. 30.

CLODIUS, R. L., and MUELLER, W. F. (1961), 'Market structure analysis as an orientation for research in agricultural economics', *J. farm Econ.*, vol. 43.

EVELY, R., and LITTLE, I. M. D. (1960), *Concentration in British Industry*, Cambridge University Press.

HOLDREN, B. R. (1965), 'Competition in food retailing', *J. farm Econ.*, vol. 47.

MORGAN, H. E. (1965), 'Concentration in food retailing', *J. farm Econ.*, vol. 47.

NELSON, P. E., and PRESTON, L. E. (1966), *Price Merchandising in Food Retailing: A Case Study*, IBER, Berkeley.

SOSNICK, S. (1958), 'A critique of concepts of workable competition', *Q. J. Econ.* vol. 72.

Part Three
Costs, Margins and Efficiency

Marshall (Reading 11) lists several reasons why large-scale retail units tend to displace small outlets and why some smaller shops may nevertheless survive. One approach to the determination of the optimal size of retail units is to estimate average cost at different levels of output. Dean (Reading 12) found that cost in departments (of a department store) was affected by a number of factors, but that average cost generally was unchanged or even declined as sales increased. Douglas (Reading 13) investigates three types of cost for US retailing firms: the cost of goods sold, total operating cost and the cost of capital.

Many measurement problems and difficulties of interpretation arise in these types of studies. Winsten and Hall (Reading 14) discuss the conceptual and econometric problems of measuring productivity and optimal size for retail units. Similar problems arise when retail gross margins are studied to throw light on the relative efficiency of firms in different regions and countries. Hall and Knapp (Reading 15) doubt whether gross margins should be used, in isolation of other variables and information, to compare levels of efficiency. By contrast, Hughes and Pollard (Reading 16) offer an explanation as to the features which contribute towards variations in gross margins among retail units engaged in a similar activity.

11 A. Marshall

Large and Small Trading Establishments

A. Marshall, *Principles of Economics*, Macmillan, 1890, book 4, chapter 11, section 6 (pp. 287–9 of 6th edn, 1936).

The advantages which a large business has over a small one are conspicuous in manufacture, because, as we have noticed, it has special facilities for concentrating a great deal of work in a small area. But there is a strong tendency for large establishments to drive out small ones in many other industries. In particular the retail trade is being transformed, the small shopkeeper is losing ground daily.

Let us look at the advantages which a large retail shop or store has in competing with its smaller neighbours. To begin with, it can obviously buy on better terms, it can get its goods carried more cheaply, and can offer a larger variety to meet the taste of customers. Next, it has a great economy of skill: the small shopkeeper, like the small manufacturer, must spend much of his time in routine work that requires no judgment: whereas the head of a large establishment, and even in some cases his chief assistants, spend their whole time in using their judgment. Until lately these advantages have been generally outweighed by the greater facilities which the small shopkeeper has for bringing his goods to the door of his customers; for humouring their several tastes; and for knowing enough of them individually to be able safely to lend them capital, in the form of selling them goods on credit.

But within recent years there have been many changes all telling on the side of large establishments. The habit of buying on credit is passing away; and the personal relations between shopkeeper and customer are becoming more distant. The first change is a great step forwards: the second is on some accounts to be regretted, but not on all; for it is partly due to the fact that the increase of true self-respect among the wealthier classes is making them no longer care for the subservient personal attentions they used to require. Again, the growing value of time makes people less willing than they were to spend several hours in shopping; they now often prefer to spend a few minutes in writing out a long list of orders from a varied and detailed price-list; and this they are enabled to do easily by the growing facilities for ordering and receiving parcels by post and in other ways. And when they do go shopping, tramcars and local trains are often at hand to take them easily and cheaply to the large central shops of a neighbouring town. All these changes render it more difficult than it was for the small shopkeeper to hold his own even in the provision trade, and others in which no great variety of stock is required.

But in many trades the ever-growing variety of commodities, and those rapid changes of fashion which now extend their baneful influence through almost every rank of society, weight the balance even more heavily against the small dealer, for he cannot keep a sufficient stock to offer much variety of choice, and if he tries to follow any movement of fashion closely, a larger proportion of his stock will be left stranded by the receding tide than in the case of a large shopkeeper. Again, in some branches of the clothing and furniture and other trades the increasing cheapness of machine-made goods is leading people to buy ready-made things from a large store instead of having them made to order by some small maker and dealer in their neighbourhood. Again, the large shopkeeper, not content with receiving travellers from the manufacturers, makes tours either himself or by his agent in the most important manufacturing districts at home and abroad; and he thus often dispenses with middlemen between him and the manufacturer. A tailor with moderate capital shows his customers specimens of many hundreds of the newest cloths, and perhaps orders by telegraph the selected cloth to be sent by parcels' post. Again, ladies often buy their materials direct from the manufacturer, and get them made up by dressmakers who have scarcely any capital. Small shopkeepers seem likely always to retain some hold of the minor repairing trades: and they keep their own fairly well in the sale of perishable food, especially to the working classes, partly in consequence of their being able to sell goods on credit and to collect small debts. In many trades however a firm with a large capital prefers having many small shops to one large one. Buying, and whatever production is desirable, is concentrated under a central management; and exceptional demands are met from a central reserve, so that each branch has large resources, without the expense of keeping a large stock. The branch manager has nothing to divert his attention from his customers; and, if an active man, with direct interest in the success of his branch, may prove himself a formidable rival to the small shopkeeper; as has been shown in many trades connected with clothing and food.

12 J. Dean

Cost Functions in Department Stores

J. Dean, 'Department store cost functions', in O. Lange *et al.* (eds.), *Studies in Mathematical Economics and Econometrics in Memory of Henry Schultz*, University of Chicago Press, 1942, pp. 222–54.

1 Introduction

An empirical study of the operating behavior of the individual enterprise should supply factual information for verification of theoretical formulations. This is a counsel of perfection, however, and at the present level of development of economic science much of the value of this type of empirical study lies (1) in determining whether the assumptions underlying the economic theory of the individual firm are sufficiently typical, extensive, and realistic to have descriptive usefulness and to admit of empirical verification and (2) in developing statistical techniques which will in time permit the effective use of the results of theoretical research in the solution of economic problems.

The systematic theoretical analysis of the form of the cost function of the individual firm was a by-product of the attempt to clarify the relation between cost curves and industry supply curves under the assumption of perfect competition. This assumption, however, was not only unrealistic in an institutional sense, but it oversimplified the problem of cost and output determination by implying that the only part of the marginal cost curve relevant for output decisions is the rising section. The development of the economics of imperfect competition represented, therefore, a significant improvement in the theoretical background of empirical research, since by dispensing with the postulates of perfect competition it reduced the assumptions necessary to the theory of costs to the familiar technical laws of diminishing returns and variable proportions, and the psychological postulate of economically rational behavior.

When the assumption of perfect competition was dispensed with, however, it immediately became necessary to analyse that category of expenditure which was devoted to influencing the individual firm's demand function. The conditions of equilibrium for the individual firm were restated to include selling cost as a variable category of expenditure exhibiting a functional relation to sales.[1] In the formal solution of the

1. See Smith (1934–5), and Shone, in the same volume. On polyperiodic production see Carlson (1936, chapter 6).

equilibrium condition, it is assumed that selling expense and expenses of production in the narrow sense can be separated and the amount of each determined independently. By definition, the two may be clearly distinguished on a functional basis; selling costs are accordingly expenditures designed to alter the shape or position of a firm's demand function, while costs of production proper consist only of those outlays technically necessary to produce a given physical quantity of a particular product.[2]

Empirically, it may in some cases be possible to perform the operations which are required to separate cost data into these two categories. When the business organization whose costs are being analysed is specialized to supplying selling service, however, the basis of the distinction itself becomes uncertain. This is true because the assumption made in theoretical writings that a 'given demand' for a good exists apart from the conditions under which the good is presented to the public is only realistic for very homogeneous and frequently purchased commodities. More usually, it is impossible to isolate 'demand' from selling or promotional cost which create or modify it.

Promotional activities designed to crystallize and focus demand constitute a large part of the total operations of a department store. To some extent such promotion may quite properly be regarded as a utility-creating function, constituting an integral part of output of a retail store, namely, its sales service.[3] Moreover, promotional activities pervade every accounting category of department-store cost and contribute to every aspect of stores' sales-service product. Thus even if the basis of distinction were clear, the practical difficulties of extricating promotional costs from pure production cost in the data would probably be insuperable.

The solution adopted for this difficulty was to consider all merchandising costs as costs of production. A more general argument may be made out for this procedure on the ground that selling expenditure can only augment the sales of the affected commodity by increasing its utility to consumers; more strictly, selling expenditure converts a given physical commodity into

2. Shone (1934–5, p. 225) has used the term 'allocated costs' for costs of production because they 'vary directly with output, and their redistribution, increase, or decrease for any given output is excluded by hypothesis. On the other hand, the unallocated expenditures (selling costs) may be incurred in any form, increased or decreased, in order to alter the price and the output of the product defined by the allocated costs'.

3. Particularly for goods that are purchased infrequently, the advertising, displays, demonstrations, and advice of sales-persons required before a vague desire is transformed into a sale of goods may be viewed as creating a utility for which consumers are willing to pay. Even newspaper advertising may be considered as contributing to the store's sales service since it acquaints the consumer with prices and qualities of goods available, and since its 'tone' may augment the prestige satisfaction derived from the merchandise.

a different and more desirable economic good, and may accordingly be regarded as a cost of production in its most rigorous sense.[4]

Whatever may be the merits of this argument, its acceptance points to an additional source of embarrassment and difficulty in this study. If we are to consider that selling expenditures change the character and utility of the product, the unit of output is no longer homogeneous as selling costs vary. A cost function derived from accounting data over a period of time during which selling expenditure constituted a varying proportion of cost would therefore relate to a product which was not homogeneous throughout the sampling period.

This non-homogeneity of output arises from the fact that promotional cost does not bear the simple technical relation to output that pure production cost does. The amount of selling costs it is advantageous to incur presumably depends upon (1) the position and slope of the firm's demand function and (2) the effectiveness of selling expenditure in modifying this demand function, rather than upon technical conditions of production. In the present case, however, since selling costs and costs of production are inseparable, the quantities of output and of selling expenditure cannot be determined independently, although some variation in the proportion of selling expenditure to strictly productive expenditure is undoubtedly possible. Especially in a department store dependent upon its prestige, promotional expenditures for spacious salesrooms, sales advice, and elaborate display are an essential requirement for the maintenance of sales volume. The situation approximates closely joint production in industry.

The possibility that the proportion of selling to production costs may be kept fairly stable by certain institutional conventions or standards should therefore not be overlooked.[5] In such a case, the output would be fairly homogeneous, and the cost function discovered would be more likely to possess the stability necessary for purposes of prediction.

To recapitulate, the ambiguity surrounding the concept 'unit of sales service', which may properly be considered the product of a retail enterprise, made it impossible to separate selling costs from costs of production

4. Cf. Knight (1921, p. 339): 'In so far as they [changes in wants] result from a deliberate expenditure of resources, they become as all other economic operations. . . . In fact, as we have previously observed, the advertising, puffing or salesmanship necessary to create a demand for a commodity is causally indistinguishable from a utility inherent in the commodity itself'.

5. Considerable stability in the store's standards with respect to sales personnel, fixtures, delivery, returns, and internal displays would be expected in view of the importance of prestige in this particular store's merchandising policy. Prestige is an important aspect of product differentiation in the oligopolistic department-store market in which the firm competes.

proper. The inclusion of a variable and perhaps indeterminate quantity of the former results in heterogeneity of output through time. The cost function determined by our procedures cannot therefore be compared precisely with the static model of cost theory. All that can be claimed is that it shows the relation between a composite cost and some admittedly imperfect index of output.[6] Its heuristic value will, therefore, be confined to providing a description of merchandising costs when certain operating conditions have been stabilized in order to isolate the influence of output on cost.

As this suggests, with the exception of the inclusion of selling costs among costs of production, every attempt was made to make this empirical situation investigated conform to the static model for the short run. The investigator must wrest from his dynamic data something as nearly approaching a static function as possible if he wishes to find cost or demand functions which are conformable to those upon which so much valuable theoretical elaboration has been based. Such a procedure increases the usefulness of the findings for purposes of estimating costs and also makes their interpretation more clear. Once the basic relation between costs and output has been established, it becomes relatively simple to adjust for the effect of changes in operating conditions, such as shifts in wage rates, material prices, etc., when desired. Of course, changes which lead to factor substitution cannot be handled in this way, since the cost function itself will be altered.

The main problems in determining the cost-output relation arose from the necessity of breaking down available accounting data into the categories of fixed and variable costs as defined in theoretical writings and the selection of procedures for 'rectifying' the data in order to remove the effect upon cost of changing conditions of production. No completely satisfactory solution could be found to these problems in some instances, even though no attempt was made to analyse the cost functions of the department store as a whole.[7] Only three carefully selected departments in a large metropolitan store were studied, and in these departments no analysis was made of the behavior of aggregate operating costs. Since the allocation of overhead costs to these units is necessarily arbitrary, it was obviously impossible to make any economically significant estimate of the department's true aggregate cost. Fortunately, the critical questions of cost theory center on marginal rather than average costs, although a knowledge of average costs is indispensable to the individual firm in computing its profits. In the present study, therefore, all allocated general store overhead costs were excluded. The analysis was confined to the following cost

6. For a further discussion of the index of output see section 2C.

7. Two papers concerning empirical studies of other department stores should be mentioned in this connection: van Dyk (1940), and Whitman (1940).

elements: (1) advertising (2) salespeople's salaries (3) other departmental salaries (4) inside delivery (5) outside delivery and (6) direct departmental expense. Obviously some of these departmental costs are to a degree fixed, but the inclusion of such items does not affect the determination of marginal cost and yields average cost behavior useful for certain types of managerial decisions. The resulting estimates of marginal costs are subject to error because of the failure to include certain general store expenses which may bear some relation to the departments' volume. Moreover, some items which have been included may have little relation to volume but are administered, allocated, or recorded in such a fashion as to show a spurious correlation with sales volume. For example, several of the indirect advertising cost items which are allocated to departments on the basis of dollar sales may appear to possess a closer relation to volume than is in fact the case.[8] Similarly, the closeness of the relation of inside delivery cost to volume may be exaggerated by the method of computing this cost.

2 Methodology

The major methodological problems in deriving empirical cost functions from accounting records arise from the necessity of purging the data of the effects of dynamic influences which were at work during the observation period.

In order to get an adequate number of observations, monthly data were analysed for sixty consecutive months, covering the years 1931–5 inclusive. In attempting to isolate the static components of these data, three chief methods of freeing the cost data from the distorting influences of extraneous variables were employed. First, by careful selection of the establishment, departments, cost items, and time period investigated, certain factors which would have obscured the cost-volume relation were held constant. Second, the influence of another group of factors was allowed for by using them as independent variables in the multiple-correlation analysis. Third, the effects of several disturbing forces were removed directly from the data by familiar rectification procedures.

A Collection of data

1. *Selection of establishment.* Among distributive enterprises department stores are of particular significance because of their quantitative importance in distribution and because of the variety of merchandise carried. In searching for an establishment to cooperate in a study of this type, a large

8. The indirect advertising costs allocated to departments on the basis of dollar sales include direct mail, compositions and cuts, art work, interior decoration, car advertising, Foster Bureau, fashion shows, magazines, addressograph, window-dressing and sign-writing, and salaries of advertising office.

metropolitan department store was found which had kept comparable and unusually comprehensive accounting and statistical records over a period of years. Furthermore, the management was sufficiently interested in research to understand the importance of this study to economics and to see its practical usefulness in business administration.

2. *Selection of departments.* Selection of the selling departments which would be most suitable for statistical cost analysis was made after an examination of each department with reference to the following criteria:

(a) The sales volume should vary from month to month in such a fashion as to give a wide range of volume and a fairly uniform coverage of this range;
(b) The heterogeneity of the merchandise sold in the department should be at a minimum, so as to simplify the problem of finding a suitable output index;
(c) The character of the merchandise and the nature of the transaction should be relatively uniform from month to month, in order to minimize changes in the meaning of the output index through time;
(d) The department should be relatively large, to maximize the managerial significance of the study and minimize the effects of indivisibility of input factors;
(e) The changes in layout, general method of operation and managerial personnel during the period of analysis should be at a minimum, in order to approximate short-run cost functions by holding technology and plant scale as nearly constant as possible.

On the basis of these criteria, three departments were selected for study: hosiery, women's shoes and medium-priced women's coats.

3. *Selection of the time period for analysis.* Since the objective of this investigation is to determine statistically the behavior patterns of short-run selling cost, it is desirable to study the effects upon cost of changes in operating conditions in a situation which precludes the possibility of bringing certain of the input factors into optimum adjustment – a situation in which some cost elements offer effective resistance to adjustment to the prevailing operating conditions. Analyses of monthly or weekly observations of cost and operating conditions satisfy this condition, since many input factors in the department store cannot be adjusted to these relatively rapid changes in output and other circumstances. Monthly observations appeared more suitable than weekly observations for this purpose since fewer arbitrary cost allocations are involved because most of the statistical and accounting records of the firm were in terms of months. In addition, random and irrelevant fluctuations are more likely to be averaged out by taking the longer period.

In determining the years to be selected for study, the following criteria were applied:

(a) Changes in the space occupied, in layout, in general methods and in the management personnel should be at a minimum;
(b) Accounting records should be comparable throughout the period of analysis;
(c) A sufficient number of months should be included to permit valid statistical analyses;
(d) There should be sufficient independent fluctuations in demand, and consequently in output, to give a fairly wide range of observations of both cost and output.

Using these criteria as a basis for selection, the best years for analysis appeared to be 1931, 1932, 1933, 1934 and 1935, which made available sixty monthly observations.

B Direct rectification of data

Changes in operating conditions which could be removed directly are:

1. Time lag between the recording of cost and of the volume of output to which the cost contributed.
2. Variation in the number of selling days in a month.
3. Changes in salary rates and material prices.
4. Seasonal variation not associated with sales volume.

1. *Time lag*. The time lag between the recording of cost and of operating conditions which give rise to the cost was found to be appreciable for advertising only. During the years in question, however, this lag had been foreseen by the store and to a certain extent removed from the data in the process of recording the cost. Any advertising which occurred on the last day of the month was charged to the following month, on the supposition that it was to the sales of the second month that such expense contributed. This procedure assumes that the largest part of the effect of advertisement is felt on the day following its appearance and that the part which is carried over to the subsequent day is so sharply diminished as to be negligible for practical purposes. Consultation with store executives indicated a consensus that this assumption is correct. The removal of a recording lag, therefore, appeared unnecessary.

2. *Number of selling days*. Variation in the number of selling days per month undoubtedly exerts an influence on the magnitude of cost, but the relation is neither proportionate nor constant because of the differential effect of length of month on the several subdivisions of total variable cost. Salaries of buyers are constant regardless of the length of the month.

Salaries of the sales-persons, stock persons and clerical help are paid on a weekly basis and allocated to each month on the basis of the proportion of the overlapping week falling in the month. These costs, however, are not directly proportional to number of selling days, because of holidays, for which full salaries are paid. Other items, such as inside delivery, outside delivery, and departmental direct expense vary somewhat with number of selling days, but this variation results indirectly from the influence of the number of selling days on the volume of sales rather than directly from the length of the work month.[9]

It may be concluded, then, that the number of selling days is a factor affecting both the dependent variable, cost, and certain independent variables. But since none of these relations can be considered proportional, the number of selling days should, therefore, be employed as an independent variable in the multiple-correlation analysis, in order to avoid the distortion and spurious correlation which would arise from proportional correction in the original data.

3. *Changes in input prices.* Changes in salary rates and material prices are also likely to cause variation in cost behavior over a period of time. In determining whether correction for these changes is necessary and, if so, how it should be effected, several important questions arise:
(a) Were there significant changes in wage rates and material prices during the period under study?;
(b) Are the observed changes in rates separable from the changes in cost which are due to variation in volume of sales?;
(c) Can an index of wage changes be found that will reflect changes in the labor market alone and not the fluctuations associated with improvement of the skill of the individual?[10]

An analysis of the variations in the salaries of sales-persons over the period under consideration revealed that the average salary in each of the departments declined throughout 1931 and 1932 and most of 1933, then remained fairly constant, with a slight tendency to rise during 1934 and 1935. The magnitude of this fluctuation, however, was not great. Furthermore, it was not a blanket reduction but was highly individualized. The desirability of removing the effects of this change in average salary from the cost data depends essentially upon whether the salary cost per unit of

9. Sales volume is probably not proportional to the number of selling days, since the occurrence of holidays often results merely in a time redistribution within a relatively short period and not a loss of sales. Hence, even the cost items most closely related to volume do not vary proportionately with the length of the month.

10. It is important to distinguish between changes arising from career advancement of the individual (i.e., improved selling effectiveness) and those associated with changes in factor prices.

sales was significantly affected. If this cost has not changed during the period, then the adjustments in salary rates have been approximately proportional to the changes in sales volume and have thus brought about what is, in effect, a constant piece rate. A study of the average salesperson's salary cost per dollar of sales for each of the three departments showed that this rate did remain substantially constant. On the basis of this evidence of approximately constant factor prices per service unit, it was concluded that no correction was needed.[11]

Inside delivery cost figures were not corrected because a large proportion of their total was made up of salaries which were so administered as to defy index-number correction for the same reason discussed under salary rectification and because the materials used in this activity were so diverse that construction of an accurate price index would have been more costly than the improvement in accuracy would justify in view of the relatively small magnitude of these expenditures.

Correction of outside delivery, which was all handled by an independent delivery company during the period of study, was unnecessary because the package rate had remained unchanged over this period.

Advertising cost was found to vary mainly in response to changes in newspaper linage rates. Of advertising expenditure, 70 per cent was for newspaper advertising, and an average of 83 per cent of this proportion was paid for actual space (the remainder being for copywriting and illustration); so that about 60 per cent of advertising expense was proportionately dependent upon linage rates. The three departments in question were remarkably similar to the store as a whole with respect to the distribution of advertising expense.

Since there were significant changes in newspaper rates over the period of analysis, it was necessary to devise a correction index to eliminate the effect of these variations. A monthly index of the composite space-rate fluctuations for all the newspapers in which advertising was purchased was constructed and applied to 60 per cent of the original advertising cost data. These corrected data were then combined with the uncorrected

11. Rectification of other kinds of salaries was regarded as undesirable for several reasons. Variation in the salary of buyers and assistant buyers in the departments in question over the years studied was small. In two departments the same buyer, at almost the same salary, was employed during practically the entire period. In the other department the salary changes which accompanied the change of buyers were not great. The changes which did occur were supposedly a reflection of increases in the 'effectiveness' of the buyer rather than changes in the labor market. However, the buyers' labor market is so imperfect and the measurement of 'effectiveness' of merchandising executives so ineffective that little solace can be derived from this possibility. Nevertheless, the absence of objective bases for rectification of these costs made it seem more questionable to try to correct them than to leave them as recorded.

40 per cent to give a new series of cost figures from which the influence of rate changes had been removed.[12]

From the above discussion it is clear that rectification of most cost items for changes in wage rates or prices was found to be either unnecessary or unpractical so that only advertising cost was rectified for rate changes.

4. *Seasonal variation.* Although seasonal variation in cost may be regarded as deriving primarily from fluctuation in the volume of sales, it is to a lesser degree attributable to changes in other conditions. Since in this study volume is the principal causal factor to be associated with cost, only the seasonal variation not arising from changes in physical volume and in average value of sale should be removed from the data. It was decided, therefore, first, to study the net relation of cost to number of transactions and average value of transaction, and then to isolate and remove that part of seasonal cost not correlated with this relation.

The familiar Bean-Ezekiel technique of establishing the net regression of cost on number of transactions and average value of transaction was employed.[13] Cost residuals from these net relations exhibited a seasonal pattern. In order to correct for this, an additive type seasonal index was computed,[14] which was used to correct the costs of the coat and shoe departments. The seasonal pattern of the hosiery department was not sufficiently clear to warrant such correction.

Because of the regularity of seasonal changes in many aspects of department-store merchandising, the seasonal index arrived at in this way appears to correct the cost data for a number of distorting influences which could not be successfully removed individually. Differences in the

12. The index employed was a weighted arithmetic average of price relatives based on January 1931 rates, with total linage purchased in the base year as the weighting factor. Although these weights are not constant throughout the five-year period for each newspaper, the composite result differed negligibly from an index weighted with the five-year average annual linage.

13. Cost residuals from these net relations were first plotted as a time series to ascertain whether there was any trend in the residuals or any perceptible shift in the seasonal pattern during the period of study, or whether the magnitude of the residual deviation was systematically different for different years. This analysis indicated that no significant trend, shifting seasonal, or variation in absolute magnitudes characterized the years studied.

14. The index was constructed by taking the arithmetic mean of the absolute deviations for each month. This figure was then added to or subtracted from the original observations. The use of an additive, rather than a multiplicative, index was the logical outgrowth of employing an additive process in establishing the relationship of cost to number of transactions and average value of transaction. Moreover, the preliminary analysis indicated that the magnitude of the residual deviation was not proportional to the total cost, which further confirmed the choice of an absolute rather than a relative method of rectification.

amount and character of sales service performed, for instance, appear to have for some departments a regular seasonal pattern which accords with the observed net seasonal variation in costs.[15]

Although variation in the number of selling days in a month was not a strong enough influence to show significant correlation with cost, its effect may be partly reflected in the residual seasonal pattern. February, a short month, shows higher than average costs in all departments. July and August, short months because the store closed Saturday, show high seasonal costs. Lags between the month in which sales effort was expended and the month in which the transaction is recorded appear to differ from month to month in a fairly regular pattern. For example, February, being the beginning of the style season for coats, carries missionary work and even actual sales completion for transactions not recorded until the following month. Similarly, November is loaded with some expense of training new girls or carrying over trained personnel preparatory to the holiday peak. Vacations, which caused cost distortion difficult to remove directly, appeared also to be included in this blanket rectifier, for they occur only in the months of July and August, and in these months costs are seasonally high. Thus the blanket correction of seasonal variation appears, happily, to cover a variety of specific causes for cost distortion which could not be removed individually.[16]

C Analysis of relations

1. *Selection of index of output.* In choosing the measurement unit that best represents output of retailing service, both physical volume of sales and dollar volume of sales were considered. The index that most accurately reflected the effect of physical volume upon the cost of the departments appeared to be the number of transactions. Number of units seemed less acceptable since sales-service effort was not believed to increase proportionately in selling several units in one transaction. Sales service, moreover, seems to be directly associated with the number of transactions when a department has a fairly homogeneous 'product'; and some items of cost, such as inside and outside delivery, are so incurred and allocated as to be closely related to transaction volume.

An alternative measure of output, dollar value of sales, possessed some

15. E.g., lower standards of service during the Christmas rush and during the January clearance sales may partially explain the low costs of these two months in the coat department. Differences in the character of the merchandise are also seasonally regular and would be expected to affect cost. The low costs of May and June in the coat department, for instance, are attributed by executives to sales of summer wraps which require relatively little sales service.

16. The effect of this correction as well as of most rectification is to increase the correlation between costs and sales volume.

advantages because some items of cost, such as advertising, appeared more directly related to value of sales than to number of transactions. On the whole it was felt, however, that value of sales did not represent as acceptable a measure of output as number of transactions, especially as it was possible to reduce monthly figures for number of transactions to a comparable basis by holding average value of transaction constant. While a complete correlation analysis was made using value of sales as the output index, the results were not as satisfactory as those obtained by using number of transactions with average value of transaction held constant. These results will not be presented in detail here.[17]

The size (money value) of the transaction had a clearly defined influence upon cost, even though its variation arose both from the number of units sold and from the size (money value) of these units. Records for the period of study did not permit a precise distinction between the two sources; but it seems evident that for the coat and shoe departments most of the fluctuations in cost came from differences in the value of units, whereas for the hosiery department most were attributable to differences in the number of units sold. Regardless of which of these influences predominates, the size of transaction probably affects cost materially. Even when the number of units is the same, more time is likely to be required for the sale of an expensive item than of a cheaper one.

The only available index of size of transaction was the average dollar value per sale. Since this measure reflects the effect of variation in dollar sales when number of transactions is held constant, it indirectly introduces value volume into the multiple-correlation analysis. This index is, however, subject to the same defects as dollar sales, namely, that it reflects changes in the retail price level, shifts in popularity among price lines, and changes in the nature of the article sold. Nevertheless, it appears to be a fairly satisfactory measure of an important cost influence.[18]

17. Cost deviations from the net regression curves of number of transactions and average value of transaction were plotted against dollar volume of sales in order to determine whether this factor was significantly correlated with the residual variation in cost not accounted for by the net regression curves. The application of this test indicated that the inclusion of dollar volume of sales as an additional independent variable in the multiple-correlation analysis was unnecessary. The influence of number of transactions and average value of transaction upon cost accounted for all the cost variation associated with dollar volume of sales, leaving no net correlation between the cost residuals and the latter.

18. As has been noted, differences in the character of transaction were held to a minimum by selecting departments whose products were relatively homogeneous and whose sales service was similar for different types of articles. A large part of the remaining variation was probably removed by the use of a monthly time interval and by correction for seasonal pattern. Nevertheless, it is likely that important residual differences remained, part of which are reflected in average value of transaction.

2. *Selection of additional independent variables.* In addition to output as measured by volume of transactions, and average value of transaction, the following cost influences were tentatively selected as independent variables for the correlation analyses on the ground that they appeared to influence cost significantly and that they could be measured and treated statistically, but that their effect could not be safely removed by rectification of the original data:[19]

(a) difference between actual and anticipated volume;
(b) intramonth variability in volume of transactions;
(c) number of selling days having unfavorable weather;
(d) number of selling days per month;
(e) change in volume from previous month;
(f) fluctuations in business conditions.

(a) *Difference between actual and anticipated volume.* The departure of actual sales from anticipated sales seems to have an important effect upon the costs of a department largely because of the difficulty of adjusting the working force to a violently fluctuating sales volume. The existence of a versatile contingent sales force which can be shifted among departments and of a trained alumni corps available for part-time work makes possible fairly accurate adjustment of sales-persons and stock-personnel to the sales volume to the extent that sales can be correctly forecasted. But if actual sales fall below planned sales, the adjustment is defective, and cost per sale rises.

The difference between budgeted sales and actual sales was considered as a possible measure of inaccurate forecasting but was subsequently found unacceptable because of incomplete records. The most promising of the alternative indexes of forecasting inaccuracies appeared to be the ratio of each month's sales to the sales of the corresponding month of the pre-

19. Two other cost influences were given consideration: rate of stock turnover and the proportion of inexperienced workers employed. Inquiry indicated, however, that the effect of inventory turnover was likely to be confined to cost and profit items not included in the analysis, e.g., interest, storage space and mark-downs.

The proportion of inexperienced sales-people employed did not appear to exert a serious influence on cost for several reasons: (1) the low rate of labor turnover in these departments; (2) the store's policy of developing a reserve of experienced extras and a versatile flying squadron of sales-people trained to work in several departments; and (3) the policy of starting inexperienced girls at low salaries and raising salaries only as their sales increase.

No suitable index of inexperienced personnel could be found. Average length of service is an inexact measure because of marked individual differences in learning speed and because it does not reflect a new clerk's previous training in selling the same merchandise at other stores. Selling cost per sales-person was equally unsuitable, since there appeared to be no correlation between length of service and the ratio of salary to sales.

ceding year, since the earlier year's volume is usually a most important consideration in making plans for the current year's sales.

(b) *Intramonth variability in volume transactions.* Another important cause for variation in cost was thought to be fluctuation in sales volume within the time period selected as the unit of analysis. This fluctuation is of three main types: week-to-week variation, day-to-day variation within the week, and hour-to-hour fluctuation within the day. Fluctuation in volume affects cost partly because of the difficulty of adjusting the sales force to changes in need for its services. Intramonthly fluctuations may influence month-to-month differences in cost in two ways: (1) by departure from a predictable pattern of variation or (2) by such extreme irregularity of variation as to make adjustments impossible even when correctly anticipated.[20] An examination of each type of fluctuation indicated that variability of sales within the month would probably fail to account for differences in cost between months.[21] Nevertheless, an index of variability was computed for one department to test this conclusion. Day-to-day fluctuation was chosen as most likely to be important and easiest to measure. An index of the variability in number of sales transactions was constructed by expressing the difference between the highest day and the lowest day of the week as a ratio of the lowest day.[22]

(c) *Weather.* Weather was thought to influence cost not only through its effect upon sales volume but also through its effect upon the predictability of sales. Bad weather, by suddenly driving sales below estimated volume, may make unnecessary the services of sales-persons and stock-persons previously employed.

Two kinds of adverse weather conditions can be distinguished: unseasonable weather and disagreeable weather. Since the former's disturb-

20. To a certain extent, successful adjustment depends upon ability to forecast sales accurately. Nevertheless, the problem is larger than this, for it also relates to the limited divisibility of production factors; e.g., the hour-to-hour fluctuations in business cannot be completely met by hourly adjustments in the selling force.

21. Although the pattern of hour-to-hour variation had not been accurately determined, it was thought by executives to be approximately the same from month to month. The day-to-day variation within the week had been subjected to an analysis which showed that, although the fluctuations were marked for the departments under study, the pattern did not appear to differ significantly from month to month. Week-to-week fluctuation showed marked differences among months; but this type of variability could be more easily coped with because regularity of the seasonal pattern made it more exactly predictable and because a week is a long enough period to permit tolerably accurate adjustment of personnel needs.

22. This method was based on the assumption that relative variation within the week was more significant than absolute variation. To have measured deviations from the expected pattern of fluctuation might have been preferable but was considered too laborious.

ing effect upon cost was probably not great,[23] and since it was difficult to obtain an objective measure of unseasonable weather for the period under study, measurement of this phenomenon for use as an independent variable was abandoned.[24]

Disagreeable weather appears to affect costs by causing large day-to-day variations in sales which are not accurately predictable early enough to permit adjustments of selling and stock force. An index was constructed by tabulating for each month the number of days with extreme temperature (above 85° or below 15°) or with rainfall during store hours.[25]

(d) *Number of selling days per month*. Direct rectification of data for length of work month was, upon analysis, considered both unnecessary and unpractical. As a check upon the conclusion that its effect was negligible, number of selling days per month was tested as an independent variable.

(e) *Change in volume from previous month*. The position of a point on a static cost function is assumed to be unaffected by the position of previous observations; that is, the cost-output relation for one period is not supposed to be influenced by the output of the previous period. Our cost function, however, may not correspond precisely to this model, since rigidities of various sorts may cause the cost associated with a given output to be different when this output has been attained by an increase from the previous level than by a decrease. To examine the reversibility of the empirical cost function, the magnitude and direction of change in output from that of the previous month was tested as an independent variable.

(f) *Fluctuations in business conditions*. It might be supposed that fluctuations in general business conditions would influence costs in the present

23. Whether unseasonable weather results in actual loss of sales or merely in postponement is of no consequence here, for concern is only with the extent to which it may cause errors in planning personnel needs.

24. Average variation of temperature from the normal for past years is not satisfactory, for it does not spot the timing and number of unseasonable days; while buyers' records are incomplete and are likely to rationalize unfavorable showings.

25. By studying daily sales records over the five-year period, in conjunction with average noontime temperature, it was found that, on the average sales fell off when the noontime temperatures was 85° or higher in summer and 15° or lower in winter. The number of selling days with temperature above or below these critical points was therefore determined for each month of the period under study.

The effects of precipitation were studied by comparing daily sales with records of rain and snow during store hours. Snow appeared to have little or no ill effect upon sales whereas rain was frequently associated with subnormal sales. The number of days in which it rained during store hours in each month was therefore included in the index of bad weather. Duplications between the two criteria of bad weather were then eliminated, leaving a net count of the number of selling days with disagreeable weather in each month. This involved equal weighting of days regarded as uncomfortable from each of these conditions, but no *a priori* or empirical evidence was available to indicate other weights.

study mainly through changes in the various input prices and through variations in number of transactions and in the average value of transactions. By rectifying the data to remove the influence of changes in wage rates and prices, it was hoped to remove the greatest part of the 'irrelevant' variation in costs attributable to what will be called, for lack of a better term, 'the business cycle'. The remaining effect of cyclical influences upon cost behavior was roughly tested by plotting the cost residuals of a graphic correlation analysis in chronological order to observe periodic fluctuations.

3. *Testing the influence of independent variables.* In the preceding section certain cost influences were tentatively selected as independent variables for the correlation analyses on the grounds that they appeared to influence cost significantly, that they could be measured and treated statistically, and that their effect upon cost could not be safely removed by rectification of the original data. Number of transactions and average value of transaction were chosen as measurement units for physical output. In addition, the following sources of cost variation were analysed:

(a) difference between actual and anticipated volume;
(b) intramonth variability in volume of transactions;
(c) number of selling days having unfavorable weather;
(d) number of selling days per month;
(e) change in volume from previous month;
(f) fluctuations in business conditions.

Two criteria were applied in selecting from this list the independent variables for the least-squares multiple-correlation analysis: (1) the factor must have an independent influence upon cost not accounted for by some other variable and (2) the factor must not be highly correlated with any other independent variable.

By a preliminary graphic analysis it was possible, first, to ascertain whether any net relation existed between cost and each of the tentative causal elements; second, to define the general character of this relation; and, third, to determine the degree of intercorrelation among the independent variables.

The net relations were tested by employing each factor as an independent variable in graphic multiple-correlation analyses of total departmental cost. Introduction of the independent variables in the order of their believed importance[26] made it possible to establish by successive approximation the net relation between cost and those items which proved most important and to test the correlation between each factor

26. The hierarchy was based upon opinion of executives plus closeness of simple correlation as determined by inspection of scatter diagrams. Space limitations prevent introduction of these and the multiple-correlation charts in this presentation.

and the cost variation not attributable to a more closely correlated variable.[27] A clear net relation to cost was found for both number of transactions (X_2) and average value of transaction (X_4).[28] Cost deviations from these net regression curves were plotted against each of the remaining independent variables, to determine whether the factor was significantly correlated with the residual variation in cost not accounted for by the net regressions of X_2 and X_4.

The number of selling days per month was found to have no net correlation with cost in any of the three departments after the cost variation associated with X_2 and X_4 had been removed. Although the effect of the factor upon sales volume was clear, its net effect upon cost was not; and it was, therefore, not included among the independent variables.

The percentage change in number of transactions from the corresponding month of the previous year likewise showed no net correlation with cost for any department studied and was rejected as an independent variable.

Although unfavorable weather (as measured by the number of selling days per month that were rainy or uncomfortably hot or cold) appeared to have a clear effect upon sales volume, this index showed no statistically significant net relation to cost for any department. Apparently its only effect upon cost was through its effect upon sales volume; it therefore not used in the least-squares analysis.

Daily variability in number of sales transactions likewise failed to show a statistically significant net relation to cost in each department and was, therefore, not included among the independent variables.

Change in volume from that of the previous month showed no net relation to cost, thus roughly showing the continuity or reversibility of the cost function. No cyclical pattern was found in the cost residuals from the X_2 and X_4 net regressions. This indicated that no additional correction for cyclical changes in supply prices and wages was needed and that the observed cyclical fluctuations of cost were primarily accounted for by fluctuations in physical and dollar volume of sales.[29]

To summarize, by determining graphically the net regression of each

27. The order of introduction may have a significant effect upon results, hence the care with which the variables were arrayed (cf. Malenbaum and Black 1937, pp. 66–112).

28. 'Average value of transaction' will hereafter be referred to as 'average gross sale' in deference to department-store terminology.

29. Seasonal variation, on the other hand, did not exhaust its influence on cost by working through number of transactions and dollar value of sale. Rather it apparently exercised an independent additional influence since the cost residuals from the net regression of X_2 and X_4 had a subdued but well-defined seasonal pattern. Instead of including the seasonal factor as a third independent variable, however, the residuals were used to rectify the original cost data. This procedure is discussed under 'Data Rectification'.

prospective independent variable on cost, a significant relation was found between cost and two factors: number of transactions (X_2) and average gross sale (X_4). Dollar volume of sales (X_3) showed a strong gross relationship but was adequately represented in the multiple-correlation analysis by X_2 and X_4. A well-defined residual seasonal pattern of cost variation was discovered and was removed from the data by a correction index. No net relation to cost, however, was found for the following factors:

(a) change from corresponding month of previous year;
(b) number of selling days per month;
(c) number of selling days per month having unfavorable weather;
(d) day-to-day variability in volume of transactions;
(e) business conditions.

4. *Determining the intercorrelation of independent variables.* The degree of intercorrelation among the independent variables was first explored by means of scatter diagrams, which provided a sufficiently accurate indication for these purposes.

Number of transactions (X_2) and average gross sale (X_4) showed no correlation for the coat and shoe departments. For hosiery no correlation was found for the years 1932, 1933, 1934 and 1935, but for the year 1931 a clear relation appeared to exist.

The high correlation which existed between some of the rejected independent variables and number of transactions (X_2) accounts, in part, for lack of any relation between these variables and cost after the effect of volume variation had been removed.[30]

3 Findings

The preceding sections have dealt with problems of collecting, rectifying and analysing the data in order to find the net relation between cost and output, with other influences held constant. In this section the findings of the study are presented.

Three departments of a retail store were studied: the women's medium-priced coat department, the women's hosiery department and the women's shoe department. The cost analysed for each department excluded general

30. Both the number of selling days per month and disagreeable weather, for example, were clearly correlated with volume of sales, although multiple-correlation analysis revealed no additional independent effect upon cost. Likewise, the original data revealed a clear cyclical pattern in volume of transactions and in average dollar value of transaction. Yet there was no significant residual cyclical variation in corrected cost over and above that attributable to X_2 and X_4. Both number of transactions (X_2) and average gross sale (X_4) had a strong seasonal pattern. It was, in fact, this high intercorrelation which precluded correction of the original data for the full seasonal influence. The residual seasonal pattern which served as a basis for the correction index was not, however, correlated with X_2 or X_4.

store allocated expenses and was confined to an aggregate of the monthly expenses of advertising, sales-people's salaries, other department salaries, inside delivery, outside delivery and direct expenses. This aggregate cost, hereafter referred to as 'combined cost', was studied in three forms: as a total of the monthly expense (total cost), as the average expense per unit of sale (average cost), and as the increment in total cost associated with an additional unit of sale (marginal cost).

Previous experiments in methodology have indicated that more useful and accurate estimates of cost behavior can be obtained by analysing cost in terms of total expense for an accounting period than in terms of expense per unit of sale.[31] Cost behavior was, therefore, analysed in terms of totals before converting the findings into average and marginal terms. Empirical cost functions were obtained by least-squares multiple regression analysis of corrected monthly observations.

A Cost as a function of number of transactions

We shall first summarize the findings concerning cost behavior associated with variations in output as measured by number of transactions (the influence of average gross sale being allowed for) since this was accepted as the most useful measure of output.[32] The total, average, and marginal cost functions will be shown for the coat, hosiery, and shoe departments.

In order to keep absolute cost magnitudes confidential, both cost and output measures were transformed into index numbers. Number of transactions will henceforth refer to number of units of transaction index, and average and marginal costs must be understood to refer to the index unit. Average gross sale will also refer to index units rather than to dollars.

1. *Coat department.* The following partial regression equation for total cost was obtained for the coat department:[33]

$$X_T^C = 16\cdot835 + 1\cdot052X_2 - 0\cdot00194X_2^2.$$

It shows total cost increasing in a convex curve which rises at a declining rate as physical volume increases, as portrayed in Figure 1.

31. Cf. Joel Dean (1936).

32. A strong gross relation between dollar volume of sales (X_3) and both seasonally corrected and uncorrected cost was evidenced for each department. The relation of total cost appeared to be convex downward for coats and shoes (falling marginal cost), and linear for hosiery (constant marginal cost). Since dollar volume is more commonly used in store management than is physical quantity, a least-squares analysis of its relation to cost was made which confirmed these graphic results. Simple correlation was indicated because deviations from the gross regressions did not have a significant relation to average gross sale or to other factors.

33. The following subscripts and superscripts are used in these equations: T = total cost, A = average cost, M = marginal cost; C = coat department; H = hosiery department; S = shoe department; X_2 = index of number of transactions; X_4 = index of average gross sale.

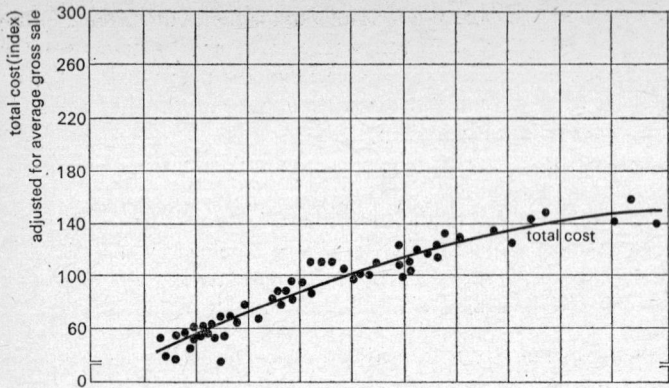

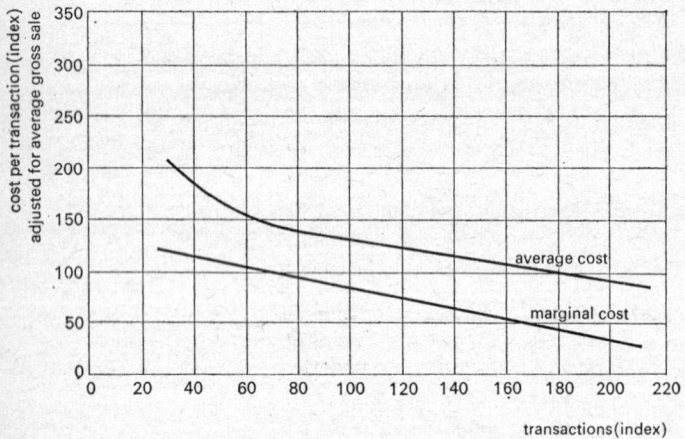

Figure 1 Coat department : total, average and marginal combined cost derived from partial regression on transactions

The behavior of average cost was determined by conversion of the corresponding total cost function rather than by direct correlation analysis of unit cost observations. It shows transaction cost declining in a hyperbolic curve as physical volume increases, as may be observed in Figure 1, and seen from the following equation:

$$X_A^C = 1 \cdot 052 + 16 \cdot 835/X_2 - 0 \cdot 00194 X_2 .$$

The marginal cost per transaction unit declines at a constant rate, as physical volume increases, in a function described by the following equation:

$$X_M^C = 1 \cdot 052 - 0 \cdot 00388 X_2 .$$

2. *Hosiery department.* For the hosiery department the least-squares equation for the net relation between cost and number of transactions, while holding the average gross sale at its mean, is

$$X_T^H = 55 \cdot 554 + 0 \cdot 347 X_2 .$$

The graph of the equation, which indicates that total cost rises at a constant rate as number of transactions increases, is shown in the upper half of Figure 2. Inspection of the latter figure reveals that the observations upon which the curves are based are so unevenly distributed that the

Table 1 **Hosiery department: estimated total, average, and marginal cost* for various units of transactions (X_2) with the index of average gross sale constant at its mean**

Transactions (index)	Estimated total cost (index)	Estimated average cost (index)	Estimated marginal cost (index)
60	76·374	1·273	0·347
80	83·314	1·041	0·347
100	90·254	0·903	0·347
120	97·194	0·810	0·347
140	104·134	0·744	0·347
160	111·074	0·694	0·347
180	118·014	0·656	0·347
200	124·954	0·625	0·347
240	138·834	0·578	0·347
280	152·714	0·545	0·347
320	166·594	0·521	0·347

* Derived from the equations:
$$X_T^H = 55 \cdot 554 + 0 \cdot 347 X_2$$
$$X_A^H = X_T^H/X_2 = 0 \cdot 347 + 55 \cdot 554/X_2$$
$$X_M^H = 0 \cdot 347$$

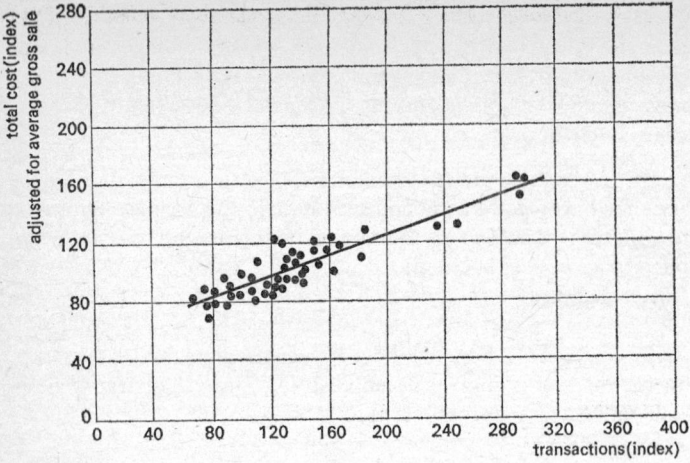

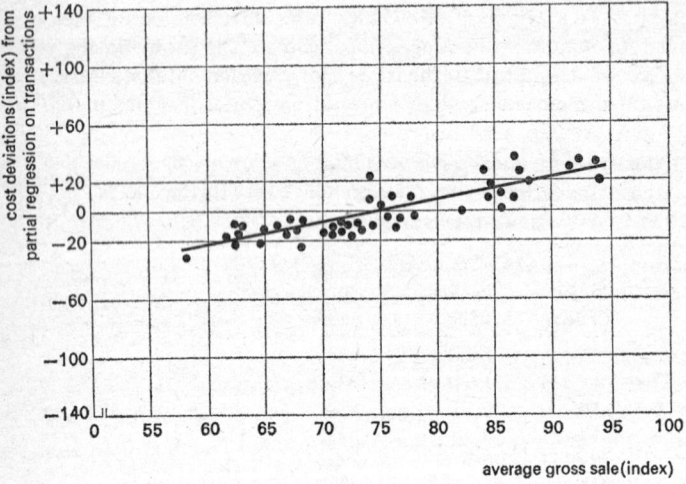

Figure 2 Hosiery department: partial regressions of total combined cost on transactions and average gross sale

relation was well established only between the transactions index figures of 80 and 170, and only tentatively defined for the range between 170 and 300.

The equation for average cost per sales transaction as related to number of transactions, when the average gross sale is held constant, is

$$X_A^H = 0.347 + 55.554/X_2 .$$

In tabular form this function is presented in Table 1. Examination of the table shows that average cost per transaction unit falls at a declining rate as physical volume of sales increases and tends to approach a constant at the extreme range of cost observation.

The marginal cost of one additional hosiery transaction was found to be constant at 0.347.

3. *Shoe department.* For the shoe department the net relation between total cost and number of transactions (X_2), when the average value of transaction is held constant at its mean, is depicted by the following partial regression equation:

$$X_T^S = 32.137 + 0.925 X_2 .$$

The graph of this function (Figure 3) indicates that total selling cost of the department increases at a constant, although not proportionate, rate as the physical volume of sales rises.

The average cost per transaction unit for women's shoes declines, as would be expected, when the number of transactions increases. This relation, when average value of sale is constant at its mean, is shown in the following equation:

$$S_A^S = 0.925 + 32.137/X_2 .$$

The graph of the function is shown in Figure 3, where it may be contrasted with the total cost function.

The estimate of the marginal cost of an additional transaction index unit for the women's shoe department appears to be constant, throughout the observed range of physical volume, at 0.925.

B Cost as a function of average gross sale

The findings for cost functions when number of transactions is accepted as the index of the output (with average gross sale held constant) which were presented in the preceding section need to be supplemented by examination of the influence of another aspect of output. The significance of the net relation between the average gross sale and cost indicates that output should be considered as two-dimensional and may increase either in the direction of more transactions or greater average size of the transaction. Accepting size of transaction (average gross sale) as the measure of

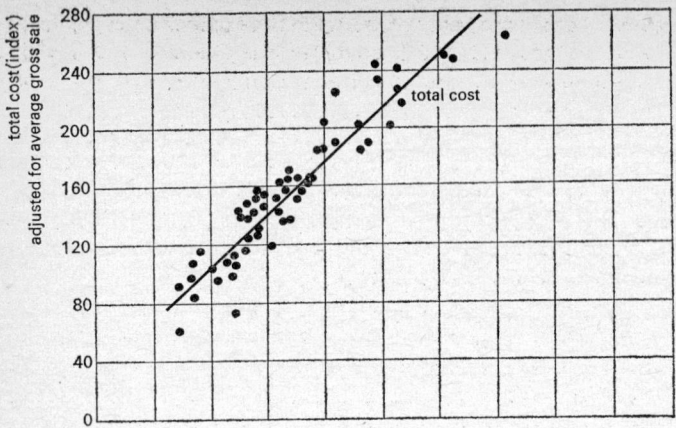

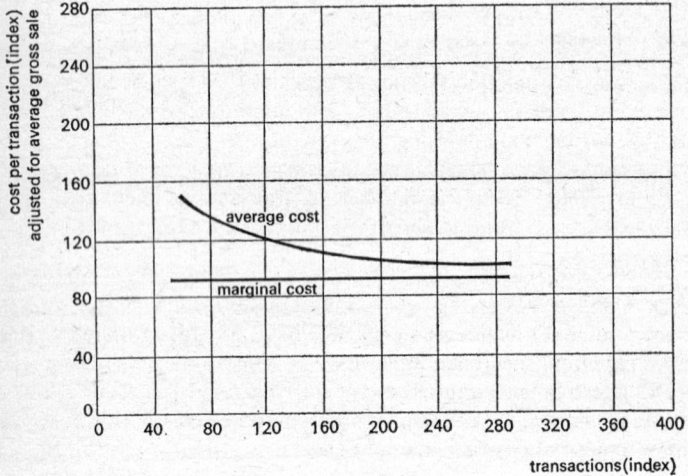

Figure 3 Shoe department: total, average and marginal combined cost derived from partial regression on transactions

Table 2 **Budget coat department: estimated total, average, and marginal cost* for various magnitudes of the index of average gross sale (X_4) with index of transactions constant at its mean**

Average gross sale (index)	Estimated total cost (index)	Estimated average cost (index)	Estimated marginal cost (index)
50	75·292	1·506	0·787
60	83·162	1·386	0·787
70	91·032	1·300	0·787
80	98·902	1·236	0·787
90	106·772	1·186	0·787
100	114·642	1·146	0·787

     * Derived from the equations:

$X_T^C = 35\cdot942 + 0\cdot787\,X_4$

$X_A^C = X_T^C/X_4 = 0\cdot787 + 35\cdot942/X_4$

$X_M^C = 0\cdot787$

output, and holding number of transactions constant at its mean, we obtain the results summarized in this section.

1. *Coat department.* The net functional relation between total cost of the coat department and average gross sale (with number of transactions constant) is shown by the following least-squares partial regression equation:

$X_T^C = 35\cdot942 + 0\cdot787X_4$.

Total cost tends to increase at a constant rate with the size of the average gross sale. Table 2, which was obtained by substituting in the above regression equation, shows this relation in the form of estimated total cost for various values of average gross sale.

The average cost per index unit of average gross sale, as average gross sale varies and number of transactions remains constant, is shown by the following expression:

$X_A^C = 0\cdot787 + 35\cdot942/X_4$.

The cost per unit increase in the monthly average value of transaction is constant at 0·787 over the observed range.

2. *Hosiery department.* For the hosiery department the equation obtained for the net relation between total costs and average gross sale, when the effect of number of transactions is allowed for, is

$X_T^H = -13\cdot889 + 1\cdot557X_4$.

Table 3 **Hosiery department: estimated total, average, and marginal cost* for various magnitudes of the index of average gross sale (X_4) with index of transactions constant at its mean**

Average gross sale (index)	Estimated total cost (index)	Estimated average cost (index)	Estimated marginal cost (index)
50	63·961	1·279	1·557
60	79·531	1·326	1·557
70	95·101	1·359	1·557
80	110·671	1·383	1·557
90	126·241	1·403	1·557
100	141·811	1·418	1·557

* Derived from the equations:
$$X_T^H = -13·889 + 1·557 X_4$$
$$X_A^H = X_T^H/X_4 = 1·557 - 13·899/X_4$$
$$X_M^H = 1·557$$

The curve of this equation found in the lower half of Figure 3 shows that cost increases with the size of the average gross sale at a constant rate. As in the case of number of transactions, the wide dispersion of the observations casts some doubt on the validity of a linear relation.

The average cost per index unit of average gross sale, when the number of transactions is held constant, is described by the following equation:

$$X_A^H = 1·557 - 13·889/X_4 .$$

The tabular representation is shown in Table 3.

The additional cost of increasing average gross sale by one index unit for the month was found to be 1·557.

3. *Shoe department.* The functional relation of total cost and average gross sale, with transactions constant, for the shoe department, is shown by the equation:

$$X_T^S = -23·427 + 0·837 X_4 .$$

Total cost increases at a constant rate with the value of average gross sale, when physical volume is held constant at its mean.[34]

The average cost per unit of average gross sale, with physical volume constant at its mean and size of gross sale varying, is shown by the following expression:

$$X_A^S = 0·837 - 23·427/X_4 .$$

34. Graphic correlation analysis paralleled the least-squares findings by revealing the same type of net relation, although the uneven and scattered distribution of the observations from which the relations were obtained somewhat restricts the reliance to be placed in these functions.

The cost of a dollar increase in average value of transaction is constant at 0·837.

C. Cost as a function of number of transactions and average gross sale

The findings concerning the combined effect upon cost of the two aspects of output – number of transactions and average gross sale – will be briefly presented in this section.

For the coat department the combined effect of number of transactions (X_2) and average gross sale (X_4) on total cost is shown by the following multiple-regression equation:

$$X_T^C = -35·440 + 1·052X_2 - 0·00194X_2^2 + 0·787X_4 .$$

The standard error of estimate, adjusted for degrees of freedom, was 7·901. The close relation of cost to the independent variables is shown by the value of the coefficient of multiple correlation, 0·980, and by the coefficient of multiple determination which indicates that about 96 per cent of the variance in rectified cost was accounted for by the independent factors.

The combined effect of number of transactions (X_2) and average gross sale (X_4) upon total cost of the hosiery department is described by the following equation:

$$X_T^H = -60·764 + 0·347X_2 + 1·557X_4 .$$

The confidence which can be placed in the relation described above is indicated by the standard error of estimate of 8·140, the coefficient of multiple correlation of 0·957, and the coefficient of multiple determination of 0·91.

For the shoe department the combined effects of number of transactions (X_2) and average gross sale (X_4) upon total cost is shown by the following multiple-regression equation:

$$X_T^S = -146·776 + 0·925X_2 + 0·837X_4 .$$

Provided that the basic conditions of the sampling period remain unchanged, considerable confidence can be placed on the above relations, as is evidenced by a standard error of estimate of 16·624, a coefficient of multiple correlation of 0·965, and a coefficient of multiple determination of 0·93.

4 Interpretation of findings

The findings of an empirical study of the individual firm should constitute some kind of an evaluation of what theorists have been saying with regard to its economic behavior. However, such an appraisal would imply that the situation described by the statistician is strictly comparable to that generally postulated by the theorist. The actual situation investigated, in fact, deviates from the theoretical norm in two important respects, namely, first, by the inclusion of selling costs in cost of production and second, by the failure to purge the statistical data of all sources of dynamic nonconformity to the static model. Some brief comments will be made on these limitations of the findings in sections *A* and *B* before an attempt is made in sections *C* and *D* to explain and rationalize the results observed.

A Inclusion of selling costs

As was mentioned above, the costs examined in this study were not confined to what is usually designated as cost of production proper. *A priori*, of course, there are equally good, if not better, reasons for supposing that marginal selling expenditure increases with intensified selling activity as there are for expecting that marginal cost of production rises with output. First, with more intensive utilization of fixed equipment returns per unit of input presumably decrease. Second, each additional unit of promotional cost has diminishing effectiveness since it becomes necessary, in order to increase sales, to detach customers with increasing degrees of personal affiliation and loyalty to rival firms, or to make present customers spend an ever increasing share of their incomes.[35]

Although our findings may be strongly influenced by the presence of costs designed to modify the existing demand functions, the relation of such costs to sales may not be revealed in our data. A spurious correlation between selling expenditure and sales could result from independent fluctuations in demand and from market-sharing, since it obviously is not possible to attribute all shifts in the store's demand functions during the period of analysis to its promotional activities. It is conceivable that selling costs in a mature competitive retail market have the effect of maintaining the store's share of the total demand – a demand which shifts seasonally and cyclically in response to changes in custom, in tastes and in income.

It would be impossible to establish the relation between number of sales transactions and expenditure on advertising without eliminating variations in sales resulting from varying effectiveness of advertising, from changes in demand and from other irrelevant factors. The same holds true of other elements of promotional expenditure. Consequently, our results cannot be interpreted as measuring the influence of the diminishing effectiveness of promotional expenditures as a firm's market is expanded at the expense of rivals.

35. 'When a field is fertilized or a pig fed, the profit per dose decreases with the quantity of doses, and it is time to stop when profit and dose have the same value. Similar phenomena of fatigue appear when we feed a market, which may also be considered as a kind of living being....' (Jantzen, 1939, p. 6).

The inclusion of both selling costs and pure costs of production in the empirical cost function, furthermore, indicates that the product, a unit of sales service, is not entirely homogeneous, since selling activity which increases sales may be considered to have enhanced the utility of commodities offered. However, there may be considerable stability in the proportion of selling costs to total costs.[36]

An additional reason for suspecting that the unit of output, sales service, may not be homogeneous over the observation period and may be correlated with the physical transaction rate is the fact that sales service per transaction is likely to diminish during busy seasons. As a consequence of this, the decline of marginal cost as the volume of transactions increases may merely reflect deterioration of sales service standards.[37] If this is the case, and if this deterioration has a tendency to decrease future marginal revenue, the management may regard falling marginal cost as a danger signal, indicating that sharply rising marginal promotional expenditure may be necessary in the future.[38]

B Statistical sources of nonconformity

Besides the problems involved in promotional activity, there also exist certain statistical sources of possible nonconformity of the empirical situation to the theoretical model in addition to those mentioned in the sections dealing with methodology.

36. It was not possible to isolate the promotional or selling constituent in the various accounting categories of cost. Nevertheless, in the coat and hosiery departments the behavior of newspaper advertising costs (which approximate pure promotional costs, indicated the existence of a proportional relation to output. In a graphic correlation analysis the functions appeared to be linear and to pass through the origin, although the scatter was wide, particularly for high outputs. An ill-defined curvilinear function was found for the shoe department. It seems reasonable, moreover, to expect substantial constancy of store standards over time, which would further buttress the assumption of approximate constancy of promotional components of cost. The results of this partial analysis are not conclusive, however, because of the failure to stabilize demand and other impinging conditions.

37. The corrected data employed are intended, however, to represent a fairly uniform quantity of sales service. Day-to-day and hour-to-hour variation in sales service was probably averaged out by taking monthly totals rather than daily or weekly totals, and the effect of seasonal variation in sales service was at least partially removed by means of the index of seasonal variation.

It is possible that the form of the cost function obtained was altered by the seasonal correction of the cost data. This appears unlikely, however, because the influence of volume on cost was removed before constructing the seasonal index, by the process described in section 2B.

38. Since the cost components entering into sales service are not independent of marginal revenue, it is therefore possible that declining marginal cost indicates that the department has passed the output which will maximize revenue over a period of time extending more or less indefinitely into the future.

It is possible that, had a smaller observation unit been chosen (e.g., days or weeks instead of months), a more conventional cost function would have been obtained. If uncorrected data had been used, the expectation would be that the longer the time unit chosen the less would be the slope of the marginal cost curve, since marginal costs are a function of the time period allowed for adjustment to changed rates of output. If rectification of the data has been successful, however, adjustments of a long-period or quasi-long-period character have been eliminated, so that there should be no discrepancy between a function based on monthly findings and one based on a shorter time period.

From the purely technical viewpoint, it should probably be mentioned that the total cost functions are not defined beyond question as being straight lines or parabolas. The unexplained scatter of observations is great enough to permit a cubic of the traditional form to be fitted in each case. However, the curvature would be so slight as to be insignificant from a managerial viewpoint, so that it could scarcely affect any economic conclusions which might be derived from the linear and parabolic functions. In each instance a higher-order function than that selected was fitted and subjected to critical ratio tests, which indicated that the more complex function did not fit the data significantly better than that chosen.

C Excess capacity

If the plant of these three departments were systematically under-utilized during the observation period, marginal costs might appear to be constant or falling over the whole length of the curve because of an inadequate range of observations.

Over-building as a result of errors of optimism in estimating the position and inclination of demand functions is not a plausible explanation for over-capacity, since department-store layouts are relatively easy to modify when such errors become apparent. This explanation, moreover, does not take account of the possibility that selling expenditures may eventually shift the demand functions so that capacity is fully utilized.

The equilibrium position of a department may be one of apparent excess capacity only. The fact that the magnitude of selling expenditures affects both the cost function and the demand function results in complex interrelations that may yield equilibrium at a point on the demand surface that appears to represent under-utilization of capacity. Delays in the responsiveness of demand to various kinds of promotional expenditures, together with complexities of polyperiodic production, may accentuate this condition. Store prestige may, furthermore, force some departments to operate at less than their departmental optimum capacity. An over-elaborate layout and stock in particular departments could also result from the effort of the store to maintain comparable standards of sales service, variety of merchandise, display, etc., in all departments of the store. Store 'good will' may thus necessitate a minimum size for the departments studied, greater than that justified by the average position and slope of their demand functions during the period examined.

We have no evidence that the observed outputs were those which would have maximized profits under these complicated conditions. In view of the complexity of the relations between cost and revenue, it is not surprising that this store conformed to the general pricing policy of department stores which is based on the 'cost plus a given percentage' principle rather than on an attempt to calculate optimum price on the basis of inter-related cost and revenue functions. The 'cost-plus' policy would yield the price and output which was 'optimum' for any momentary situation only accidentally and might result in a systematic under-utilization of plant which would confine observations to the constant section of the marginal curve.

D Technical explanations for constant marginal costs

A variety of technically plausible explanations can be given for findings of constant marginal costs in the hosiery and coat departments and falling marginal costs in the shoe department. Marginal costs may be constant if it is possible to 'sectionalize' the activities of a firm; that is, if the factors employed can be grouped into small operating entities, each of which can be utilized to equal advantage, and each of which represents the optimum combination of factors.[39] In practice, of course, a plant cannot be completely sectionalized, since some factors, if only the management and organization, are fixed in the short run. As long as fixed factors are present, the law of diminishing returns will cause costs to rise over some portion of the marginal cost curve.

Second, the declining phase of the marginal cost curve will be particularly important if the fixed factors are not completely adaptable to varying inputs of the variable factors and if, in addition to 'lumpiness' of the fixed factors, there are organizational economies available when larger amounts of the variable factors are used. The inclination of the curve will depend on the degree of technical 'flexibility' to be found. An inflexible plant would have a U-shaped marginal cost function with a sharply defined minimum; greater flexibility would be present if outputs less or greater than the optimum could be obtained without entailing rapidly rising marginal cost.[40]

39. Cf. Joseph (1933, pp. 390–98).
40. See a recent article by Stigler (1939, pp. 305–28), for a discussion of the concepts of adaptability and flexibility. Stigler has pointed out that technical flexibility may be

It is probable that the type of marginal cost function found in empirical studies can be explained by investigating (1) the degree to which sectional divisibility of the plant has been attained and (2) the degree of technical rigidity which exists.

In a department store technical rigidities are probably not so great as would be found in a manufacturing enterprise. The fixed elements of cost include, from the standpoint of the individual department, the general standards and reputation of the store, the location, in the present instance the size of the departmental layout, and to a certain extent the service of the buying and managerial staff. However, it is probable that buying and managerial service varies with output, even when no recognition of such variation is given in salaries or number of people employed. To this relatively small component of fixed factors might be added units composed of the optimum combination of selling service, advertising, delivery expense, etc. The degree of 'sectionalization' thus attained might offset, for considerable variations in output, the tendency to diminishing returns. Moreover, since there are few highly specialized input factors in a technical sense the degree of flexibility is probably great.

In conclusion, since the demand and cost functions are not independent when promotional expenditures are being made, it would be necessary in order to get a determinate solution to the problem of the optimum price and output not only to separate promotional costs from cost of production proper or to determine a functional relation between them but also to determine: (1) The relation between selling costs and the demand function. (2) The time lag between the incurring of the selling expenditure and its effect on demand. (3) The relation between the output-price adjustment in one period and the demand function in successive periods. (4) The inter-relation among the demands for various products both within and outside this department (e.g., 'loss leader' and 'ensemble' buying). (5) The reaction of rivals to the firm's price, output, and promotion policies.

---

deliberately provided by building a plant in a way which will maximize profits over time through efficient operation over the expected range of outputs, even if this involves the sacrifice of the optimum technical adjustment for any one output.

References

CARLSON, S. (1936), *A Contribution to the Pure Theory of Production*, Ph.D. dissertation, University of Chicago.

DEAN, J. (1936), *Statistical Determination of Costs, with Special Reference to Marginal Cost*, University of Chicago Press.

JANTZEN, I. (1939), 'Increasing returns in industrial production', *Nordisk tidsskrift for teknisk økonomi*, March–June.

JOSEPH, M. F. W. (1933), 'A discontinuous cost curve and the tendency to increasing returns', *econ. J.*, vol. 43.

KNIGHT, F. H. (1921), *Risk, Uncertainty and Profit*, Houghton Mifflin (LSE reprint, 1933).

MALENBAUM, W., and BLACK, J. D. (1937), 'The use of the short-cut graphic method of multiple correlation', *Q. J. Econ.*, vol. 52.

SHONE, R. M. (1934–5), 'Selling costs', *Rev. econ. Stud.*, vol. 2.

SMITH, H. (1934–5), 'Advertising costs and equilibrium', *Rev. econ. Stud.*, vol. 2.

STIGLER, G. (1939), 'Production and distribution in the short run', *J. polit. Econ.*, vol. 47.

VAN DYK, P. (1940), 'Cost functions in merchandising', paper delivered at research conference of Cowles Commission in Colorado Springs, Colorado.

WHITMAN, R. H. (1940), 'Cost functions in the department store', delivered at annual meeting of the American Economic Association, Philadelphia.

13 E. Douglas

Size of Firm and Cost Structure in Retailing

E. Douglas, 'Size of firm and the structure of costs in retailing', *Journal of Business*, vol. 35, 1962, pp. 158–90.

In the economic analysis of the firm, considerable attention has been directed toward the structure of short-run and long-run costs, based on various assumptions concerning the technological requirements of the industry, and on the relationship of costs to the size of firm. A classic exposition of these cost patterns is that of Jacob Viner (1931) in which he related decreasing and increasing short-run costs to long-run decreasing, constant, and/or increasing costs, employing the concept of an envelope long-run cost curve which embraces short-run cost curves for firms, or plants, of increasing size. Brems (1952) has dealt with the problem of discontinuities in cost functions. Two basic questions to which such theoretical descriptions and analyses have been directed are:

1. What determines the actual size of a firm in a given market situation?
2. What is the optimum size?

Through the analysis of accounting records and of engineering cost data, businessmen and others have sought an empirical method of determining efficiency and profits at various levels of output and capital investment. A review of such studies prior to 1941 may be found in the volume prepared by the Committee on Price Determination for the Conference on Price Research of the National Bureau of Economic Research (1943). More recent studies include those of Bain (1954) for twenty manufacturing industries, Borts (1960) for sixty-one Class 1 railway firms, Moore (1959) for chemical and metal industries, Blair (1948) for tire manufacturers, and Bressler (1945) for milk plants. In each of these an attempt was made to derive empirical cost functions which would show the variations in short-run and/or long-run costs associated with variations in volume of sales or capital investment and, from this, to draw certain conclusions concerning the optimum size of firm or plant. Eiteman and Guthrie (1952) attempted to obtain similar information from businessmen's responses to a mail questionnaire. Joe Bain (1959, pp. 145–86) and J. Johnston (1960, pp. 44–168) have summarized much of the available data on empirical cost analysis, particularly in manufacturing.

Cost analysis in retailing

Most studies of retailing costs have been concerned with the breakdown of costs among various 'functions' – that is, stockholding, selling, transportation, location, accounting, buying – or among various productive factors – for example, labor, management, merchandise, other capital, site – and with the relation of these costs, separately and in total, to the size of the retail establishment.[1] While the growth of chains has stimulated interest in the cost structure of the retail firm, most studies of retail costs have been concerned with costs of stores rather than of firms.

Either sales or transactions have served as the measure of output in retailing, and to these have been related wages and salaries, number of employees (selling, non-selling and total), gross margins, total operating expenses, and capital or portions of capital investment (e.g., stocks). The more recently developed Harvard system of expense-center accounting has focused attention upon physical inputs and outputs in terms of workload (output in physical units), productivity (output in physical units related to input in physical units, measured by mark-ons), and pay-rate (cost per physical unit of output) (McNair and May, 1953).

Purpose of this study

It is the purpose of this study to consider, first, the general problem of empirical cost analysis of firms and the particular problems peculiar to retail firms and, second, the relation of empirical data on three basic costs of retail operation to the size of firm. The three variables to be considered are cost of goods sold, total operating costs and cost of capital. We shall focus attention upon the retail firm rather than the retail store and, because of the availability of data, shall restrict our empirical analysis to retail corporations.

1 Problems of empirical cost analysis of cross-sectional data

Is it possible to employ cross-sectional data for firms of different sizes operating during the same period of time in substantially similar market situations and, by observation of cost differences among these firms, determine the parameters which describe the relation between costs of pro-

1. Authors of empirical and theoretical studies of retailing costs include Bakkenist and Beutick (1957), Bass (1956), Bellamy (1946a, b and c), Cohen (1952), Dean (1942a and b), Galbraith and Holton (1955), Hall and Knapp (1955 [Reading 15]; 1957), Jefferys *et al.* (1954), Jervis (1953), Plant and Fowler (1939), Pollard and Hughes (1955a and b), and Wiegmann *et al.* (1955). In addition, trade associations, accounting firms and credit agencies frequently collect and publish operating cost data for specific types of retail establishments. These examples do not include studies of aggregate retailing costs such as those of Barger (1955) and others described in Vaile *et al.* (1952, pp. 630–79).

duction and volume of output? If so, it would then be possible to test our assumptions concerning the shape of short-run and long-run cost curves as well as to determine objectively whether a firm is or is not operating at its most efficient scale.

General problems of cost analysis

This type of empirical analysis is plagued with a number of pitfalls which students of cost analysis have observed.[2] We can group these problems into four categories: (1) measures of size, (2) the estimation of costs, (3) the lack of homogeneity of firms, and (4) the regression fallacy.

1. *Measures of size.* The concept of economies to scale is in terms of a physical output which is homogeneous and measurable. Most firms, however, are multiproduct or multiservice, and output is ambiguous. If physical units of output cannot be computed, size approximation must be based on volume of sales, capital investment, number of transactions, gross margin, or similar measures. Estimates in terms of dollar volume may, however, confound physical output with other forces operating to determine market values. For this reason the concept of scale may not be simple to translate into empirical terms.

2. *The estimation of costs.* Interpretation of cost data must be in terms of the nature of those data. Accounting data depend in part upon the accountant's method of cost estimation. This is especially true where costs are imputed or assigned to particular elements from some aggregative dollar figure. The possibility of spurious costs arising from arbitrary cost allocation was one of the critical issues in the A & P case of more than a decade ago and is germane to the problem under consideration here. To the extent that costs are determined by accounting methods rather than by market transactions, questions of cost determination and allocation are crucial in the interpretation of empirical data. This is particularly important for integrated firms which may operate certain activities at an accounting 'loss' which are not in fact a market 'loss'.

Another related problem is that of profits. Should costs of production be considered equal to total receipts, on the grounds that profits are the 'cost' of entrepreneurial investment? Or should they exclude all or a portion of accounting profits? If the equity of stockholders is large, answers to these questions can make considerable difference in the nature of accounting cost data.

Suppose, however, that all costs used are based on values determined through market transactions. Are these appropriate data for the deter-

2. See particularly Borts (1960), Friedman (1955), Johnston (1958, 1960), and Walters (1960).

mination of the structure of the short-run and long-run cost curves of the industry? Friedman (1955) has pointed out that if these firms operate in markets which are purely and perfectly competitive, the prices paid for factors of production will be equal for all firms. Differences will, therefore, reflect mistakes or imperfections. In this case, the data enable us to judge the efficiency of the capital market rather than the efficiency of the firms' managements. If competition is sufficiently effective, firms will tend to move to an optimum size, and empirical data are useless in showing what costs would have been at other levels of output.

3. *Homogeneity of firms.* Interfirm cost comparison assumes that the firms being compared are homogeneous with respect to both output and the productive factors used. This does not mean that all firms use all factors in the same proportions but that they have equal access to all in the markets and will select the optimum proportion.

We know, however, that two firms are not identical and may, in fact, show great differences. In retailing, for example, while services of two stores may be very much alike, they will differ in certain fundamental respects. Even more important, managerial abilities will vary from one firm to another. 'Big' management may require a big firm; 'little' management will be appropriate to a small firm. Chamberlin (1948) has pointed out that this is not so much an objection to the relating of productive factors to the size of firm as it is to the omission of proportionality as one of the variables to be considered in optimum size.[3] For a given size of firm, there is an optimum proportion of resources; for a given proportion, there is an optimum size. The problem in empirical cost analysis is, therefore, to see that cross-sectional data are from firms either with homogeneous output and factors or with identifiable differences in output and factor proportions.

4. *The regression fallacy.* Friedman (1955) has stated the elements of the regression fallacy in empirical cost analysis. It is based upon the fact that there is a difference between the expenditure which is observed for a given level of output and the minimum cost of producing that output. While in the short run a firm will attempt to achieve an optimum cost given its profit, survival, sales, or other objectives, unforeseen changes in demand may force it to deviate from its planned level of output. Actual costs are incurred in anticipation of a given level of output. The relation of costs to planned output is not the same as their relation to unplanned output. Costs are likely to show some rigidity in the face of fluctuations in demand, particularly if the firm is seeking an average optimum cost over several short-run periods. Unused capacity during periods of lower-than-planned

3. See additional discussion by McLeod and Hahn (1949) and Chamberlin (1949).

sales and intensive use of capacity during periods of greater-than-planned sales will result in actual cost-revenue relationships different from those which would have occurred had planned outputs and planned costs been experienced.

In Figure 1, for example, the short-run cost is represented by CC' and is comprised of a series of cost-output relations of which a and b are two examples. But a and b may seldom occur in actual business experience. Rather, as firms experience over- and under-capacity with varying volumes of sales, their short-short-run cost curves may look like de and fg, moving slightly above and slightly below a or b and reflecting the rigidity in certain

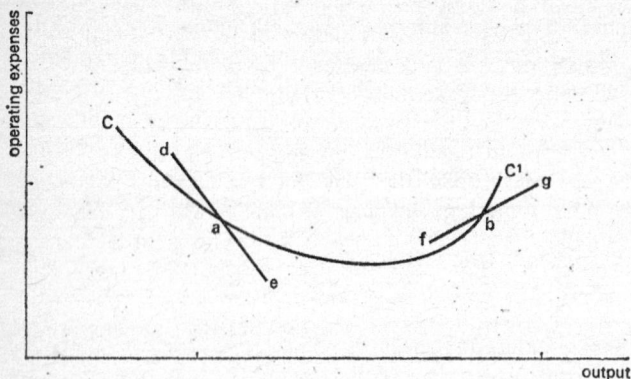

Figure 1 Short-run and short-short-run operating costs and output

costs as volume varies above and below that at the planned output levels a and b. Empirical measurement of cost relations at any given moment in time may, therefore, yield points on the lines de or fg rather than on CC'. If the firm is operating on that portion of its short-run cost curve which has a positive cost elasticity – that is, to the right of the point of lowest unit cost – the slope of the short-short-run curve will be less than that of the theoretical short-run curve. If, on the other hand, the firm is operating on that portion of its average cost curve which has a negative slope – that is, at less than its point of lowest unit cost – its short-short-run curve will have a greater negative slope than will the short-run cost curve (see Figure 1).

We can state the problem in another way. The cost curves of economic theory represent the minimum cost of producing each output. The short-run curve assumes a given plant, while the long-run curve assumes that all factors of production are variable. But for both curves the costs are *ex ante*. Accounting costs are *ex post* and are unlikely to be the same as *ex ante* costs.

For this reason, some writers have proposed that engineering cost estimates, which are *ex ante*, be substituted for the less satisfactory accounting costs in empirical cost analyses.

Special problems of retail cost analysis

Each of the four problems mentioned above applies to the analysis of retailing costs as well as to those of other industries. The first two, however, – measurement of size and estimation of costs – are peculiarly complicated in the retail field.

Measurement of size of a firm for the purposes we are considering is probably best done in terms of units of physical output. In retailing, however, the outputs are services, and these are almost impossible to measure in real units. Also, differences between firms in the quantity and quality of services rendered make interfirm comparisons difficult. One solution has been to measure dollar volume of sales, which assumes that there is a more-or-less standardized bundle of services associated with each dollar of sales, or number of transactions, which makes the same assumption with respect to each transaction. In some cases, gross margin has been used as a measure of output (Hall and Knapp, 1955 [Reading 15]; 1957; Pollard and Hughes, 1955a and b). The usefulness of any one of these measures depends upon the variability in services rendered with respect to sales, transactions, or margins.

The estimation of costs and their interpretation in relation to output are extremely complicated in retailing. This arises from the fact that a large portion of the retail firm's costs of operation is 'selling costs', in contrast to 'production costs'. Production costs are those incurred to meet a given demand. Selling costs are those incurred to change the position and/or slope of the demand curve.[4]

Joel Dean has pointed out the problems of cost analysis which arise from the relative importance of selling costs in the total budget of the retail firm (1942a) [Reading 12]. If costs are incurred to change demand, then we must say that a part of the output of retailing is the change in demand. This practice, identified with monopolistic competition, may repre-

4. The importance of this phenomenon in retailing is illustrated by data from department stores reporting to the National Retail Merchants' Association for 1957. Sales people's salaries and advertising represented 25–34 per cent of the gross margin of department stores of six size groups (1958, pp. 37, 63, 89, 115, 141, 167). While sales people's salaries are only partly 'selling' costs in the sense in which we define them, they are partially that, and advertising expenditures are almost totally selling costs. To the extent that retail firms are engaged in the production of 'selling' services, and to the degree that there are differences between firms in the quantity and quality of these services, homogeneity in output is lacking, and problems are created in cross-sectional comparisons.

sent a service for which consumers are willing to pay. Margaret Hall has interpreted its prevalence as evidence of a willingness on the part of the consumer to surrender his control over demand by submitting to the indoctrination of advertising, thereby making it unnecessary to make his own decision (1949, pp. 76–8). Whether seller-imposed in an imperfect market or demanded by consumers, such practices create an intermingling of costs and revenue which greatly complicates the determination of optimum size.

One relevant cost element is absent from retail accounting data. These are consumer buying costs which may vary from firm to firm, depending upon the extent to which marketing functions are performed by the consumer or by the retailer. Suppose, for example, that a small retail firm services a small trading area and minimizes transport costs for customer shopping and retail delivery costs for merchandise sold. It is possible that the firm may show high operating costs relative to sales because of its small scale of operations but that the total marketing cost to the consumer is lower than is indicated by the firm's operating cost ratio. This is probably not so serious an analytical problem for the firm as for the store, however. A firm can decentralize its local outlets in order to achieve optimum customer buying costs. Interstore comparisons, on the other hand, may embrace these differences in the allocation of marketing functions.

Conclusions concerning empirical cost analysis

Given these rather serious criticisms of empirical cost analysis, is it possible to make sufficient adjustments in our data or analytical methods to permit the use of empirical cost data in the analysis of firm size? Or should such analyses be considered too useless to aid in the formulation of either private or public policy?

It would appear that certain adjustments can be made in the data or in the analytical procedure which would make possible some useful interpretations of empirical costs. Cost estimation can be improved by the use of engineering cost data. Where accounting data must be used, their bias toward higher or lower cost elasticities should be recognized in interpreting the observed relationships. Homogeneity of firms can be controlled to some extent by the choice of criteria for the universe to be studied. Finally, the effects of the regression fallacy can be minimized by substituting time-series analysis for cross-sectional analysis, thus showing the movement of a firm or sample of firms toward an optimum. Borts (1960) has also employed analysis of variance as a check on the error introduced by the regression fallacy. Specifically, he has stratified sixty-one railway firms by region and by size. For each class size, he has computed marginal cost, average cost, and elasticity of cost. Marginal cost and elasticity of cost between size classes have also been computed to determine the presence of the regression. Thus, while the problem is not eliminated, some estimate of its size is obtained.

The limitations of available data and the problems of interpretation make it absolutely necessary that empirical analysis be undertaken with considerable caution. Friedman (1955), who has been particularly sensitive to the problems of empirical cost analysis, proposes that we concern ourselves not with the question of what size firm has minimum costs but with the question of what effect changes in various market circumstances would have upon the size distribution of firms. What effect, for example, would a change in the availability of investment capital have upon the size of firms? Or what is the probable effect of changes in the supply of goods in wholesale markets upon the size of firms in retail markets? Similarly, Stigler (1951), by focusing upon cost relationships within vertically related firms as the industry of which they are a part experiences expansion or contraction of its market size, has pointed to the importance of examining shifting cost relationships as demand changes.

Keeping in mind the limitations of accounting data and their bias toward elasticity-coefficients different from those which would obtain were the data what our theory assumes, and focusing upon the interrelations of costs, we believe that cross-sectional cost analysis makes it possible (1) to obtain crude approximations of the optimum size or sizes of retail firms, (2) to observe the shifting relationships among various cost components as the size of firms varies, and (3) to compare cost structures and estimated optimum size among retail firms handling quite different types of merchandise. Because of the analytical problems, we shall be concerned primarily with the *directions* in which cost structures shift or differ rather than with the absolute or relative levels of those structures and shall regard our findings concerning optimum size as suggestive rather than definitive.

2 Procedure

We shall describe the nature of our data, their limitations and their statistical treatment.

The data

The Internal Revenue Service of the United States Treasury Department publishes annually certain selected statistics from a sample of corporation income-tax returns (1959, 1960a and b). Most of the data for this study were taken from the report for the fiscal year 1956–7 (1959, pp. 50–53). All corporations reporting for that year were grouped by the Internal Revenue Service into three groups on the basis of net income. A sample was selected from each of the three groups and certain statistical data from

Table 1 **Condensed operating statement of all reporting retail corporations and source of data, 1956–7**

Item	Amount ($000s)	Source
Gross sales and gross receipts from operations*	98,377,830†	Given
Cost of goods sold and of operations	73,521,313‡	Given
Gross margin	24,856,517	Computed
Operating expenses	23,800,514	Computed
Net operating profit	1,056,003	Computed
Other income	1,461,760	Computed§
Compiled net profit	2,517,763	Given

* Gross sales, less returns and allowances, were reported when inventories were an income-determining factor. Gross receipts from operations were reported when inventories were not an income-determining factor.

† Of this amount, $881,214,000, or 0·9 per cent, were gross receipts from operations which were not based on inventories.

‡ Of this amount, $351,212,000, or 0·5 per cent, were cost of operations related to receipts which were not related to inventories.

§ Computed from total compiled receipts (given) *minus* gross sales plus gross receipts (given).

this sample were published. Sampling rates prescribed were 1·00 for those with sales of $1,000,000 or more, 0·20 for those with sales of $100,000 to $1,000,000, and 0·10 for those with sales of less than $100,000. Sampling rates actually achieved were 1·00, 0·18, and 0·09, respectively (1959, p. 4).

For corporations in the sample, data are summarized for selected items of the balance sheet and operating statements and reported for industries and certain subgroups within those industries. Retail-trade corporations are classified as food, general merchandise, apparel and accessories, furniture and house furnishings, automotive dealers and filling stations, drug, eating and drinking, building materials and hardware, and other. By imputation, it has been possible to reconstruct from the data reported the essential elements of the operating statement – that is, gross sales, cost of goods sold, gross margin, operating expenses, net profit – of corporations in each of the nine groups and for all retail corporations combined as well as for corporations of different asset sizes within each of these groups (see Table 1).

Summary data from the operating statement for 1956–7, plus the reported capital stock and surplus from the balance sheet, are the basis for this analysis. In addition, comparable statistics reported by retail food and general merchandise corporations for 1957–8 (1960a, p. 56) were also analysed to determine whether the observed cost-revenue relationships were stable over a two-year period.

Limitations of the data

Certain limitations are inherent in the data employed, and these are important in the choice of method of statistical treatment and in the interpretation of findings. We shall consider these in two groups: (1) characteristics of the sample, and (2) the form in which operating data were reported.

1. *Characteristics of the sample.* It is difficult to arrive at a theoretically satisfactory definition of a firm which is unambiguous empirically. The problem is particularly apparent when published reports of the Internal Revenue Service are used.

In the first place, detailed operating data were reported for corporations only. Summary statistics for proprietorships and partnerships as well as corporations were reported for the first time for 1957–8 (1960b, pp. 7, 11, 14). In that year corporations represented only 9 per cent of the total number of retail firms reporting. Of the 1,983,494 retail firms reporting, 77·6 per cent were proprietorships and 13·4 per cent were partnerships. However, corporations accounted for 52·6 per cent of the $199,533,238,000 gross sales reported, while proprietorships accounted for 33·4 per cent and partnerships for only 14 per cent. If comparable ratios for 1956–7 were about the same, we are dealing in this study with only about one-half the gross retail sales for that fiscal year and are restricting our attention to corporations, with large corporations sampled at a disproportionately high rate.

Second, while our data include information for corporations only, all such firms are not necessarily comparable in an economic sense. The small corporation may function much as a small partnership or proprietorship. If, for example, there is a melding of family and business activities in the small corporation, with heavy withdrawals of income or assets by owner-managers, the firm's objective and the criteria by which its owners judge its success will be quite different from those which we assume dominate decisions in the larger corporate enterprise. These small firms could have been eliminated from our analysis of interfirm differences had we known the nature of their behavior and the size groups into which they fall. In the absence of an objective basis for such exclusion, we have made calculations for all corporations for which data were reported. However, the possibility of this distinctive form of business behavior should be taken into account when examining the experience of small firms.

Third, the problem of identifying and comparing comparable firms is aggravated by consolidated financial reports in published data of the Internal Revenue Service. Since 1947, corporations have been allowed to submit consolidated returns where certain conditions of interfirm relationship existed. For the year 1956–7, a single income-tax return could be submitted for two or more corporations if (a) the parent corporation owned at least 80 per cent of each class of nonvoting stock, excluding preferred stock, of at least one member of the group, or (b) these same proportions of stock of each other member of the group were owned within the group (1959, p. 5).

The trade group, consisting of both retail and wholesale corporations, submitted 286,252 returns for the year 1956–7. Of these, 826, or 0·289 per cent, were consolidated returns, representing 2,806 subsidiaries. Although such returns were a small percentage of the total, they may have distorted the comparability of reports for firms of different sizes. It is probable that consolidated returns were more frequent for large firms. Moreover, changes from year to year in the legal requirements for such reporting would limit possibilities for achieving comparability of size classifications through time.

2. *The form in which operating data were reported.* While reports of the Inland Revenue Service contain considerable detail, they involve classifications and consolidations which complicate the analysis.

First, the operating statement for reporting corporations had to be reconstructed from reported data in the manner described in Table 1 for all retail corporations. The computation of gross margin was, of course, straightforward. Other income was computed by subtracting gross sales and gross receipts from total compiled receipts. This estimation made possible the computation of operating expenses and net operating profit. The accuracy of this imputation procedure depends upon the precision and consistency of classification by the reporting corporations and upon the accuracy with which we have interpreted the definitions of categories as reported by the Internal Revenue Service.

Second, published data of the Internal Revenue Service were for firms grouped according to total assets, and this made impossible the estimation of statistical cost functions from individual observations. Estimating equations fitted to grouped data do not differ in any systematic way from equations fitted to ungrouped data. For this reason, we have not attempted to derive statistical cost functions but have instead utilized cruder estimates of elasticity.

Third, the groups varied considerably in the number of firms reporting. An average for one group may have represented three thousand corporations, while that for another group may have been based on the experience of only two or three firms. Some of the cells for the largest firms were very thinly populated, reducing the reliability of estimates for firms of these sizes.

The extent of this problem is indicated in Table 2 where the number of corporations reporting is indicated for each of the nine types of retail firms. There were fewer than ten firms in several of the cells used in this study. In these size groups, cost and sales experience peculiar to a single firm could have had considerable influence on the average studied. This limits our confidence in the generality of the cost-revenue relationships found for such firms in a single year. Additional observations are possible only by using data for more than one year. Where numbers of firms are small, therefore, it is particularly useful to determine whether the relationships observed show stability through time so long as the additional influences related to time itself can be effectively isolated.

Another limitation of our data concerns the basis upon which groups were established for the published reports. Size classifications were based upon the volume of assets. Since sales rather than assets appeared to be the better basis for identifying the size of retail firms for purposes of cost analysis, the asset groupings were used as a crude basis for achieving a sales stratification.

Some aspects of the relationship between sales and assets are suggested by Table 2 in which the average gross sales of corporations in each of the fourteen asset sizes are given, along with the average assets reported for each group. When the group means of assets and sales were plotted on double logarithmic paper, a marked linear relationship was apparent. The table indicates roughly an equal rate of change for the two variables. The most conspicuous exceptions were small furniture and house-furnishings corporations whose asset size increased more rapidly than sales up to about $150,000 total assets, automobile dealers and filling stations in the asset sizes from about $250,000 to $10,000,000 within which increasing volume of assets was associated with a lower than average rate of sales increase, and eating and drinking and 'other' retail corporations which showed somewhat greater irregularity in the asset-sales relationship than did other types.

These data suggest that the use of total assets as a basis for stratification by size yields results not greatly unlike those which would have occurred had sales volume been used as the basis for classification. Ungrouped data might, however, produce different results, and this inference from the data at hand can only be tentative.

Data treatment

Operating statements have been reconstructed for the nine types of retail corporations in accordance with the procedure described in the section

Table 2 **No. of retail corporations of various types and gross sales and total assets per corporation computed from reports to Internal Revenue Service, July 1956–June 1957**

Type of retail corporation and item	Total	Under $25 (Group 1)	$25 and under $50 (Group 2)	$50 and under $100 (Group 3)	$100 and under $250 (Group 4)	$250 and under $500 (Group 5)	$500 and under $1000 (Group 6)
Total retail trade:							
No. of corporations	157,543	38,392	31,245	34,540	34,141	11,429	4754
Average gross sales ($000s)	624	57	113	212	462	1051	2067
Average assets ($000s)	223	13	36	71	157	343	682
Food:							
No. of corporations	11,531	3437	2220	2027	2192	851	355
Average gross sales ($000s)	2154	86	201	398	826	1657	3244
Average assets ($000s)	433	13	35	72	158	349	697
General merchandise:							
No. of corporations	8400	1506	1539	1800	1842	702	393
Average gross sales ($000s)	2337	33	93	173	358	739	1438
Average assets ($000s)	1217	10	36	72	159	352	707
Apparel and accessories:							
No. of corporations	20,643	4379	5426	5300	3753	986	442
Average gross sales ($000s)	326	42	90	157	335	685	1394
Average assets ($000s)	154	14	37	71	152	340	690
Furniture and house furnishings:							
No. of corporations	15,142	3329	2654	3359	3867	1165	514
Average gross sales ($000s)	278	51	111	183	291	524	934
Average assets ($000s)	162	12	36	71	155	341	669
Drug:							
No. of corporations	6292	1478	2193	1691	698	113	48
Average gross sales ($000s)	334	64	115	199	374	889	2180
Average assets ($000s)	119	16	36	69	148	331	707
Building materials and hardware:							
No. of corporations	19,201	2717	3072	4748	5695	2006	633
Average gross sales ($000s)	326	45	88	155	310	692	1364
Average assets ($000s)	167	14	36	72	160	343	682
Automotive dealers and filling stations:							
No. of corporations	28,032	4074	3289	6113	8780	3519	1665
Average gross sales ($000s)	851	92	172	324	719	1637	3053
Average assets ($000s)	200	12	37	73	160	346	678
Eating and drinking:							
No. of corporations	19,996	10,006	4621	3169	1628	351	147
Average gross sales ($000s)	172	57	105	199	374	818	1317
Average assets ($000s)	64	13	35	69	151	343	670
Other:							
No. of corporations	28,306	7466	6231	6333	5686	1736	557
Average gross sales ($000s)	259	45	97	171	346	724	1379
Average assets ($000s)	120	13	36	71	154	337	672

Total assets per corporation (000's)

$1000 and under $2500 (Group 7)	$2500 and under $5000 (Group 8)	$5000 and under $10,000 (Group 9)	$10,000 and under $25,000 (Group 10)	$25,000 and under $50,000 (Group 11)	$50,000 and under $100,000 (Group 12)	$100,000 and under $250,000 (Group 13)	$250,000 or more (Group 14)
2054	510	252	150	32	19	16	9
3987	7739	15,880	35,037	83,263	182,291	289,384	1,727,426
1483	3447	6875	15,802	34,859	67,892	141,079	543,901
273	70	56	29	8	6	4	3
7412	13,480	26,413	62,824	130,679	348,604	453,574	2,567,045
1523	3352	6874	15,664	34,821	70,720	114,410	396,584
316	120	78	56	20	11	11	6
3093	6732	13,145	28,641	66,745	107,130	236,869	1,307,617
1578	3591	6892	16,010	34,612	68,443	153,412	617,560
232	75	27	18	3	2		
3062	6502	15,941	37,564	62,661	96,738		
1503	3458	6602	17,466	34,688	56,383		
183	39	20	12				
1798	4490	7542	22,047				
1426	3517	7460	15,979				
32	22	8	8	1			
4614	9765	21,303	40,629	96,084			
1605	3270	6981	16,594	40,630			
260	53	14	3				
2455	5502	8962	16,042				
1460	3311	6424	13,591				
497	73	16	5			1	
5330	8680	9746	23,221			210,288	
1426	3315	6292	12,572			112,094	
41	14	12	7				
3647	10,999	13,591	27,654				
1519	3641	6980	15,557				
220	44	21	12				
2563	5424	14,334	17,180				
1456	3535	6866	14,001				

above, and these have been converted into ratios of sales. In addition, profit ratios have been computed in relation to capital stock and surplus. Finally, crude elasticity coefficients have been computed showing relative changes in (1) gross margins and sales, (2) cost of goods sold and sales, (3) operating expenses and sales, (4) compiled net profits and sales, and (5) compiled net profits and capital stock and surplus.

Where cost- or profit-elasticities were computed with respect to sales, we have used sales volume as a measure of quantity of output. This was necessary because we do not have available information on physical units of output in retailing.

Elasticities computed are arc elasticity coefficients. They represent the estimated elasticities of a straight-line relationship between the average of two groups of firms classified by asset size. For example, Table 5 (see below) shows that firms in asset-group 6 had average sales of $1·4 million in 1956–7 and those in asset-group 7, $3·1 million. Table 6 (see below) indicates that the average elasticity for operating expenses with respect to sales for these two asset groups was 1·019 in that year. This means that the average firm whose sales increased from about $1·4 million to $3·1 million

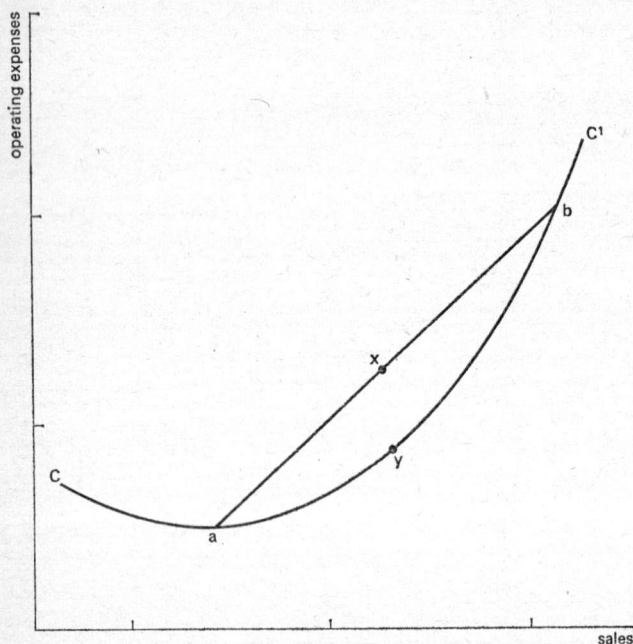

Figure 2 Computation of operating expenses for point and arc elasticity coefficients

experienced an increase in operating expenses of 1·019 per cent for each 1·000 per cent increase in sales. Similarly, a firm whose sales decreased from $3·1 million to $1·4 million had, on an average, a 1·019 per cent decrease in operating expenses with each 1·000 per cent decrease in sales. We have 'centered' this elasticity coefficient at a sales volume of $2·3 million, midway between the average sales of each of the two sizes of corporations.

This is a very crude elasticity coefficient. It embraces a $1·7 million average change in sales and does not show elasticity variations which may have existed within that sales range. Suppose, for example, that the cost curve between $1·4 million and $3·1 million sales appeared as in Figure 2. The average elasticity coefficient which we have computed in our example is for a sales volume of $2·3 million, midway between $1·4 million (a) and

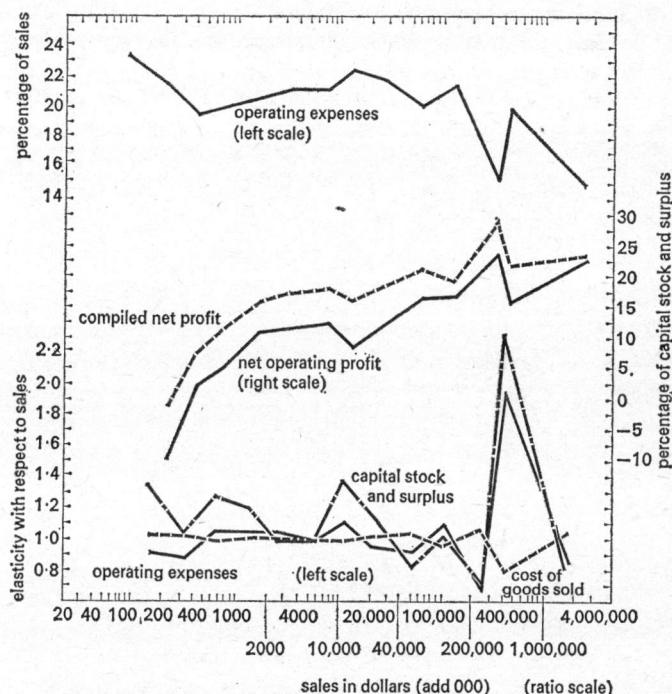

Figure 3 Retail food corporations: operating expenses as percentage of sales; net operating profit and compiled net profit as a percentage of capital stock and surplus; and elasticity of cost of goods sold, operating expenses, and capital investment with respect to sales, 1956–7

$3·1 million (b). It is the elasticity at x rather than at y on the operating cost curve.

The alternative to the estimation of such crude elasticity coefficients would have been the fitting of mathematical curves to the original observations and the determination of point elasticities. This was not done because the data reported by the Internal Revenue Service were grouped and not amenable to the precise derivation of estimating equations. We have already pointed out the tendency for accounting data to yield elasticities which are higher or lower than they would be if *ex ante* cost data were utilized. By using grouped data and computing arc elasticity coefficients, we have added further to this tendency. In addition, the breadth of sales brackets employed in the grouping of data prevents the precise identification of the sales volume to which the computed coefficients should be imputed. For these reasons, our estimates are only approximations of the elasticities in which we are interested.

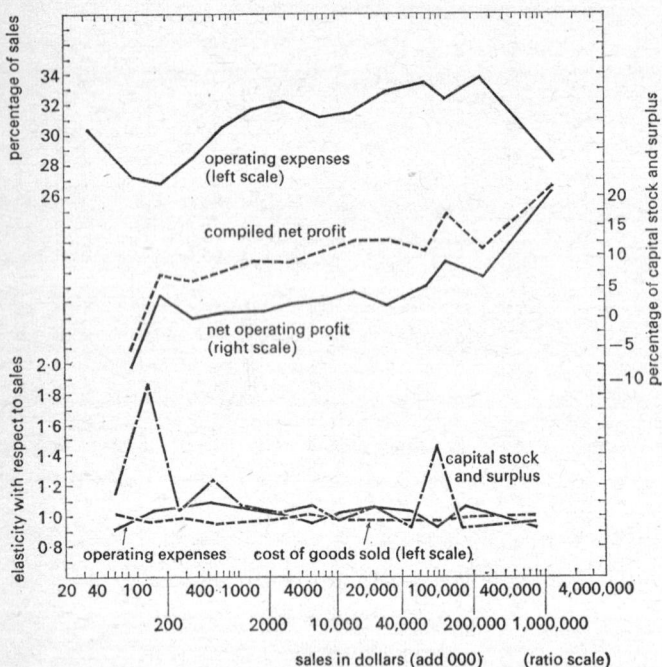

Figure 4 Retail general merchandise corporations: operating expenses as percentage of sales; net operating profit and compiled net profit as percentage of capital stock and surplus: and elasticity of cost of goods sold, operating expenses, and capital investment with respect to sales, 1956–7

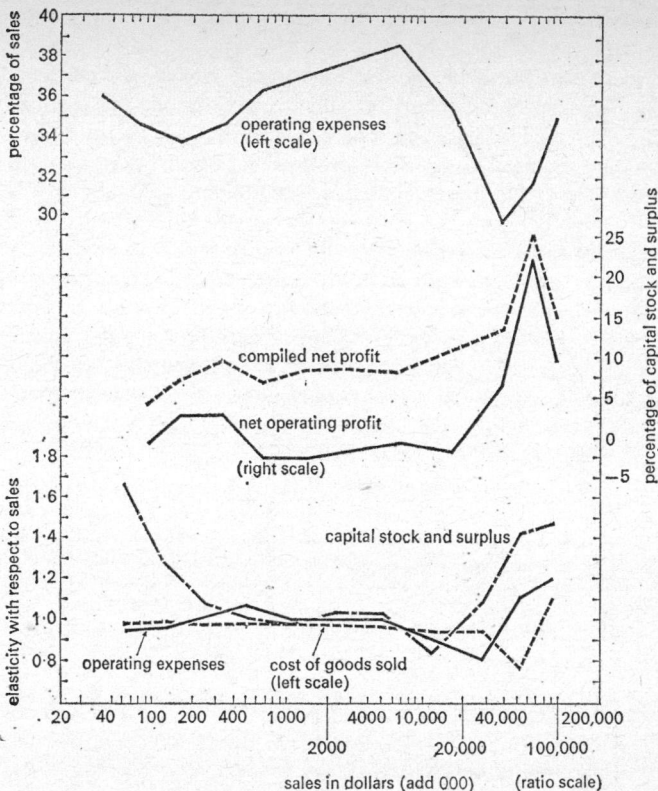

Figure 5 Retail apparel and accessories corporations : operating expenses as percentage of sales ; net operating profit and compiled net profit as percentage of capital stock and surplus ; and elasticity of cost of goods sold, operating expenses, and capital investment with respect to sales, 1956–7

3 Analysis of findings

Our computations yielded operating statements and elasticity coefficients for each of the nine retail trade groups and for all retail corporations for 1956–7. Because of the considerable detail involved, we have included summary tables of operating statements and elasticity coefficients for only retail food and general merchandise. We have extended the tables of elasticity coefficients to cover 1957–8 as well as 1956–7 (see Tables 3–6). For greater clarification of the relationships involved, we also give summary charts for five types of retail corporations for 1956–7: food, general

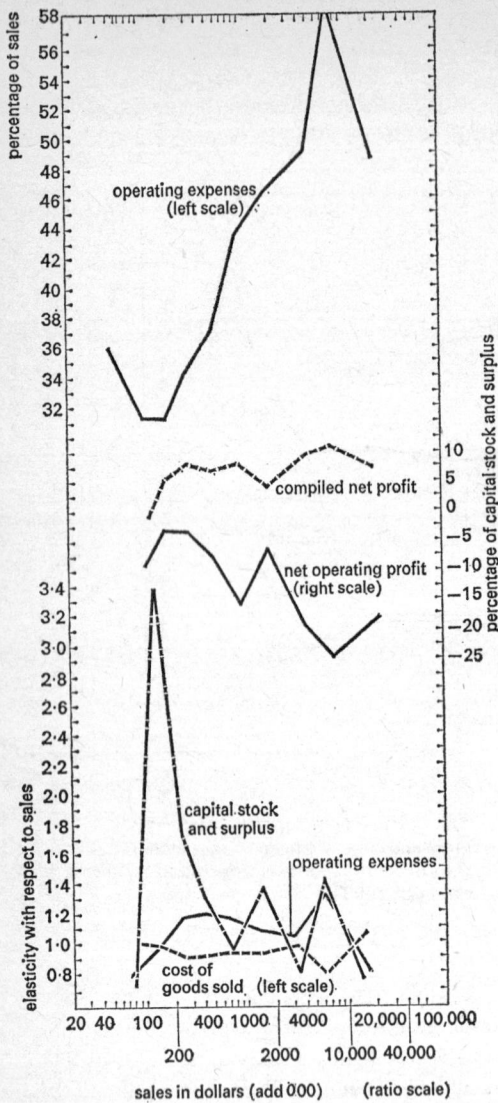

Figure 6 Retail furniture and house furnishings corporations: operating expenses as percentage of sales; net operating profit and compiled net profit as percentage of capital stock and surplus; and elasticity of cost of goods sold, operating expenses, and capital investment with respect to sales, 1956–7

merchandise, apparel and accessories, drug, and furniture and house furnishings. Each of these charts shows (1) operating expenses as a percentage of gross sales, (2) elasticity coefficients at various sales levels for cost of goods sold, operating expenses and capital investment, and (3) net operating profit and compiled net profit as a percentage of capital invest-

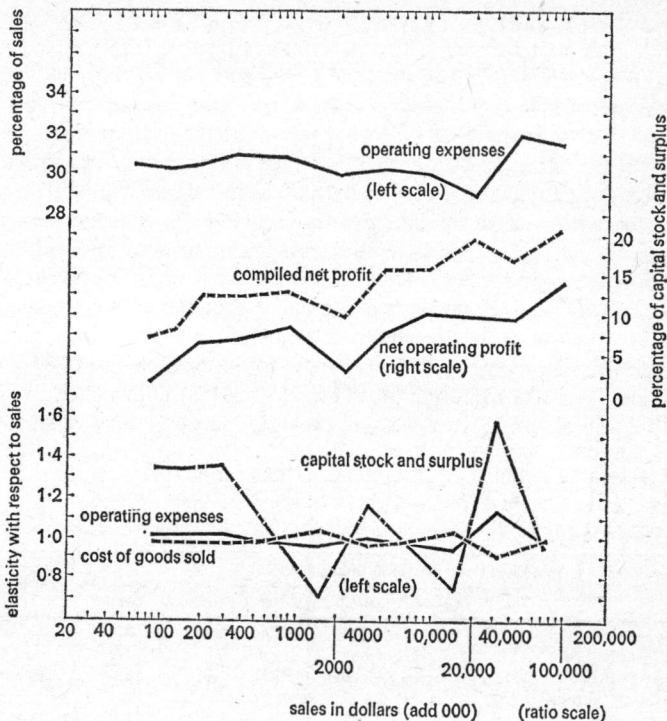

Figure 7 Retail drug corporations : operating expenses as percentage of sales ; net operating profit and compiled net profit as percentage of capital stock and surplus ; and elasticity of cost of goods sold, operating expenses, and capital investment with respect to sales, 1956–7

ment (see Figures 3–7). We have also included some statements of findings concerning other types of retail corporations not included in the tables and charts shown here. Finally, there are two summary tables which identify the sales volume at which each of the elasticity coefficients reached its lowest point and at which the ratio of profits to capital investment was highest (Tables 7 and 8).

Interpretation of results

We can illustrate the interpretation of our results by using retail food corporations as an example. From Table 3 we see that the average retail food corporation whose assets were between $500,000 and $1,000,000 had sales in 1956–7 of $3,244,000 and a capital investment of $354,000. Their gross margin was 22·36 per cent of sales, average expenses 21·10 per cent, and average compiled net profit 1·90 per cent. Total profit was 17·37 per cent of capital stock and surplus. Table 4 compares firms of this particular group with those immediately above and immediately below it in size. Firms just below it in size – that is, those whose assets were $250,000 to $500,000 – had average sales of $1,657,000 in 1956–7 (from Table 3). Table 4 tells us that in that year when firms moved from asset-group 5 to asset-group 6, each 1·000 per cent increase in sales had associated with it 1·031 per cent increase in operating expenses, 0·991 per cent increase in cost of goods sold, and 0·988 per cent increase in capital stock and surplus. This is an average percentage increase between these two sales levels for this year, and we have 'centered' this average at the sales volume midway between $1·7 million and $3·2 million, or $2·45 million.

What do these elasticity coefficients mean? In the example just cited, we can say that when a corporation moved from the $1·7 million sales group to the $3·2 million group, its operating expenses increased *more* relatively

Table 3 **Operating statement and capital stock and surplus of retail food corporations imputed from reports to Internal Revenue Service, July 1956–June 1957**

| Item | Total assets per corporation (000s) | | | | | | |
	Total	Group 1*	Group 2	Group 3	Group 4	Group 5	Group 6
No. of corporations	11,531	3437	2220	2027	2192	851	355
Average gross sales per corporation ($000s)	2154	86	201	398	826	1657	3244
Capital stock and surplus per corporation ($000s)	233	5	15	30	78	183	354
Gross sales : capital stock + surplus	9·26	18·96	13·56	13·23	10·58	9·08	9·16
Percentage of gross sales :							
Cost of goods sold	79·85	77·69	79·39	80·39	79·35	78·16	77·64
Gross margin	20·15	22·31	20·61	19·61	20·65	21·84	22·36
Operating expenses	18·49	23·41	21·34	19·45	20·07	20·63	21·10
Net operating profit	1·66	−1·10	−0·73	0·16	0·58	1·21	1·26
Other income	0·45	0·30	0·63	0·40	0·55	0·52	0·64
Compiled net profit	2·11	−0·80	−0·10	0·57	1·13	1·73	1·90
Percentage of capital stock and surplus							
Net operating profit	15·40	−20·87	−9·89	2·17	6·10	10·93	11·50
Compiled net profit	19·55	−15·12	−1·32	7·43	11·97	15·69	17·37

than did its sales. On the other hand, its cost of goods and capital investment increased relatively less than sales. Table 3 further reveals to us that the *net* effect of these combined changes was probably favorable *to the firm,* for the compiled net profit increased from 15·69 per cent of capital investment to 17·37 per cent. If the sales movement were in the opposite direction, from $3·2 million to $1·7 million, operating expenses decreased relatively more than did sales, while cost of goods sold and capital investment decreased relatively less than sales.

If we are seeking efficiency, we shall prefer elasticity coefficients as low as possible as we move from smaller to larger sizes, and the point at which the coefficient is lowest will represent the 'best' size for the performance of that particular phase of the firm's operation within the size brackets embraced by high coefficients which precede and follow the low coefficient. For example, if we examine operating expense coefficients for retail food corporations in 1956–7, we find in Table 4 that between sales volumes of about $10 million and $100 million, elasticity coefficients fell from 1·101 to a low point of 0·917 for firms with sales of about $50 million. Beyond $50 million, the coefficient rose to more than 1·000. Within this size range, firms of about $50 million appeared to have the most advantageous operating costs in that year. This was also true in 1957–8.

But within this size range, we find that elasticity coefficients for cost of goods sold were lowest for the very small firms (about $10 million sales) or the very large firms (about $100 million sales) but higher for intermediate

| Total assets per corporation (000s) | | | | | | | |
Group 7	Group 8	Group 9	Group 10	Group 11	Group 12	Group 13	Group 14
273	70	56	29	8	6	4	3
7412	13,480	26,413	62,824	130,679	348,604	453,574	2,567,045
801	1858	4134	8348	17,671	34,504	64,546	231,077
9·25	7·26	6·39	7·53	7·40	10·10	7·03	11·11
77·62	76·41	76·35	77·70	76·33	82·35	77·85	83·12
22·38	23·59	23·65	22·30	23·67	17·65	22·15	16·88
21·03	22·43	21·78	20·10	21·44	15·31	19·90	14·85
1·35	1·16	1·87	2·20	2·23	2·34	2·25	2·03
0·59	1·03	0·96	0·58	0·39	0·52	0·78	0·06
1·94	2·19	2·83	2·78	2·62	2·86	3·03	2·09
12·50	8·45	11·95	16·56	16·49	23·64	15·78	22·60
17·98	15·89	18·09	20·94	19·36	28·84	21·27	23·32

* Asset groups identified in Table 2.

Table 4 Arc sales and net investment elasticity coefficients for retail food corporations reporting to Internal Revenue Service, July 1956–June 1957, and July 1957–June 1958

Item and year	Groups 1 and 2*	Groups 2 and 3	Groups 3 and 4	Groups 4 and 5	Groups 5 and 6	Groups 6 and 7	Groups 7 and 8	Groups 8 and 9	Groups 9 and 10	Groups 10 and 11	Groups 11 and 12	Groups 12 and 13	Groups 13 and 14
Average gross sales ($000s):													
1957	144	300	612	1242	2451	5328	10,446	19,947	49,619	96,752	239,642	401,089	1,510,310
1958	145	298	634	1304	2499	5296	11,540	22,162	45,497	96,774	224,088	409,080	1,643,192
Elasticity coefficients:†													
Gross margin and sales:													
1957	0·915	0·967	1·029	1·077	1·032	1·001	1·082	1·003	0·939	1·074	0·728	1·837	0·894
1958	0·962	0·880	1·001	1·057	1·143	1·013	0·858	1·140	1·021	0·941	0·830	1·344	0·923
Operating expenses and sales:													
1957	0·901	0·872	1·039	1·036	1·031	0·996	1·101	0·959	0·917	1·080	0·685	1·963	0·882
1958	0·933	0·883	0·938	1·032	1·154	1·002	0·869	1·119	0·960	0·964	0·819	1·316	0·921
Cost of goods sold and sales:													
1957	1·023	1·018	0·985	0·979	0·991	1·000	0·975	0·999	1·018	0·978	1·065	0·788	1·023
1958	1·010	1·024	1·001	0·985	0·960	0·996	1·038	0·961	0·994	1·017	1·041	0·912	1·018
(Operating expenses + cost of goods sold) and sales:													
1957	0·996	0·989	0·996	0·991	0·999	0·999	1·003	0·990	0·988	1·000	0·999	1·004	1·001
1958	0·993	0·995	0·988	0·994	1·001	0·997	1·003	0·994	0·987	1·006	1·001	0·987	1·001
(Capital stock + surplus) and sales:													
1957	1·329	1·033	1·268	1·198	0·988	0·989	1·368	1·172	0·827	1·022	0·710	2·318	0·805
1958	1·576	0·944	1·197	1·186	1·102	0·974	1·024	1·400	1·004	0·629	1·096	1·387	0·811
Compiled net profit and (capital stock + surplus):													
1957	−1·039	3·531	1·385	1·267	1·140	1·038	0·866	1·142	1·187	0·903	1·513	0·526	1·054
1958	−1·732	2·916	1·973	1·172	1·015	1·083	0·988	1·009	1·390	0·912	1·107	0·678	1·060

* Asset groups identified in Table 2.

† The elasticity of gross margin relative to sales is computed by the formula:

$$E_{gm,s} = \frac{(GM_2 - GM_1)/(GM_1 + GM_2)}{(S_2 - S_1)/(S_1 + S_2)},$$

in which $E_{gm,s}$ = the elasticity of gross margin with respect to sales, GM = gross margin, and S = gross sales. Subscript 2 is for the group with the larger average sales volume and subscript 1 for the group with the smaller average sales volume. All other elasticity coefficients are computed by similar methods.

sizes in 1956–7. This was reversed in 1957–8, with firms of intermediate sizes, particularly those of about $20 million sales volume, showing the lowest cost of goods elasticities. Capital elasticities were lowest for the $50 million firms in 1957–8, and for the $100 million firms in 1957–8.

Our elasticities do not enable us to compare operating experience of corporations of one size with that of firms of greatly different sizes but merely of firms of adjacent sizes. Elasticities which show continuously falling and then rising values can establish the size limits within which decreasing and increasing costs are being experienced for that segment of the retail corporations of that type. The lowest coefficient identifies the most efficient size for that function within that particular range of sizes.

The elasticity coefficient of capital investment with respect to sales warrants special comment. We have not attempted to estimate 'cost' of capital but have assumed that the relative amount of capital is an accurate indication of cost. This assumption may be incorrect for several reasons. In the first place, there may be economies (or diseconomies) to scale in the acquisition of capital, while our assumption implies that these do not exist. Further, there may be differences between firms in the amount of risk associated with each dollar of investment. This is of particular importance in evaluating return on capital investment. Two firms with the same capital stock and surplus may have quite different asset structures. If one retail firm, for example, has a portion of its assets in real property, while another has an equivalent portion in larger inventories, the risk on these two may not be the same. Because of greater risk, the return on investment may be larger for the firm which owns its own buildings. Our analysis assumes equivalent risk and may not, therefore, represent the situation accurately. A third qualification concerns the possibility that a part of the cost of capital is in the form of debt. There is evidence that this is true for firms of certain sizes.[5] A better measure of the cost of capital would be:

$$\text{Cost of capital ratio} = \frac{\text{profit} + \text{interest}}{\text{long-term debt} + \text{stockholders' equity}}.$$

The measure which we employ here excludes both interest and long-term debt as elements in the cost of capital ratio.

A single cost is not, however, the most important thing to consider. It is the combination of costs – cost of goods sold plus operating expenses plus cost of capital – which constitutes the basis for overall efficiency, for a

5. For example, bonds and mortgages payable for all active retail corporations combined ranged between 4·1 per cent and 14·3 per cent of long-term debt plus stockholders' equity, with larger percentages in firms of medium and very large size and smaller percentages in small and large corporations. Computed from United States Treasury Department (1959, p. 50).

firm may often substitute one cost for another. Therefore, the total operation is the basis upon which overall efficiency must be judged. Table 7 shows that retail food corporations had their highest profit ratio at $349 million sales in 1956–7 and that this was related to favorable operating expense and capital investment elasticity coefficients with respect to sales.

We have used profits as an indication of overall efficiency. This raises interesting and important questions concerning evaluation of a firm's operations. Our choice of criteria will depend in part upon our orientation – that is, whether we are considering the objectives of the firm or the objectives of society. We shall concern ourselves at this point with the objectives of the firm and shall explore questions concerning the social implications of our findings at a later point.

Are profits an adequate indication of efficiency from the firm's point of view? While economic theorists have traditionally accepted profit maximization as the objective of the firm, a considerable body of literature has challenged the reality of this objective. William Baumol (1959), for example has suggested that, instead of profit maximization, we should consider an objective of maximum dollar sales subject to a minimum profit constraint. Others have suggested that stability, survival, security, size of firm and

Table 5 Operating statement and capital stock and surplus of retail general merchandise corporations imputed from reports to Internal Revenue Service, July, 1956–June, 1957

Item	Total assets per corporation (000s)						
	Total	Group 1*	Group 2	Group 3	Group 4	Group 5	Group 6
No. of corporations	8400	1506	1539	1800	1842	702	393
Average gross sales per corporation ($000s)	2337	33	93	173	358	739	1438
Capital stock and surplus per corporation ($000s)	836	4	12	44	95	235	481
Gross sales : Capital stock +surplus	2·80	9·24	7·64	3·92	3·79	3·14	2·99
Percentage of gross sales :							
Cost of goods sold	65·19	72·74	73·82	72·20	71·44	69·20	67·87
Gross margin	34·81	27·26	26·18	27·80	28·56	30·80	32·13
Operating expenses	30·81	30·48	27·18	26·83	28·54	30·54	31·73
Net operating profit	4·00	−3·22	−1·00	0·97	0·02	0·26	0·40
Other income	1·78	0·62	0·43	0·88	1·60	2·23	2·75
Compiled net profit	5·78	−2·60	−0·57	1·85	1·62	2·49	3·15
Percentage of capital stock and surplus :							
Net operating profit	11·19	−29·93	−7·69	3·80	0·07	0·83	1·19
Compiled net profit	16·16	−24·13	−4·37	7·27	6·15	7·82	9·42

* Asset groups identified in Table 2.

psychic income may be equally important objectives of corporate entrepreneurs.[6] If, however, we concern ourselves with the question, not of entrepreneurial objectives, but of how management would judge the efficiency with which it uses the resources at its disposal, we are justified in accepting the profit–capital ratio as indicative of operating efficiency, and we shall do so in the analysis of these data.

Findings

Observation of average operating ratios and of cost elasticity coefficients for nine types of retail trade and for all types combined reveals certain significant facts concerning the size of retail corporations.

1. Operating expenses are not alone a sufficient basis for judging efficiency in retailing. Although often used as a measure of efficiency, operating costs should be evaluated in combination with buying costs and capital investment. Our data do not, however, permit the separate analysis of selling costs and consumer buying costs.

Furniture and house-furnishings corporations were an unusually interesting case in which operating expenses were an inadequate indication of profitability. Figure 6 shows that expenses as a percentage of sales rose with increasing volume of sales except for the very smallest and very largest firms. Table 8 further indicates that the points of largest compiled net profits were associated with favorable elasticities for cost of goods sold

Total assets per corporation (000s)							
Group 7	Group 8	Group 9	Group 10	Group 11	Group 12	Group 13	Group 14
316	120	78	56	20	11	11	6
3093	6732	13,145	28,641	66,745	107,130	236,869	1,307,617
1042	2043	4612	10,497	22,604	46,025	94,854	470,780
2·97	2·80	2·85	2·73	2·95	2·33	2·49	2·78
67·00	67·62	66·95	66·29	64·73	63·66	63·41	63·68
33·00	32·38	33·05	33·71	35·27	36·34	36·59	36·32
32·24	31·31	31·56	32·92	33·54	32·38	33·94	28·55
0·76	1·07	1·49	0·79	1·73	3·96	2·65	7·77
2·37	2·83	2·98	3·90	2·02	3·32	1·89	0·55
3·13	3·90	4·47	4·69	3·75	7·28	4·54	8·32
2·27	3·01	4·24	2·16	5·11	9·20	6·61	21·57
9·29	10·95	12·74	12·80	11·06	16·94	11·32	23·11

6. See, e.g., Myrvoll (1948), Holbaeck-Hanssen (1960, pp. 75–6), and Boulding (1955, pp. 862–83).

Table 6 Arc sales and net investment elasticity coefficients for retail general merchandise corporations reporting to Internal Revenue Service, July, 1956–June, 1957, and July, 1957–June, 1958

Item and year	Groups 1 and 2*	Groups 2 and 3	Groups 3 and 4	Groups 4 and 5	Groups 5 and 6	Groups 6 and 7	Groups 7 and 8	Groups 8 and 9	Groups 9 and 10	Groups 10 and 11	Groups 11 and 12	Groups 12 and 13	Groups 13 and 14
Average gross sales ($000s):													
1957	63	133	266	548	1088	2266	4912	9938	20,893	47,693	86,938	172,000	772,243
1958	71	134	269	548	1067	2143	4596	10,071	22,292	46,667	85,962	175,929	787,942
Elasticity coefficients:†													
Gross margin and sales:													
1957	0·955	1·108	1·033	1·099	1·056	1·032	0·978	1·028	1·023	1·047	1·061	1·008	0·997
1958	0·942	1·116	1·056	1·090	1·017	1·053	0·980	1·031	0·963	1·116	1·047	1·010	0·998
Operating expenses and sales:													
1957	0·900	1·016	1·060	1·089	1·050	1·019	0·966	1·011	1·049	1·019	0·928	1·053	0·931
1958	0·758	1·087	0·978	1·130	1·076	0·995	1·047	1·025	0·990	1·060	0·953	1·050	0·937
Cost of goods sold and sales:													
1957	1·016	0·960	0·987	0·957	0·974	0·984	1·011	0·986	0·988	0·975	0·966	0·995	1·002
1958	1·013	0·952	0·992	0·961	0·993	0·974	1·009	0·985	1·018	0·939	0·974	0·994	1·001
(Operating expenses + cost of goods sold) and sales:													
1957	0·984	0·975	1·007	0·997	0·998	0·996	0·996	0·994	1·008	0·990	0·953	1·015	0·979
1958	0·940	0·991	0·988	1·013	1·020	0·981	0·992	0·998	1·009	0·980	0·966	1·014	0·980
(Capital stock + surplus) and sales:													
1957	1·147	1·888	1·043	1·228	1·068	1·010	1·066	0·976	1·050	0·916	1·469	0·919	0·959
1958	1·780	1·420	1·032	1·186	0·979	1·170	1·070	0·932	1·009	1·047	1·325	0·896	0·971
Compiled net profit and (capital stock + surplus):													
1957	0·418	2·900	1·608	2·198	1·249	0·993	1·168	1·211	1·006	0·822	1·508	0·458	1·234
1958	−1·234	+3·327	2·259	0·952	0·120	1·643	0·867	1·338	0·995	1·047	1·268	0·691	1·318

* Asset groups identified in Table 2.

† See n. †, Table 4.

Table 7 **Levels of sales (in millions of dollars) at which selected cost factors were inelastic and net profit ratios were high, retail food and general merchandise corporations, 1956–7 and 1957–8**

Item	Food 1956–7	Food 1957–8	General merchandise 1956–7	General merchandise 1957–8
Sales volumes at which elasticity coefficients were low:*				
Cost of goods and sales	1·2	2·5	0·1	0·1
	10·5	22·2	*0·5*	0·5
	96·8	*409·1*	9·9	2·1
	401·1		86·9	10·1
				46·7
Operating expenses and sales	0·3	0·3	4·9	0·3
	5·3	11·5	*86·9*	2·1
	49·6	45·5	772·2	22·3
	239·6	*224·1*		86·0
	1510·3	1643·2		787·9
(Capital stock + surplus) and sales	2·5	0·3	9·9	1·1
	49·6	5·3	47·7	10·1
	239·6	96·8	172·0	*175·9*
	1510·3	1643·2		
Sales volumes at which ratios of compiled net profits to (capital stock + surplus) were high,† and variables‡ associated with each, ranked in order of importance§	7·4	7·3	1·4	0·4
	Capital	Capital	Goods	Expense
	Expense	Goods		Goods
	62·8	62·4	28·6	2·9
	Capital	Expense	Goods	Goods
	Expense	Goods		Expense
				13·8
	348·6	*317·0*	107·1	Capital
	Expense	Expense	Expense	Goods
	Capital		Goods	Expense
	2,570·0	2,785·3	*1307·6*	109·3
	Capital	Capital	Expense	Expense
	Expense	Expense	Capital	Goods
				1333·4
				Capital
				Expense

* Sales volumes identified are those at which elasticity coefficients reached a low point and were less than 1·000. Sales volumes of less than $100,000 are not considered. The lowest coefficient occurred at sales volumes indicated by italics.

† Sales volumes identified are those at which compiled net profit ratios reached a high point. The sales volume with the highest ratio is indicated by italics. Since all computations are based on group averages, it should be noted that the sales figures used to identify points of high profits are not exactly the same as those used where sales volumes are related to elasticity coefficients. Figures in the net profit row are derived from operating data for a single group of retail firms, and the sales volume given is the average of that one group. Elasticity coefficients, however, are related to the midpoints between two groups of retail firms, and the sales volumes identified are the average sales of the two groups.

‡ Expense = operating expenses; Goods = cost of goods sold; Capital = capital investment.

§ Based on elasticity coefficients less than 1·000, ranked by size of deviation from 1·000.

in smaller firms, and capital investment, in larger firms. There is, however, another important facet to the profit position of these firms. Figure 6 reveals that corporations of all sizes had a negative operating profit, while compiled net profit, which includes 'other income', became positive after sales of about $150,000. 'Other income' averaged 15·2 per cent of the gross margin of these corporations.

What is the nature of this 'other income' which is obviously of so much importance to the profitability of retail furniture and house-furnishings corporations? While details reported by the Internal Revenue Service do not indicate precisely the source of this portion of total income, it would appear that at least a part may have been interest and other charges for credit extended. Notes and accounts receivable at the end of the fiscal year were 46·4 per cent of the total liabilities of furniture and house-furnishings corporations and 27·1 per cent of sales during the year. No other type of retail firm had such high ratios. Comparable percentages for food firms were 11·2 per cent of liabilities and 2·2 per cent of sales; for building materials and hardware, 31 per cent of liabilities and 15·9 per cent of sales. It is probable, therefore, that the financing function of furniture and house-furnishings firms is implied in these data. It is necessary that all sources of profit be considered in evaluating a firm's efficiency.

2. In only a few cases did low coefficients occur at the same sales volume for cost of goods sold, operating expenses, and capital investment. Sometimes the operating expense coefficient was high while the capital investment coefficient was low. At some sales volumes buying advantage was dominant while expense and investment coefficients were far less favorable. These shifting coefficients give some insight into the nature of resource substitution in retailing. Increased capital investment may make possible operating efficiencies which are reflected in lower operating costs. Or perhaps by increasing operating expenses, it may be possible to lower the cost of goods sold.

Inverse relations between these coefficients were particularly apparent among firms with large sales volume.[7] The diverse movements of the three sets of coefficients focuses attention upon the range of substitution possibilities in the operation of the firm and upon the importance of the firm's *total* operation. The large retail corporation has a wide range of substitution possibilities, because the total resources allocated to any one phase of its operations are large enough to make additions or subtractions to one allocation economical. Capital investment can rarely be increased by one

7. Because there were fewer very large firms and because they were more likely to be highly integrated, it is possible that some of the cost data were spurious, resulting in synthetic coefficients.

Table 8 Levels of sales (in millions of dollars) at which various types of retail corporations broke even, had low elasticity coefficients for selected cost factors, and had high net profit ratios, 1956–7

Item	Type of firm — Total*	Apparel and accessories	Furniture and house furnishings	Drug	Building materials and hardware	Automotive and filling stations	Eating and drinking places	Other
Sales volume at break-even point, based on compiled net profit	0·075	0·075	0·150	†	0·125	0·525	0·075	0·075
Sales volumes at which elasticity coefficients were low:‡								
Cost of goods and sales	5·9	0·2	0·2	0·2	0·5	9·2	0·2	0·5
	59·2	4·8	1·4	0·3	1·9		7·3	2·0
	235·8	50·1	6·0	3·4				9·9
				31·0				
Operating expenses and sales	0·2	0·1	0·1	1·5	0·1	0·2	0·3	0·3
	25·5	26·8	15·0	15·5	7·2	16·5	1·1	1·1
	132·8			68·4			12·3	4·0
	1008·4							
(Capital stock + surplus) and sales	0·8	1·0	0·7	1·5	0·5	16·5	7·3	9·9
	132·8	11·2	3·1	15·5	4·0			
	1008·4		14·8	68·4	12·5			
Sales volumes at which ratios of compiled net profits to (capital stock + surplus) were high§ and variables¶ associated with each ranked in order of importance‖	182·3 Expense Capital	0·3 Goods	0·3 Goods	0·9 Expense Goods	16·0 Capital	23·2 Capital Expense Goods	11·0 Capital Goods	14·3 Capital Goods
	1727·4 Capital Expense	62·7 Goods	0·9 Goods Capital	21·3 Capital Expense				
			22·0 Capital Expense	96·1 Capital Expense Goods				

* Includes food and general merchandise corporations detailed in Table 7 plus firms of the seven types detailed in this table.

† Average corporations of all groups showed a positive profit rate.

‡ See Table 7, n. *.

§ See Table 7, n. †.

¶ See Table 7, n. ‡.

‖ See Table 7, n. §.

dollar or even one hundred dollars at a time. The large firm is in a position to make economical additions to a selected cost because even a large addition will be a relatively small percentage of the total cost.

Food corporations provide examples of this. Large profits in food retailing were associated with favorable elasticity coefficients for capital investment and operating expenses and unfavorable coefficients for cost of goods sold. It is possible that margins were narrowed for competitive reasons, thereby increasing the ratio of cost of goods to sales, but at the same time resulting in increased sales without a commensurate increase in operating expenses or investment because of such things as more intensive use of physical plant and labor.

The large firm is also able to use resources in distinctive ways to build a corporate 'image'. There may be economies to scale in this phase of retailing which manifest themselves, not in the relative level of costs, but in the relative level of the cost-revenue relationship. The small number of firms in the larger sizes makes the achievement of distinction easier. Thus, the cost structure of the firm reflects not only the outlays necessary to perform routine retailing functions but also those incurred to achieve corporate differentiation. It is possible that our averages conceal some of these inter-firm differences among large corporations.

3. While there was an optimum size, as measured by return on capital investment, for each of the nine types of retail firms studied, there were also other sizes of high relative efficiency (see Tables 7 and 8). There is, in fact, an interesting similarity between the short-run and long-run cost relationships of economic theory and those implied by our three cost estimates and the logarithm of sales (see especially Figures 3–7).

Because accounting records modify the cost relationships which would obtain were purely *ex ante* costs utilized, and because we are using grouped data and arc elasticity coefficients, it is likely that the curvature of our implied functions is not exactly the same as it would have been for functions consistent with those of the economic theory of the firm. If we assume that retail corporations typically operate under conditions of monopolistic competition with excess capacity, we would expect our empirical results to relate most often to the left side of the short-run cost curve. It has already been indicated that on this portion of the curve, the short-short-run cost curve described by accounting data would show greater inelasticity than would be true were *ex ante* costs used. Therefore, to the extent that the data used in this study relate to this portion of the short-run cost curve, we have undoubtedly overstated the slope. On the other hand, this is partially compensated for by the dampening effects of grouped data and arc elasticity coefficients.

4. It would appear that there are economies to scale in retailing but that in many lines the most efficient size is less than the largest which existed. In four lines, the largest corporations reported the highest profit ratio relative to capital: building materials and hardware, general merchandise, furniture and house furnishings, and drug. In all others – food, apparel and accessories, eating and drinking, automobile and filling stations, and other – the largest corporations had lower profit ratios than corporations of somewhat smaller size.

5. The most profitable firms varied in size from one line of trade to another. The most profitable general merchandise corporations were very large – over $1·5 billion sales. The most profitable food corporations had less than $0·5 billion in sales. Next were the medium-sized corporations – apparel and accessories and drug – with 'best' sizes of about $50–$100 million. Finally, the other types – furniture and house furnishings, building materials and hardware, automobiles and filling stations, eating and drinking, and others – tended to be small with maximum profits at sales volumes of $10–$25 million.

The basic nature of retailing is clearly revealed in these data. Retailing is an operation which is highly dispersed geographically. There is a limit to the optimum size of a given store in terms of accessibility of the store and its merchandise to customers. Large firms may develop, however, in those merchandise lines where multistore ownership and/or vertical integration offer sufficient economies or other marketing advantages. The differences in optimum size which we have noted would seem to be related to the extent to which the particular line of business would or would not lend itself to economies related to specialized management, standardization of merchandise and operating procedure, skill and scale in buying, and relative sales appeal of greater quality, price and stock diversification. It is interesting that the only type of firm which reached its maximum profit at a sales volume greater than $1 billion was characterized by the greatest amount of merchandise diversification.

6. It is not surprising that highest profit ratios were most often associated with favorable capital investment elasticity coefficients since profit ratios are stated in terms of capital investment. Nevertheless, an interesting exception appears. High profit ratios in apparel and accessories corporations were in each instance associated with favorable cost-of-goods-sold coefficients. Such firms apparently had strong buying advantages.

When profits were associated with low investment coefficients, the fact suggests a more intensive use of capital. A low coefficient means that the proportionate increase in amount of invested capital is less than the proportionate increase in sales revenue. There are, however, a few cases in

Tables 7 and 8 where large profits were associated with favorable expense or cost of goods coefficients rather than with low investment coefficients. For example, the maximum profit ratio for food corporations occurred at a sales volume of approximately $350 million. While both operating expense and capital coefficients were below 1·000 at this point, the operating expense coefficient was the more favorable. A high cost-of-goods coefficient would be reflected in lower margins, but these low margins were more than offset by efficiency in the use of capital and by low operating costs. Similarly, profits of general merchandise firms with sales of about $100 million were associated with advantageous operating expense and cost-of-goods-sold coefficients, reflecting a more extensive use of capital but with compensations in expenses and margins.

7. We can also observe differences among our nine types of retail firms in the stability of the elasticity coefficients at various levels of output. The two with the most stable coefficients were apparel and accessories and building materials and hardware. Firms with moderate fluctuations were drug, food and other retail corporations. The four types with rather great variations were general merchandise, furniture and house furnishings, eating and drinking, and automobile dealers and filling stations. Variations were greatest in capital investment coefficients.

These shifting investment coefficients suggest that there is a lumpiness in the capital-investment volume in most trades. We can illustrate this by examination of the elasticity coefficients for medium and large food firms in 1956–7 (see Table 4). At particular sales volumes, investment elasticity coefficients were extremely high: $10·5 million, 1·368, and $401·1 million, 2·318. Similar peaks occurred in 1957–8 at sales volumes of $22·2 million and $409·1 million. To move from sales of about $5 million to $10 million in 1957 required a considerable increase in capital investment. Additional increases in sales beyond that point were possible with much smaller additions to capital. Expansion from $240 million to $400 million, however, called for another wave of capital investment. These patterns indicate that scale of operations in retailing is closely tied to the volume of capital required to sustain a given volume of sales.[8]

If return on capital investment is accepted as an appropriate measure of efficiency in retailing, and if our observation of a lumpiness in the amount of capital investment required as volume of sales increases is accurate, we can conclude that additional investment in the retail firm is justified (a) if the firm is able to move quickly over the 'hump', where the investment-elasticity coefficient is high, to a greater volume of sales where the mar-

8. It is appropriate at this point to reiterate one aspect of the procedure used in this study. Firms in this study were scaled according to total assets, and sales volumes were assumed to be reflected proportionately.

ginal investment is not so great as the marginal sales, or (b) if the additional investment with a high elasticity coefficient makes possible a more than compensatory reduction in the elasticity coefficient for cost of goods or operating expenses.

Variations in capital investment coefficients from year to year suggest, however, that the relationship of this variable to sales should be examined over a period longer than one year. Not only is this cost factor a reflection of long-run expectations, but the value of capital stock and surplus from which our elasticities were computed is a book value which may not indicate accurately short-run market conditions. Additional aspects of this problem are discussed in the section which follows in which we consider year-to-year changes in elasticity coefficients.

8. There was considerable stability in the sales volumes at which food and general merchandise corporations experienced maximum profit ratios and lowest cost elasticities between 1957 and 1958 (see Table 7). Profit ratios for food firms were highest at sales volumes between $300 million and $350 million in both years, and in both years operating expense elasticities were quite low at this volume. Similarly, general merchandise firms with sales volumes of $1·3 billion had the highest profit ratios in both years, and in both years operating expenses and capital showed favorable elasticities at this volume. Other sales volumes at which profit ratios peaked were similar in the two years, with some differences apparent among smaller general merchandise firms.

While the elasticity coefficients for food corporations were remarkably stable from one year to the next, some interesting differences did occur. Among middle-sized firms, some of the low coefficients showed an upward drift to firms in the next size bracket (see Table 4). For example, a low operating expense coefficient was apparent in 1957 at a sales volume of $5·3 million. The low in 1958 was at $11·5 million. A low cost of goods sold coefficient was at $10·5 million in 1957 but at $22·2 million in 1958. A high capital stock and surplus coefficient at sales of $10·5 million in 1957 had shifted to $22·2 million in 1958, while the 1957 low at sales of $49·6 million had shifted to $96·8 million in 1958. But the largest three asset groups did not show similar shifts.

These movements toward larger-sized optima were occurring in a period of increased concentration in food retailing (1960). It would be valuable to examine similar data for other years during this entire period of increased concentration to determine if elasticity measures could throw light on some of the conditions related to the changing size of firm.

Another factor which might account for year-to-year differences in cost elasticities is the possibility that certain allocations may be determined on the basis of long-run rather than short-run conditions. This would be particularly true of capital stock and surplus which represents long-term investment which may not bear any reasonable relationship to the sales experience of a single year. There is, in fact, considerable difference in capital stock and surplus elasticities of the food corporations reporting for the two years. If firms were acquiring additional stockholders' equity for purposes of long-run expansion which had not yet resulted in increased sales, the capital elasticity would be high for that year. Other firms which were reducing surplus to maintain dividends during a period of lower profits would have shown a low elasticity. Just as there are substitution possibilities for a firm within a given year, substitutions may also be made between years. Overexpansion in one phase of operations in one year may stimulate management to compensate through greater control in a succeeding year. As we have indicated, short-short-run elasticities may differ from short-run elasticities, and short-run elasticities will be quite different from those of the long run.

General merchandise corporations showed fewer differences in elasticity coefficients from one year to the next than did food corporations (see Table 6). Again some drift to the next largest size was apparent for a few coefficients, but in general, absolute and relative levels were quite stable over the two-year period.

4 Summary and conclusions

We have reviewed the problems of analysing accounting cost data and have concluded that such analysis can be useful if the data are sufficiently refined, if the tendency toward over- or underestimation of the true coefficients is recognized, and if the deviation of actual experience from optimum experience at a given level of output can be estimated. Such analyses are particularly useful in identifying the directions in which change will occur and in indicating the internal reallocation of resources as firms experience growth. It is the direction of change and the nature of internal readjustments which have been the focal points of this study of the structure of costs in retail corporations.

On the basis of data of the Internal Revenue Service, we have analysed operating costs, cost of goods sold, capital investment and profits of nine types of retail corporations of varying sizes. Using profit ratios in relation to capital investment as the measure of firm efficiency, we have identified the sales volume at which firms showed greatest efficiency and have related those points of efficiency to cost of goods sold, operating expenses and capital investment. We have also computed three series of arc elasticity coefficients at different levels of output.

Implications for the firm

Our findings have important policy implications for retail firms. They show the existence of profit-related substitution possibilities in the use of resources in the three broad categories of activities we have examined. The relative importance of these cost elements varies at different levels of output. There is some evidence that the short-run cost curves and long-run envelope curves described in economic theory are appropriate for retail trade, though the imperfections and crudeness of our data do not make it possible for us to describe these curves mathematically. Retailing appears to be an industry of decreasing costs up to a point. In some lines of trade it appears that the largest corporations in our study were less profitable than firms which were somewhat smaller. The most profitable sales volume varied rather markedly among firms of different organizational or merchandise types.

Social implications

Are there social implications in these findings? To maximize consumer welfare, firms must not only operate at the point of greatest efficiency, but the benefits of that efficiency must be transmitted to consumers through prices or qualitative means of consumer compensation. The behavior of firms must result in efficient resource allocation.

Profit ratios alone are not a sufficient basis for evaluating firm size from a social point of view. As an example, of the nine types of retail trade examined here, we have found five – food, apparel and accessories, eating and drinking places, automobile and filling stations, and 'others' – in which the largest corporations did not have the highest profit–capital ratio. From this it might seem that the largest firms were, on an average, too big for maximum efficiency. We cannot, however, make such a statement on the basis of our data alone. Large firms may be able to obtain capital on better terms as a result of efficiencies that are socially acceptable, or they may be providing a substantially different package of goods and services entailing lower profit ratios but no less desirable performance. In the long run, or at least through a complete business cycle, their profit ratios might actually be higher than those of smaller firms even though they were lower in the two-year period studied.

Dynamic considerations may also qualify the significance to consumers of profit ratios at any point in time. If they are rooted in imperfect or monopolistic market situations, high profits represent a misallocation of resources. On the other hand, if they are short-term returns to more efficient operations in an adjusting market situation, they may foreshadow long-run social benefits as competitive adjustments are effected. It is possible that in a highly competitive market situation, small profit margins may be associated with vigorous price competition which accrues to the consumer's benefit. But it is also possible that they reflect over-investment in the industry. These diverse social meanings which may attach to a given profit ratio impel us to be cautious in interpreting empirical profit data in terms of consumer welfare.

A full social appraisal of the retail structure would require study of the competitive structure of retail markets and its impact upon the behavior of firms, as well as more precise measurement of such things as capital costs, output and the utility or disutility to consumers of the firm's selling activities. It is within this broader context that public policy should be formulated concerning such questions as increases in concentration and integration in retailing.[9] Known relationships between cost elements and size of firm, as described here, are a part of the economic intelligence needed to formulate sound public policy in marketing.

9. See for example, the recent report of the Federal Trade Commission on concentration and integration in food marketing (1960).

References

BAIN, J. S. (1954), 'Economies of scale, concentration, and the condition of entry in twenty manufacturing industries', *Amer. econ. Rev.*, vol. 44, pp. 15–39.

BAIN, J. S. (1959), *Industrial Organization*, Wiley.

BAKKENIST, S. C., and BEUTICK, D. E. (1957), 'An investigation into the costs of distribution in the grocery retail trade in the Netherlands', European Productivity Agency, *Productivity meas. Rev.*, special no., July.

BARGER, H. (1955), *Distribution's Place in the American Economy since 1869* Princeton University Press.

BASS, F. M. (1956), 'Expense and margin functions in drug stores', *J. Marketing*, vol. 20, pp. 236–41.

BAUMOL, W. J. (1959), *Business Behavior, Value and Growth*, Macmillan.

BELLAMY, R. (1946a), 'The changing pattern of retail distribution', *Bull. Oxford Univ. Inst. Stats.*, vol. 8, pp. 237–60.

BELLAMY, R. (1946b), 'Private and social cost in retail distribution', *Bull. Oxford Univ. Inst. Stats*, vol. 8, pp. 345–51.

BELLAMY, R. (1946c), 'Size and success in retail distribution', *Bull. Oxford Univ. Inst. Stats*, vol. 8, pp. 324–39.

BLAIR, J. M. (1948), 'Technology and size', *Amer. econ. Rev.*, vol. 38, pp. 121–52.

BORTS, G. H. (1960), 'The estimation of rail cost functions', *Econometrica*, vol. 28, pp. 108–31.

BOULDING, K. E. (1955), *Economic Analysis*, 3rd edn, Harper & Row.

BREMS, H. (1952), 'A discontinuous cost function', *Amer. econ. Rev.*, vol. 42, pp. 577–86.

BRESSLER, R. G., Jr (1945), 'Research determination of economics of scale', *J. farm Econ.*, vol. 17, pp. 526–39.

CHAMBERLIN, E. H. (1948), 'Proportionality, divisibility and economies of scale', *Q. J. Econ.*, vol. 62, pp. 229–62.

CHAMBERLIN, E. H. (1949), 'Reply' (to comments of A. N. McLeod and F. H. Hahn), *Q. J. Econ.*, vol. 63, pp. 137–43.

COHEN, L. (1952), 'Costs of distribution in department stores', *Manchester Sch. Econ. and soc. Stud.*, vol. 20, pp. 139–73.

DEAN, J. (1942a), 'Department store cost functions', in O. Lange *et al.*, *Studies in Mathematical Economics and Econometrics*, University of Chicago Press, pp. 222–54.

DEAN, J., and JAMES, R. W. (1942b), *The Long-Run Behavior of Costs in a Chain of Shoe Stores: A Statistical Analysis* ('Studies in business administration', vol. 12, no. 3), University of Chicago Press.

EITEMAN, W. J., and GUTHRIE, G. E. (1952), 'The shape of the average cost curve', *Amer. econ. Rev.*, vol. 42, pp. 832–8.

FRIEDMAN, M. (1955), 'Comment' (on paper by Caleb Smith) in Universities-National Bureau of Economic Research, *Business Concentration and Price Policy*, pp. 230–38, Princeton University Press.

GALBRAITH, J. K., and HOLTON, R. H. (1955), *Marketing Efficiency in Puerto Rico*, Harvard University Press.

HALL, M. (1949), *Distributive Trading: An Economic Analysis*, Hutchinson.

HALL, M., and KNAPP, J. (1955), 'Gross margins and efficiency measurement in retail trade', *Oxford econ. Papers*, vol. 7, pp. 312–26.

HALL, M., and KNAPP, J. (1957), 'Productivity in distribution with particular reference to the measurement of output', *Productivity meas. Rev.*, February, pp. 22–38.

HOLBACK-HANSSEN, L. (1960), 'Aktuelle problemstillinger og forskningsopgaver innen markeds og distribusjonsøkonomien', *Det Danske Marked*, vol. 19, pp. 72–84.

JEFFERYS, J. B., HAUSCHERGER, S., and LINDBLAD, G. (1954), *Productivity in the Distributive Trade in Europe*, Office of European Economic Cooperation, Paris.

JERVIS, F. R. J. (1953), 'Profits in large scale retailing', *Manchester Sch. Econ. and soc. Stud.*, vol. 21, May, pp. 165–75.

JOHNSTON, J. (1958), 'Statistical cost functions: a reappraisal', *Rev. Econ. Stats.*, vol. 40, pp. 339–50.

JOHNSTON, J. (1960), *Statistical Cost Analysis*, McGraw-Hill.

KRIER, J., and KRIER, H. (1954), 'Elements pour une théorie de la distribution', *Revue Economique*, pp. 342–71.

MCLEOD, A. N., and HAHN, F. H. (1949), 'Comments' (on paper by E. H. Chamberlin), *Q. J. Econ.*, vol. 63, pp. 128–37.

MCNAIR, M. P., and MAY, E. G. (1953), 'Department store expense control', *Harvard bus. Rev.*, vol. 31, pp. 113–27.

MOORE, F. T. (1959), 'Economies of scale: some statistical evidence', *Q. J. Econ.*, vol. 73, pp. 232–45.

MYRVOLL, O. (1948), 'The profit motive and the theory of partial equilibrium of the firm', reprint from *Nordisk tidsskrift for teknisk økonomi*, pp. 179–86.

National Bureau of Economic Research (1943), Conference on Price Research Committee on Price Determination, *Cost Behavior and Price Policy*.

National Retail Merchants' Association (1958), Controllers' Congress, *Departmental Merchandising and Operating Results of 1957*.

PLANT, A., and FOWLER, R. F. (1939), 'The analysis of costs in retail distribution', *Economica*, new series, vol. 6, pp. 121–55.

POLLARD, S., and HUGHES, J. D. (1955a), 'Retailing costs: a reply', *Oxford econ. Papers*, vol. 7, pp. 327–8.

POLLARD, S., and HUGHES, J. D. (1955b), 'Retailing costs: some comments on the census of distribution, 1950', *Oxford econ. Papers*, vol. 7, pp. 71–93.

Productivity Measurement Rev., 'Interfirm comparison in retail trade' (1959), European Productivity Agency, special no., September.

SMITH, C. A. (1955), 'Survey of the empirical evidence on returns to scale', in Universities-National Bureau of Economic Research, *Business Concentration and Price Policy*, pp. 213–30, Princeton University Press.

STIGLER, G. J. (1951), 'The division of labor is limited by the extent of the market', *J. polit. Econ.*, vol. 59, pp. 185–93.

United States Federal Trade Commission (1960), *Staff Report to the Federal Trade Commission: Economic Inquiry into Food Marketing*, Part 1: *Concentration and Integration in Retailing*, Government Printing Office.

United States Temporary National Economic Committee (1940), *Relative Efficiency of Large, Medium-sized and Small Business*, 'TNEC Monograph' no. 13, Government Printing Office.

United States Treasury Department, Internal Revenue Service (1959), *Statistics of Income, 1956–7: Corporation Income Tax Returns*, publication no. 16, Government Printing Office.

United States Treasury Department, Internal Revenue Service (1960a), *Statistics of Income 1957–8: Corporation Income Tax Returns*, publication no. 16, Government Printing Office.

United States Treasury Department, Internal Revenue Service (1960b); *Statistics of Income, 1957–8: U.S. Business Tax Returns*, publication no. 438, Government Printing Office.

VAILE, R. S., GRETHER, E. T., and COX, R. (1952), *Marketing in the American Economy*, Ronald Press.

VINER, J. (1931), 'Cost curves and supply curves', *Zeitschrift für Nationalökonomie*, vol. 3, pp. 23–46. Also in American Economic Association, *Readings in Price Theory*, Irwin 1952, pp. 198–232.

WALTERS, A. A. (1960), 'Economies of scale: some statistical evidence: comment', *Q. J. Econ.*, vol. 74, pp. 154–7.

WIEGMANN, F. H., CLIFTON, E. S., and SHEPHERD, G. (1955), *Comparison of Costs of Services and Self-Service Methods in Retail Meat Departments*, Research Bulletin 422, Iowa Agricultural Experiment Station.

14 C. Winsten and M. Hall

The Measurement of Economies of Scale

C. Winsten and M. Hall, 'The measurement of economies of scale', *Journal of Industrial Economics*, vol. 9, 1961, pp. 255–64.

1. In this paper we discuss a number of problems which arise in the attempt to assess the extent of economies of scale in an industry. The work was provoked by, and indeed partly comes from, a statistical study of the data collected in the various Censuses of distribution taken both in Great Britain and in the United States in recent years (Hall, Knapp and Winsten, 1961). Our quantitative findings are being published separately; here we restrict ourselves to some theoretical problems of interpretation. But because of the nature of our source of inspiration, our examples will be taken from the field of shops and distribution; they have the advantage of being familiar and also present interesting special problems. We found that the immense volume of data collected from many different trades, and covering a wide area, provided a fascinating challenge.

2. We have already published a discussion of the notion of efficiency in economics (Hall and Winsten, 1959), and it may be useful to take first an idea considered there.

Efficiency analysis is essentially a comparison of a range of entities which either exist or *could* exist. One does not always take one's standards from something that exists: sometimes one takes them from something that one merely judges as possible. Thus it is important to define in any particular investigation the group of real or possible entities which are allowed in the analysis; or, in other words, enter into the population. In defining this population one may also be defining the field of choice which is being considered as open to the units under study. Different investigators may have different ideas of the possible: i.e. of the opportunities open to the firms or units in mind. Such differences of judgment on the part of the analyst may have important effects on the statistical analysis, which thus may contain an element of the subjective, blended with its apparently objective form. It is thus important for the investigator to state his range of comparison as precisely as possible.

A second point, which arises in efficiency analysis, but is important here also, concerns the way we define the economic units which we are considering. In comparing different units, one must be quite sure what is being taken as the defining characteristic of the unit. We will take our example from distribution again; in fact it is in the econometric analysis of shops that the problem arises in its most obvious form.

At any one time a shop is a conjunction of a variety of elements and these may not stay together. There are: the firm – the legal entity, the managers, the technique used in running the shop, the site of the shop, its building, etc. (which may conceivably be included in the category of technique). These are different aspects, and as time goes on they may be separated from each other. An aggressive firm may move to a better site, yet still leave another firm to operate a shop on the old one. Or it may switch its technique at the old site – switching from counter-service to self-service for example. The management may or may not stay with the firm, or the shop. These and other examples emphasize that it is necessary to identify which aspect of the unit interests us. Of course it is possible to think of these different aspects as factors of production, but in the examples we have mentioned this does not seem a particularly constructive way of seeing the problem. We are not thinking of these factors being added at will to some productive unit apart from themselves, but rather of them as individual entities with some permanence through time, some particular one of which is taken, in fact, to define the unit. In a time-series analysis the importance of identifying these different aspects, as soon as mentioned, seems obvious. Cross-section studies, of the kind made on the basis of Census data, of a number of shops at the same time, do not call attention to this difficulty; but it is present, all the same. The problem is important because one has to interpret cross-section data in terms of response functions, as we shall see, and these will be different with the different definitions of unit. For example, the response of output to change of input with the site unchanged may be very different from that which is obtained when expansion takes place by moving to a more appropriate site. An analogous problem arises in the study of household budgets through time. Should a household be considered as associated with the 'head of the household', remaining the same unit as long as he is the same, or be associated with the same place of residence, or should it only continue to exist as long as the same people are together? The problem is often a difficult one. Here as in other places, economic problems have something in common with those of biology, where also the unit can be difficult to define. Since the nature of the response function affects the statistical interpretation of the data, so also must the definition of unit used.

3. We come now to the question of the different dimensions of scale. For the sake of definiteness we will, in what follows, think of the firm as being defined as a legal entity. Roughly these different dimensions can be classified as input dimensions and as output dimensions. Input dimensions are

such things as value of assets or size of labour force. But we are primarily interested in the different dimensions of output, since our study concerned the effects on its structure and productivity of the environment in which distribution is carried out. Dimensions of scale have often been enumerated, but usually without this distinction being made between input and output dimensions. We were, in our study, especially interested in the way enterprises adapt to the different calls on them occasioned by the different economic environments in which they find themselves. They partly adapt by adjusting their inputs to the job they want to do, i.e. their desired outputs. Thus measures of size by output would seem logically to have priority over measures of size by inputs.

The dimensions of scale of output along which a distributive unit can expand can be listed as follows:

(a) Turnover can increase, so that the unit or organization is performing more of its services per week (we might call this a greater intensity of output);

(b) The operations of the organizations may be carried out at more outlets (as when an independent shop expands to become a chain of shops);

(c) The range of operations may be widened, in the sense that the shop (or each shop of the chain) sells a wider range of goods. This is an aspect of scale that is quite prominent at the moment, as supermarkets, for example, carry ranges of goods not previously associated with grocery and in many specialists' trades the process of 'poaching', the selling of merchandise traditionally sold by another trade, is going on;

(d) The operations may be 'deepened' in the sense that the organization performs more of the services needed before the goods are consumed. A retail organization, for example, may do its own packaging, wholesaling or even manufacturing;

(e) A particular type of operation may be repeated more times. In manufacturing, production runs may be longer; in distribution, the same lines may be carried longer, with the consequent decrease in buying costs;

An aspect of scale which does not altogether fit in with those given above, but is nevertheless important is:

(f) The quantities actually bought at each transaction may be larger. This may occur either when consumers buy larger quantities of the same goods (bigger packets, for example) or more types of goods at the same time. Though it is arguable sometimes whether such a tendency increases or reduces the task performed by the retailer, this case can well be discussed under the heading of economies of scale, and can have an important effect. It is analogous to the making of a larger article in manufacturing.

C. Winsten and M. Hall 235

These are six of the dimensions of scale which can roughly be classified as scales of output. They can be combined amongst themselves in many different ways (in fact in $2^6 - 1$, i.e. sixty-three ways), and expansion will often occur along particular combinations of dimensions; for example, as a chain acquires more shops so it will tend to take over more of its own wholesaling. There are, however, other environmental factors which influence the task to be performed by the shop, but which perhaps just escape the classification as scale factors. One such is the time pattern of demand. Demand may be evenly spread or come in sharp peaks and troughs (at and between rush hours, for example). In the latter case, it may sometimes be possible to take advantage of 'economies of scale' at the peaks, without incurring corresponding losses in the troughs. Or, if, for example, the peaks and troughs are not predictable, uneven demand may lead to losses. Thus unevenness of demand is a subject close to that of economies of scale, but cannot be classified under the same head.

4. Now that we have roughly delimited what we mean (or rather, the many things we can mean) by scale of output, we must try to assess how important scale will be in determining the costs of operation. There are two ways of answering this question. The first is to study the theoretical advantages (and disadvantages) of large-scale operations. By this means we will be led to an idea of how, for example, an increase in the demand for goods from a shop might lead to a decrease in unit costs, if the management grasped the opportunities available to them. The second method is to examine the data concerning shops available from the censuses. Such data can help to answer a rather different sort of question: to what extent do economies of scale occur in practice?

Theoretical reasons for the existence of economies of scale in various types of economic organization have been thoroughly discussed in economic literature, from Adam Smith, through Babbage, to the more recent literature, of which Clark's *Economics of Overhead Costs* (1923) is a notable example. We will not list them here, but will interpolate two considerations which must be borne in mind in studying economies of scale by any means.

Firstly, the range of available techniques changes in the course of time, as do the range and price of equipment. Thus, there may be great potential economies of scale at one time and then, following the invention of new small-scale techniques, or the cheapening of previously expensive equipment, the potential productivity of the small unit may in part catch up on the larger. (This kind of thing happened in the transport industry in this country as road transport overtook rail, for example). Some such thing may happen in retailing in the future, for example as cheap automatic vending devices, suitable for use inside or outside shops, become available. In this field, as in all others, the potential economies of scale can change over time. The invention of the supermarket has certainly much increased the economies of large-scale operation in the grocery sector.

Secondly, the difficulty of the job done by an organization and the resources which have to be used to perform it must depend on the relationship of the organization to those whose work is similar or complementary. And it may well be that a series of organizations may cooperate so well that they achieve the efficiency of a large-scale operation; indeed, together they may hardly be distinguishable from a single coherent unit except in name and law. On the other hand, a large organization may easily be in the state where none of the departments knows much of what the others do, and there is little interchange between them of staff or ideas. In that case, it has very nearly broken down into its component organizations.

We come now to the problems of measuring economies of scale from census data. Such data only give a cross-section study at a particular time. Yet the relationships in which one is interested in economics are always those which are useful in describing and explaining the changes which take place from one time to another. Part of the problem will therefore be how far we can switch from cross-section studies to time-series relations. And part will be the question of indicators of input and output.

5. *The question of indicators.* The indicator to be used depends partly on the range of comparison of the study, including both the actual and potential units entering into the comparison, and also partly on the valuation to be used. In retail distribution there are a host of different services which are provided by a shop, and all of them could be considered as output. These services may be valued differently by different people. Thus if the relative proportions vary over the range of comparison, different people would have different ideas of relative output. Partly with this in mind, we restricted our range of comparison to fairly narrow limits: in fact to particular trade groups. Within such groups, the value of sales of a shop is roughly proportional to the volume of throughput, and we can take services as proportional to throughput. At the worst this imposes a valuation on services, but we think it is a valuation that gives a useful basis for discussion.[1] Of course there are other possible indicators of output: value added and gross margins are often used. If the range of comparison is sufficiently restricted, then these should be highly correlated with value of sales. If not, then all three have potential weaknesses: for example, value added may be affected by monopoly elements in pricing, sales are not affected by an increase of depth of task. Value added, although at first sight an attractive measure of output, involves, especially in retail distribution, the addition of the values of many different services. Yet different

1. However, the restriction of the range of comparison introduces an interesting statistical point, which will be noted in section 8 later.

people may value these services in different ways. Even if we could get a measure of each of these services directly we should still face the problem of bringing them to a common scale, an idea which involves valuing each of them. The value-added notion gives only one possible way of relating the valuations, that reached by the bargainings and frictions of the market, and it may in fact satisfy no individual member and thus may be irrelevant for any particular analysis.

As an indicator of input, we used persons employed. Here again there is an imposed valuation: each person is valued as equal to all others. The alternative might be to take wages as a valuation, though this can be just as arbitrary in many ways. Again we think that our valuation can form the basis of a useful discussion, though we would agree that others would too.

Once indicators (with their associated valuations) have been selected, it is still possible for units to differ in efficiency because of differences of inputs and of outputs not shown up by the indicators. They may, for example, be able to provide those services which are valued in a particular analysis as the same as others but are cheaper to provide, or use workers valued in the analysis as the same as others but cheaper to hire. These adaptations may sometimes explain the economies or diseconomies of scale we find, but the effects still exist, and should be measured. They are *not* explained away.

6. The data supplied by the census effectively give only the regressions of sales on labour, and labour on sales for particular trades. If we are willing to grant that labour is useful as the sole measure of input in distribution, and it is certainly the dominant one there, then we must question how much these regressions may tell us about economies of scale. Our primary interest is in how much an autonomous change in demand for the services of the industry will produce a change in productivity. It would thus appear at first sight that we are interested in the regression of labour on sales, the latter being the independent variable for changes through time.

But in looking at census data we are not looking at a time series, we are looking at a variety of units at the same time. And to interpret the results, we will have to have a theory of how these firms reached their relative positions on the scatter diagram of output against input. To do this we must take into account the possibility that each has in part adapted to its own peculiarities, as well as to the economic climate in which it finds itself, a climate which may be influenced by the numbers and behaviour of its competitors.

The first point has been discussed by one of us (Winsten, 1960). It is essentially related to the statistical theory associated with 'simultaneous equation' systems. If one thinks of each firm as having a characteristic production function, and supposes that those firms which are more efficient have higher production functions, they may adapt to these higher

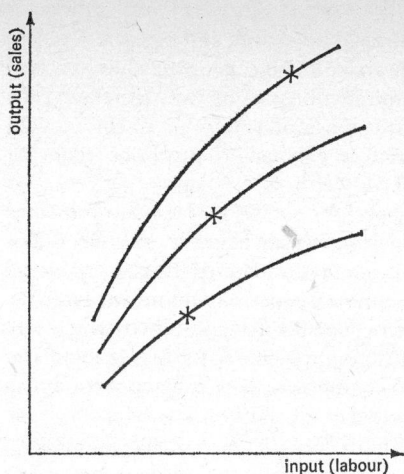

Figure 1

production functions by expanding more. This will give a tilt to the scatter diagram, exaggerating in the direction of greater economies, or less dis-economies, of scale. Simultaneous-equation theory usually assumes the firms have reached an equilibrium state. Even if they have not done so, however, we can often see what sort of qualitative effect a tendency for firms to adapt themselves in this way will have on the scatter diagram. The point is illustrated in Figure 1.

Something of the sort we have just described must surely go on, though the effect may not be too great in most trades. The market for most shops is limited and they cannot expand without incurring increasing costs, as they have to attempt to take custom from others fairly near them. These costs will, as we said above, depend on the number and actions of the competitors.

7. If we are interested in the responses in productivity of the whole trade (industry) to autonomous increases in demand, then the cross-section studies may underestimate possible economies for another reason. Since some of the costs of each firm are costs of competition, an autonomous increase in demand may give each unit access to new demand without incurring such costs. Thus it may raise the 'cross-section' production functions of many of the firms.

8. Not only this, however, but an autonomous increase in demand may bring new firms into the industry, and a decrease may remove old ones. A cross-section study only takes into account those firms that exist at the

time: it cannot in the nature of the case predict the new entrants, or those firms that may give up. Any inference from cross-section studies to time-series results will have to make allowance for this possibility. It will also have to guess whether the new entrants are more or less efficient on the average than the old. Moreover, the new entrants, being competitors with those already there, may depress their production functions again by causing them to incur extra costs of competition.

A similar point is one which is especially likely to arise when the range of competition is kept narrow. It may be that an efficient firm may find it best to expand in a way that takes it out of the scope of the comparison: a grocer may take on more lines and become a department store, for example. We do not think that this happens to a statistically important extent, at any rate over the fairly short run. But the point illustrates the disadvantages of too narrow comparisons. The best economies of scale may be those which involve a quite distinct change of nature of the unit.

9. We decided to examine the scatter diagrams for some trades in more detail, and obtained from the British Census authorities some special tabulations giving the complete scatter of sales and labour employed for some relatively homogeneous trades.[2] When we examined these, some surprising features emerged. If one examined the regression of output on input (the result was not very different if one took the regression of input on output) one usually obtained a line which showed large economies of scale at first, but then flattened off. This would at first sight accord with the *a priori* expectation that at small sizes an increase can greatly help specialization of labour: after a certain size has been reached there does not seem to be any great change in the way a shop is operated.

But if we look at the upper boundary of the scatter diagram, the result looks quite different (see Figure 2). In the cases we examined this showed a fairly steady *decline* in productivity as the size grew larger. Yet if we hoped to measure a 'best practice' line from actual data, it is to this upper boundary that we would look. And the usual theoretical discussion of 'best practice' hardly suggests such a result.

Two explanations suggest themselves. The most productive small shops usually have one immensely hard-working proprietor or manager. The smaller the shop, the more influence his work will have on its productivity. Also there are many more small shops than large ones. Thus from the small ones there is more chance that some will happen to find themselves in extreme conditions (of good site, and continuous demand, for example) that will give high productivity. This latter explanation becomes less convincing when one remembers that the larger shop can bid itself into the good positions.

2. These detailed figures are published in Hall *et al.*, 1961.

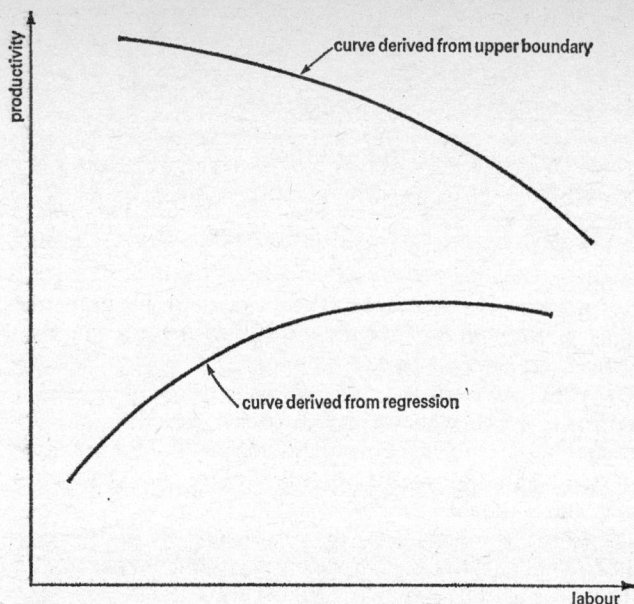

Figure 2

As for the regression line, it is strongly influenced by the number of shops of very low productivity that occur (perhaps those shops which are just starting, or are alternatively on the point of bankruptcy). As labour size increases, there are proportionately less of these. The point in section 8 above is underlined: one has to have some theory of entry to and exit from the industry, as well as one concerning the production relations within it. Both in the case of the regression lines (lines of averages) and in the case of the upper boundary line (the line of 'best performance') it is a striking fact that the usual theoretical discussions of economies of scale, since they have not acknowledged the variations in environment and efficiency of different firms, have not provided an explanation of the shapes we find.

References

CLARK, J. M. (1923), *Economics of Overhead Costs*, University of Chicago Press.
HALL, M., KNAPP, J., and WINSTEN, C. (1961), *Distribution in Great Britain and North America: A Study in Structure and Productivity*, Oxford Clarendon Press.
HALL, M., and WINSTEN, C. (1959), 'The ambiguous notion of efficiency', *econ. J.*, vol. 69, pp. 71–86.
WINSTEN, C. *et al.* (1960), 'The present position of econometrics: a discussion', *J. roy. stat. Soc.*, vol. 123, pp. 274–96.

15 M. Hall and J. Knapp

Gross Margins and Efficiency Measurement in Retail Trade

M. Hall and J. Knapp, 'Gross margins and efficiency measurement in retail trade',
Oxford Economic Papers, n.s., vol. 7, 1955, pp. 312–36.

The purpose of this article is to examine how far it is possible to use the data on margins published in the British Census of Distribution for 1950 to throw light on efficiency in retail trade.

1. Any analysis of the behaviour of a firm or industry requires clear recognition of the character of its output and of the input of the resources employed, and any empirical analysis of efficiency requires that these quantities should be measurable.

In the field of distribution statistics the application of these maxims has been hampered not only by a lack of the precise measurements needed, but also by the persistence of a certain conceptual vagueness.

Now that Census data are available for this country, a statistical groundwork for efficiency analysis has been provided. As we shall show, further progress in this field requires the collection of additional empirical data. The need for these, and the limits on what can be said on the basis of our existing information, can only be appreciated if we take care to make our concepts clear.

2. The output of a retail shop has been crudely thought of as the amount of merchandise it sells and, on this account, retail sales at constant prices have frequently been accepted as a tolerable measure of output (see for example Smith, 1948, p. 145). This practice encourages a confusion between the merchandise sold on the one hand and the activity of selling on the other. It is this last which constitutes the output of retail trade. Retail output consists of a varied aggregate, not of goods but of services, such as holding stock, serving customers, breaking bulk, providing credit, and delivery. If the amount of these services did not vary much per unit of sales, the real value of retail sales could still be used as an indirect measure of retail output. But there is no reason to suppose that the amount of retail service required to market, for example, £100 worth of tinned peas is the same as that involved in selling £100 worth of millinery. To take account of this obvious fact some analysts have, when measuring aggregate retail output, weighted real sales figures by the retail margins of various trades.

This is certainly an advance, but the validity of this procedure depends on the assumption that differences in distribution costs *measure* differences in retail output. Such an assumption would be appropriate if one were contemplating an imaginary perfectly competitive long-run equilibrium situation. However, in the context of an attempt to measure retail output and efficiency in an imperfectly competitive and changing world, to assume that distribution cost measures distributive output is clearly to beg the very question which is at issue, for it involves saying that the ratio of output to input, i.e. 'efficiency',[1] is uniformly the same throughout distributive industry.

It is natural, in these circumstances, to seek for a way of measuring the service output of distribution directly. What is involved here has been outlined by Professor G. J. Stigler as follows:

If we wished to construct an index of the aggregate output of retailing services, . . . we would have to know first the individual products of the industry: the amounts of storage, selling, wrapping, delivery, credit extension, and similar services supplied to consumers. The problems that would be encountered in enumerating these quantities are not different in nature, and perhaps not in magnitude, from those already faced, and solved in varying degree, in the commodity-producing industries. But when one seeks the prices with which to weight these services in constructing a single index, a new problem arises. Rarely is there a separate and definite retail price differential for cash payments versus a month's credit, delivery of specified frequency, or availability of rarely purchased items. These services are usually supplied jointly in variable amounts. Is the additional obstacle of the absence of an explicit price system insurmountable? I think not. There exists an implicit price system for the components of retailing service, . . . and it could be uncovered by statistical analysis of appropriate data. . . . But to construct indexes of service outputs will be a very large task (1947, pp. 15–16).

Nor is this all. The significance of direct output measurements of the type defined by Professor Stigler is limited by the fact that they do not, apparently, make allowance for variations in the environmental setting of distributive activity. The sale of a dozen oranges in a hut at the top of Snowdon need not, when reckoned at the direct output measures of the type listed by Professor Stigler, involve a quantity of distributive output very much different from the quantity involved in selling a dozen oranges from a shack in Islington. The problems involved in making allowance for such environmental differences as the density of population or their shopping habits add a further formidable layer of difficulties to the task of comparing the performances of firms or trades in retail distribution.

3. Total distributive input, like aggregate output, can only be measured

1. See also the discussion of the relationship between the ratio output/input and efficiency, below, p. 254.

by appropriately pricing and adding the values of its various physically heterogeneous component parts.

The retailer's costs, his total expenses of running his business, consist of his outlay on rent, rates, capital tied up in stocks, shop assistants, light, heat, delivery, taxes, the expense of providing credit, advertising, shop fixtures and sundries, repairs, maintenance and depreciation. In principle, we should add to this the value of the work put in by the shopkeeper, and the supply price of his 'enterprise' in running the business.

In practice, the 'gross margin', that is what the retailer charges for the merchandise he sells minus what he paid for this merchandise, is frequently taken to represent his costs. This is inappropriate in so far as the retailer is receiving an element of pure profit or is making a loss.[2]

Statistics of gross margins are sometimes broken down into the two major elements, 'operating expenses' and 'net profit'.[3] In establishments with working proprietors, which form the great bulk of retail enterprises, 'net profit' is usually reckoned without any allowance or deduction in respect of proprietors' salaries.[4] In principle, we should wish to identify three component elements of the profit accruing to proprietors, namely, (i) wages of labour and management, (ii) supply price of enterprise, (iii) pure profit – and we should wish to deduct only the third from the gross margin in order to arrive at the money value of total input. None of these three elements in 'net profit' can, as a rule, be distinguished in the available statistics.

In practice, the best that can usually be done is to take operating costs as a measure of input, judgement being used in allowing for the value of the input represented by the labour of proprietors and any other unpaid workers.[5]

2. It may be noted also that the gross margin is not equal to net value added in distribution, because some of the outlays which enter into it, e.g. shop supplies and repairs, are paid to factors of production in other industries.

3. The most useful official statistics of this kind are the biannual surveys published by the Dominion Bureau of Statistics in Canada. Their figures are secured on a voluntary basis from a carefully selected representative sample of firms.

4. In the United States Censuses for 1929, 1933 and 1935 the wage value of proprietors' services was put at an amount equal to the average annual earnings of full-time employees in the kind of business concerned. In the Canadian Census for 1941 the salaries and withdrawals of proprietors, whose practice it was to withdraw a stipulated amount of compensation from their business, was used as the basis for estimating the value of proprietors' services, and the amounts so estimated were included in operating expenses. This last method was judged to be unsuitable for use in the United States. Both the United States and Canada have discontinued the publication of operating-expense data in their Censuses of Distribution since 1935 and 1941 respectively.

5. In the discussion which follows, the difficulties of measuring the supply price of enterprise and pure profits are ignored.

A further difficulty which arises, whether the money value of inputs is given in the form of gross margins or of operating expenses, is that they will fail to correspond to real inputs where there is an element of monopsony or monopoly in the market for factors of production.[6]

4. Distribution cost is generally measured by the ratio

$$\frac{\text{gross margin}}{\text{sales}} \times 100,$$

or the percentage gross margin. In, say, retail trade as a whole, this shows what proportion of the money value of consumers' outlay is absorbed by the cost of distribution.

Now, variations in efficiency will consist of variations in the ratio

$$\frac{\text{real input}}{\text{real output}}$$

and such variations will be reflected in what we shall call the 'unit cost' of distribution.

It follows from our earlier discussion that the percentage gross margin is *not* a measure of the cost of distribution in the sense of its cost per unit of distributive output (unit cost), since this latter measure would be equal to

$$\frac{\text{gross margin} - \text{pure profit}}{\text{unit of distributive output}} .$$

It is the unit costs of distribution which are of central interest in distribution cost analysis.

5. To detect evidence of inefficiency in retail trade in the Census statistics, one must find data showing variations in the unit costs of distribution. Unit costs cannot be computed from the Census data.

The Census contains no measurements of distributive output (Board of Trade, 1954, Tables 24 and 25). It contains data on sales on the one hand, and on gross margins on the other hand. The latter is equal to the sum of distributive expenses (other than the cost of merchandise bought for resale) and profits.

Sales cannot generally[7] be used as a measure of distributive output. There is no reason to suppose that the amount of distribution services provided per unit of sales is the same in different trades. If it were, real sales would provide a measure of retail output. But there are reasons for suspecting this simple approach because there are wide and systematic variations in retail costs in different trades. There are in fact good grounds for the procedure of making inferences about comparative retail output,

6. This may often be the case in the distributive trades.
7. But see pp. 247–51.

as a first approximation, on the basis of cost data, although these are, in principle, measures of comparative distributive input. The grounds for such a procedure are partly analytical and partly empirical in character.

Economic theory suggests that in so far as a sufficiently high degree of competition prevails in distribution, the value of the distributive outputs produced by firms in the industry will tend to be equal to the payments made by firms for the resources they use. Sufficient competition will simultaneously tend, according to theory, to ensure also that the efficiency with which resources are used in distributive industry will be equal, at the margin, in all firms throughout the industry. It follows that differences in retail costs, as between trades, can be taken to reflect the existence of differences in retail output associated with a given value of sales.[8]

On the empirical side, this interpretation of distribution-cost statistics has gained support from the fact that students of distribution have felt able, in a broad way, to account for the variations to be found in the distribution expenses of different trades by pointing to differences in circumstances between them other than differences in their efficiency.[9]

Figures 1 and 2 show percentage gross margins and data on length of stock-holding in a number of roughly comparable trades in Great Britain and the United States. The pattern of variation of the margins, and even more strikingly of stock turn, can be seen to be similar in Great Britain and in the United States. This supports the view that variations in distribution costs, as between trades, broadly speaking do reflect variations in the amount of distributive output performed in them per unit of sales rather than variations in their unit costs of distribution, i.e. in their comparative efficiency, since it would be very odd indeed if the comparatively inefficient branches of retail trade were the same in Great Britain and the United States.

We are left with the conclusion that as between trades real sales cannot be taken to measure retail output.

8. This is the philosophy implied in the procedure of national income statisticians who, in measuring the output of the distributive trades, use sales at constant prices weighted by net value added in distribution as their output index. See, e.g., Reddaway (1950, p. 446).

9. Thus, Marshall (1920, p. 512) wrote: 'The retail dealer's profit on the turnover is often only 5 or 10 per cent for commodities which are in general demand, and which are not subject to changes of fashion; so that while the sales are large, the necessary stocks are small, and the capital invested in them can be turned over very rapidly, with very little trouble and no risk. But a profit on the turnover of nearly 100 per cent is required to remunerate the retailer of some kinds of fancy goods which can be sold but slowly, of which varied stocks must be kept, which require a large place for their display, and which a change of fashion may render unsaleable except at a loss; and even this high rate is often exceeded in the case of fish, fruit, flowers and vegetables.' See also Braithwaite and Dobbs (1932, pp. 270–71), and Jefferys (1950, chapter 4).

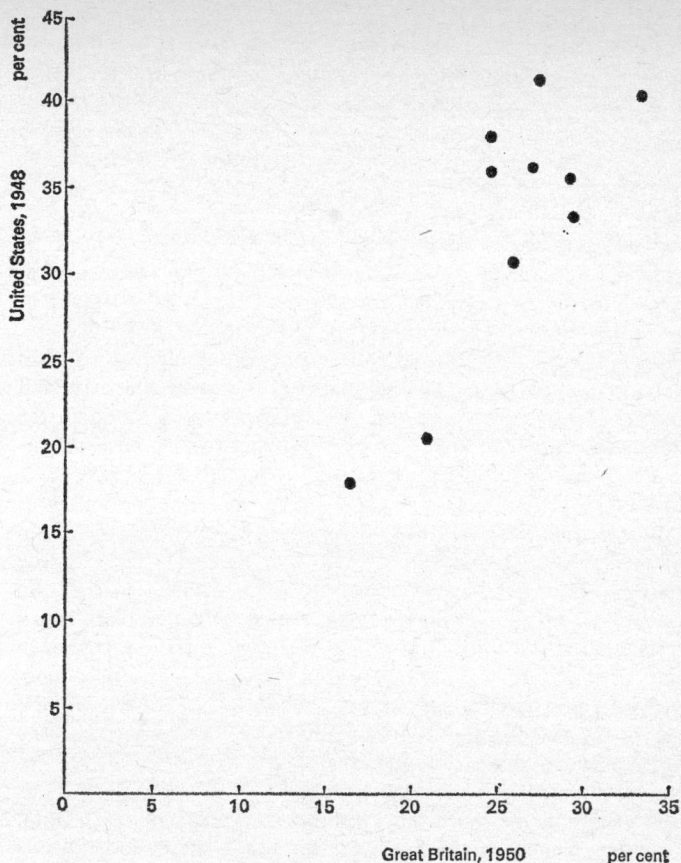

Figure 1 Great Britain, 1950, and the United States, 1948 : gross margin as percentage of sales in selected comparable retail trades

6. In contrast to the situation when different trades are compared, and as a first approximation, the amount of distributive output may be taken, within fairly narrowly defined trade groups, to vary proportionately to sales. It can easily be shown, however, that this rather artificial simplifying assumption concerning output measurement does not carry us nearer to establishing a relation between variations in percentage gross margins and efficiency in retail trade.

Tables 1 and 2 show, in a schematic manner, the way in which gross

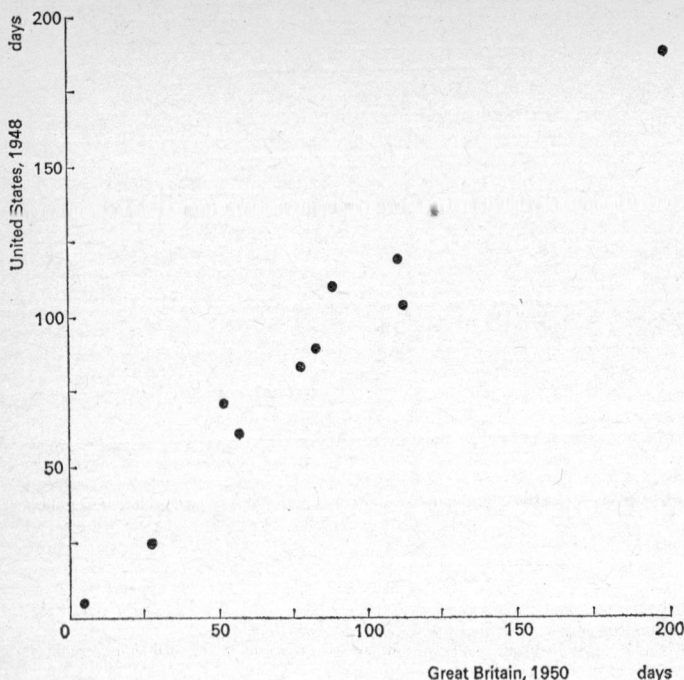

Figure 2 Great Britain, 1950, and the United States, 1948 : length of stock-holding in selected comparable retail trades

margins as a percentage of sales vary with the size of firms in each of the 73 minor trades which are the finest breakdown of retail trades distinguished in the British Census of Distribution. In both tables the same ten margin patterns are distinguished: e.g., \ means that percentage gross margins fall as the size of firms increases, and / means that percentage gross margins rise as the size of firms increases; — means that percentage margins do not vary with the size of firms. The margin patterns are shown with respect to both of the ways in which sizes of firms are measured in the Census: in Table 1, by the number of shops or establishments controlled by retail firms, and in Table 2, by the sales-size of firms. Thus the margin patterns in Table 1 gives a comparison of percentage gross margins taken in independent shops having one outlet or shop per retail firm as compared with the margins of chains of increasing size, while margin patterns in Table 2 show the variations of percentage gross margins as the turnover

Table 1 **Great Britain, 1950: retail trade[1] – percentage gross margin patterns, by increasing establishment-size of firms**

	Percentage gross margin patterns[2,3]											
	1	2	3	4	5	6	7	8	9	10 Other	11 Not available[4]	12 Total
	\	⌣	\	/	⌡	⌐	—	⌐	⌣			
Number of trades	4	..	1	15	4	2	10	7	..	7	23	73
Value of sales as % of total retail sales	4·7	..	0·3	24·9	8·4	18·0	18·4	7·2	..	9·5	8·5	100

[1] Except retail cooperative societies.

[2] The rules used in assigning trades to the margin patterns are described in a Note at the end of this article.

[3] Trades in columns 1–10 of the table are as follows: Column 1: other food; men's wear; furriers; pawnbrokers. Column 3: corn merchants. Column 4: grocers with off-licence; grocers with meat; grocers with bakery goods, with baking; grocers with bakery goods, without baking; grocers with hardware; butchers; fishmongers, poulterers; greengrocers, fruiterers; chocolate, sugar-confectioners; chocolate, sugar-confectioner–tobacconists; women's underwear; wool, art needle-work; dispensing chemists; domestic furniture; florists. Column 5: tobacconists; men's and women's wear; domestic hardware; builders' materials. Column 6: grocers; bread and flour confectioners with baking. Column 7: dairymen; greengrocerers, fruiterers with fish; cooked meat and delicatessen; chocolate, sugar-confectioner–tobacconist–newsagents; women's outfitters; milliners; soft furnishings, floor coverings; leather goods; fancy goods; department stores. Column 8: tobacconist–newsagents; boots and shoes; drapers; china, glassware; sports goods; toys; other non-food. Column 10: bread and flour confectioners, without baking; off-licences; women's outerwear; booksellers, stationers; jewellery, watches and clocks; coal; pets, pet food.

[4] 'Not available' means that only two establishment-size groups are distinguished in a trade, or that no breakdown at all is given.

Source: *Census of Distribution and Other Services, 1950*, vol. 2, Table 25.

of firms increases. It should be noted that the dispersions of the margins around the average for each size group are relatively large.[10]

Now it is frequently asserted that because of economies of scale, unit costs of distribution will fall as the size of firms increases. Yet Tables 1 and 2 show a great variety of gross margin patterns with respect to size.[11] What can we say about this?

Percentage gross margins cannot, generally, be taken to measure efficiency even within a trade,[12] and so cannot be expected to fall with rising scale of operations, for reasons which can be classified as follows:

Suppose that all firms buy both merchandise and hired factors of pro-

10. Thus, in the grocery trade, average margins of the various turnover size groups range between 11·8 per cent and 17·9 per cent. But among organizations having sales of under £1000, for instance, one-quarter have margins below 10·2 per cent and one-quarter have margins above 16·9 per cent.

11. The difference in the distribution of trades among the margin patterns according as the size of firms is measured by number of shops controlled or turnover, is discussed below, p. 253.

12. And even where retail sales are taken as a measure of retail output.

Table 2 **Great Britain, 1950: retail trade[1] – percentage gross margin patterns, by increasing turnover-size of firms**

	Percentage gross margin patterns[2,3]											
	1	2	3	4	5	6	7	8	9	10 Other	11 Not available[4]	12 Total
	\	⌣	＼	/	⌟	⌐	—	⌐	⌣			
Number of trades	7	18	2	3	12	1	1	6	12	6	5	73
Value of sales as % of total retail sales	5·0	16·4	0·2	8·9	29·5	0·1	0·2	9·3	12·3	13·3	4·7	100

[1] Except retail cooperative societies.

[2] The rules used in assigning trades to the margin patterns are described in a Note at the end of this article.

[3] Trades in columns 1–10 of the table are as follows: Column 1: boots and shoes with repairs; men's wear; second-hand clothes dealers; antique dealers; pictures; builders' materials with contracting; corn merchants. Column 2: grocers with bakery goods, with baking; fishmongers, poulterers; cooked meat and delicatessen; general shops; chocolate, sugar-confectioner-tobacconist–newsagents; tobacconists; drapers; radio, electrical goods with repairs; electrical goods with contracting; booksellers, stationers; photographic goods; domestic furniture; soft furnishings, floor coverings; secondhand furniture dealers; jewellery, watches and clocks; leather goods; fancy goods; pawnbrokers. Column 3: newsagents; furriers. Column 4: bread and flour confectioners, with baking; bread and flour confectioners, without baking; department stores. Column 5: grocers; grocers with off-licence; grocers with bakery goods, without baking; grocers with hardware; greengrocers, fruiterers; off-licences; chocolate, sugar-confectioners; men's and women's wear; wool, art needlework; radio, electrical goods; florists; other non-food. Column 6: corsetieres. Column 7: other food. Column 8: grocers with meat; butchers; china, glassware; dispensing chemists; builders' materials; pets, pet food. Column 9: chocolate, sugar-confectioner-tobacconists; tobacconist–newsagents; boots and shoes; women's underwear; infants', children's wear; domestic hardware; other retailers of chemist's goods; musical instruments; sports goods; toys; nurserymen, garden seedsmen; general secondhand dealers. Column 10: dairymen; greengrocers, fruiterers with fish; women's outerwear; women's outfitters; milliners; coal.

[4] 'Not available' means that no turnover-size breakdown is given in the trade.

Source: *Census of Distribution and Other Services, 1950*, vol. 2, Table 24.

duction at the same prices, and also sell at the same prices either because prices are maintained or controlled or because this corresponds to the individual price policy of retailers themselves, or, finally, because of competition. The percentage gross margins of all firms will be identical, but their unit costs (which exclude pure profits) may differ. Firms having lower unit costs are more efficient. It follows that where the buying and selling prices of firms are identical, data on percentage gross margins cannot, without supplementary information on the pure-profit component of the margin, tell us anything about the comparative efficiency of firms within a trade. If larger firms had lower unit costs because of economies of scale or for any other reason, their percentage gross margins would not be any lower than those of smaller firms, but their pure profits would be higher.

If all firms sell at identical prices, but buy at different prices, say, because their buying is more efficient or on account of bulk discounts, or because they have monopsonistic advantages, firms with lower buying prices will tend to show higher percentage gross margins than those having higher buying prices whether or not they are also more efficient in terms of the costs they incur in distributing a given volume of goods.[13] In this case, larger firms which obtain quantity discounts may show higher percentage margins even though they may have lower unit costs.

If all shops buy at the same prices, but competition in retailing is imperfect and fixed price systems are not universal, it is possible for prices to be different in respect of sales of identical goods accompanied by equal quantities of distributive service. In this situation, variations in percentage gross margins calculated on the *buying* cost of goods sold would reflect variations in unit costs or efficiency of distribution, if pure profit were nil and if prices were reduced in proportion to distribution costs in the more efficient firms.[14] Such situations may be quite widespread in practice, since imperfect competition plus limited price competition may well be common occurrences in distribution. But it must be remembered that before such a situation could be identified, it would be necessary to supplement any data on percentage gross margins corresponding to it with independent information establishing the facts concerning buying and selling prices and the degree of imperfect competition. (It will be noticed that this case is, by definition, not compatible with our simplifying assumption that sales should be proportional to distributive output, although it does imply that distributive output is proportional to the cost of goods bought by retailers.)

If different firms both buy and sell at different prices, for some combination of the reasons given in the foregoing, there is no reason to expect any systematic pattern in percentage gross margins, and no ground for connecting variations of percentage gross margins with unit costs of distribution.

It is necessary to recognize that the simplifying assumption we made earlier, namely, that the amount of distributive output provided by firms within a given trade varies proportionately with the volume of goods distributed, is itself of limited validity. Three reasons for this may be listed:

First, the amount of distributive output necessarily associated with the distribution of a given value of goods bought by retailers may vary with the composition of goods for resale. Unless, therefore, all firms in a single trade sell goods of very similar commodity composition, costs and with

13. This is further explained in detail in footnote 15.

14. The variations of percentage gross margins *on sales* corresponding to the variations of cost and efficiency envisaged in the text are given by the formula $1/(1-c/e)$ where c equals buying cost per unit of goods sold and e distribution costs per unit of goods sold.

them percentage gross margins of shops may vary even though all shops are equally efficient.

Secondly, the quantity of luxury service provided to consumers with goods of a given wholesale value and composition may vary in different shops within a single trade. This also can give rise to variations in costs and gross margins among firms of equal efficiency.

Thirdly, firms classified for practical purposes as retailers belonging to a single trade may assume, to varying extents, what are normally regarded as wholesalers' distributive functions. This will tend to raise the gross margins and also the costs of establishments belonging to firms which assume a relatively greater part of wholesalers' distributive functions even though their unit costs of distribution may be lower than, or equal to, those of other retailers.

It is clear from this that the Census information on percentage gross margins cannot, in itself, tell us anything conclusive about the comparative efficiency of firms even when the data refer to a single trade defined in a fairly narrow way.

Thus, whatever the gross margin patterns in Table 1 and Table 2 show, it is possible that unit costs do fall with increasing size of firm in each and every one of our 73 trades. For any particular pattern of margin variations is compatible with falling unit costs of distribution provided that the varying patterns are associated with suitable variations in buying and selling prices, in distributive output per unit of sales, and of pure profits per unit of sales as the size of firm increases. By the same token, it is possible to make assumptions which would make the observed patterns of margin variations consistent with constant or rising unit costs of distribution as the size of firms increases. This question cannot be conclusively settled without much further empirical research.

Nevertheless, detailed examination of the data on variations of margins within single trades does suggest further lines of inquiry on which investigation might be concentrated. Table 1 shows that percentage gross margins are constant or rise in the majority of trades as one moves from independent shops to chains with a larger number of outlets. This is quite compatible with the larger chains obtaining larger economies of scale, since where the economy consists in the chains obtaining bulk discounts they will tend to show higher or constant percentage gross margins whether or not they pass these economies on to the consumer in the form of lower prices.[15] However, these margin patterns evidently invite further

15. The influence of quantity discounts on percentage gross margins can be brought out by making a *ceteris paribus* assumption, as follows:
Suppose that a chain has the same operating expenses per unit of a given assortment of merchandise and the same rate of net profit on turnover as an independent, thus

investigation, since very little is known about the extent and size of quantity discounts, comparative net profit rates, and prices of chains as against independents.[16]

Table 2 shows a very different distribution of trades among the margin patterns. This is due to the fact that the classification by size of turnover has the effect of revealing the variations in margins of independent (single-unit) retailers of varying sales size in considerable detail, while in Table 1 these variations are all compressed in the overall average margin shown for independents. In contrast with the picture which emerges in Table 1, the result of the classification in Table 2 by turnover-size is to shift the majority of trades into categories of margin patterns which show percentage gross margins falling with size over a significant range of independent shops of smaller sizes. The idea that this range of observations in the various trades reflects variations in unit costs is supported, on the face of it, by the fact that in thirty one out of forty six trades in which margins decline with increasing size of independents, over at least the smaller-size groups of the independents, the rate of stock turn increases as percentage

---

passing on any buying economies to the consumer. Suppose that the chain obtains a quantity discount of 20 per cent for buying one hundred times as much. Then the percentage gross margin of the chain will be higher, as follows:

	Cost of goods bought (£)	Total expenses (£)	% Profits on turnover	Total profits (£)	Retail sales value (£)	% Gross margin
Independent	800	150	5	50	1000	20
Chain	64,000	15,000	5	4158	83,158	23

If the chains sell at the same prices as independents, we have:

	Cost of goods bought (£)	Total expenses (£)	% Profits on turnover	Total profits (£)	Retail sales value (£)	% Gross margin
Independent	800	150	5	50	1000	20
Chain	64,000	15,000	21	21,000	100,000	36

It follows that chains will only have lower percentage gross margins than independents if they take a lower rate of net profit or have lower operating costs than independents.

It also follows that margins will be constant where lower profit rates and/or lower operating costs happen to offset the influence of bulk discounts. Such a result will come about if conventional margins are adhered to or enforced throughout a trade.

16. It is interesting to note that in the United States the percentage gross margins of chains were found to be lower than those of independent shops in the inter-war period. Cf. Bellamy (1946, pp. 330–31).

gross margins decline.[17] This in itself is not, however, conclusive, since it is possible that the composition of goods sold in shops of different sizes in the same trade varies, e.g. the smaller shops sell a greater proportion of higher margin goods, or they give more service. The high margins of the smallest independents are probably in fact attributable at least in part to inefficiency and imperfect competition, but there is no way of establishing the extent of this inefficiency from the Census data. Any attempt to do this would require field studies of an intensive kind.

7. It follows from the foregoing that 'to isolate the factors which make for efficiency or inefficiency in distribution' is a much more complicated task than the authors of a recent contribution to this journal imply (Pollard and Hughes, 1955, p. 71). The central argument put forward by Pollard and Hughes seems to consist of the following propositions:

(a) Efficiency in distribution can be measured by distributive costs as represented by percentage gross margins (pp. 71, 78–9, 86, 89).

(b) Sales per person engaged increase with the sales-size of establishments and also, though to a less extent, with the size of establishments as measured by persons engaged per shop.[18]

(c) There is a negative correlation between sales per person engaged and percentage gross margins, both as between trades and within single trades. Consequently, 'the influence of "labour efficiency" on distributive costs can hardly be exaggerated' (p. 79).

(d) As sales per person engaged depend on the size of establishments (or firms), it follows that small shops are inefficient. This is also argued directly on the basis of a table showing that 'distributive costs, as measured by gross margins, are lowest in the middle size ranges, rise with the larger size ranges, but are highest in the smallest size' (pp. 78–9).

None of these propositions seems acceptable, as they involve various sorts of errors in interpretation.

17. The trades in question are: grocers; grocers with off-licence; grocers with bakery goods, without baking; greengrocers, fruiterers; greengrocers, fruiterers with fish; chocolate, sugar-confectioners; chocolate, sugar-confectioner–tobacconist–newsagents; boots and shoes; boots and shoes with repairs; women's outerwear; women's outfitters; milliners; infants, children's wear; men's and women's wear; wool, art needlework; domestic hardware, ironmongery; radio, electrical goods; radio, electrical goods, with repairs; electrical goods with contracting; booksellers, stationers; dispensing chemists; domestic furniture; antiques; musical instruments; sports goods; toys; builders' materials; corn merchants; nurserymen, garden seedsmen; pets, pet food; general second-hand dealers. For the purposes of this analysis, the data for organizations of increasing turnover-size up to and including the group having 1–25 establishments per organization have been regarded as relevant to independents.

18. Pollard and Hughes (1955, pp. 73–5). Sales per person are calculated by taking two part-time workers as equal to one full-time worker.

First, as we showed above (pp. 242–52), it is a fundamental misconception to suppose that distributive costs, as represented by percentage gross margins, can serve as measures of unit costs or efficiency in distribution.

Second, while it is true that sales per person engaged increase with the sales-size of establishments, detailed examination of the data by individual trades shows that it is by no means always the case that sales per person engaged increase with size of establishment as measured by persons engaged per shop.[19]

Thirdly, while it is true that there is a negative association, as among different trades, between variations in sales per person and percentage gross margins, any inference that there are corresponding differences, as between trades, in the efficiency with which labour is used, is unwarranted. Nor is it correct to infer that high margins are *caused* by low sales per person. Both phenomena may be the reflection of a common cause quite unrelated to the issue of efficiency. The most obvious cases in point here are the low figures for sales per person and the high percentage margins which are both found in the various retail kinds of business in which productive activities like baking, repairing, etc., are carried on, together with retail distribution. It is clear that in these cases relative output per person is higher than the relative sales-per-person figures indicate, and the high-percentage gross margins in these trades reflect this very fact.[20] In general, the association between sales per person and percentage gross margins among trades needs to be analysed fully, by considering the determinants of each.

Moreover, it is not the case at all that there is a negative correlation

19. The reverse occurs in some thirteen trades out of the seventy-one minor kinds of business distinguished in Table 11 of the Census. In these trades, which account for 24·1 per cent of total retail sales, sales per man fall consistently as the persons-engaged size of establishments increases. The trades in question are: grocers with bakery goods; bread and flour confectioners; cooked meat and delicatessen; chocolate, sugar-confectioners; chocolate, sugar-confectioner–tobacconists; chocolate, sugar-confectioner–tobacconist–newsagents; tobacconists; tobacconist–newsagents; newsagents; electricity showrooms; dispensing chemists; sub-post offices with minor retail sales; department stores. If department stores are excluded, these trades account for 17·8 per cent of total retail sales.

In seven other trades the smallest size groups (as measured by persons engaged) attain sales per person higher than the average for all employee sizes together. In twenty-two trades, the relationship between sales per man and the persons-engaged size of establishments is irregular.

Pollard and Hughes show only data for retail trade as a whole, and for the grocery group.

20. In these trades, at least, where 'sales efficiency' is low, services rendered are relatively high. In the face of such examples it is difficult to share the scepticism of Pollard and Hughes about the probability of finding low sales efficiency accompanied by high retail-service output (1955, p. 89).

between sales per person engaged and percentage gross margins *within* single trades. While it is true that sales per person regularly increase with the sales-size of organizations (firms), at any rate up to rather large sizes of organization, it is not the case that the pattern of margin variations is regularly of the L-shaped type which would correspond to this. As Table 2 shows, the margin patterns with increasing turnover size within single kinds of business show a wide variety of shapes.[21]

Fourthly, the conclusion that small firms are inefficient, while possibly quite true, cannot be deduced from the evidence given, partly because the gross margins of small firms are in fact often not high in relation to the margins of larger firms within the same trade, and partly because percentage gross margins do not, in any case, provide a reliable measure of efficiency.

8. The negative tone of this article should not be interpreted as implying that the study of Census data is of no use in the analysis of retail efficiency. We endorse the view supported by the Census of Distribution Committee that:

> You cannot start to make any examination of relative efficiency until you have got something like the Census of Distribution to start from, but you have got to do a lot more work and discussion and research and investigation before you can reach any tolerable conclusions about the comparative efficiency or inefficiency in various fields . . . a Census could chiefly be justified as providing a groundwork on which enquiries into this difficult subject could more reliably be conducted (1946, p. 3, paragraph 16).

21. The rules used in assigning trades to margin patterns in Tables 1 and 2 were as follows: (1) If percentage gross margins within a trade all fell within a range no more than 5 per cent above the lowest percentage margin, the trade was allocated to pattern No. 7, *unless* the percentage gross margins consistently rose or fell with size. In the latter cases, trades were allocated to patterns Nos. 1 or 4. (2) A minimum 5 per cent difference at the extreme observations was also the criterion applied in deciding on the allocation of trades among patterns Nos. 2, 3, 5, 6 and 9. (3) The definition of patterns ignores the position of the points of inflexion relative to the size-of-firm variable. The breakdowns by size shown for the various trades vary as among trades but were taken as found in the Census. (4) The patterns 1–9 were found to be 'smooth' in the sense of being uninterrupted in thirty-six out of forty-three trades in Table 1 and in thirty out of sixty trades in Table 2. In the other cases, the patterns were 'smoothed' when possible, provided that the number of interruptions to patterns was not more than one in four of the total number of observations in a trade. 'Smoothing' was considered possible when, on taking the weighted average of an observation with an adjacent observation on *either* side, the interruption disappeared.

References

BELLAMY, R. (1946), 'Size and success in retail distribution', *Bull. Oxford Univ. Inst. Stats*, vol. 8, pp. 324–39.

Board of Trade (1954), *Census of Distribution and Other Services, 1950*, vol. 2, HMSO.

BRAITHWAITE, D., and DOBBS, S. P. (1932), *The Distribution of Consumable Goods*, Routledge & Kegan Paul.

JEFFERYS, J. B. (1950), *The Distribution of Consumer Goods*, Cambridge University Press.

MARSHALL, A. (1920), *Principles of Economics*, 8th edn, Macmillan.

POLLARD, S., and HUGHES, J. D. (1955), 'Retailing costs: some comments on the Census of Distribution, 1950', *Oxford econ. Papers*, vol. 7, pp. 71–93.

REDDAWAY, W. B. (1950), 'Movements in the real product of the United Kingdom, 1946–1949', *J. roy. stat. Soc.*, vol. 113, pp. 435–55.

Report of the Census of Distribution Committee (1946), Cmnd 6764, HMSO.

SMITH, H. (1948), *Retail Distribution*, 2nd edn, Oxford University Press.

STIGLER, G. J. (1947), *Trends in Output and Employment*, National Bureau of Economic Research.

16 J. D. Hughes and S. Pollard

Gross Margins in Retail Distribution

J. D. Hughes and S. Pollard, 'Gross margins in retail distribution', *Oxford Economic Papers*, n.s., vol. 9, 1957, pp. 75–87.

The Census of Distribution for the year 1950 makes it possible, for the first time, to raise the discussion on margins, costs, and profits in retailing from the level of guesswork and *a priori* reasoning to that of measurement. The Census returns, though analysed with great care and presented in considerable detail, are not without their weaknesses: small shops, in particular, sometimes omitted to reply to certain questions or sent in returns which were highly suspect.[1] The following notes, in which we attempt to draw several conclusions from the published figures of gross margins[2] and labour costs, should be read with this proviso in mind.

1

It might have been expected that in most trades the gross margins of shops carrying a similar range of goods would not show very wide variations. Many articles are marked up by a conventional margin at least in the short run; others are subject to resale price maintenance or were (in 1950) subject to government price control. Although, in a wide range of goods, the large buyers enjoy the benefits of discounts for bulk, many of them, chain stores and variety stores among them, claim to pass on the benefits

---

1. For the influence of this factor on the returns on margins, see especially *Census of Distribution and Other Services, 1950*, 1954, p. xii. All references in this paper are to this volume of the Census.

2. Gross margins were not obtained from direct information, but were derived from the figures of sales, purchases, and stocks, according to the formula $S+(I_1-I)-P = GM$, where S = sales during the year, I = stocks at the beginning of the year, I_1 = stocks at the end of the year, P = purchases during the year, and GM = gross margin. The rate of gross margins is quoted as $\{S+(I_1-I)-P\}/S$, expressed as a percentage. Gross margins include both costs and profits of distribution and for the purposes of this paper may be conceived as being made up in the following way: $GM = W+C+R$, where W stands for wages, C for all other costs, such as rents, lighting, heating, equipment, loan services, insurance, and advertisement, and R for net profit. It will be noted that losses through deterioration of goods or in 'sales' are accounted for by reductions in S and do not enter into GM or C. 'Residual margins', discussed in section 4 below, are composed of $C+R$.

of bulk buying to the consumer; so that even in their case, if their claim is correct, the actual gross margin need not be expected to differ greatly from that of small unit shops.

Contrary to these expectations, the gross margins tabulated in the Census show very large dispersions, not only as between shops selling similar goods, but also as between shops of similar size selling similar goods. Table 1, listing for purposes of example shops in the sales range of £2500 and under £5000 p.a., in a few selected trades in which resale price maintenance

Table 1 **Dispersion of gross margins in shops of similar size: selected trades[a]**

| | Gross margins % of sales | |
	Median	Quartile deviation
Grocers	11·8	2·2
Butchers	19·8	2·8
Tobacconists	10·8	4·0
Boots and shoes	23·0	3·6
Radio, electrical goods	26·5	5·0
Booksellers, stationers	25·5	7·4
Chemists' goods (no dispensing)	24·1	5·9
Coal	20·6	4·0

[a] In all cases, shops with sales of £2500 and under £5000 p.a.

or government price control were important in 1950, shows the extent of the dispersion of gross margins.

This wide range of gross margins even in the least likely cases may have a number of possible explanations.[3]

1. Varying degrees of monopoly exist both in wholesale buying and retail selling. Although prices of some goods may, in fact, be highly competitive,[4] there are many commodities outside the range of price maintenance for which some retailers are, in fact, able to sell at a higher mark-up than others. Buying prices may also vary, especially where manufacturing units are small.[5]

2. Even in the most narrowly defined sub-groups of trades in the Census returns, it has not been possible to avoid grouping together shops which sell goods or services of different kinds or in different proportions. The divergence is caused by a number of factors.

3. See also the notes in the *Census*, vol. 2, p. xii.
4. e.g. for greengroceries, see Gornall (1954) and Allen and Rutherford (1954).
5. e.g. Wray (1954).

(a) The 'bundles' of goods sold may not be identical: this is particularly evident in mixed groups, as, for example, among 'tobacconists-newsagents'. Where the normal margins of the different groups of commodities sold differ markedly, the variations in the proportions of commodities sold are certain to lead to marked variations in the shops' average margins. Some opportunities for such variations are shown in Table 2.

Table 2 Sales patterns of selected 'composite' shops

Sub-group	Mean gross margin (%)	Main commodity sold	% of total sales	Gross[6] margin (%)	Other commodities sold	% of total sales	Gross[6] margin (%)
Tobacconists, newsagents	13·8	Cigarettes, tobacco, etc.	59·7	9·2	Books, newspapers, etc.	32·5	20·3
Chocolate, sugar confectionery, tobacconists	13·3	Ditto	62·1	9·2	Choc, sugar confect., ice-cream	32·3	23·5
Grocers with hardware	16·5	Groceries	52·0	14·7	General ironmongery	36·0	25·1
Grocers with meat	20·1	Meat	51·0	20·9	Groceries	40·0	14·7

(b) Differences in the quality of the range of goods normally sold by retailers may, to some extent, help to explain differences in margins though in many trades the 'mark-up' is conventional, irrespective of quality.

(c) In cases of branded goods subject to r.p.m., the permitted margin may differ widely as between manufacturers. Thus the policy of a manufacturer who advertises heavily on a national scale and is able to force the retailer to stock his goods even at a low margin may be contrasted with the policy of granting the retailer a generous margin in order to induce him to push the particular commodity.

(d) Of total retail sales of £4941 million, nearly £71 million consists of receipts from services, and a further £24 million represents sales of meals. The provision of a large proportion of services by some shops, and a negligible proportion by others, may cause considerable variations in nominal gross margins in several trades. For example, the receipts from services and meals as percentages of total sales in the sub-groups listed below were as follows:

6. This is, itself, a mean of the gross margins among 'pure' or almost 'pure' shops specializing in the commodity group, which may in turn be made up of goods carrying different margins.

Receipts from services as percentage of total sales

Radio, electrical goods	8·2
Radio, electrical goods with repairs	34·2
Electrical goods with contracting	49·6
Booksellers, stationers	3·5
Soft furnishings	4·7
Jewellery, watches and clocks	10·9

Receipts from meals served as percentage of total sales

Bread and flour confectionery with baking	2·5
Women's outfitters	1·5
Cooked meat and delicatessen	1·7

(e) Certain retail organizations specialize in selling goods on trade terms. The 16,865 firms (mostly firms of considerable size) which reported sales of goods on these terms represented 4·2 per cent of the number of firms included in the Census. 34 per cent of their sales, valued at £140 million (of which £89 million went to other retailers for resale), were made on trade terms.

Similarly, certain firms sell regularly on hire-purchase or other instalment terms. A total of 25,611 shops, accounting for nearly 14 per cent of total turnover (excluding Cooperative Societies) were reported as belonging to this category in 1950. This type of trading was particularly prevalent among shops in men's and women's wear (38 per cent),[7] radio, electrical goods (80 per cent), gas and electricity showrooms (100 per cent), domestic furniture (80 per cent) and department stores (59 per cent). The alteration of gross margins owing to either of these methods of trading is unlikely to affect different shops to the same degree.

(f) In certain trades deterioration of stocks is of some importance. Reductions in selling prices owing to deterioration, or in regular 'sales' periods, may introduce a further disturbing factor.

2

The Census returns do not allow us to analyse more closely these influences on retail gross margins, nor do they permit an estimate of their relative importance. There are, however, some aspects of the statistics presented which may repay further analysis. In particular, a study of the average gross margins of firms grouped by size in different trades shows up a number of regularities which may be significant, even though the differences between size groups are generally of lesser moment than the differences between upper and lower quartiles within the size groups.[8]

7. Turnover of shops reporting sales on these terms as percentage of all sales of the sub-group.

8. It should also be noted that the data given are those for 'Organizations', not shops.

The rough-and-ready assumption that shops within the same trade, but of different size, would show gross margins either constant or rising steadily with size (to allow for bulk buying) is not borne out by the returns. The Census enumerates altogether seventy-four sub-groups of retail trades.[9] Of these, twenty-two, representing 14·6 per cent of total sales, are too small, or are not presented in a sufficient number of size groups, to permit statistical analysis; three show no discernible trend;[10] four show gross margins rising with increasing sales; and seven have gross margins which fall with size. Of the remaining thirty-five sub-groups, four are kinked or 'L-shaped' (i.e. fairly level with a pronounced rise in the largest sizes), and the gross margins among the other thirty-one have a pronounced 'U-shape', i.e. high margins for very small and very large firms and low margins for the medium sizes. This last category is by far the most important: the thirty-one trade sub-groups account for 45·9 per cent of total sales. Its variations in gross margins are shown in Table 3.[11]

The 'U-shaped' curve of gross margins is thus predominant in retail trade.[12] The compilers of the Census, who appear to have noticed this predominance, attempt to explain it in part by pointing out that returns for shops of the smaller sizes were often incomplete (margins for one-sixth of them had, in fact, to be estimated) while the large organizations might also include wholesaling and 'sometimes engage in manufacture' (p. xii), so that only the medium sizes should be taken as representing normal margins. This explanation does not seem entirely satisfactory. The missing returns of the small units were estimated by assigning to them the average figures of their type and size, and no conclusions can be drawn as to the way in which they diverge from the actual figures. As far as the largest size group was concerned, some 'central office and warehouse' activities could be separated from their retailing activities; those that were included amounted to less than 1 per cent of total sales (Appendix F, Table D, p. 315). Similarly, many productive processes could be separated from the returns,

---

Large size may thus refer to chain stores as well as large-unit shops, and even medium-sized firms may either be made up of several small shops or own one shop only.

9. Including Cooperative Societies.

10. These were dairies, coal, and dispensing chemists.

11. The assigning of 'curves' to series made up of a small number of data is to some extent subjective, depending on differing definitions of significance: Hall and Knapp (1955, Table 2, columns 2, 5 and 9) [Reading 15], found no fewer than forty-two trades, accounting for 58·2 per cent of total sales, with contours which we would term 'U-shaped'. While some of the difference is accounted for by their inclusion of trades for which we considered the data insufficient or which were insignificant, there were also some differences of interpretation.

12. The four trades with 'L-shaped' curves are not fundamentally different; see below.

while those that could not be deducted appear to have been included in the returns from large and small organizations alike, and there is little reason to believe that they affected the returns of the largest firms more than those of the others. A total of only 97,000 persons, out of 2,386,000 persons engaged in retail trades, were returned as 'mainly engaged in making goods' (Appendix B, paras. 12–14, pp. 302–3).

While in certain trades some weight must be given to the weaknesses in the returns, described by the compilers of the Census as an explanation of the higher recorded margins of the larger firms, these weaknesses cannot account for the whole of the characteristic 'U-shape' of the gross margin curve. It is more reasonable to suppose that the large firms, receiving the benefits of bulk purchase, do not pass them all on to the consumer, while the small firms, buying at unfavourable rates, either recoup themselves by charging higher prices or limit their stock to goods with high margins. The middle size groups, which include the bulk of the shops 'with working proprietors', are working on the lowest gross margins.

Table 3 **Variations of gross margin with size of organization: thirty-one retail trade groups***

No.	Size groups (turnover in £ p.a.)	twenty-three trades† Av. g.m. for these trades = 100	eight trades‡ Av. g.m. for these trades = 100
1	Under £1000	112·7	112·6
2	£1000 but under £2500	106·1	103·7
3	£2500 but under £5000	98·7	95·9
4	£5000 but under £10,000	95·7	94·4
5	£10,000 but under £25,000	94·8	93·7
6	£25,000 but under £50,000	95·4	104·3
7	£50,000 but under £100,000	97·7⎫	112·8
8	£100,000 and over	114·3⎭	

* The table was constructed by calculating, within each trade, the variation of each size group from the mean of the whole trade, expressed as a percentage, and then taking the unweighted mean of these percentages for each size.

† These twenty-three trades have been separated out from the thirty-one since details for size group No. 7 are available for them, but not for the others. They are: grocers; grocers with off-licence; grocers with bakery goods and baking; grocers with bakery goods, no baking; grocers with hardware; fishmongers and poulterers; greengrocers, fruit, fish; delicatessen; chocolate, sugar confectionery, tobacco; tobacco, newsagents; boots and shoes; women's underwear; women's outfitters; men's and women's wear; wool, art needlework; drapers; domestic hardware, ironmongery; radio, electrical; books, stationery; domestic furniture; soft furnishings, floor coverings; sports goods; pawnbrokers.

‡ The eight trades are: milliners; china, glassware; radio, electrical goods and repairs; musical instruments; toys; fancy goods; florists; nurserymen.

The four trades with 'L-shaped' gross margins were not, in principle, dissimilar from the thirty-one trades described here. In all four cases there were strong reasons in the price control by the government or by an Association, or in active competition,[13] for keeping the prices of the smallest shops in line with the rest; bulk purchases or wholesaling activities accounted for the high margins of the large firms.

Similar factors seem to be operating in three of the four trades with rising margins with size, namely, off-licences and bread and flour confectionary goods with and without baking. Among Cooperatives, the fourth group, the small Societies are generally limited to sales of groceries and similar goods on which margins are low, while the averages of the larger Societies are raised by sales of clothing and furniture which have considerably higher gross margins.

Seven trades with falling gross margins are left for consideration. Shops selling jewellery, watches and clocks, in which margins are particularly high for the smallest size group, are clearly affected by the high proportion of repair work undertaken by them. In shops selling 'leather goods' and among furriers the small unit partly represents a handicraft manufacturing establishment, and in part exacts higher prices for real or imagined exclusiveness.[14] At the other end of the scale, the large firms in these three trades are mostly multiple chains with a different kind of appeal and a different type of trading. The position in 'men's wear' and 'women's outerwear' is not dissimilar. The small shops exact high prices for exclusive service or to compensate for their inefficiency, or they offer manufacturing services; the largest firms are excellent examples of multiple chains which exert their appeal by low margins which are passed on to the consumer in the form of low prices. Their success is impressive. In 'men's wear' the firms with sales over £1 million are nineteen in number, with 2463 branches; their share of the total trade is 35 per cent; in 'women's outerwear' there are seven firms with 462 establishments in that size group, accounting for 39·5 per cent of total sales. 'Corn merchants' may show falling margins because of the large proportion of bulk sales at discounts made by the large dealers. 'Chocolate, sugar confectionery, tobacconists, newsagents' form the last group in this category. They sell a great variety of goods and services, and the high margins of the small shops may mainly represent a large proportion of high-margin goods or newspaper delivery services.[15]

13. Among greengrocers and fruiterers (cf. Gornall, 1954; Allen and Rutherford, 1954). The other three trades are grocers with meat, butchers and 'builders' materials'.

14. It is difficult to understand the appeal of the twenty-six furriers' shops with sales of under £1000 a year. What sorts of furs were they selling?

15. The very high margins of 'pure' tobacconists are not easily explained (except by doubting their returns), in view of the rigid r.p.m. in the trade. Members of the trade

While the foregoing discussion of the patterns of variations of gross margins with turnover size may not, in the absence of detailed field studies, permit any valid conclusions on differences in efficiency, it does suggest some significant conclusions on the constituents of gross margins. In particular, in the case of the large size groups of several trades, it appears likely that large margins, that is, high costs of distribution, do not necessarily correspond to a high level of distributive service per unit sold, but indicate the existence of profit margins above the normal.

This conclusion necessarily rests on 'the simplifying assumption ... that the amount of distributive output provided by firms within a given trade varies proportionately with the volume of goods distributed' (Hall and Knapp, 1955 [Reading 15], p. 251) in each of the turnover size groups. Hall and Knapp (1955, [Reading 15]), who use this simplifying assumption to develop part of their argument in the article quoted, then go on to limit its validity for three reasons:

(a) the heterogeneity of goods sold,
(b) the 'quantity of luxury service provided',
(c) the assumption of wholesaling functions by some retailers. (1955, see this volume, pp. 251–2)

We have enlarged in section 1 above on (a) and (b), together with other factors not mentioned by Hall and Knapp, as explanations of the wide dispersions of gross margins ruling within similar firms of similar size; there does not, however, seem to be any reason to suppose that these factors would necessarily vary regularly with different size of turnover.

The third point referred to, the carrying out of wholesaling functions, may account for increased gross margins in the larger size groups, though, as we attempted to show above (p. 262), not to the extent the two authors seem to suggest. Of particular importance in this context is the fact that the sharp rise in gross margins in the firms of large size occur in some trades only; in others, in which the wholesaling functions are just as common, gross margins do not rise with size, and in several cases they are lower in the largest firms. It seems, therefore, that large and regular differences in gross margins remain unexplained even after the three factors enumerated above have been taken into account.

3

By giving separate data for 'organizations with working proprietors' and 'organizations without working proprietors', the Census of Distribu-

have suggested to us that these shops may concentrate on brands with high margins, or may buy tobacco in bulk and make up their own brands. Neither explanation is entirely satisfactory for the very wide difference which exists between shops selling under £5000 p.a. and the remainder.

tion reveals another striking feature of gross margins in retailing. A comparison of the gross margins of both types of organization for the different sections of retail trade shows that in most cases they are higher for the 'organizations without working proprietors'. This is true whether the comparison in the case of a particular trade is between organizations in the same size group or between the average gross margins of all sizes for both types of organization.[16] The relationship in some of the main groups of trades is illustrated in Table 4.

From Table 4 it is clear that the difference in gross margins between the two types of organization is generally about 10 per cent, when organizations of the same size in similar groups of trades are compared.[17]

Table 4 **Gross margins of 'organizations without working proprietors' as a percentage of those 'with working proprietors'**

No.	Size group (turnover in £ p.a.	Grocery	Other food	Confectionery, tobacconists, newsagents	Clothing	Furniture	Chemists
1	Under £1000 ⎫	108	⎧119	136	99	104⎫	100
2	£1000 but under £2500 ⎭		⎩111	109	106	108⎭	
3	£2500 but under £5000	108	111	104	112	112	100
4	£5000 but under £10,000	115	113	102	118	117	104
5	£10,000 but under £25,000	114	112	108	114	108	101
6	£25,000 but under £50,000	109	106	116	112	111	103
7	£50,000 but under £100,000	103	105	108	111	106⎫	
8	£100,000 but under £250,000	108	104	117	110	109 ⎬	96
9	£250,000 but under £500,000	114	128⎫	104	⎧110⎫	109⎭	
10–11	£500,000 and over	110	108⎭		⎩ 95⎭		
Mean		126	114	109	104	110	104

The mean difference between the two types of organization (given at the bottom of the table) varies considerably in different trades. This is so because the working proprietor is generally found in the small and medium-sized firm, while most of the firms without working proprietors are large.

16. For convenience of presentation our discussion of this relationship in the text is made in terms of the main groups of retail trade. A detailed comparison of the subgroups of trades shows 282 cases in which the margins of the working proprietors were lower, three in which they were equal, and eighty-one in which they were higher. The eighty-one exceptions were often in the largest size groups of some trades, or in trades where the working proprietor is obviously doing repair work.

17. If the comparison is made for 'all retail trades' a deceptively wide disparity (averaging 20 per cent) appears between the gross margins of the two types of organization. This is because the firms with working proprietors predominate in the sections of retail trade with relatively low margins (e.g. in 'grocery', 'other food' and 'confectionery, tobacconists, newsagents' they account for 64·6 per cent of total turnover, with an average gross margin of only 16·8 per cent).

In some important trades (e.g. clothing), as we have seen, the gross margins in the largest size groups tend to be lower than those in the middle size groups, but in most trades the largest-sized organizations show higher margins than the smaller.

The exceptions to this relationship of gross margins between the two types of organizations are not numerous. The only retail trade group in which the average gross margin is actually lower (by 3 per cent) for 'organizations without' than for those 'with working proprietors' is 'coal, builders' materials, corn'. The explanation lies in the lower gross margins of the largest organizations in the group than those of the smaller organizations in which the working proprietors predominate. If comparison is made between the two types of organization in the same size groups in this trade group, the 'organizations without working proprietors' have gross margins 10 per cent higher[18] than those 'with'. The other important exceptions occur in the largest-size groups of some trades, where the gross margins of 'organizations without working proprietors' are very slightly lower than those with working proprietors. The main trades concerned are in the 'clothing', 'chemists' goods, photographic goods', and 'jewellery, leather and sports goods' groups, where the existence of multiples (in some cases with low margins) as the main form of large-scale organization may blur the differences between the two types of organization.[19]

More striking still than these exceptions is the fact that even in the largest sizes of organization, in which one would expect the difference between an organization with a working proprietor and one without to be minimized, the gross margins of the former are generally 9–10 per cent lower than the latter's. From the point of view of the cost of retail distribution, the generally lower gross margins of the organizations which have working proprietors is a feature of some importance.[20]

4

'Gross margins' in retail distribution include not only profits, but all the costs of retailing. It is not possible to break down gross margins into all their constituent parts on the basis of the Census returns, but one major cost item can be isolated and deducted: the labour cost. Labour costs are not available for all retail firms; only those without working proprietors (or 'unpaid helpers') were able to isolate wage and salary payments from other sources of income from shopkeeping. The firms for which these wage

18. Unweighted mean.
19. The very slight differences in margins throughout the 'chemists' goods, etc.' group are undoubtedly the product of resale price maintenance.
20. An analysis of these differences in gross margins between the two types of organization is to be found in Hughes and Pollard (1956).

and salary costs are given in detail account for 55·4 per cent of total retail sales, and although this group includes most of the large shops and multiples but very few of the small shops, each size group within the major sub-groups of trades may be taken as sufficiently representative of its type to warrant further investigation into the relationship of size, trade and margin. This section is therefore devoted to a discussion of the 'residual margin', left after the wages bill has been deducted from gross margins, in the retail firms without working proprietors.

Table 5 indicates the relationship between gross margins, the wages and salaries bill and residual margins.[21]

'Grocery' has been separated from the rest of retail trade in this table because its wage and salary costs increase fairly steadily with size of organization, whereas they fall with increasing size in other sections of retail trade. In both cases the sales per person engaged rise sharply with

Table 5 **Gross margins, wages and salaries, and residual margins in retail organizations without working proprietors**

| Size group (as for table 4) | (Expressed as percentage of turnover) | | | | | |
| | Grocery | | | All other retail | | |
	G.M.	W./Sal.	Residual	G.M.	W./Sal.	Residual
1 and 2	15·2	8·4	6·8	28·6	15·5	13·1
3	14·7	7·3	7·4	26·7	13·7	13·0
4	15·3	8·1	7·2	26·7	14·2	12·5
5	16·2	9·1	7·1	25·9	13·7	12·2
6	16·3	9·3	7·0	25·5	12·7	12·8
7	16·1	9·1	7·0	24·6	11·6	13·0
8	17·6	10·1	7·5	24·5	11·2	13·3
9	19·3	10·8	8·5	24·6	10·9	13·7
10 and 11	18·0	10·0	8·0	24·7	10·6	14·1

size of organization, but in the grocery trades low labour efficiency[22] is more than compensated for by low wages costs, while in other sections of retail trade it is not fully compensated for by the differences in the wages paid in different sizes of organization.

Thus the small shops in every trade group have low sales per person employed, which are usually reflected in high labour costs in relation to

21. Table 28 of the Census of Distribution gives these data for the main groups and sub-groups of retail trade.

22. The term 'labour efficiency' is used here to denote the sales per person employed per annum. See Hughes and Pollard (1955). See also the discussions of the criteria of efficiency in distribution in Hough (1949, pp. 49–66); Hall and Knapp (1955a, p. 76, n. 1); Roberts (1955, p. 78); Pasdermadjian (1954, pp. 80 ff).

turnover. We should, therefore, expect the higher gross margins of the small units to be absorbed in large measure by their wages bills, leaving them a residual margin, to meet profits, rents and other costs, near or below the average of all shops. Such is, in fact, the case in thirty-three out of the forty-five sub-groups of retail trade large enough for statistical analysis. In fourteen of these, in which residual margins of small shops are much below the average, it would appear that high labour costs and poor purchasing terms are likely to be balanced by low rents and services provided or low returns to owners, or a combination of the two.[23] In the remainder (nineteen trades), the less favourable labour costs are passed on to the customer in the form of normal margins, which in the case of small shops often mean higher retail prices.

In the remaining twelve sub-groups of trades the residual margins of the small shop are still high. Four of these sell goods which are largely price-maintained: booksellers and stationers, grocery with hardware, tobacconists and builders' merchants. In view of the high labour costs in small shops this high residual margin is even more puzzling than their high gross margin, but neither has an easy explanation under r.p.m., which would prevent them from charging higher prices. It is conceivable that the small shops (especially in the two first-named trades) concentrated on stocking only those articles on which a high margin can be earned; but it is difficult to escape the conclusion that some of the returns of small shops are highly suspect.[24] The other eight trades are typically those in which retailers make many of their own prices: they are grocery with bakery goods and baking, women's outerwear, soft furnishing, musical instruments, fancy goods, leather goods, pets and pet food and pawnbrokers. In their case, the customer is likely to pay an exceptionally high price in the very small shop, whether or not this is compensated for by convenience of location or services rendered.[25]

At the other end of the scale are the very large shops and the multiple firms with turnovers of £25,000 or £50,000, p.a. and over. Their 'labour efficiency' is in every case at or above the average, and their gross margins are also high. As a result, their residual margins drop in no case below the average, and are generally well above it.

Large retailing firms of both types (large shops and multiples) have generally a different cost structure from the small shops. Rents and certain

23. This group includes, among others, fishmongers, footwear, men's wear, men's and women's wear, women's outfitters, drapers, domestic furniture and hardware, coal and florists.
24. Suspicion is increased when the smallest firms of butchers and corsetieres are found to have returned an average year-end stock of £1 in value per firm.
25. We are indebted for this point, as for other comments on the paper, to B. Yamey.

types of equipment costs and overheads are likely to be relatively higher[26] and are, in part, substitutes for the higher labour costs to be found in small units. Residual margins, as used here, are, therefore, likely to include precisely those costs which bear heavily on the large firms. Where these residual margins are near the average, they are likely to represent low returns to the proprietors or high technical efficiency. In either of these cases the benefits of large-scale organization are passed on to the consumer. There were sixteen out of the forty-five sub-groups in this category in 1950. In four of them, the largest firms showed a markedly slower turnover than firms of other sizes, but the adverse effects of large stocks on retailing costs cannot be calculated with any accuracy and are in any case likely to be small. The other twelve sub-groups showed stock turns at or above the average. Among these sixteen trades in which large-scale enterprise appears to benefit the consumer in the form of lower prices are fishmongers, footwear, men's wear, dairy and greengrocers, fruiterers: all are trades in which the large firm is represented by the multiple rather than by the single large shop.

In the other twenty-nine sub-groups, the residual margins of the large firms rise remarkably steeply (Table 6), after showing little variation in the other sizes.

Table 6 **Variations of residual margins with size of organization: (index)[27]**

Turnover	Under £2500	£2500 and under £5000	£5000 and under £10,000	£10,000 and under £25,000	£25,000 and under £50,000	£50,000 and over
19 trades	84	87	85	83	83	107
10 trades	84	83	87	90	112	

In addition to benefiting from low labour costs and more favourable purchase prices, which are common to virtually all large firms, in nine trades the largest size of firm also showed a very favourable rate of stock turn.[28] The large residual margins point to the fact that these advantages tend to be swallowed up by higher costs or by higher net returns (or both) and do not benefit the consumer.

The argument of this brief review of gross margins and residual margins in retail trade may be summarized as follows:

26. In multiple shops, rents are likely to be particularly high; in large unit stores, rents are lower, but costs of services, equipment, advertisement, etc., are high.

27. The table is constructed as Table 3 above. Average g.m. in each trade = 100.

28. These include clothing (women's outfitters, women's underwear, men's and women's wear, drapers), domestic furniture and radio and electrical goods, a mixture of large shops and chains.

1. There is a wide dispersion of margins within all trades and size groups as classified in the Census. This appears to be partly the result of imperfect competition, and partly of the heterogeneity of goods and services provided, by different shops, however narrowly the Census sub-groups are defined.

2. A comparison of the margins of retail organization by size of turnover shows distinct regularities. In trades accounting for nearly half the total retail sales the gross margins are lowest in the medium-size groups (turnover £5000 to £50,000) and rise progressively towards the extremes.

3. Shops with working proprietors have generally lower margins than similar shops without working proprietors, the difference being, in most cases, of the order of 10 per cent.

4. When wages costs are deducted from the gross margins of firms without working proprietors, the residual margins also show certain regularities when the firms are grouped by size. In twenty-nine out of forty-five sub-groups, the largest firms have residual margins some thirty per cent higher than the rest; in the remaining sixteen sub-groups, where the large firm is normally a multiple, this rise in residual margins is not found.

References

ALLEN, G. R., and RUTHERFORD, M. E. E. (1954), 'Fruit and vegetable prices in a large city', *J. indust. Econ.*, vol. 2, pp. 221–5.
Census of Distribution and Other Services, 1950 (1954), vol. 2, Retail and Service Trades, General tables, HMSO.
GORNALL, E. (1954), 'Some aspects of the retail greengrocery trade in an industrial working class district', *J. indust. Econ.*, vol. 2, pp. 207–20.
HALL, M., and KNAPP, J. (1955a). 'Numbers of shops and productivity in retail distribution in Great Britain, the United States and Canada', *econ. J.*, vol. 65, pp. 72–88.
HALL, M., and KNAPP, J. (1955b), 'Gross margins and efficiency measurement in retail trade', *Oxford econ. Papers*, vol. 7, pp. 312–26.
HOUGH, J. A. (1949), 'Retail sales per employee', *Manchester Sch.*, vol. 17, pp. 49–66.
HUGHES, J. D., and POLLARD, S. (1955), 'Retailing costs', *Oxford econ. Papers*, vol. 7, pp. 71–93.
HUGHES, J. D., and POLLARD, S. (1956), 'Note on managerial incomes in retail distribution', *Manchester Sch.*, vol. 24, pp. 68–76.
PASDERMADJIAN, H. (1954), *The Department Store*, Newman Books.
ROBERTS, C. (1955), 'Labour productivity and utilization in capitalist and cooperative shop trading', *J. indust. Econ.*, vol. 4, pp. 78–80.
WRAY, M. (1954), 'Fashion in the women's outerwear industry', *Westminster Bank Rev.*, November.

Part Four
Characteristics of Retail Operations

Many of the characteristics of retailing mentioned in the Readings by Mill and Marshall can be incorporated into formally rigorous models. Baumol (Reading 17) demonstrates that product differentiation by a a retailer must concern itself not only with the characteristics of the products sold but also with the service characteristics of the retail outlet, all within the environment of diverse consumer preferences. Where the location of retail units is a significant variable in attracting consumers, Huff (Reading 18) shows how consumer utilities may be reflected in alternative locations involving differences in travelling time, the size of a shopping facility, and the type of shopping trip undertaken. By focusing on one other variable in the consumer's behavioural response, Baumol and Ide (Reading 19) demonstrate the implications, in terms of costs and profits for the retailer and of costs for the consumer, of extending the inventory range. Cairns (Reading 20) provides a similar analysis of the problem, when the retail assortment is adjusted, of maintaining a profit-maximizing balance between changes in the use of space and increments in gross profits.

17 W. J. Baumol

Optimal Product and Retailer Characteristics[1]

W. J. Baumol, 'Calculation of optimal product and retailer characteristics: the abstract product approach', *Journal of Political Economy*, vol. 75, 1967, pp. 674–85.

In an unpublished paper Professor A. R. Oxenfeldt (1966) has recently called to our attention the fact that the standard models of the firm do not treat some of the most critical decision problems that arise under monopolistic competition. These models do not tell us how sellers deal with the diversity of consumer tastes that characterize most real markets and how, consequently, the firm decides on a competitive strategy that encompasses the specifications of its products and the 'marketing mix' that constitutes the distinctive personality of its selling effort. It has long been recognized that these are issues that loom very large in the mind of management – often much more so than the routine pricing decisions that are the focus of most standard models. Yet it has often been felt that they are too amorphous and too difficult to define for their effective incorporation in a model that is analytically tractable.[2]

Utilizing a relatively new analytic framework which I call the 'abstract product approach', this paper provides a model that undertakes to describe the calculation of an optimal selling posture: the choice of product characteristics and retailer stance that respond most effectively to diverse consumer tastes and the characteristics of products and firms that are already in the market. It illustrates in a small-scale case how the calculation can actually be conducted and describes a programing formulation that can be used in the general case. The computation does require data on consumers' tastes and costs of alternative strategies that are not always readily available. Yet reasonable approximations to the requisite data are potentially obtainable by standard means such as the market survey. And the required information is far more accessible than are the figures needed in areas of

1. Since the completion of this paper there has appeared a pathbreaking new analysis by Kelvin Lancaster (1966) applying a similar point of view to a closely related area. For a discussion of some of the other benefits offered by the abstract product approach and an application, see Quandt and Baumol (1966).

2. There have, however, been a number of interesting writings on the subject. See, for example, Hans Brems (1951) and Lawrence Abbott (1955). See also Harold Hotelling (1929). A highly suggestive game-theoretic analysis has been provided by Robert Reichardt (1962).

analysis considered to be on the verge of becoming operational. Here I have in mind, for example, investment decision models, many of which call for relatively firm notions on the future stream of returns that is offered by each candidate investment project.

The objective of the model provided here, then, is rather ambitious. It seeks to analyse in theoretical terms some of the most fundamental decision problems that arise out of monopolistic competition and the diversity of buyers, products and competitive strategies. In addition, it points the way to an approach to the matter that is tractable computationally and that offers some hope for eventual application.

However, the analysis evades completely one important aspect of the problem – the effects of oligopolistic interdependence. As is the case with so many models of the firm that seek to show how optimal decisions are arrived at, my construct simply ignores this vital issue and quite illegitimately assumes away the countermeasures to which our company's competitors are likely to be led by its decisions.[3]

1 Characterization of consumer and seller diversity

Though it is obvious that there is diversity in the tastes of consumers, the manner in which these differences are sometimes characterized is most inconvenient for analytic purposes. One consumer may be extremely price conscious, while another may assign a good deal of weight to the courteous and considerate service provided by a retailer. Yet these differences are not absolute, as some descriptions might seem to suggest. For example, it is plausible that the first of the preceding customers would ignore minimal price differences if service in the slightly more expensive shop were also vastly better.

Willingness to substitute one desired attribute for another, provided the exchange rate is right, is of course representable with the aid of the individual's indifference map, and we shall use this device here. For simplicity of exposition it will be assumed that (in the two-variable cases) each person's indifference curves are a set of parallel straight lines, so that the marginal rates of substitution among store or product attributes will be taken to be constant, at least over the relevant range. Hence, any individual's indifference map can be characterized completely with the aid of a single parameter: the slope of any one of his indifference curves. When the analysis is generalized to deal with n attributes of a product or store, the straight-

3. For a treatment of the subject of oligopolistic interdependence in product design, see Reichardt (1962). See also Martin Shubik (1959, pp. 295–308). One reader suggested an approach to this matter in which each firm solves its own problem, uses the same reasoning to calculate the responses of competitors, on this basis recalculates its own decision, etc. I have no idea whether these calculations by different firms would yield consistent results or whether the process would be convergent.

line indifference curves must clearly be replaced by families of parallel $n-1$ dimensional hyperplanes which are then determined uniquely by the values of their $n-1$ partial derivatives. In the n-attribute discussion this linearity assumption will enable the analysis to remain within the realm of *linear* integer programing, and so it will play a role considerably more significant that mere expository convenience.

Though in Section 5 we will turn to an n-attribute analysis, the discussion of the next few sections will deal with the two-dimensional diagram – the two-attribute case. In Figure 1 we have such a diagram, and along its

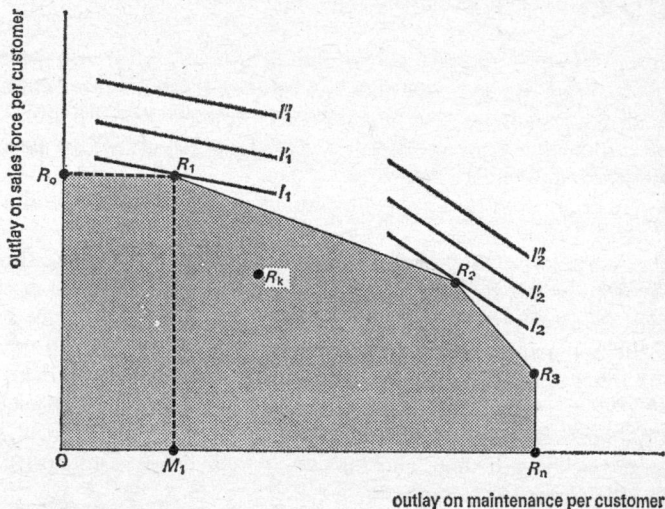

Figure 1

axes we measure two illustrative attribute variables for a retailing establishment: expenditure (per customer) on store renovation and maintenance and expenditure (per customer) on sales force, each of which is assumed to improve the desirability of the store to the shopper. A noteworthy example of other attribute measures we might have used instead of the preceding is the variable $1/p$, where p is some index of the store's price level, so that a *ceteris paribus* rise in $1/p$, that is, a fall in p, will be desired by the customer who does not judge quality by price and is not taken by snob appeal.

2 Equilibrium of the consumer: abstract commodities and retailers

For our analysis it is convenient to describe a store or a product entirely as an abstract bundle of attributes such as those which have just been discussed. This is the essence of the abstract product approach, which ignores the explicit identity of any item that it is analysing and considers it only as an attribute bundle. Thus in Figure 1 a store or a product is characterized *completely* by a point in the diagram (which we may call its 'strategy point'). Point R_1, for example, represents a retailer whose strategy consists of the expenditure of OM_1 dollars on maintenance and OR_0 dollars on his sales force. The diagram also shows two other retailer or commodity strategy points, R_2 and R_3, representing two other selling outlets or two other goods. The parallel lines labelled I_1, I_1' and I_1'' are indifference curves of one customer, while those marked I_2, I_2' and I_2'' are indifference curves of another.

Since the absolute slope of the I_1 lines is less than that of R_1R_2, the straight line connecting points R_1 and R_2, customer 1 will attain maximal satisfaction by shopping at store 1. For this customer points R_2 and R_3 lie on lower indifference curves than does R_1. Similarly, because the slope of consumer 2's indifference curves is between that of R_1R_2 and that of R_2R_3, customer 2 will, if he is rational, shop at store 2. No one will shop at a 'dominated' store such as k, whose attributes place it at a point R_k below and to the left of any point on the line segment (R_1R_2) connecting two other store points, because any consumer can reach a higher level of satisfaction by shopping at one or the other of the stores (1 or 2) represented by the end points of that line segment.

This, in essence, describes the determination of the equilibrium of the consumer. We can summarize its properties with the aid of the following conventions: exclude from consideration dominated store points such as R_k at which no one will shop, and number the remaining store strategy points in order from left to right, R_1, R_2,..., R_{n-1}. Let R_0 and R_n be fictitious 'dummy' store points, where R_0 is the point on the vertical axis directly to the left of R_1 and R_n is the point on the horizontal axis directly below the rightmost store point, R_{n-1} (which is R_3 in the diagram). Note first that, together with the axes, R_0, R_1, R_2,..., R_n must constitute the boundary of a convex region. Let S_j be the (absolute) slope of one of individual j's indifference curves, and let $S_{i,i+1}$ be the (absolute) slope of the line segment R_iR_{i+1}. Then we have the following result that completely characterizes the equilibrium of the consumer:

Theorem 1
Sufficient condition: a rational consumer j will always shop at store i if $S_{i-1,i} < S_j < S_{i,i+1}$. Necessary condition: j will not shop at store i unless $S_{i-1,i} \leqslant S_j \leqslant S_{i,i+1}$.

The rationale of this result should be obvious on examination of the diagram.

3 Total demand for a product or a store

It is now simple, in principle, to determine the demand which will be attracted by a store's or a product's characteristics. It is convenient – though, as we will see, not necessary – to assume that a customer's total demand for the items in question is relatively fixed – he is merely concerned with the choice of store in which to purchase or the choice among the competing products meeting his general specifications. Then we may consider a customer who is willing to purchase $2k$ units as the equivalent of two customers, with the same indifference-curve slopes, each one purchasing k units, and, correspondingly, an increase in demand by any one customer may be translated as a rise in the number of buyers present in the market.

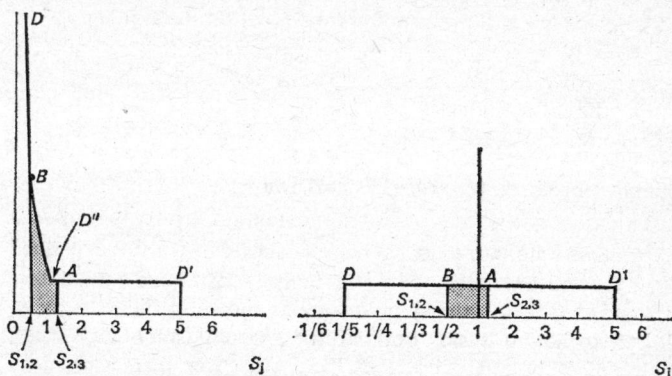

Figure 2

Utilizing this definition of 'a customer', one can construct a diagram showing the distribution of customers as a function of the slope of their indifference curves (Figure 2, *left*). This distribution is represented by DD', whose peculiar shape will be explained presently. The area under the curve between any two points S_a and S_b on the S_j (horizontal) axis represents the total number of customers (total sales to customers) whose indifference-curve slopes lie in the interval $S_a \leqslant S_j \leqslant S_b$.

In the diagram we show specifically the points $S_{1,2}$ and $S_{2,3}$ corresponding, respectively, to the slopes of line segments R_1R_2 and R_2R_3 in Figure 1. Since, by theorem 1, all individuals whose indifference curves have slopes falling in this interval will shop at store 2, we see that the sales volume of this store will be given by shaded area $S_{1,2}S_{2,3}AB$. Similarly, store 1 will obtain all customers corresponding to the available area to the left of point $S_{1,2}$, and store 3 will obtain the demand given by the area under the DD' curve to the right of point $S_{2,3}$.

This is all there is to say on the determination of demand for each store. A word should be said, however, about the peculiar distribution function DD' utilized in Figure 2, *left*, because this provides some illumination on the nature of the relevant demand function. I have assumed here as a standard of reference that the slopes of customers' indifference curves are in a sense uniformly distributed between, say, $S_J = \frac{1}{5}$ and $S_J = 5$. However, in our standard-of-reference case it seems appropriate to suppose that customers' preferences are more or less symmetrically distributed between the two attributes represented by the axes in Figure 1. That is, there should be about as many indifference maps with slopes less than unity as there are with slopes greater than unity. Thus, to show a uniform distribution in the usual way, one would have to distort the horizontal axis by extending the portion of that axis lying to the left of point $S_J = 1$, in the manner shown in Figure 2, *right*. If one then transforms the diagram back to a normal axis, the DD' curve is distorted in the manner shown in Figure 2, *left*, because the area under the curve to the left of point $S_J = 1$ must be the same as the corresponding area in Figure 2, *right*.[4]

4 The optimal competitive stance of a business firm

We can address ourselves now to the optimal strategy of a firm that is about to open a new store or launch a new product. For reasons explained in note 5, we assume that there are initially (at least) two other competitors in the area and that their strategy points are as shown in Figure 3 by R_1 and R_2. It is clear that our store's optimal strategy point cannot lie beneath and to the left of the boundary line $R_0R_1R_2R_n$. Moreover, there is no motivation for management to spend the money necessary to take it beyond point R, which lies directly to the right of R_1 and directly above R_2. For at R our company dominates both its competitors, and, if they undertook no countermoves, he could take away all their customers. Thus all the relevant strategy points for our company must lie in the triangular region R_1RR_2.

Let TT' be a locus of all strategy points in the relevant triangular region involving a constant total expenditure on maintenance (M) and sales force (F). In our case, since we are measuring these variables in terms of the

---

4. The equation for the portion of the DD' curve in Figure 2, *left*, that lies to the left of point D'' is $y = f(S_J) = k/S_J^2$.
Proof. Write $S_J = q$ for the abscissa of any point to the left of $S_J = 1$ and $S_J = p$ for the abscissa of any point to the right of this. Moreover, let k be the ordinate of any point on the horizontal segment of DD'. We require the area under DD' between $S_J = q$ and $S_J = 1$ to be the same as the area between $S_J = 1$ and $S_J = p$, where $p = 1/q$. This requires for all q that $-f(q)dq = f(p)dp$, for $p = 1/q$, $q \leqslant 1$. Since $f(p) = k$, this means $f(q) = -kdp/dq = k/q^2$, which is our result.

expenditure devoted to them, line TT' has the equation $M+F$ = constant, and it has a slope of minus one.[5]

One can then, as will be shown presently, determine what point on TT' yields a maximal sales volume to our firm. Suppose this optimal point is A, which therefore represents the optimal strategic stance for our company given the constant level of expenditure specified by TT'. If one next considers the various other possible expenditure levels (various shifts in TT'), the set of corresponding optimal points such as A forms a locus EE'. This is the company's expansion path, describing the variation in its optimal strategic stance for different expenditure levels.

Let us now examine a simple though rather artificial example to describe the numerical computations involved in the determination of the optimal points. The main purpose of the derivation, of course, is to illustrate the nature of the calculation, not to obtain a result that pretends to be representative. Some readers may prefer to skim over its details or to proceed directly to the generalized n-attribute formulation in programing terms that is provided in the next section.

In Figure 3 the x and y co-ordinates of points R_1, A and R_2 are shown in the following table:

	R_1	A	R_2
y	10	9	2
x	1	3	8

Thus, we have as the absolute slopes S_{1a} and S_{a2} for line segments R_1A and AR_2, respectively, $S_{1a} = (10-9)/(3-1) = \frac{1}{2}$ and $S_{a2} = \frac{7}{5}$. With a rectangular distribution of the sort represented in Figure 2, we consider first the area under the curve DD' between points $S_j = 1$ and $S'_j = S_{a2} = \frac{7}{5}$,

---

5. We can see now why our analysis assumes that (at least) two firms are already in the market before our company starts to plan its entry. In terms of our model there is no optimal strategy for a monopoly firm. For with total demand given it would capture the entire market with any sort of reasonable facilities or product characteristics. It would, however, find it profitable to make itself sufficiently attractive to discourage the entry of new competitors. This would mean that its strategy point, R_1, would have to be at a considerable distance from the origin. Fear of retaliation aside, it would pay a second firm to locate its strategy point just above or just to the right of R_1. Thus, in Figure 3, consider any strategy point A for our second firm on iso-expenditure line TT'. By theorem 1, this company will capture more of the market the smaller the absolute slope of R_1A, for it will then get the business of all customers whose indifference curves are steeper than this. But the slope of R_1A decreases monotonically as A approaches T. Note that this result is independent of the position of R_1. One concludes that there are only two motivations for our second seller to differentiate himself from seller 1: first, he may want to avoid retaliation by seller 1, and, second, he may want to prevent a third entering firm from cutting him off from the market, just as he had previously done to seller 1. If he had picked a point just to the right of R_1, he would have been as vulnerable to this sort of move as seller 1 was initially.

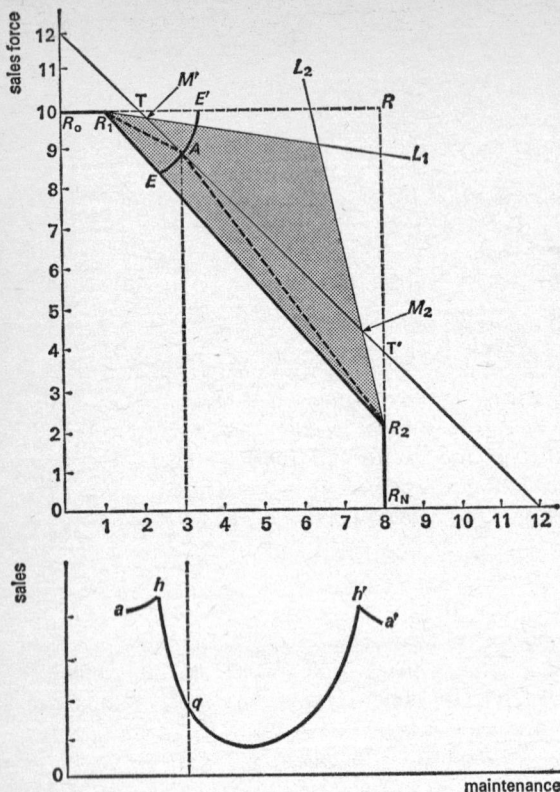

Figure 3

which is clearly $k(S'_j - S_j) = k(\frac{7}{5} - 1) = \frac{2}{5}k$. Similarly, the area under the curve to the left of $S_j = 1$ will be $k[(1/S_{1a}) - 1] = k(2-1) = k$. Hence at point A total demand will be the sum of these two areas $= k + \frac{2}{5}k = \frac{7}{5}k$. This is represented by point q on the sales curve aa' shown toward the bottom of Figure 3.

From this observation we can proceed to the derivation of the entire demand relationship. Let P be any point on TT', and let its co-ordinates be (x, y). Then the absolute slopes of R_1P and PR_2 are, respectively,

$$S_{1P} = \frac{10-y}{x-1} \quad \text{and} \quad S_{P2} = \frac{y-2}{8-x}. \qquad 1$$

Since for any point on TT' we have $y = 12 - x$, these slopes become by substitution

$$S_{1P} = \frac{x-2}{x-1} \quad \text{and} \quad S_{P2} = \frac{10-x}{8-x}. \qquad \qquad \mathbf{2}$$

Now as point P moves toward the right along the iso-expenditure curve TT', both of the preceding slopes will obviously increase in absolute value. The rise in S_{1P} will result in a loss in customers by theorem 1, for any customer j whose indifference curves have the slope S_j will cease shopping at our store once S_{1P} exceeds S_j. However, while the rise in S_{1P} loses customers whose S_j is small, the simultaneous rise in S_{P2} brings in new customers whose S_j was formerly greater than S_{P2} in absolute value. Thus, every rightward move of point P has two counteracting effects on demand: it brings in some new customers, and it loses some old ones. This is only to be expected, for as a store changes its attributes it will attract those customers who value highly its new characteristics and will drive away the purchasers who preferred the alternative store image.

However, the peculiarity of our assumed demand distribution places a limit on this balancing process. For our illustrative premise is that $\frac{1}{5} \leqslant |S_j| \leqslant 5$ (see Figure 2). Hence, once point P moves so far to the right that $S_{2P} = 5$, any further rightward move will yield no new customers – it will only drive away the old ones. This will occur[6] where the abscissa of point P is 7·5 (point M_2 in Figure 3). Hence the firm will never move to any point on TT' to the right of M_2. More generally, if we consider iso-expenditure curves other than TT', it will never pay the company to move to any point outside the relevant shaded region that lies to the left of line segment[7] R_2L_2, for any such point P will involve a slope $S_{P2} > 5$. Similarly, the company will never consider any point P on TT' to the left of M_1 where $x = 2\cdot25$, or any point P on any iso-expenditure curve that lies above line segment R_1L_1, for at any such point the slope S_{1P} would be less than $\frac{1}{5}$ in absolute value, and so an upward move from line M_1L_1 to such a P would bring in no new customers, since, by Figure 2, there are no potential purchasers with a marginal rate of substitution lower than this.[8]

We may now examine the shape of the demand curve corresponding to M_1M_2, the relevant segment of TT'. By theorem 1, demand (D) at any point P can be obtained with the aid of equation 2 by considering separately the areas (in Figure 2) to the left and to the right of the unit slope point, $S_j = 1$. This gives us

---

6. For by **2** this is the point where $5 = S_{P2} = (10-x)/(8-x)$, so that $40-5x = 10-x$, that is $x = 7\cdot5$.

7. By **1** the equation of R_2L_2 is given by $S_{P2} = (y-2)/(8-x) = 5$ so that $y = 42-5x$.

8. By **1** the equation of R_1L_1 is $S_{1P} = (10-y)/(x-1) = \frac{1}{5}$. By **2**, point M_1 is the point on this line at which $x+y = 12$, so that $(x-2)/(x-1) = \frac{1}{5}$, that is, $5x-10 = x-1$, and so $x = 2\cdot25$.

$$D = k\left(\frac{1}{S_{1P}} - 1 + S_{P2} - 1\right)$$
$$= k\left(\frac{x-1}{x-2} - 1 + \frac{10-x}{8-x} - 1\right) \qquad\qquad 3$$
$$= \frac{k}{x-2} + \frac{2k}{8-x}.$$

This is our desired demand function. To determine some of its properties we differentiate it to obtain

$$\frac{dD}{dx} = \frac{2k}{(8-x)^2} - \frac{k}{(x-2)^2}.$$

Hence, by inspection, we see that the second derivative must be positive[9] when $2 < x < 8$, since any increase in x increases the positive term and reduces the negative term in dD/dx. Thus the portion of the demand curve corresponding to points on $M_1 M_2$ will have the form shown by hh' in Figure 3 and will have only an interior minimum.[10] This result is totally independent of the particular values chosen for the co-ordinates of the competitive points R_1 and R_2. The entire demand curve will have the shape given by aa', and the optimal point will clearly be one of the two peaks h or h' (in this case it will be point h).[11]

5 Extension to an n-attribute calculation

We turn now to the generalization of our analysis to the n-attribute case. The form of our approach suggests that the firm's optimality calculation can be transformed into a linear- or non-linear-programing computation. The boundary $R_0 R_1 R_2 ... R_n$ in Figure 1 looks just like that of the feasible region in a linear-programing calculation, and the imbedded maximization calculations of the individual consumers at once suggest the decentralized-decision approach of decomposition theory. It turns out that a programing

9. More formally, $d^2D/dx^2 = 4k/(8-x)^3 + 2k/(x-2)^3 > 0$ for $8 > x > 2$.

10. Note the relationship to the conclusion by Hotelling (1929) that in spatial competition in a linear world competitors would tend to select adjacent positions in the center of the line. Abbott (1955, p. 184) points out that this sort of conclusion is 'apparently the result of the highly artificial assumption that demand terminates abruptly at each end of the line, rather than tapering off at the outer fringes', and of the 'assumption that an increase in the distance between buyer and seller does not diminish the quantity bought'.

11. For points to the left of h the equation for the demand curve is obtained by substituting $\frac{1}{3}$ for S_{1P} in equation 3, while the equation for $h'a'$ is obtained by substitution of 5 for S_{P2} in equation 1. The values of quantity of demands at the two candidate maxima, h and h', are determined by substitution of their x values into 3 to obtain
$D_h = k(1/0 \cdot 25 + 2/5 \cdot 75) = 4\frac{8}{23}k$;
$D_{h'} = k(1/5 \cdot 5 + 2/0 \cdot 5) = 4\frac{2}{11}k$.

approach to the matter does work, though it is not precisely what seems to be suggested by our figures. In mathematical terms our n-attribute problem may be described as follows:

Let x_{ij} represent the proportion of consumer i's shopping done at store j (or for product j), so that we would expect $\sum_j x_{ij} = 1$ for any consumer i $(i = 1, 2,..., m)$, $(j = 0, 1, 2,..., n)$; let a_{jk} be the value of attribute k provided at store j or by product j $(k = 1, 2,..., r)$; finally, let u_{ki} be the marginal utility[12] of attribute k to consumer i. In order to permit *linear*-programing methods to be used in the following discussion, these marginal utilities are assumed to be constant, so that customers' indifference maps are again taken to be composed of families of parallel hyperplane indifference surfaces.

The objective of our store, say, store zero, is to choose values of the a_{0k} which will

$$\left.\begin{array}{l}
\text{maximize} \quad \sum_i x_{i0} \\
\text{subject to the budget constraint} \\
g_0(a_{01},..., a_{0r}) \leqslant B_0 \\
\text{and the non-negativity requirement} \\
\text{all } a_{0k} \geqslant 0.
\end{array}\right\} \qquad \textbf{4}$$

The x_{ij}, the demands by the various customers i for the product of store j, are determined by the m subsidiary maximization calculations:[13]

$$\left.\begin{array}{l}
\text{maximize the utility of customer } i: \\
\sum_j \sum_k a_{jk} u_{ki} x_{ij} \quad (i = 1, 2,..., m) \\
\text{subject to}^{14} \\
\sum_j x_{ij} \leqslant 1 \quad \text{and all} \quad x_{ij} \geqslant 0.
\end{array}\right\} \qquad \textbf{5}$$

12. This can be expressed as a ratio to u_{si}, the marginal utility of any arbitrarily chosen standard attribute s. Then we need deal only with ordinal utility and marginal rates of substitution, which, as in the earlier portion of the paper, are constant as a result of the assumed constancy of the u_{si}.

13. In this calculation the values of all competitors' attribute variables, a $(j \neq 1)$, are taken to be given in advance. Thus we once again evade the issues raised by oligopolistic interdependence.

14. The inequality in the constraint $\sum x_{ij} \leqslant 1$ makes it possible for the consumer to end up at any point inside the feasible region. This already provides some degree of flexibility to consumer demand. In any event, it should be observed that the analysis does *not* require total demand either of the individual consumer or of the market as a whole to be fixed and predetermined. Variability of demand can be introduced by means of two simple devices: (a) an increase of demand by any one consumer (say a trebling of his demand) may be described as the entry into the market of two additional consumers with similar utility functions; (b) new customers may be taken to flow in from store n, which is a fictitious retailing establishment offering zero prices and zero outlays on other attributes. That is, retailer n becomes the location of all potential customers who do not initially shop at any real store in the analysis but who might be induced to shop at our store (zero) if it makes itself sufficiently attractive.

The solution of the consumer's decision problem **5** is trivial, for it is a single-constraint linear-programing problem in the variables x_{ij}. Since the constraint coefficients are all equal to unity, if there is a unique maximum we must have the following solution:

$$x_{iw} = 1 \quad \text{for}$$
$$\sum_k a_{wk} u_{ki} = \max \left(\sum_k a_{jk} u_{ki} \right);$$
$$x_{ij} = 0 \quad \text{for} \quad j \neq w.$$

The seller's decision problem **4** is not so easily solved, however, since it involves some relatively difficult combinatorial allocation problems. In effect, each time management reallocates its resources to cater to the tastes of one set of consumers, it is likely to alienate some other set of its clientele. The problem is to find some way to balance these gains and losses and thus to design a systematic procedure which leads to an optimal solution.[15] Several simplifications can help us to make the problem more tractable. First, we redefine the a_{jk} to represent the amount of *money* spent by firm j on attribute k. Then the budget constraint takes the simple linear form

$$\sum_k a_{0k} \leqslant B_0. \qquad\qquad 6$$

Second, as a matter of convenience in application it is helpful to divide the set of consumers into subsets such that any two consumers in the same subset have reasonably similar utility functions. We will let y_{ij} be a variable whose value is unity if customers in set i find it advantageous to shop in store j and whose value is zero otherwise, and let s_i be the number of dollars to be spent by this customer set per unit of time. As a final preliminary we observe that customers in set i will purchase from our store (zero) if[16]

$$\sum_k a_{0k} u_{ki} \geqslant \max_{j \neq 0} \left(\sum_k a_{jk} u_{ki} \right),$$

that is, if store zero offers consumers i greater utility than is made available by any other retailer, j. However, all values on the right of the inequality

15. Note the structural resemblance of our problem to the Colonel Blotto game in which a player can capture a chunk of territory or an installation by assigning to it more of his pieces than his opponent has placed there. Our calculation problem is rendered somewhat more difficult, since in it the weight (utility) assigned to different pieces (dollars of attribute expenditure) varies from territory to territory (consumer to consumer), and one piece (attribute expenditure) can simultaneously serve several consumers. On the other hand, the Blotto game takes into account the full problem of competitive strategy, while our discussion assumes all rivals' decisions (product designs and retailing characteristics) to be determined in advance. On the Blotto problem see D. W. Blackett (1954, pp. 55–60).

16. This inequality disposes of the possibility of ties by assuming arbitrarily that if a customer is indifferent between store zero and another retailer he will shop at the former. The economics of the situation really offers us no information which enables us to deal with the problem more reasonably. A variety of conventions can be used to dispose of ties – for example, we can assume that if w stores each offer the same utility to customers in subset i, then $1/w$ of these customers will go to each of those retailers.

are known in advance, since both the utility coefficients, u_{ki}, and the competitors' attributes, a_{jk}, are given. Hence we can write $\mathrm{Max}_{J \neq 0} \left(\sum_k a_{jk} u_{ki} \right) = K_i$ for the utility of the best alternative offered to consumers in set i by store zero's competitors. The condition under which these customers will shop at store zero thus becomes

$$\sum_k a_{0k} u_{ki} \geqslant K_i. \qquad\qquad 7$$

It is now possible to combine the maximization problem of our seller with those of each customer-set into a single mixed-integer program:[17]

Maximize $\sum_i s_i y_{i0}$ subject to

$$\sum a_{k0} \leqslant B_0,$$
$$y_{i0} \leqslant 1,$$
$$\sum_k a_{0k} u_{ki} \geqslant y_{i0} K_i,$$
all $a_{0k} \geqslant 0, \quad y_{i0} \geqslant 0,$
y_{i0} integer.

Here the first constraint is company zero's budget constraint, **6**, and the three constraints $y_{i0} \leqslant 1$, $y_{i0} \geqslant 0$, and y_{i0} integer guarantee that this variable can take only one of two values: either zero or one. However, it is the third constraint which constitutes the heart of the translation into a single program. It (together with the objective function) serves to guarantee that $y_{i0} = 1$ if condition **7** is satisfied and that $y_{i0} = 0$ otherwise. The reason this constraint has that effect is easily explained. The objective function guarantees that $y_{i0} = 1$ will always be chosen instead of $y_{i0} = 0$ if the former value does not violate the constraints of the problem. But if $y_{i0} = 1$, the right-hand term in our third constraint, $y_{i0}K_i$, simply becomes K_i, and this constraint is then identical with requirement **7**. Hence we will have $y_{i0} = 1$ if and only if **7** is satisfied. If, however, **7** is not satisfied, so that $y_{i0} = 1$ is not feasible, then $y_{i0} = 0$ is the only possible alternative. In that case the third constraint is, in effect, annulled by being transformed into the trivial requirement[18] $\sum a_{0k} u_{ki} \geqslant 0$. We see, then, that the form of the third constraint is such that it is changed into **7** if $y_{i0} = 1$, while the constraint, for all practical purposes, becomes inoperative if $y_{i0} = 0$, exactly as the analysis requires.

Computational approaches to this sort of mixed-integer-programing problem have recently been developed. In particular, a partitioning approach invented by Benders seems to be a promising way to deal with the

17. I am indebted to M. Balinski for suggesting this approach to the problem.

18. If some of the u_{ki} are negative, for example, if store expenditure on 'background music' offends some customers, even this last weak requirement may not automatically be satisfied. In that event the constraint $\sum a_{0k} u_{ki} \geqslant y_{i0} K_i$ can be replaced by the more general form $\sum a_{0k} u_{ki} \geqslant K_i - M(1 - y_{i0})$ with M sufficiently greater than K_i. Obviously if $y_{i0} = 1$ this again reduces to **7**, while if $y_{i0} = 0$ the right-hand side of the inequality reduces to $K_i - M$, so that $\sum a_{0k} u_{ki}$ is constrained only to exceed this negative number.

matter (see Benders, 1962, and Balinski, 1965, esp. pp. 271–4 and 268–90). The procedure has the advantage that, should the calculation prove too long and expensive, it can be stopped at an intermediate step to obtain an approximating feasible solution along with an estimate of its distance from the optimum.

6 Concluding comments

We have developed a model that constitutes an approach to the analysis of the optimal strategy of product design and retailer-characteristic determination. These decisions are, of course, at the heart of product differentiation and are among the most crucial issues faced by company managements.

The analysis has drawn its methods from several lines of analysis, perhaps the most important being the abstract-product approach (in which goods and retail establishments become just bundles of attributes). This is the very fruitful method that was first contributed by Kelvin Lancaster (1966) and independently arrived at by R. E. Quandt and the present author (Quandt and Baumol, 1966). The source of the problem studied in this paper is to be found in Oxenfeldt's more empirical view of the firm (1966), and for its calculations our investigation turned to the methods of integer programing. Thus from this variety of strands there emerges what may be a promising approach to a problem that seems previously to have appeared to be intractable, so that despite its obvious importance it has heretofore produced a comparatively scanty literature.

References

ABBOTT, L. (1955), *Quality and Competition*, Columbia University Press.
BALINSKI, M. L. (1965), 'Integer programming: methods, uses, computation', *manag. Sci.*, vol. 12, pp. 253–313.
BENDERS, J. F. (1962), 'Partitioning procedures for solving mixed-variables programming problems', *Numerische Math.*, vol. 4, pp. 238–52.
BLACKETT, D. W. (1954), 'Some blotto games', *Naval Res. Logistics Q.*, vol. 1, pp. 55–60.
BREMS, H. J. (1951), *Product Equilibrium under Monopolistic Competition*, Harvard University Press.
HOTELLING, H. (1929), 'Stability in competition', *econ. J.*, vol. 39, pp. 41–57.
LANCASTER, K. J. (1966), 'A new approach to consumer theory', *J. polit. Econ.*, vol. 74, pp. 132–57.
OXENFELDT, A. R. (1966), 'Broad outlines of a new model of markets: buyer and seller diversity', Columbia University, (mimeographed).
QUANDT, R. E., and BAUMOL, W. J. (1966), 'The demand for abstract transport modes: theory and measurement', *J. regional Sci.*, vol. 6, pp. 13–26.
REICHARDT, R. (1962), 'Competition through the introduction of new products', *Zeitschrift Nationalökon.*, vol. 22, pp. 41–84.
SHUBIK, M. (1959), *Strategy and Market Structure*, Wiley.

18 D. L. Huff

Optimal Retail Location

D. L. Huff, 'A programmed solution for approximating an optimum retail location', *Land Economics*, vol. 42, 1966, pp. 293–303.

The purpose of this article is to present a computer-programmed solution for approximating an optimum location of a proposed retail development. The problem involves calculating, for a set of potential locations, the net operating profit of each and then selecting from among this set that particular location at which the net operating profit is greatest, i.e., optimum.

The solution to the problem rests, in part, on two basic assumptions. First, the unique spatial position of each location has an effect on the potential sales that can be achieved. Second, the size of each location limits the scale of operation that can be considered for a proposed retail development and, as a consequence, has an effect on the development's potential sales as well as its operating costs. Therefore, proposed scales of operation at a given location will be constrained by a maximum size limit.

Given a specified number of potential locations for a proposed retail development within a particular geographical area, the sequential steps involved in estimating the optimum location are as follows:

1. Estimate sales values associated with specified scales of operation (up to the maximum size limit) for an initial potential location.
2. Specify the operating costs corresponding to each scale of operation.
3. Calculate net operating profit values for the initial location by simply subtracting the operating costs determined in step 2 from the corresponding sales values estimated in step 1.
4. Single out the maximum, that is the largest, net operating profit from among the specified scales of operation at the initial potential location.
5. Continue to calculate and single out maximum net operating profit values for each of the remaining potential locations; and
6. Select the optimum potential location by selecting that particular location which possesses the highest net operating profit.

Consumer demand

The critical calculation in the above-mentioned sequence is the sales estimate. In order to arrive at such an estimate, a model of consumer choice has been formulated. Naturally, a certain degree of abstraction is necessary in analysing such a complex subject as consumer behavior. There are innumerable variables pertinent to any given choice situation. In addition, countless possible relationships among such variables exist. Therefore, the objective here has been to formulate a comparatively simple model that possesses only a few important variables related to one another in a specified manner so as to produce predictions reasonably well and consistently.

Terms and definitions

The following basic elements are incorporated in the model of consumer behavior:

1. A set of alternative locational choices represented as set J.
2. A subset of alternative locational choices which is represented as J_0. The subset J_0 of alternatives represents available alternatives which are in accord with a consumer's tastes and preferences. Any given alternative within the subset J_0 is represented as j (where $j = 1,...,n$).
3. A positive 'payoff' function u_j associated with each alternative location indicating its 'utility' to a consumer.

Basic propositions

Given the preceding elements, the following propositions are set forth:

1. The probability P of a given alternative j being chosen from among all alternatives in the subset J_0 is proportional to u_j. That is,

$$P_j = \frac{u_j}{\sum_{j=1}^{n} u_j} \qquad\qquad 1$$

such that, $\sum_{j=1}^{n} P_j = 1$ and $0 < P_j \leqslant 1$.

2. The ratio between the probabilities of a consumer's choosing any one of two particular locations does not depend on the existence of other locations. This ratio is called the ratio of utilities of the two locations to a consumer. Therefore,

$$\frac{P_{j_1}}{P_{j_2}} = \frac{u_{j_1}}{u_{j_2}}$$

3. The properties of the pair (P_{j_1}, P_{j_2}) that determine the utility in (u_{j_1}, u_{j_2}) are (1) the 'size' S_j of a given shopping facility (an individual store, shopping center, etc.); and (2) the distance T_{ij} in time units from a consumer's travel base i to j.

4. The utility u_{ij} of a shopping facility is directly proportional to the ratio S_j/T_{ij}^{λ} where λ is constant. That is,

$$P_{ij} = \frac{u_{ij}}{\sum\limits_{j=1}^{n} u_{ij}} = \frac{S_j/T_{ij}^{\lambda}}{\sum\limits_{j=1}^{n} S_j/T_{ij}^{\lambda}}, \qquad\qquad 2$$

where P_{ij} = the probability of a consumer from a given statistical area[1] i travelling to a given shopping facility j; S_j = the size of a shopping facility; T_{ij} = the travel time involved in getting from a statistical area i to shopping facility j; and, λ = a parameter which is to be estimated empirically to reflect the effect of travel time on various kinds of shopping trips.

5. The expected number of consumers at a given statistical area i shopping at facility j is proportional to the number of consumers at i multiplied by the probability that a consumer at i will select j for shopping. Therefore,

$$E_{ij} = P_{ij}\, C_i \qquad\qquad 3$$

where E_{ij} = the expected number of consumers at i that are likely to travel to the shopping facility j; and, C_i = the number of consumers at i.

The expected average annual expenditures for a given product or product class by the consumers from a given statistical area i shopping at a particular retail facility j are equal to the expected number of consumers at i shopping at j multiplied by the average annual amount budgeted by such consumers for the product or product class in question. That is,

$$A_{ij} = E_{ij}\, B_{ik} \qquad\qquad 4$$

where A_{ij} = the expected average annual expenditures A for a given product or product class by the consumers at i shopping at j: and, B_{ik} = the average annual amount budgeted B by consumers at i for a given product or product class k.

The model of consumer behavior that has been presented should be assessed on the basis of two principal considerations: 1. its conceptual or theoretical content, and 2. its predictive capability.

Theoretical content

Consumer behavior as indicated by the probabilistic model reflects that the consumer is not able to discriminate among choices perfectly. As a consequence, the consumer is incapable of maximizing, i.e., choosing one alternative exclusively. This contention is based on two fundamental notions. First, when the perceived differences among alternative choices are small, the consumer finds it difficult to discriminate among them and there-

1. A statistical area may represent residential block grouping, census enumeration districts, squares within a constructed grid, etc.

fore chooses somewhat randomly. Secondly, and most important, since the consumer is uncertain as to the true conditions associated with the fulfillment of his shopping expectations at various alternative facilities, he tends to check on his intuitive beliefs; i.e., engages in an information-seeking process by also making choices from the other alternatives. This accounts for the proposition that, if a consumer is confronted with the same choice situation a number of times, he will tend to choose among such alternatives in some constant proportion; therefore, a 'relative utility' can be assigned to each. It should be mentioned, however, that, in any empirical examination of consumer choice behavior in which probabilities have been estimated, some variation from the actual observed behavior is almost certain to exist. However, if sufficient continued observations are made, it is contended that the actual behaviour will closely approximate the expected as derived from the model.

Consumer behavior as just described differs markedly from traditional economic theory in that the latter maintains that the consumer will always choose one particular alternative (that which is 'most desirable') with probability 1; therefore, all other alternatives possess probability zero. Utility, by definition, is thus identical with the rank of an alternative. Such a theory does not seem realistic. It is difficult to imagine consumers possessing perfect knowledge and the ability to discriminate among choices perfectly.

Predictive capability

Historically, models similar to the one advanced in this paper have been found to be quite successful in the analysis of spatial phenomena. Spatial interaction between points of origin and places of destination has been found to vary directly with some function of the 'attraction' of the places of destination and inversely with some function of the distance separating the points of origination and destination (Corrothers, 1956, pp. 94–102). Furthermore, the results of an empirical study using the model presented here proved to be quite favorable (for example, see Huff, 1962).

Composition and structural properties

The rationale underlying the use of the two variables (the size of the shopping facility S_j, and the time involved in getting from a consumer's travel base to a given shopping facility T_{ij}), the parameter λ, and the functional relationships that have been specified is worthy of discussion.

A consumer does not know in advance whether a particular shopping facility will definitely fulfill a specified purchase desire. However, a consumer does have an *a priori* knowledge of the probability that various shopping centers might satisfy his shopping demands. Such a probability is based, for the most part, on the number of items of the kind that he desires and feels are carried by various shopping facilities. Presumably, the greater the number of items carried by such facilities, the greater is the consumer's expectation that his shopping trip will be successful. Therefore, consumers will show a willingness to travel further distances for various goods and services as the number of such items available at various shopping centers increases. It would be extremely time-consuming and laborious to ascertain the number of different types of goods offered by various shopping facilities in any empirical application of the model. This factor can be approximated by using the square footage of selling space devoted to the sale of such items.

The utility of a shopping facility to a consumer is also influenced significantly by the effort and expense that is perceived to be involved in travelling to alternative shopping facilities. The anticipated costs of transportation, the effort involved in preparing for as well as making the trip, and other opportunities that must be foregone tend to detract from the utility of a shopping facility. This condition simply reflects the notion of opportunity costs. That is, the consumer has only so much time that he can devote to various activities in any given time-period if he is going to accomplish any one of them. Consequently, if he devotes more time to one activity at the expense of others, the costs of those foregone opportunities rise sufficiently to act as a check against further time losses. Therefore, a shopping facility's utility or value to a consumer is inversely related to the effort and expense involved in getting from the consumer's point of origin to a given shopping facility. Since the effort and expense involved with a shopping trip are inextricably linked with time, a suitable measure of these factors would be the travel time involved in making a given journey.

Consumers also display differences in terms of their willingness to travel various distances for different types of products. This accounts for the distance exponent λ. These variations can be attributed chiefly to the value differences that various goods and services possess to consumers.

Firm demand

The total expected annual sales for a given retail facility can be computed now that a formulation exists for estimating individual consumer preferences. Such a computation involves simply summing all those consumers who prefer a given retail facility. Total sales for a given retail facility would thus be the sum of the expected average annual expenditures to be spent at such a facility for a particular product or product class that have been estimated for the consumers from each of the statistical areas. That is,

$$T_J = \sum_{i=1}^{m} A_{iJ} \qquad\qquad 5$$

where T_j = the total T expected annual sales for a given retail facility j; m = the number of statistical areas.

Operating costs and profit

The next step after estimating the expected annual retail sales of a facility of a specified size at a potential location is to estimate the operating costs and profit associated with such a facility. It is assumed, as was mentioned in the beginning of this article, that the operating costs of a retail facility are a function of its size. Precise data depicting the relationship between operating costs and various scales of operation (size levels) must be determined empirically for different kinds of retail activities. Such a task is beyond the scope of this study. However, it seems reasonable to expect that the nature of this function would conform closely to conventional cost behavior. That is, total operating costs would tend to increase quite rapidly with initial increases in the scales of operation. But, with further increases in size, economies of scale that reduce the rate at which such costs increase come into effect. However, increases in firm size finally result in diminishing returns and operating costs begin to increase at an increasing rate.

Once the operating costs associated with specified size levels are known, the maximum expected operating profit at a proposed facility at a potential location can be determined. This is accomplished simply by subtracting the operating costs from the expected sales estimates corresponding to each specified size level up to the stipulated size limit. The size level that yields the highest, i.e. maximum, operating profit is singled out for each potential location under consideration. The optimum location is that particular location at which the operating profit is highest from among all the potential locations.

Need for the computer

It is obvious that the calculations necessary to provide the profit estimates for any one location would be a formidable task if they had to be computed manually. When a large number of potential locations are involved, the task is simply not feasible. Fortunately, the use of the computer makes it possible for such a task to be undertaken. The computer program used for the case problem that follows possesses sufficient capability to search an entire city for an optimum location.[2]

A case study

The steps that have been described for approximating an optimum retail location can be better understood by relating them to a case study. There-

2. A copy of this program may be obtained from The Center for Regional Studies, The University of Kansas, 210 Summerfield Hall, Lawrence, Kansas 66044.

fore, let us consider a hypothetical problem in which an optimum location is desired for a proposed supermarket in a city with a population of 50,000 persons. The basic information necessary for analysing the problem is as follows: (1) the number of competitors (existing stores), (2) the sizes of existing stores, (3) the number of potential locations, (4) the maximum store size allowed at each potential location, (5) the size increment that is to be used for calculating the sales estimate at each potential location, (6) the profit margin percentages corresponding to various store sizes, (7) the number of statistical areas, (8) the number of households within each of the statistical areas, (9) the food expenditures per household of each statistical area, (10) the travel times involved in getting from each of the statistical areas to each of the existing and potential locations, and (11) the appropriate value for λ. The hypothetical city in question currently has seven retail food stores. The sizes of these stores, measured in terms of square footage of selling space, are indicated in Table 1.

Eligible potential locations for the proposed supermarket are limited to twenty-two due to commercial restrictions and the number of sites available within these commercially zoned areas. Furthermore, these potential locations vary in size and thus have different limits with respect to the size of store that can be built at each. The spatial distribution of the existing stores as well as the potential locations are shown in Figure 1. Table 2

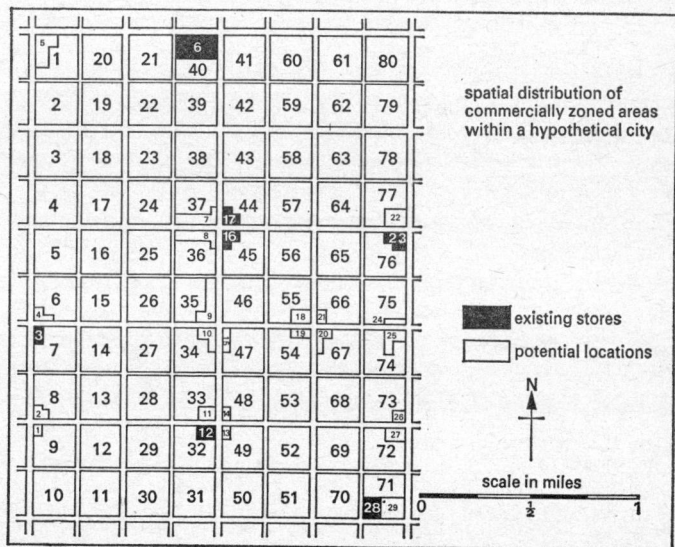

Figure 1

indicates the maximum size store that can be built at each potential location.

A size increment of 5000 square feet shall be used for calculating the sales estimates at each potential location. The relationship of store size to the margin on sales, expenses and net operating profit is indicated in Table 3.

Table 1 **Sizes of the existing stores**

Location no.	Sales area (sq. ft)
3	5000
16	25,000
12	10,000
16	15,000
17	15,000
23	15,000
28	20,000

Table 2 **Maximum size limit of each potential location**

Location no.	Maximum sale area capacity (sq. ft)
1	10,000
2	15,000
4	15,000
5	25,000
7	25,000
8	25,000
9	25,000
10	20,000
11	15,000
13	15,000
14	15,000
15	15,000
18	15,000
19	10,000
20	15,000
21	10,000
22	25,000
24	5000
25	20,000
26	10,000
27	15,000
29	25,000

Table 3 **Relationship of size of store to margin on sales, expenses, and net operating profit***

| Sq. ft of sales area | Operating facts (Expressed as a % of sales) | | |
	Margin on sales	Expenses	Net operating profit before taxes
5000	17·3	15·6	1·7
10,000	17·4	16·0	1·4
15,000	17·6	16·4	1·2
20,000	17·7	16·9	0·8
25,000	17·9	17·3	0·6

* These data do not reflect actual percentage figures pertaining to food stores. They have been compiled solely for illustrative purposes.

Within the boundaries of the hypothetical city under study, a grid was constructed containing eighty squares. These squares represent the statistical areas from which consumer purchases originate, i.e., the i's in the model. Hypothetical values portraying the number of households, average annual incomes per household, and the average annual food expenditures per household for the eighty statistical areas are shown in Table 4. Simply

Table 4 **Number of households, household income and food expenditure: per household**

Statistical unit no.	No. of households	Average annual income per household ($)	Average annual food expenditures ($)
1	100	5200– 7500	1400
2	100	5200– 7500	1400
3	60	7500–10,000	1600
4	120	5200– 7500	1400
5	100	5200– 7500	1400
6	120	5200– 7500	1400
7	320	3900– 5200	1200
8	420	5200– 7500	1400
9	80	7500–10,000	1600
10	40	15,000–over	2000
11	60	10,000–15,000	1800
12	80	7500–10,000	1600
13	380	5200– 7500	1400
14	260	3900– 5200	1200
15	160	3900– 5200	1200
16	140	3900– 5200	1200

Table 4 – *continued*

Statistical unit no.	No. of households	Average annual income per household ($)	Average annual food expenditures
17	120	5200– 7500	1400
18	80	7500–10,000	1600
19	120	5200– 7500	1400
20	120	5200– 7500	1400
21	260	3900– 5200	1200
22	120	5200– 7500	1400
23	140	5200– 7500	1400
24	480	3900– 5200	1200
25	720	under– 3900	1000
26	360	3900– 5200	1200
27	300	3900– 5200	1200
28	120	5200– 7500	1400
29	100	5200– 7500	1400
30	80	7500–10,000	1600
31	80	7500–10,000	1600
32	120	5200– 7500	1400
33	120	5200– 7500	1400
34	200	3900– 5200	1200
35	360	3900– 5200	1200
36	460	3900– 5200	1200
37	600	3900– 5200	1200
38	120	5200– 7500	1400
39	160	5200– 7500	1400
40	100	3900– 5200	1200
41	360	5200– 7500	1400
42	100	5200– 7500	1400
43	160	5200– 7500	1400
44	360	5200– 7500	1400
45	320	3900– 5200	1200
46	400	3900– 5200	1200
47	260	3900– 5200	1200
48	120	5200– 7500	1400
49	100	7500–10,000	1600
50	80	7500–10,000	1600
51	120	5200– 7500	1400
52	100	5200– 7500	1400
53	120	5200– 7500	1400
54	220	5200– 7500	1400
55	280	5200– 7500	1400
56	260	5200– 7500	1400
57	120	5200– 7500	1400

Table 4 – *continued*

Statistical unit no.	No. of households	Average annual income per household ($)	Average annual food expenditure
58	140	5200– 7500	1400
59	100	7500–10,000	1600
60	120	7500–10,000	1600
61	80	10,000–15,000	1800
62	80	10,000–15,000	1800
63	140	7500–10,000	1600
64	140	5200– 7500	1400
65	160	5200– 7500	1400
66	320	5200– 7500	1400
67	280	5200– 7500	1400
68	220	5200– 7500	1400
69	180	5200– 7500	1400
70	120	5200– 7500	1400
71	60	3900– 5200	1200
72	180	3900– 5200	1200
73	300	3900– 5200	1200
74	260	3900– 5200	1200
75	340	5200– 7500	1400
76	160	5200– 7500	1400
77	140	5200– 7500	1400
78	120	7500–10,000	1600
79	100	10,000–15,000	1800
80	60	15,000–over	2000
—	Total 15,260	—	—

as a matter of convenience, straight-line distances from the centers of the statistical areas to the existing and potential locations were calculated and substituted for travel times. It is obvious that, if this were an actual empirical study to determine an optimum location, straight-line distances would be poor substitutes for travel times. Differences in the transportation network can have a marked effect on the accessibility and thus the sales of retail locations. In conjunction with the distance figures, a value of 3·00 shall be used for λ.

Given the preceding constraints and conditions, the problem now is to determine which location from among the set of potential locations given will yield the greatest expected operating profit for the proposed supermarket. A computer program incorporating the sequential steps shown in Figure 2 was written and utilized for generating the appropriate profit

Start.

I. Read in:

1. The total number of existing retail developments.
2. The total number of prospective locations.
3. The square footage of selling space of each existing retail development.
4. The maximum limit of selling space (sq. ft.) allowed for a retail development at a prospective location.
5. The initial size level as well as the increment in selling space (sq. ft.) pertaining to each retail development at each prospective location.
6. The net operating profit percentage associated with each of the specified levels of selling space.
7. The total number of consumer statistical areas.
8. The total number of households located within each statistical area.
9. The average annual per household income of each statistical area.

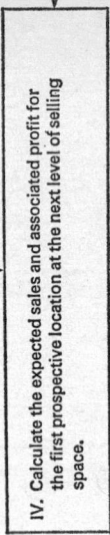

IV. Calculate the expected sales and associated profit for the first prospective location at the next level of selling space.

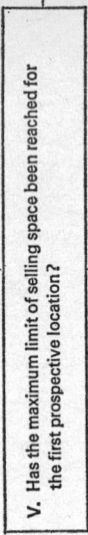

V. Has the maximum limit of selling space been reached for the first prospective location?

no

yes

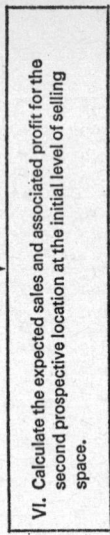

VI. Calculate the expected sales and associated profit for the second prospective location at the initial level of selling space.

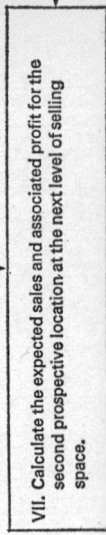

VII. Calculate the expected sales and associated profit for the second prospective location at the next level of selling space.

VIII. Has the limit of selling space been reached for the second prospective location?

no

10. The average annual per household expenditure of each statistical area spent on various classes of products.

11. The travel time from each statistical area to each of the existing retail developments as well as to each of the prospective locations.

yes

IX. Calculate the expected sales and associated profit for the next prospective location at the initial level of selling space and for each of the succeeding levels of selling space until the maximum limit of selling space is reached.

II. Estimate the total expected sales for a potential retail development of a size equal to the initial level of selling space and located at the first prospective location.

X. Have the expected sales and associated profits been calculated for all of the prospective locations?

no

yes

III. Calculate the net operating profit for the retail development specified in Step II by multiplying the net operating profit percentage associated with the initial level of selling space by the expected sales figure estimated for the first prospective location.

Stop

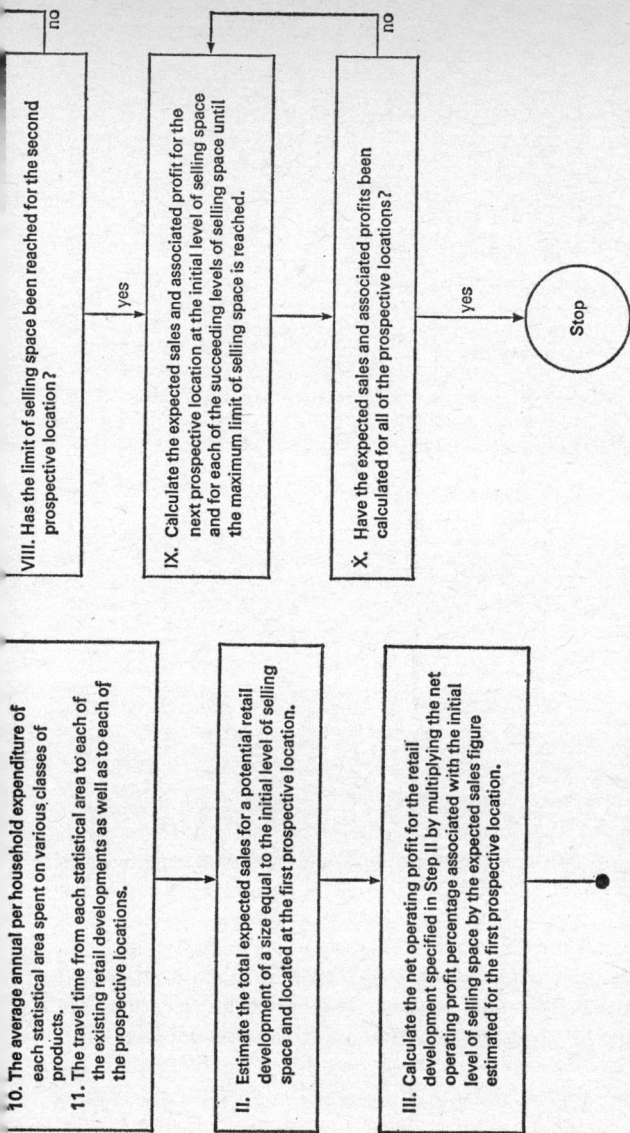

Figure 2   Sequential steps in analysing the optimum location problem

Table 5 **Maximum expected profit of each potential location**

Potential location number	Store size (sq. ft)	Estimated annual sales ($)	Estimated annual profit ($)
1	10,000	1,689,467	23,653
2	10,000	1,804,388	25,261
4	15,000	2,271,148	27,254
5	15,000	900,777	10,809
7	15,000	3,548,983	42,588
8	15,000	3,685,787	44,299*
9	15,000	3,624,525	43,494
10	15,000	3,439,659	41,276
11	15,000	2,620,976	31,452
13	15,000	2,352,961	28,236
14	15,000	2,567,757	30,813
15	15,000	3,388,635	40,664
18	15,000	3,278,031	39,336
19	10,000	2,693,793	37,713
20	15,000	3,156,840	37,882
21	10,000	2,661,994	37,268
22	15,000	1,614,255	19,371
24	5000	1,427,008	24,259
25	15,000	1,427,597	27,859
26	10,000	1,458,566	20,420
27	15,000	1,599,215	20,391
29	15,000	826,742	9921

* Optimum location.

estimates. The estimates stemming from this calculation are depicted in Table 5. It can be seen that location 8 represents the optimum location. If a store is built at this particular location, it should be 20,000 square feet in size, and it should yield $4,313,813 in annual sales and $258,829 in net operating profit.

It is interesting to compare the market shares before and after the inclusion of the proposed supermarket. By excluding a potential location and calculating the expected sales and profits among the existing locations, the market shares would be as shown in Table 6. If the optimum location is included and the necessary calculations are repeated, it can be seen that the market shares would change rather dramatically. This change is also shown in Table 6. Each existing location would give up some of its former sales to the proposed store. Not all of the existing stores would be affected the same, however. Those stores located in close proximity to the proposed store would receive the greatest impact. This clearly illustrates the dynamic

Table 6 Market shares before and after the inclusion of the prospective store

Location number	Store size (sq. ft)	Excluding prospective store		Including prospective store	
		Estimated sales	Proportion of total sales	Estimated sales	Proportion of total sales
8	15,000			3,685,787	0·20
3	5000	2,024,284	0·10	1,785,010	0·09
6	25,000	3,024,413	0·14	2,687,476	0·13
12	10,000	2,688,001	0·13	2,425,511	0·11
16	15,000	4,238,105	0·22	2,854,486	0·14
17	15,000	3,927,448	0·20	2,750,254	0·13
23	15,000	2,582,328	0·12	2,393,570	0·11
28	20,000	1,847,418	0·09	1,749,902	0·09
Total	—	20,331,996	1·00	20,331,996	1·00

aspects of location in the retail field. As new firms enter and existing firms exit, the competitive field reflects these changes by the market shares each firm receives in any given time-period.

Concluding remarks

The probability model that has been presented in this paper is a simple yet seemingly powerful tool for estimating sales of prospective retail firms. Through the use of this model and the assistance of a computer, it is possible to search a very large geographical area for an optimum retail location. The estimates stemming from such investigations provide investors with a more rational basis upon which to assess potential investment opportunities. Furthermore, if future changes in the size and distribution of population and income are estimated, as well as the likely changes in the transportation network for a particular region, the investor is also able to assess future investment possibilities.

A word of caution, however, should be noted in conjunction with the use of the model. Mathematical models are not infallible. They are, by necessity, simplified constructs of some aspect of reality. It is impossible for such constructs to include all the possible factors that may have a bearing on a particular problem. Therefore, decision-makers should be aware that there are variables other than those specified in the model that affect the sales of a retail firm. The reputation of a firm, the newness of the store, the merchandise it carries, the services it offers, etc. are but a few examples of additional variables. As a consequence, human judgment should also play an important role in decisions of this type. Furthermore, the model does not consider important questions pertaining to the site at a potential location.

It is obvious that there are a number of important factors related to the site itself that can influence the volume of sales that can be expected from a given location. Visibility and accessibility, as well as the nature and condition of adjacent property, have a bearing on the sales that can be expected. Therefore, it is important that supplemental techniques for appraising the site be used in conjunction with the general sales estimate afforded by the model. Generally, such techniques are of a qualitative character and thus, again, human judgment plays an important role in arriving at an adjusted sales estimate.

References

CORROTHERS, G. A. P. (1956), 'An historical review of the gravity and potential concepts of human interaction', *J. Amer. Inst. Planners*, May, pp. 94–102.

HUFF, D. L. (1962), *Determination of Intra-urban Retail Trade Areas*, Real Estate Research Program, University of California.

19 W. J. Baumol and E. A. Ide

Variety in Retailing[1]

W. J. Baumol and E. A. Ide, 'Variety in retailing', *Management Science*, vol. 3, 1956
pp. 93–101.

Many marketing problems which promise to be amenable to the techniques
of operations research have apparently not been subjected to systematic
analysis. This article is a first attempt at an analysis of one such area –
the number of items stocked by a retailer and its relation to his sales, his
costs and his profits.

The analysis of the relations among these variables permits the development of criteria for an optimal variety of items; that is, of expressions which
can indicate to the retailer whether an increase or a reduction in the number
of commodities, styles and brands which he offers for sale will enhance his
profits. The discussion also throws some light on a number of well-known
retailing phenomena like the growth of suburban shopping centers and
supermarkets. By and large, these results are reassuring rather than startling.

The tentative nature of the model cannot be overemphasized. Its structure has purposely been greatly simplified. In particular, linearity has been
assumed wherever it does not seem to conflict directly with the properties
which the expressions are intended to describe. It is, therefore, noteworthy
how often non-linearities have imposed themselves on the model or have
arisen out of the mathematical manipulations.

1 Equilibrium of the consumer
1 The gains from increased variety

A shopper does not know in advance (with certainty) whether he will
obtain what he wants by entering a particular shop, i.e. whether it does or
does not carry some of the items he desires. Generally, there will be one or
several alternative sets of items, the availability at acceptable prices of any
one of which will make the shopping trip successful in the consumer's
view. The greater the number of items carried by the store he enters, the

1. This article is a product of the empirical and theoretical investigations carried out
in connection with the Alderson & Sessions Basic Research Program. For a description of the other aspects of the program see: *Cost and profit outlook* (1956, vol. 9, no. 2
and no. 3); *Printers' Ink* (20 January 1956, p. 25); *Business Week* (12 November, 1955,
p. 58).

greater, ordinarily, is the consumer's reason for expecting that the shopping trip will in this sense be successful. Of course, this is only true so long as any additional items carried are not known to exclude all commodities desired by the consumer. For example, a known addition to a store's line of paints will not help attract necktie shoppers.

This can readily be translated into probabilistic terms. Let N be the number of different items, i.e., the number of varieties, sold by the retailer. Then we may write

$$p(N) \qquad\qquad\qquad\qquad\qquad\qquad\qquad\qquad\qquad\qquad\qquad 1$$

for the probability that the consumer will find some set of items in the store which will make his trip successful. On the usual convention, we have $0 \leqslant p(N) \leqslant 1$ where, for example, $p(N) = 1$ means certain foreknowledge of success. In the absence of specific customer information about the nature of the items carried in the store, $p(N)$ will be close to unity only if the customer is easily satisfied or if N is very large.

Since an increase in the number of items stocked is taken to increase the probability of success in shopping, we also have $dp/dN \geqslant 0$.

It must be emphasized that since we are here not primarily interested in the influence of prices and advertising, they are both assumed to remain unchanged throughout. In particular, they are taken to be unaffected by the number of items stocked by the retailer. Of course, this is not likely to occur in practice. The influence of both these variables is clear. When there is a decrease in prices or an increase in informative advertising, there will be an increase in the probability of successful shopping trips, for consumers are then more likely to know which store carries the items they want and are more likely to find them offered for sale at acceptable prices.

2 The costs of shopping

In going to some particular store the customer incurs some costs. Some of these represent the cost and trouble of transportation. If the distance of the consumer from the store is D, we assume that for him these costs are strictly proportionate to D and are given by $c_d D$ where c_d is a constant.

Moreover, the difficulty of shopping increases with the number of items stocked by the store – the more items stocked the further we must walk to get to the spot where some items are kept. Roughly speaking, the average distance walked to an item may be expected to increase as the square root of the number of items carried by the store if it is all located on one story since area increases as the square of the radius of a circle or the length of the sides of a rectangle. For similar reasons, if the store operates with a multi-story building we might expect these costs to vary as the cube root of the number of items offered for sale. For our purposes, we shall assume that these costs are directly proportionate with the square root of the number of items stocked, and are given by $c_n\sqrt{N}$.

Finally, there are costs which do not vary with the number of items sold or the consumers' distance from the store. Simply taking the initiative to shop involves time and effort as well as opportunity costs, including other shopping opportunities foregone. For example, a shopper knows that by spending the day shopping, she may be giving up a chance to catch up with her darning or to spend a quiet evening at home. For some who enjoy shopping this cost, c_i (and perhaps c_n), may be negative. It should be emphasized that c_i is defined as a total, not an average cost, and includes the opportunity cost of foregoing other alternative shopping trips.

Thus the costs of shopping to the consumer are assumed to be given by the sum of these three classes of cost, i.e., by

$$c_d D + c_n \sqrt{N} + c_i. \qquad\qquad 2$$

3 The demand function

Presumably the decision to shop or not to shop at a given retail outlet will result from a weighing of the probability of success as given by **1** against the costs of shopping **2**. We assume that the typical consumer does this simply by assigning unconsciously subjective weights w and v (both of which are taken to be positive) to the two components and then seeing which is the larger. The constants v and w are viewed as being invariant over a collection of stores offering similar types of assortments. Here the relevant probability function $p(N)$ is presumably subjective and its relation to the objective probability function is a matter for empirical investigation.

Thus the consumer will not shop at this store unless for him

$$f(N, D) = wp(N) - v(c_d D + c_n\sqrt{N} + c_i) \qquad\qquad 3$$

is positive.[2] The function $f(N, D)$ is a measure of the consumer's expected net benefit from entering the store in question and shows how this will vary with D, his distance from the store, and N, the number of items offered for sale there.

We can now examine the effect of variation in the number of items carried. An increase in the variety of items handled by the store will involve an increase in the probability of success but it will also increase shopping costs. We must see how $f(N, D)$ will vary with N. Direct observation yields the following results:

(a) When the number of items stocked is small the function will be negative. Specifically, $f(0, D) < 0$ since, when nothing is stocked by the store, the

2. Since c_i takes account of foregone opportunities to shop elsewhere (i.e., $f(N, D)$ is a measure of *net* benefits), the value of f will be negative for any store which does not offer the consumer maximum expected gross benefit.

probability of success $p(0) = 0$; and hence the term of which w is the coefficient, and which is ordinarily the only non-negative term in 3, becomes zero. This point amounts to the trivial observation that it does not pay to shop in an empty store.

(b) For very large values of N, f will also be negative since the first term in 3 can never[3] exceed w while $vC_n\sqrt{N}$ grows indefinitely large.

(c) For intermediate values of N and small values of D, f will be positive if w is sufficiently large relative to v, i.e. if the probability of finding what he wants is weighted sufficiently highly by the customer relative to shopping cost.

(d) In this case if the expression is assumed to be continuous throughout, i.e., if $p(N)$ is continuous, f must attain at least one maximum in the intermediate range.

(e) After f has passed its maximum, the term $-vC_n\sqrt{N}$ will ultimately dominate the expression. Since this term decreases at a decreasing rate (positive second partial derivative with respect to N), this must eventually also be characteristic of f.

(f) Marginal and average values of f will be negative for low values of N. They will subsequently become positive and finally decline to a negative value again after reaching a maximum.

4 Economic implications

These conclusions have several rather common-sense economic implications:

(a) Increased variety is an advantage to a consumer only up to a point. Ultimately a store may stock so large a variety of items that shopping costs become prohibitive. This suggests why Sears Roebuck might find it profitable to catalogue many lines which Macy's will not carry. By issuing separate catalogues for different lines some mail-order houses have been able to reduce c_n further and thereby have made an even larger N feasible.

(b) The minimum number of items necessary to induce a consumer to shop at a given store will increase with D, his distance from that store. This is simply the plausible assertion that the high shopping costs of a distant consumer can only be overcome by a high probability of a successful shopping trip.

(c) The optimum variety from the consumer's point of view, i.e., that value of N for which $f(N, D)$ is a maximum, is independent of his distance from the retailer. This was assumed directly in the form postulated for the func-

3. Of course, this is really only an artifact resulting from the linearity of the expression and the constancy of the model's coefficients but it seems also to be rather reasonable, especially in view of what follows.

tion f. For the term in $f(N, D)$ which contains D does not contain N. This term will therefore drop out when we solve for the optimum N by setting $\delta f/\delta N = 0$.

(d) For every value of N, there will be a maximum consumer distance from the store beyond which it will not pay this consumer to purchase from this shop. The net benefit is a function also of the place of residence of the consumer. Thus about each store and for a particular net benefit, i.e., for a particular value of $f(N, D)$, we may conceive of a contour line or indifference curve associated with a locus of residence about the store. The maximum shopping distance is given by the equation of the indifference curve which offers the consumer zero net benefit from shopping at this store. This maximum distance is obtained by setting $f(N, D) = 0$ (zero net benefit) and solving for D to yield

$$D_m = \frac{w}{vc_d}p(N) - \frac{1}{c_d}(c_n\sqrt{N} + c_i). \qquad 4$$

More economic implications of our model will be indicated in the next section.

2 The retailer's demand situation
1 The aggregate demand function

From the point of view of the retailer, a function very much like $f(N, D)$ may be taken to determine the proportion of the population which shops at his establishment. This may be related directly to sales in the following manner: suppose, once a customer decides to shop at this particular store, the number of items he buys is independent of the number of items available. This assumption is clearly false and we shall modify it later. This premise implies that the volume of a store's sales will depend directly on the number of individuals who can be induced to shop there, i.e., on a relationship like 3. At any distance from the retailer, sales will, in the simplest circumstances, vary directly with the proportion of the population which decides to shop at this outlet. This is strictly in accord with our decision to employ linear assumptions wherever possible. In this case, the proportion of the population residing at a distance D from the store which will decide to shop at this store is given by a function similar in form to $f(N, D)$. Let us take capital letters to indicate the parameters in the new function analogous to those represented by lower case letters in f. The new function may then be written

$$F(N, D) = WP(N) - V(C_d D + C_n\sqrt{N} + C_i) \equiv A(N) - VC_d D, \qquad 5$$

where $A(N) = WP(N) - V(C_n\sqrt{N} + C_i)$. It should be noted that since $VC_d D$ does not vary with N both $F(N, D)$ and $A(N)$ will be similarly affected by changes in the value of N. It should also be observed that while f and F are similar in form the latter should be derived independently from the data rather than from some process of aggregation of the f's of different shoppers.

To determine the volume of sales, we must also know something about the density of population in the area surrounding the store; that is, the distribution of population within the area whose boundaries are given by the relationship gotten by substituting the parameters of F for those of f in **4** and which lie within a distance D_m from the store. We discuss only two very simple possibilities in line with our determination to simplify the model to the utmost:

Case a. population per square mile is everywhere given by the constant K so that population within an area of radius D_a is $K\pi D_a^2$.

Case b. the store is located at the point of greatest population concentration, and population density, K/D varies inversely with the distance from the retailer. The area lying within a distance D_a from the store is πD_a^2. The population within the circular area of radius D_a is given by

$$\int_0^{\pi D^2} \frac{K}{D}\, d\,\text{Area} = \int_0^{D_a} \frac{K}{D}\, 2\pi D\, dD = 2\pi K D_a.$$

First consider Case a. Here

$$\text{Sales} = \int_0^{D_m} F(N, D)\, d\,\text{Population}$$

$$= \int_0^{D_m} [A(N) - VC_d D] 2\pi K D\, dD$$

$$= 2\pi K \left[A(N)\frac{D^2}{2} - VC_d \frac{D^3}{3} \right]_0^{D_m}$$

$$= 2\pi K D_m^2 \left(\frac{A(N)}{2} - VC_d \frac{D_m}{3} \right).$$

Now from **4** and **5**

$$D_m = A(N)/VC_d.$$

Substituting this in our results yields[4]

$$\text{Sales} = \frac{2\pi K}{V^2 C_d^2}\, A(N)^3(\tfrac{1}{2} - \tfrac{1}{3}) = \frac{1}{3}\frac{\pi K}{V^2 C_d^2}\, A(N)^3 = \tfrac{1}{3} VC_d \pi K D_m^3. \qquad \textbf{6}$$

4. This result can be made intuitively plausible as follows: $A(N)$ is an index of any one customer's inducement to purchase when he is located near the store. It also determines the maximum shopping distance – i.e. the radius D_m is proportionate to $A(N)$ – specifically $D_m = A(N)/VC_d$ by **4**. Because population is taken to be uniformly distributed, the number of persons in the area will be proportionate to πD_m^2. Since total sales equals sales per person times the number of persons, they will be given by a constant multiplied by $A(N)\pi D_m = A(N)^3\pi/(VC_d)^2$ which is essentially our result.

Turning now to Case b,

$$\text{Sales} = \int_0^{D_m} [A(N) - VC_d D] 2\pi K \, dD$$

$$= 2\pi K \left[A(N)D - \frac{VC_d D^2}{2} \right]_0^{D_m}$$

Thus[5]

$$\text{Sales} = 2\pi K D_m \left[A(N) - \frac{VC_d D_m}{2} \right] = \frac{\pi K}{VC_d} A(N)^2 = VC_d \pi K D_m^2. \qquad 7$$

In both cases sales will vary directly with the maximum customer distance, in one case as the cube of that distance and in the other as the square of that distance.

2 Economic implications

These results also enable us to discuss the relationship between the expected sales of the retailer and the number of lines he offers for sale directly in terms of $A(N)$. This, as can be seen from 5 will vary with N as does $F(N, D)$ or, by analogy, $f(N, D)$ whose shape we have already analysed. We are thereby led to a number of economic conclusions.

(a) An increased number of items will at first yield increasing average returns, then decreasing marginal and average returns. Finally, it will yield negative marginal returns.

(b) This means that, even neglecting considerations of retailer costs, it will not pay a store to proliferate limitlessly the variety of items it carries. There will be some maximum value of sales which can be found by setting the derivative of 6 and 7 with respect to N equal to zero.

(c) The existence of a range of rising average sales deserves attention. This conclusion asserts that not only will total sales be increased up to a point by an increase in the variety stocked but the sales *per item carried* will also rise. Increased variety will then be attracting a disproportionate number of additional customers.

(d) Our results are obviously in line with the common-sense explanation of the reason why large retailers tend to locate at metropolitan centers since high population density means a large value of K.

(e) The results are consistent with the recent increase in emphasis on dece-

5. This implies that sales would be positive for very large or small values of N when $A(N)$ is negative, which is clearly nonsense. This peculiarity arises because $A(N)$, sales per customer would supposedly have negative values at these values of N whereas in fact sales can never be less than zero. It would be more appropriate (though the complication is not worth it) to employ instead of $A(N)$ the function with discontinuous derivative given by $A(N)$ for intermediate values of N but which is zero elsewhere.

tralized retailing and large suburban shopping centers. In terms of our model this can be accounted for in two ways – the increased movement of population toward the suburbs which involves a rise in the K pertaining to the suburban relative to the metropolitan dealers, and the increasing difficulty of driving into and parking in cities which in our model involves increases in C_d and C_l for the metropolitan dealers. This suggests that C_d and C_i are themselves functions of population density.

(f) The analysis also fits in with the supermarket phenomenon in grocery retailing. The size of these giant stores can partly be explained by their relatively low C_n – the relative ease with which a consumer can get at additional items which results from the layout permitted by their spaciousness and from their self-service arrangements. Parking lots offer a relatively low C_l. The supermarkets' methods of handling and prepackaging also reduces their inventory and handling costs, and this, as shall be seen in the next section, tends to make for a high value of N, the number of items stocked.

Supermarkets are still increasing the number of items they handle and going into the sale of toiletries, housewares, clothing and appliances. However, it is our impression that no very great further increase in the number of items carried is to be expected in the absence of a marked autonomous or induced change in the value of the coefficients.

3 Purchases per customer and the number of items stocked

So far, we have retained the false assumption that purchases per consumer are independent of the number of items stocked by a retailer. Yet up to a point the more items stocked the more likely is a consumer to run into things he had not been planning to buy on this trip but which on being observed become irresistible. This may well serve as a partial offset to the ultimately diminishing returns to an increased number of items carried. But there would appear to be limits to this offset. The customer may not be able to look over more items in a very large store than in a moderately large store simply because of time limitations. After some point, further increases in N may then yield no further increases in sales per customer, though it is conceivable that this value of N is well beyond the relevant range.

3 The profit maximizing variety
1 The retailers' costs

To determine an optimum variety from the point of view of the retailers' profits we must include in our model a discussion of the effects of changes in variety on his costs. These effects will primarily involve inventory and handling costs.

In inventory theory, it is customary, as first approximation, to deal with inventory costs as follows (see, for example, Whitin, 1953, pp. 31–3): let E be the mean expected sales volume of all commodities per period, r be the handling, clerical and other related costs of each reordering, T be the warehousing costs per item per period and I the quantity ordered for inventory each time stocks are replaced. Suppose, moreover, that inventory is replaced when, and only when, stocks on hand fall to level R. Then inventory costs per commodity are, on these simplest assumptions, given by

$$\frac{E}{I}r + \left(\frac{I}{2} + R\right)T. \qquad\qquad 8$$

The first term represents the cost of keeping the inventory replenished, for E/I is the number of times during a period that inventory will be depleted if sales go on at a steady rate. Since r is the cost of reordering once, then total reordering cost will be r multiplied by E/I, the number of times reordering will take place. The second term in 8 represents warehousing cost since the quantity of the commodity held in stock will vary between $I+R$ and R so that the average level of inventory will be approximately $(I/2)+R$.

Costs can be minimized by picking an appropriate level of I. Setting the first derivative of 8 equal to zero yields the well known result $I = \sqrt{2Er/T}$. Substituting this in 8 gives minimum

$$\text{cost per item} = \frac{Er}{\sqrt{\left(\frac{2Er}{T}\right)}} + \frac{T}{2}\sqrt{\left(\frac{2Er}{T}\right)} + RT$$

$$= \sqrt{(2rTE)} + RT.$$

In the simplest circumstances, the total cost of carrying N items will be equal to fixed costs, Q plus N times the cost of handling one item plus the additional costs resulting from the increased complexity of handling a variety of items. We may then take this cost to be given by

$$Q + N\sqrt{(2rTE)} + NRT + a\sqrt{N} \qquad\qquad 9$$

where the last term is again given a square-root form on the argument that the average distance to any one item will increase as the square root of the number of items so long as all handling takes place in a one-story building.

We can combine 9 with our previous expression for E, the expected mean sales per commodity to obtain an expression for minimum retailing costs. Using 7 rather than 6, for illustrative purposes, total sales are $\pi K/VC_d A(N)^2$ so that average sales will be this expression divided by N.

Substituting this for E in **9** and writing $b = \sqrt{(2\pi KrT/VC_d)}$ yields as the expression for minimum retailing cost

$$Q + b\sqrt{(N)}A(N) + NRT + a\sqrt{N}. \qquad \qquad \textbf{10}$$

2 *The retailer's profits*

We may now obtain an expression for the retailer's total profits by subtracting his total costs **10** from his total revenues which can be obtained by multiplying the sales volume **7** by an appropriate price index. Let $s = (\pi K/VC_d)p^*$ where p^* is the price index; then

Profits $= sA(N)^2 - Q - \sqrt{(N)}[bA(N) + a] - NRT$.

As we have seen, we may expect $A(N)$ to have two positive roots at which points nothing will be sold and so profit will be negative. In between we may expect for reasonable values of the coefficients that the expression for profits will somewhere rise to a maximum which we can find by setting the first derivative equal to zero. This will indicate the optimum variety in his merchandise from the point of view of the retailer.

In particular, it is easy to see that the higher the handling and inventory costs, i.e., the higher a, r and T (and hence, the higher the value of b) the lower will be the optimal value of N, i.e. the smaller the variety it will pay to stock.

As in many operations research analyses the results have been formulated in terms for which there is no simply obtained quantitative empirical counterpart. In applying results like these, improvisation and ingenuity will no doubt be required to obtain even approximations to the true parameters. Moreover, this very preliminary model will no doubt have to be modified and tailored case by case to fit the facts of the situation, and even then computed results will have to be interpreted and employed only with extreme caution.

Reference

WHITIN, T. M. (1953), *The Theory of Inventory Management*, Princeton University Press.

20 J. P. Cairns

Demand Elasticity, Opportunity Costs and Retail Assortment

J. P. Cairns, 'A note on demand elasticity, opportunity costs and additions to the retail assortment', *Journal of Industrial Economics*, vol. 10, 1962, pp. 238–42.

In a recent article (1957, p. 30 [Reading 4]) Richard Holton suggested that the elasticity of demand is the main consideration determining whether or not a new item will be added to the assortment carried by a retail store. 'To qualify for admission to the product-mix . . . a candidate item *must* [my italics] have a relatively inelastic demand. It is this requirement which seems to be of overwhelming importance in influencing the choice of new lines.'

It is true that, in the case of supermarkets, the store-type specifically considered by Holton, most of the recent (principally non-food) additions to the product-line have had high percentage margins and therefore, it may be inferred, rather inelastic demands, at the price set. But it seems misleading to attribute the addition of such items to this low elasticity, which is only one of the factors relevant to the decision whether or not to add an item.

Consider two new item candidates for a store's assortment and assume that the acquisition cost of a unit of each is the same, and constant. Assume, as seems reasonable, that operating costs are not affected by the addition of either item, so that the acquisition cost of each is its marginal cost, and these are, therefore, for the two items identical and constant. For each item there is a family of demand curves relating quantity sold to the price, the demand curves moving to the right, as the amount of space allocated to the item is increased. Suppose a given amount of space is available for a new product. The profit-maximizing price for each item can then be determined. Although the product with the less elastic demand (at the price selected) will produce a greater profit per unit of product sold, the product with the more elastic demand may well produce a greater profit for the amount of space allotted to it. If this is so, the profit-maximizing retailer should add, if it is in fact profitable to add a new item, the item with the more elastic demand.

Whether or not it is profitable to add a new item to a retailer's assortment will depend upon the relationship between the gross profit increment attributable to the new item and the opportunity cost of adding the new item; this opportunity cost will be the decrement in gross profits that results when the space made available to the new item is withdrawn from some existing item, or combination of items.[1] The amount of selling space available to a retailer may be regarded as fixed, so that the addition of a new item involves a reduction in the space available for, and hence sales of, some other item (or items), sales of an item being an increasing function of the amount of space allocated to it. Were the sales of an item in the assortment *not* an increasing function of the space assigned to it, i.e. if sales were either a constant or declining function of space, the retailer would be 'wasting' valuable space. Hence, the gross profits earned from these other, displaced, items will decline. A new item will be added, therefore, only if the smallest possible decrement in gross profit is less than the attainable increment in gross profit. It is the profitability of alternative uses of space that should be of interest to the retailer, and the elasticity of demand for the product occupying the space is only one of the factors influencing such profitability. The relevant factors are (1) the rate of sales per time-period, and (2) the absolute profit per unit of product. Elasticity of demand enters the picture only through its influence on the ratio of selling price to acquisition cost, i.e. on the profit per unit of product.

This analysis may be clarified with the help of Figures 1 and 2. Consider Figure 1. Let RK be the acquisition cost, and also the average and marginal cost of each of two possible new items, a and b. Let $D_a D_a$ be the demand curve for product a, if a 'unit of retail space' is allocated to it, and let

1. Holton's analysis is vitiated by his failure to consider the opportunity cost of adding new items. In his Figure (reproduced on p. 317), as new products are added to the retailer's assortment, there is no shift in the demand curves for the products already stocked, such a shift being the essence of the opportunity cost. He must, therefore, be assuming (a) that the demand curve has, in each case, been drawn on the basis of the ultimate equilibrium assortment and space allocation, or (b) that sales of an item are not a function of the amount of space allocated to it, and do not, to be specific, decline as the space is reduced. That assumption (b) is unreasonable seems obvious in view of the energy manufacturers devote to getting the amount of space granted their products increased. If (a) has been assumed, this is not made clear. He writes, for example, 'if he [the retailer] were to *divert* [my italics] some of his capacity from the first product to the second'. But the diversion of capacity involves the diversion of space, and hence there must be some effect on the demand curve D_1, and on each succeeding demand curve, as the next item is added.

'Given the marginal cost function MC, the retailer will first invade the product market for which the demand is least elastic. If he were to remain a single-product retailer, he would expand output of the initial product to O_a, where marginal cost and marginal revenue are equated. But if he can enter the market for the second product, it is clear that profits can be increased if he were to divert some of his capacity from the first product to the second since at any price lower than OP_1 the marginal profit on the first product is less than the marginal profit on the first units of the second product. Similarly the retailer will proceed to invade all those product markets in which marginal revenue exceeds marginal cost, so adjusting prices as to equate to marginal cost the marginal revenues for all items handled.' (1957, p. 18).

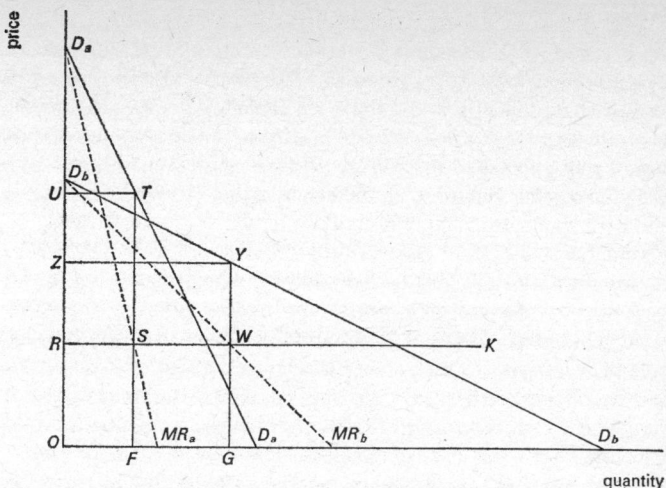

Figure 1 Profitability of two products per unit of space

$D_b D_b$ be the comparable demand curve for product b. Assume that the profit-maximizing prices, as determined by the marginal, or acquisition, cost curve, and the marginal revenue curves are set at OU for product a, and OZ for product b, so that OF units of a, and OG units of b would be sold, at the indicated prices, if a unit of retail space were allocated to either

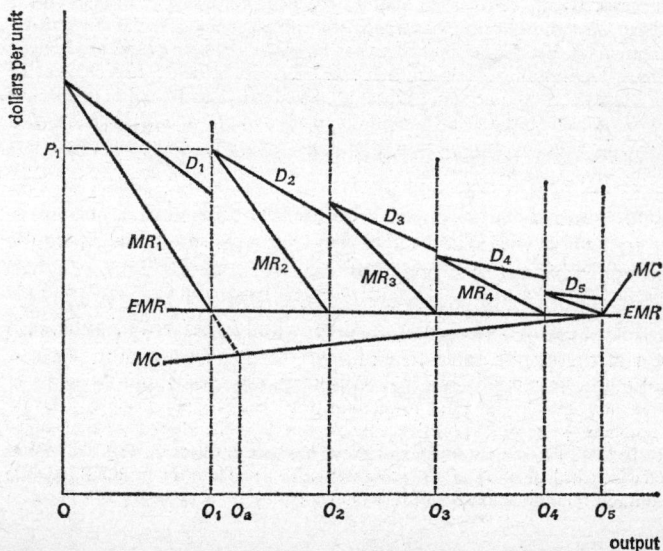

one. The gross profit per unit of space, if allocated to product a, is $RSTU$; the gross profit per unit of space, if allocated to product b, is $RWYZ$. If $RWYZ < RSTU$, it will be profitable to add b rather than a, although the demand for b is more elastic. We assume, of course, that the sales of all other items in the assortment – except the item which has been deprived of a unit of space – are not affected by the addition of either a or b.

The opportunity cost of depriving some other product of this unit of space must also be considered. The opportunity cost of a unit of space is the gross profit this space produces when allocated to the least profitable item now in the assortment; this may be treated as a constant amount. This opportunity cost of a unit of space produces a declining cost curve (in the form of a rectangular hyperbola) per unit of product a or b. Three such

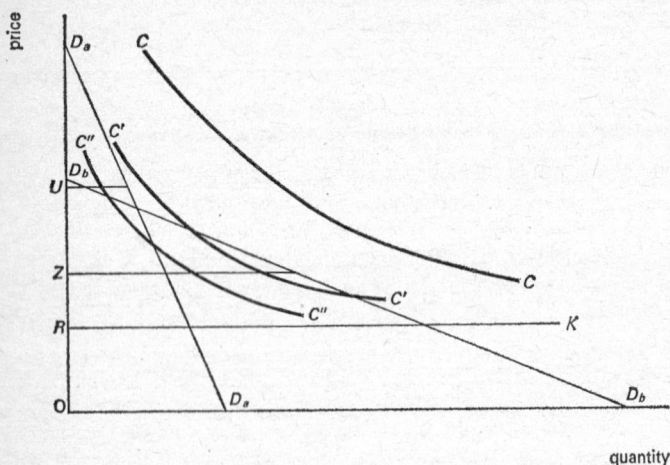

Figure 2 Retail assortment additions and opportunity costs

declining opportunity cost curves have been drawn in Figure 3, and have been added to the acquisition cost curve RK, to produce an average (acquisition plus opportunity) cost curve. In the case of curve CC, it is profitable to add neither a nor b; in the case of curve $C''C''$ either a or b may profitably be added; in the case of $C'C'$, it is profitable to add b, but not a. Thus, the introduction of the opportunity cost of space into the analysis may convert (as in the case of CC) apparently profitable into non-profitable product additions.[2]

2. In the method of analysis employed in Holton's Figure 1, the cc case would be the result of such a leftward shift of D_1 as space were withdrawn from the product that the apparent profitability of adding the product for which D_2 is the demand curve would vanish.

It may be concluded, therefore, that a comparison of demand elasticities is not sufficient to determine which of more than one new product should be added to the retailer's assortment. Nor is the elasticity of demand the most important factor in determining whether or not a new product should be added at the (inescapable) cost of reducing the amount of space assigned to, and therefore the sales of, and gross profits derived from, some product already carried in the assortment.

Note by Professor Richard H. Holton

Mr Cairns' point is well taken. But the problem of rational selection of merchandise in the retail store is a very complicated one, involving not only space allocation but also the allocation of capital available for investment in inventory. A solution to the problem is offered in my article (1961). The appendix to the article, prepared by Saul H. Hymans, presents the formal solution.

References

HOLTON, R. H. (1957), 'Price discrimination at retail: the supermarket case', *J. indust. Econ.*, vol. 7, pp. 13–32.

HOLTON, R. H. (1961), 'A simplified capital budgetary approach to merchandise management', *California Merchandise Manag.*, Spring.

Part Five
Other Aspects

Gould and Preston (Reading 21) investigate the economic effects of resale price maintenance in terms of the setting of optimal prices and gross margins. They discuss the size and number of retail outlets, the degree of competition in the manufacturer's markets, and the amount of service supplied by the retailers.

Davis (Reading 22) points out that under certain conditions trading stamps do have a predictable effect on prices, and that the effects on consumer welfare are debatable.

Bauer (Reading 23) describes and discusses certain features of the distributive trades in a less developed country, notably the multiplicity of traders and intermediaries and the highly labour-intensive character of trading.

21 J. R. Gould and L. E. Preston

Resale Price Maintenance and Retail Outlets

J. R. Gould and L. E. Preston, 'Resale price maintenance and retail outlets'
Economica, n.s., vol. 32, 1965, pp. 302–12.

Resale price maintenance (r.p.m.), the marketing practice by which the producer or brander of products requires subsequent resellers to offer them at minimum or stipulated prices, has been a subject of discussion and analysis for over a quarter century. There does not, however, seem to exist in the literature any formal analysis of the optimal choice of price and margin by a manufacturer (brander) practising r.p.m. The purpose of this article is to investigate some aspects of this problem in the context of a simple model.

Our analysis leaves out of account the two most frequently advanced explanations of r.p.m., each of which involves an assumption of a cartel or of cartel-like behaviour at either the manufacturing or the retailing level.[1] We investigate here the possibility that r.p.m. might be introduced on the initiative of a single manufacturer dealing with a large group of competitive retailers. Any discussion of price policy must assume some degree of monopoly power on the part of the policy-making firm. We consider here a model in which a single-product monopolist manufacturer sells directly to a large number of competitive single-product retailers, each operating under identical conditions of demand and cost. Throughout, the discussion is in terms of static, long-run equilibrium analysis.

Under the conventional assumptions about the determinants of market demand and production costs, the monopolist manufacturer has no incentive to practise r.p.m. Given the market demand schedule, the manufacturer's average revenue schedule is determined by deducting the retail margin directly from the demand price.[2] Since the highest average revenue curve

1. The most popular, and historically probably the most important, hypothesis is that r.p.m. indicates the existence of a retail cartel. Orthodox retailers, striving to protect themselves against price-cutters and against defections within their own ranks, combine to coerce manufacturers into the establishment of prices and margins. A second hypothesis attributes r.p.m. to cartel-like behaviour among manufacturers; a price-understanding among producers is protected against disturbance due to price-warfare at the retail level.

2. The retail margin is defined as the difference between retail price and manufacturer's price to retailers.

will be that associated with the smallest retail margin, the manufacturer has no incentive to increase the margin through r.p.m. Perfect competition and free entry among the retailers will ensure that the retail margin per unit is just equal to the minimum average retail operating cost per unit, the competitive long-run equilibrium solution. No smaller margin can be offered without forcing the retailers into bankruptcy; any larger margin simply reduces the profits of the manufacturer.

At least two hypotheses have been offered to explain the existence of r.p.m. within such a market structure. 1. The 'outlets hypothesis': final demand for the manufacturer's product is a function of both its price and the number of retailers.[3] 2. The 'service hypothesis': final demand for the manufacturer's product is a function of both its price and the amount and quality of service rendered by the retailers.[4] In this article, we deal primarily with the first, and then draw in the second to suggest the relationship between them.

In the next section we consider the relationship between the magnitude of the retail margin and the size of retail outlet. This relationship is used in the following sections to analyse the implications of the outlets hypothesis, (a) with perfect competition at the manufacturing level, (b) with a monopolist manufacturer *not* practising r.p.m., and (c) with a monopolist manufacturer *practising* r.p.m. Perfect competition among retailers is assumed in all three cases.[5] Finally, we discuss the service hypothesis.

The relation between the margin and the size of retail outlet

A convenient method of analysing the relation is to compare the unit margin with average retail operating costs. Average retailing costs are the sum of the price charged by the manufacturer to retailers plus average operating costs: retail price equals the price charged by the manufacturer plus the unit margin. Long-run equilibrium with freedom of entry and exit requires that average retailing costs equal retail price, that is, average operating costs equal the unit margin.

In long-run competitive equilibrium, without r.p.m., the unit margin and the size of the retail firm are independent of the policy of the manu-

3. For example, Yamey (1954, pp. 49–52). The hypothesis can be supported *a priori* by the following arguments: the consumer is likely to make more impulse purchases if exposed to temptation more frequently; the inconvenience of shopping (e.g. travelling) is reduced; information about the product is more widely disseminated.

4. Yamey (1954, pp. 52–8); Telser (1960, pp. 89–96).

5. It may be objected that some of the justifications for the outlets hypothesis mentioned in footnote 3 above seem inconsistent with the assumption of perfect competition in retailing. However, the assumption eases the task of exposition, and we believe the alternative assumption of monopolistic competition would not affect the results. See also note 6.

facturer. This proposition is illustrated in Figure 1, where AC and MC refer to the operating costs of retailing, omitting the cost of goods purchased for resale. Average costs will tend to the minimum, the unit margin (M_1) will equal minimum average costs, and the size of the retail firm will be determined at Q_C.

The introduction of r.p.m. makes it possible for the manufacturer to raise the margin above the minimum level, say, to M_2. Clearly, there are two possible firm sizes, Q_R and Q_R', consistent with the existence of such a margin and the absence of abnormal profits. However, only Q_R, the smaller size, represents a satisfactory solution. Suppose that by chance all retailers reached a size of Q_R' when the margin was set at M_2. Marginal cost would be above marginal revenue (M_2), and profit maximization would suggest a reduction in scale. This is a feasible move, and would indeed lead to a temporary increase in profits until new retail competitors appeared in the market. The entry of new firms would, of course, continue as long as there were any abnormal profits available, which means that firm size would continue to decrease until it reached Q_R. At Q_R, marginal cost is below marginal revenue, and retailers would wish to reduce prices to expand sales. However, they are precluded from doing so by r.p.m. Thus, the falling phase of the average retail operating cost curve (the heavy line in Figure 1) may be said to define the size of the retail firm as a function of the unit margin established by the manufacturer practising r.p.m.[6]

Conventional price theory would lead us to expect that an excess of marginal revenue over marginal cost would be eliminated, either by secret price cuts or by the incurring of additional costs – such as, for example, the cost of special services or advertising – in an attempt, however futile, to expand sales. Our separation of the effects of margin adjustment under r.p.m. on the number of the outlets from its effects on the volume of retail service is partially an analytical convenience. However, we believe that the size/margin relationship set forth above may be justified alone

6. This formulation of the retail-margin/size relationship may be extended to include both the case of monopolistic, rather than perfect, competition among retailers (e.g. through differences in locations) and the case of multi-product retailing. Under large-group monopolistic competition, the size of the retail firm in the absence of r.p.m. would be determined by a tangency solution at an output below minimum average operating costs. Otherwise the analysis is essentially similar to the perfect competition case. Multi-product retailing may be included under any of a number of possible assumptions. The simplest is that the retailer requires some minimum aggregate margin for each product stocked. Under this assumption, the margin/size relationship is defined by a rectangular hyperbola, the area of the interior rectangle determined by the total margin criterion. In both of these cases, the relationship between increasing margins and declining size of the retail firm is maintained. In the multi-product case, 'size' refers, of course, to the retailer's sales of the individual product, not to the total size of the retail firm.

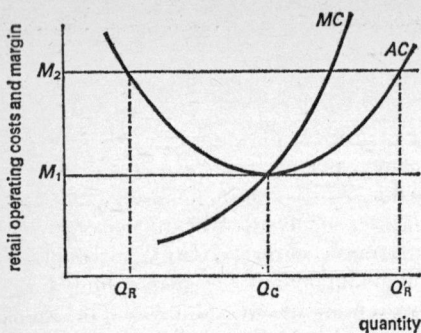

Figure 1

under some circumstances. Our model assumes 1. that the manufacturer is fully successful in maintaining r.p.m., and 2. that the retailer believes that additional expenditures on his part will not increase his sales volume, even at the expense of other retailers. Such circumstances might easily prevail in the retailing of convenience goods such as cigarettes. More generally, we may regard this as the limiting case with retail demand totally unresponsive to selling costs.

The outlets hypothesis

The hypothesis that final aggregate market demand is a function of both price and the number of retail outlets is illustrated by the series of demand curves in Figure 2. Each successively higher curve is associated with a larger number of outlets. Equal increments to the number of outlets are assumed, and the curves are drawn increasingly close together to indicate a diminishing impact of these increases on total demand.

We now discuss the long-run equilibrium adjustments, both in manufacturing and retailing, in these demand conditions. We continue to assume

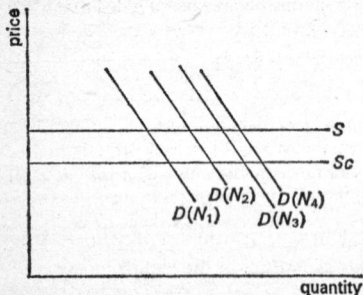

Figure 2

competition in retailing, but consider several assumptions about market structure and policy in the manufacturing sector.

1 Perfect competition in manufacturing; no r.p.m.

For convenience, we assume constant long-run industry costs at both levels. Thus, the supply curve for the manufacturing sector can be depicted in Figure 2 by the line S_C (drawn at a price equal to the minimum average cost of manufacturing), and the final market supply curve by the line S (drawn at a price equal to the minimum average cost of both manufacturing and retailing). Market price and retail margin are, by assumption, cost-determined. The equilibrium adjustment of market quantity and the number of retail outlets can be described by reference to Figure 3.

In Figure 3, the curve DS is the locus of points showing the number of retailers generating a particular market demand curve and the quantity at which supply is equal to demand on that curve at the market price. The curve is drawn to rise at an increasing rate, reflecting a hypothesized diminishing effectiveness of increases in the number of outlets.

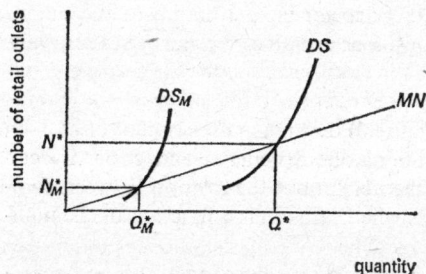

Figure 3

In the absence of r.p.m., the equilibrium size of the retail unit is determined by *minimum* average costs ($=$ retail margin), and is therefore unique. Thus, there is a determinate relationship between the total quantity sold in the market and the number of retail firms. This relationship is shown in Figure 3 by the line MN, a ray through the origin. MN is the locus of points showing the number of retailers that can exist in long-run competitive equilibrium for any quantity sold in the market, or conversely the total quantity that any equilibrium group of retailers can offer for sale.

Full equilibrium requires both that the quantity demanded should equal the quantity supplied, and that retailers should be in long-run equilibrium. The equilibrium number of retailers and volume of market transactions are given by the intersection of the DS and MN curves, N^* and Q^*.[7]

7. We need to add the plausible stability condition that for an intersection N^*, at $N < +N^*$, the equilibrium quantity traded is greater than the quantity necessary to

This intersection can be thought of as the equilibrium demand and supply of retailers under conditions of perfect competition and constant industry (not firm) costs.[8]

2 A monopolist manufacturer not practising r.p.m.

A similar analysis can be carried out for the case of a monopolist selling to perfectly competitive retailers, and not practising r.p.m. The relation between the equilibrium number of retail outlets and the total quantity sold, the MN curve, is unaltered. We can derive a DS curve for the monopolist in a manner similar to the case of perfect competition among manufacturers. From the demand curve corresponding to each N we deduct the retail margin. This margin must equal minimum average retail operating costs in equilibrium. For each resulting average revenue curve we find the profit-maximizing quantity which is plotted as DS_M in Figure 3. Full equilibrium requires both that the retailers should be in equilibrium and that for any given N the monopolist should be maximizing profits, and is thus indicated by the intersection of DS_M and MN.

The shape and position of DS_M depend on the nature of the monopolist's cost and revenue functions. For example, the steeper the upward slope of the marginal cost curve, the steeper will be the DS_M curve. Similarly, the position of the DS_M curve in relation to the DS curve for competition in manufacturing (as in Figure 3) depends on the nature of costs in the industry. On simple assumptions about demand and costs, we can derive a somewhat paradoxical theorem about the relation between competitive and monopolistic outputs when demand is a function of the number of retail outlets.

When demand is *not* a function of the number of retail outlets, it is a well-known result that, assuming constant costs and linear demand, monopoly output will be exactly one half the competitive output (see Robinson, 1933, p. 145). Making the same assumptions, and by a similar argument, we have drawn DS_M so that, at any N, quantity is half the competitive quantity. Since both the DS_M and MN curves slope upward to the

---

maintain N retailers in long-run equilibrium; and vice versa for $N > +N^*$. That is, the DS curve must cut the MN curve from below. For example, there might be no demand at the market price where there are less than some positive number of retailers; in this case the DS curve would have a positive intercept on the vertical axis. Given the shapes of the two curves, if they intersect at all, they will intersect twice. Only the second intersection is a stable equilibrium.

8. Higher, but constant, costs would be reflected in a higher DS curve, and increasing long-run industry costs would cause the DS curve to rise more steeply. If long-run costs increases were accompanied by increases in the optimal scale of the retail unit – as, for example, they would be if retail site costs rose due to scarcity – the MN curve would become concave downward as well.

right, Q^*_M will be *less* than half Q^*, that is, the introduction of the outlets hypothesis entails an even bigger contraction of output by the monopolist in comparison with perfect competition.

3 A monopolist manufacturer practising r.p.m.

The market adjustment reached by the manufacturer practising r.p.m. will be an equilibrium one in the same sense as the competitive and monopolistic adjustments shown in Figure 3, with the important exception that the manufacturer can select his own margin. With the margin now a variable, we must draw an MN curve for each possible margin and the corresponding size of retail outlet. This is illustrated in Figure 4, where M_0N represents the quantity-number relationship at the competitive margin, and M_1N and M_2N the relationship at successively higher margins.

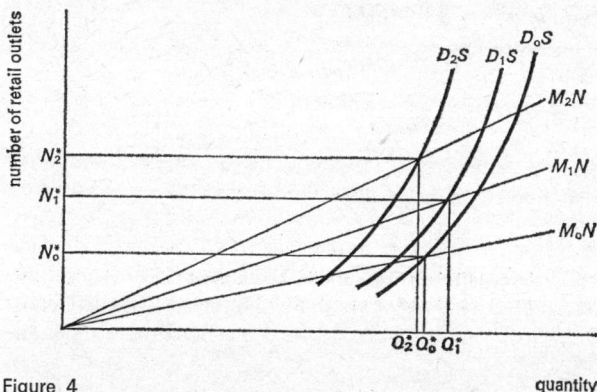

Figure 4

Similarly, just as in Figure 3 we drew a DS curve postulating the competitive margin, we can draw D_1S and D_2S postulating the margins corresponding to M_1N and M_2N respectively.

Given the size of the margin, the intersection of the relevant pair of DS and MN curves represents an equilibrium at which the manufacturer is maximizing profits and the retailers are in equilibrium. The monopolist will choose the margin and thus the intersection which maximizes his profits.[9]

9. There is an alternative method of setting out the analysis which has some advantage because in a more familiar form. We can convert the demand surface of Figure 2, in which market demand was related to price, quantity and the number of outlets, to a surface showing price, quantity and retail margin. This second surface is constructed on the assumption that retailers are in equilibrium with respect to their numbers for a given industry output. This transformation may be briefly explained in relation to Figure 5. Given the equal-numbers demand curve $D(N_1)$, select a particular combination of price and quantity (P_1 and Q_1). This quantity divided by N_1 gives the size of retail

The implications of the model

It is not surprising that few definite predictions about the effects of r.p.m. (as compared with a monopolist not practising r.p.m.) can be made on the basis of the preceding analysis without making strong assumptions about the revenue and cost functions. Some quite general conclusions can be drawn, and for the rest, we shall use the model to exhibit some interesting cases.

Conditions favourable to r.p.m.: even when demand is a function of the number of retailers it is, of course, by no means necessary that a manu-

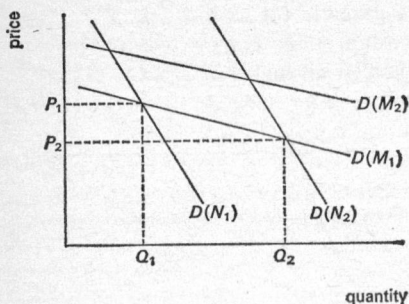

Figure 5

firm, which, if there is to be equilibrium in the retail market, must be receiving a margin (say M_1), determined by the relation shown in Figure 1. Proceeding to the next highest equal-numbers demand curve $D(N_2)$ we can determine the quantity consistent with M_1 and N_2, given equilibrium in retailing, and the corresponding price (say P_2 and Q_2). In this way we can derive an equal-margin demand curve $D(M_1)$. An entire family of such curves could, in principle, be derived; successively higher curves would be associated with increasing margins and, for any given price or quantity, with larger numbers of smaller retail units.

From a particular equal-margin demand curve, the determination of optimal price and quantity is straightforward. The manufacturer simply deducts the relevant margin to determine his average revenue curve, then obtains his marginal revenue curve, whose intersection with marginal cost determines the profit-maximizing output. For this given margin both the manufacturer and (by the construction of the equal-margin demand curve) the retailers are in equilibrium at this point.

Evidently, so long as (a) increases in the retail margin decrease the size of retailer, and (b) increases in the number of retailers result in increases in market demand, the equal-margin demand curves will shift out as the retail margin is increased. When either of these effects is exhausted, the limits of market demand will have been reached. However, the average revenue curves of the manufacturer will reach their outer limit and start to shift downward earlier as a result of the subtraction of ever larger margins from the retail price. If the average revenue curves do not cross, then the maximum maximorum for the manufacturer will be found on the highest of the average revenue curves. In any event, it is clear that the manufacturer can, in principle, calculate the maximum profit price-output for each margin and thus choose the optimal margin.

facturer will find it profitable to practise r.p.m. The strength of the relations may be such that M_0, the competitive margin, is the most profitable. What can we say on the basis of this model about the circumstances in which we would expect to find r.p.m. practised by a monopolist? Obviously, quantity demanded should be strongly responsive to changes in the number of retailers. Less obviously, the shape of the retail cost curve is important. The number of outlets should be responsive to increases in the margin (the 'cost' of securing more outlets); this requires that a small increase in margin should considerably reduce the equilibrium size of retail outlet, which in turn requires that the average retail operating cost curve slope gently at outputs below the point of minimum average cost, that is, that economies of scale in retailing should be present but not too marked.

The size and number of retail outlets: we should expect r.p.m. to result in a larger number of smaller retailers. That retail outlets should be smaller follows from the consideration that the immediate object of r.p.m. is to raise the retail margin above the competitive level, and the relation, developed above, between the margin and the equilibrium size of outlet. The equilibrium number of retailers must increase because, otherwise, with the same or a smaller number of retailers and a larger margin, the manufacturer's average revenue curve would be below that given by the competitive margin, and his profits would be greater if he did not practise r.p.m.

The wholesale and retail prices: it is often somewhat casually argued that r.p.m. raises prices because retail margins are higher, and a profit-maximizing manufacturer will not absorb any of the increased margin by reducing his price to retailers. In Figure 6 we illustrate a case in which the

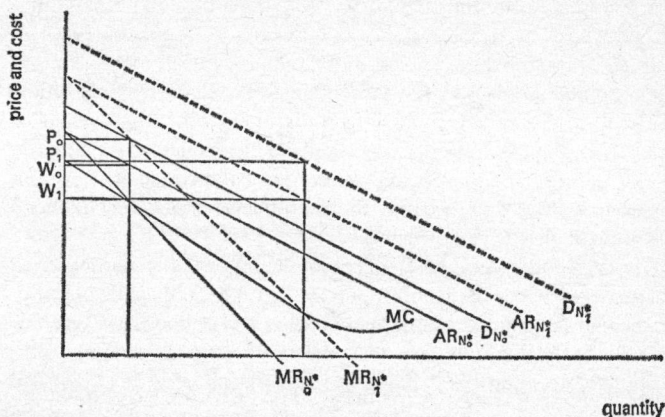

Figure 6

manufacturer practising r.p.m. finds it profitable to reduce his price below the level without r.p.m. The diagram is to be interpreted in relation to Figure 4. The solid lines show the profit-maximizing diagram relevant to the full equilibrium position given that the margin is at the competitive level, M_0, that is the intersection of M_0N and D_0S at N_0*. The broken lines represent the demand conditions for full equilibrium when the margin has been raised to (say) M_1 by r.p.m., and thus represent conditions at N_1*. The marginal cost curve is common to both sets of circumstances.

If we measure profit by the area contained by the vertical axis, the relevant marginal revenue curve and the marginal cost curve, it can be seen that M_1 is the more profitable margin, and that it will pay the manufacturer to raise the margin above the competitive level by r.p.m. Nevertheless, we can see that both the wholesale price (W_1) and the retail price (P_1) will be lower than in the absence of r.p.m. (W_0 and P_0).[10]

This case is formally similar to the standard analysis of the effects of an increase in demand on a monopolist's price (Robinson, 1933, chapter 4). As is well known, a circumstance conducive to a fall in price is that marginal costs be falling, and it is this case which we have illustrated in Figure 6. Another favourable circumstance is that the elasticity of demand at the new profit-maximizing quantity shall be greater than at the old.

There seems no obvious reason to believe that, in itself, the institution of r.p.m. will affect the marginal cost curve in any way. All we can say is that if marginal costs of manufacturing are falling, then r.p.m. is less likely to raise prices and they may even fall. It should be emphasized that it is marginal cost that is relevant here. The empirical evidence, while supporting the view that constant average costs over a wide range of outputs are common in manufacturing industry, does not confirm the hypothesis that falling marginal costs are widespread (see, for example, Johnston, 1960).

On the other hand, it can be argued that r.p.m. may itself make demand more elastic. Some market-research studies suggest that the responsiveness of purchasers to price changes is partially a function of their knowledge of price levels. If so, r.p.m. may increase elasticity of demand by spreading knowledge of the price of the product, because of the wider distribution, the uniformity of price and because the manufacturer is more likely to feature the uniform price in advertising.

The quantity trades: since the object of r.p.m. in this model is to increase demand by wider distribution, intuition suggests that the quantity traded on the market is greater under r.p.m. This is very likely the case, but not necessarily so. It is quite easy to construct a counter-example, but, since we can give no plausible explanation of the kind of shift in demand

10. In contrast to this case, the more familiar arguments that r.p.m. reduces retail prices depend on the assertion that retail margins are *reduced* by r.p.m.

needed to produce this result, we do no more than mention it as a logical possibility.

In assessing the importance of the foregoing results, the limited nature of the model should be borne in mind. Specifically, it deals with a particular kind of market structure, and but one of the several hypotheses which have been advanced to explain r.p.m.

The service hypothesis

A second explanation for the practice of r.p.m. by manufacturers is that for some goods the quantity demanded is a function of the amount of retail service provided, and that the amount of such service can be increased by raising the retail margin (see Yamey, 1954, and Telser, 1960). In effect, the retail margin is viewed as a selling cost for the manufacturer, and the manufacturer may well increase such costs in order to increase his profits. It is apparent that this hypothesis could be made part of a model of similar structure to the outlets-hypothesis model. We do not elaborate such a model here, but we indicate some possible inter-relations between the outlets and service hypotheses.

Changes in the amount of retail service may well have an impact on the size of retail outlet and thus on the number of outlets. *A priori*, one might conceive of service activity giving rise to constant costs per unit of sales and thus not changing the optimal scale of the retail unit (for example, distribution of informational literature to purchasers); in this case, an increase in market demand arising from the increased service might draw new retail firms into the market. More important, one might conceive of service activity that gave rise to economies of scale, with costs higher but decreasing per sales unit – such as public demonstrations, addition of specialized personnel – and thus to an increase in the optimal scale of the retail outlet. These possibilities suggest that an increase in service activity brought about through r.p.m. might generate changes in the number of retailers, or vice versa.

Thus, in an industry where the level of market demand was related both to the volume of retail service and to the number of outlets, a manufacturer might find that the increase in margin provided through r.p.m. might increase either the amount of retail service or the number of outlets, or some combination of the two. Choice among such alternatives would rest, of course, upon a comparison of the aggregate margins involved and the profits generated. Of particular interest, the desire of a manufacturer to restrict the growth of numbers below the maximum level and to channel part of any increase in margins into an increase in retail services might explain the adoption of another marketing practice, retail franchising. Through a franchise system, a monopolist manufacturer or brander may both introduce a maintained price structure, with margins in excess of *minimum* average costs, and also control the character and amount of surrounding services to varying degrees. The increased cost of services may, in fact, convert the cost-margin position of the retailers into a minimum cost equilibrium, so that the franchise system becomes a substitute for r.p.m. rather than an auxiliary practice.[11]

11. Somewhat similar issues to those examined here are raised in the analysis of the franchise distribution of automobiles in the US in Pashigian (1961), especially chapters 2 and 4; and Koo (1959). See also Stekler (1960) amd Koo (1960).

References

JOHNSTON, J. (1960), *Statistical Cost Analysis*, McGraw-Hill.
KOO, A. Y. C. (1959), 'A theoretical note on the dealer–manufacturer relationship in the automobile industry', *Q. J. Econ.*, vol. 73, pp. 316–25.
KOO, A. Y. C. (1960), 'Reply', *Q. J. Econ.*, vol. 74, pp. 333–7.
PASHIGIAN, B. P. (1961), *The Distribution of Automobiles*, Prentice-Hall.
ROBINSON, J. (1933), *The Economics of Imperfect Competition*, Macmillan.
STEKLER, H. (1960), 'Comment', *Q. J. Econ.*, vol. 74, pp. 330–3.
TELSER, L. G. (1960), 'Why should manufactures want fair trade', *J. Law and Econ.* vol. 3, pp. 86–105.
YAMEY, B. S. (1954), *The Economics of Resale Price Maintenance*, Pitman.

22 O. A. Davis

The Economics of Trading Stamps

O. A. Davis, 'The economics of trading stamps', *Journal of Business*, vol. 32, 1959, pp. 141–50.

A recent boom in trading stamps has centered the public's attention upon that industry. Several state legislatures have been the sites of bitter battles between pro-stamp and anti-stamp factions. It is only natural that policy-makers should question what is 'behind' the stamps, wondering if the public is being cheated and whether or not stamps are 'socially desirable.'

Several articles have appeared during the last three years on the trading-stamp controversy (Haring and Yoder, 1956; Simon, 1957; Vredenburg, 1956a; Beem, 1957; and the comment on Beem's work, Strotz, 1958). Most of these articles have been descriptive or factual in nature and, although possibly excellent in themselves, have not attempted to provide a theoretical analysis of the trading stamp. The purpose of this paper is to provide such an analysis, with a view to answering several of the controversial questions. Our method is to examine the effects of stamps upon a representative firm and to use the results for an economy-wide analysis.

The merchant can use trading stamps to generate a larger profit through two connected but conceptually separate methods. First, he may use stamps as a discriminatory device. Second, he may use stamps to generate a greater volume of business. We shall examine briefly each of these devices and then pass to the more interesting question of the effect of stamps upon prices.

Stamps as volume producers

Some firms, especially grocery stores which purchase their stamps from an independent company, do not use stamps as discriminatory devices. These firms consider the most profitable use of stamps to be that of generating a larger volume of business.

There are two volume-producing aspects of trading stamps. In the first place, stamps may be used as a price-cutting mechanism. To illustrate this point, consider a consumer who makes a purchase at a store which gives trading stamps. When the stamps are redeemed, he has received, in effect, a lower price, since he gains goods or cash in addition to his original purchase. Now consider the case of a firm which faces a negatively sloped demand curve. A greater volume can be produced simply by moving down the demand curve through the lowering of price. If the installation of trading stamps is viewed by the consumer as a reduction in price, then this aspect alone will tend to produce a greater volume. However, if firms price 'rationally' – that is, if prices are set so as to make marginal revenue equal marginal cost – this aspect of trading stamps must be deemed unimportant, for it must be assumed that prices were originally at a higher than equilibrium level so that the firm could profitably employ stamps as a price-cutting measure. Such an assumption could hardly be warranted in a free market, and it is doubtful that firms in such a market would desire to cut prices by a method that would add to costs.

On the other hand, if we consider certain institutional realities of our distributive system, stamps as a price-cutting mechanism appear feasible. For example, resale-price-maintenance laws place restrictions upon the market. If the price is set above the competitive level, over-investment in the industry will result, and each firm will find that its position is not 'optimum' in that marginal revenue (price) will be greater than marginal costs. In such a situation incentive exists for the individual firm to cut prices and expand volume. Although the fair-trade laws prevent a direct slashing of prices, trading stamps offer a method of 'chiselling', for, although the quoted price would remain the same, stamps mean that the consumer can obtain a rebate so that the price is effectively lowered. Since other firms cannot retaliate by cutting prices, their only recourse is trading stamps. If the trading-stamp company is reluctant to grant a 'franchise' to more than one store of a given type in any one market area, then the initial firm that introduces stamps gains a lasting advantage, as consumers rarely care to save more than one type of stamp.

Needless to say, resale-price-maintenance laws are not the only institutional rigidity that makes trading stamps attractive to firms. Cartel arrangements, nationally advertised prices, and any other phenomenon that results in price being set above the competitive level create a situation that is favorable to the price-cutting aspect of trading stamps.

However, trading stamps cannot be dismissed as a simple price-cutting mechanism. Like advertising, stamps are designed to affect the individual's choice of stores. There are, however, important differences between stamps and advertising. Advertising attempts to create demand by spreading knowledge and bringing the item or store in question to the consumer's attention. Trading stamps seek to focus attention on the firm by creating in the consumer an interest in the stamp itself. Trading-stamp psychology states that, once the consumer begins to save a particular type of stamp, he will be motivated to return to the same store in order to obtain his stamp. Many stamp companies will send out free stamps to a firm's prospective customers when a stamp plan is introduced, assuming that this practice will induce some persons to save stamps.

There is an element of uncertainty connected with the trading stamp – it is difficult to determine its value. To the individual consumer the value of the stamp is determined by its 'puchasing power', or the value of the goods that the stamp can command. However, the problem is not so simple as it would seem. Should the value of the articles in question be computed at the manufacturer's resale list price, the department-store price, or a discount-house price? Then, too, the stamp price and the money price (computed by either of the three methods) tend to vary widely according to which consumer article is specified. A recent study by the Department of Agriculture (1957, p. 6) indicated that the value of a book of stamps varied from $1·70 to $5·22, which represented a discount from 1·13 to 3·43 per cent per dollar of expenditure. Other studies have come up with slightly different results, but these figures should be sufficient to establish the main point. It is difficult for the consumer to determine the value of his stamps. The more the consumer tends to overestimate the value of the stamp or the more value the consumer tends to place on stamps, the more we may expect the stamp to influence his choice of stores.

A motivation study by Klass (1956) indicates that stamps are much more important to the consumer than most statistical surveys reveal. His study reports that, although surface attitudes may indicate only a casual acceptance of stamps by the consumer, subsurface attitudes tend to bear out the fact that consumers attach considerable importance to stamps. For example, not only were stamp-savers found to believe that they enjoyed a reputation for being economical and thrifty, but they regarded premiums as free gifts not connected with the price of their merchandise. Klass also found that stamps fill definite psychological needs, providing goals toward which the shopper can work, and that over three-fourths of those who collect stamps feel that most consumers would be very unhappy, even to the point of taking their trade elsewhere, should a store that gives stamps cease the practice. The results of this study seem to indicate that at least some consumers derive a positive utility from the act of saving stamps itself.

There are other, more speculative, reasons to believe that consumers place considerable importance on stamps. Since women are commonly recognized as the most important stamp-savers, let us consider, for example, a home in which the man handles the money and the wife has to make a special request for household items but is allowed money for the groceries. In this case, stamps afford a method whereby the wife can get desired items without having to make a request for additional money. The same reasoning applies when family finances are handled through a budget. If the husband carefully inspects the budget, the wife may employ trading stamps to get certain items, and at the same time she might win admiration for her 'thriftiness'.

The reason for this extended discussion is to demonstrate that the very purpose of trading stamps is to influence the customer's choice among stores. Thus, like advertising, the theoretical meaning of this aspect of trading stamps is to shift the demand curve facing the firm. It is obvious that stamps do not have to affect the choices of all relevant consumers to be effective. It is only necessary that some individuals desire stamps to cause a shift in the demand curve.

Trading stamps themselves, considered alone, are undoubtedly an additional expense to the retailer. The relevant question is whether the additional expense can be offset in other areas of cost. In this connection there would seem to be two forces working in opposite directions. Some retailers claim that the imposition of a stamp plan allows advertising expenses to be reduced. They also claim that there is less need for low-priced specials and other forms of premium promotion.[1] This argument would indicate that at least a portion of stamp costs can be offset. On the other hand, it would seem that trading stamps would tend to increase such areas as bookkeeping expenses; and, in self-service markets, check-out operations might be slowed, calling for additional expenses. Thus the question of what trading stamps do to costs is left theoretically open. However, we should note that few persons would claim that stamps would reduce total costs. The most frequent argument states that average costs may remain the same only if volume is expanded sufficiently. This argument assumes that the firm is operating on a declining portion of its average cost curve, that trading stamps raise this curve, but that stamps may cause such an expansion in volume that average costs remain the same after adoption of the stamp plan.[2]

The evident conclusion is that, if the expansion in volume produces enough revenue to more than cover whatever additions to costs that the stamp plan creates, it is advantageous for the firm to install such a plan.

Stamps as discriminatory devices

It is generally agreed that, in order for discrimination to exist, the firm in question must be faced with a down-sloping curve over at least some range of output. When the firm finds itself in such a position, it may discover that it is advantageous to 'separate the markets' and charge two different prices. In this way volume may be generated and profits increased.

1. So far as I know there are no studies to back up the claim of these retailers, but there is evidence to show that some retailers consider stamps as an alternative to the usual forms of premium promotion (see Vredenburg, 1956b, pp. 106–7, and Campbell, 1956, pp. 8 and 16).

2. See Vredenburg (1956b, pp. 62–74), for the outstanding example of this opinion.

Trading stamps offer a method whereby a retail merchant may carry on a subtle form of price discrimination.[3] Retail merchants operate in this country under standard prices; that is to say, a price is quoted and not bargained, as is the practice in some European and South American countries. As earlier discussion indicated, from the consumer's point of view, when trading stamps are offered and later redeemed the price is effectively lowered. To illustrate discriminatory possibilities of this point, consider two consumers who make identical expenditures upon identical items in a given store. If one redeems his stamps and the other does not, then one has, in effect, received a lower price, since, with an identical expenditure, he has received an additional quantity of goods or perhaps even a cash rebate.

The mere fact that a merchant gives stamps is not, however, *prima facie* evidence that he intends to use stamps as a discriminatory device. Since many of the trading stamps issued are purchased from independent stamp companies, the merchant who gives stamps with each sale will not benefit from any resulting discrimination. He has already bought and paid for the stamps. In such cases the benefits resulting from non-redemption would accrue to the stamp company. In a competitive market for the stamps themselves, we could expect non-redemptions to be reflected in lower prices for the stamps and increased values in redemption goods.

The merchant may use the discriminatory aspect of stamps to his advantage through one of two methods. First of all, if the merchant happens to operate his own stamp plan, as do several chain stores, then the benefits of discrimination return directly to him. If the merchant uses the stamps of an independent company, he may still discriminate by giving stamps only to those customers requesting them or by asking each customer whether he saves stamps.

It may be possible for a merchant to use stamps as a discriminatory device, but it remains to be determined whether it is advantageous for him to do so. Let us consider a firm with some degree of monopoly power.[4] We shall assume that this monopolist operates his own stamp company and thus is able to adjust the redemption value of his stamps so as to give the 'optimum discount'.

In Figure 1 we shall measure price and cost along axis OY and quantity of output along axis OX. The line labelled D represents the demand curve,

3. Since the plan of this paper is to separate conceptually the two obviously related aspects of trading stamps, this section of our analysis will consider stamps as a purely discriminatory device.

4. In this article we use the term 'monopolist' (a firm with monopoly power) to describe any firm facing a down-sloping demand curve. This definition includes so-called monopolistic competition and does not imply a lack of any competition. We are merely interested in the case where the firm has some control over price, as control would seem to be 'necessary' as far as discriminatory practices are concerned.

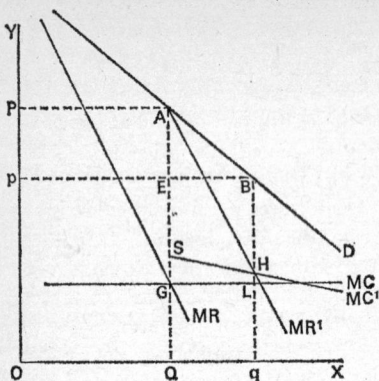

Figure 1

and the line labelled *MR* is the marginal revenue curve. The marginal cost curve is labelled *MC*; and, for purposes of simplicity, we have drawn it as a horizontal line.

In the absence of a stamp plan or a discriminatory device, profit-maximization criteria indicate that the monopolist would desire to place OQ on the market at price OP. Now assume that a stamp plan is introduced. Previously, the portion of the demand curve below point A was not relevant to the monopolist. However, with the use of discrimination, he may gain additional revenue. Assume, for example, that he employs his plan in such a manner that no stamps are given on his old 'custom', that is, that portion of his sales represented by the demand curve above point A. We have a new marginal revenue curve, represented by the line labelled MR^1, for that portion of the demand curve below point A. This curve bears the same relationship to demand as does the usual marginal revenue curve.

However, the introduction of stamps, unless compensated by the reduction of other expenditures, must alter the cost situation of the firm. For the purposes of this model we shall assume that stamps are an uncompensated cost. Since the firm usually gives stamps on the basis of per-dollar receipts, cost of a stamp plan is directly related to total revenue. Graphically, total stamp cost rises until total revenue is at its maximum, that is, until marginal revenue is zero; then it falls. The first derivation of this total-stamp-cost curve, or marginal stamp expenditure, can be algebraically added to the firm's marginal cost curve to determine the alteration that the stamp plan places upon the firm's marginal cost schedule. Since the firm in our model gives stamps only on that portion of the demand curve to the right of point A, the marginal cost curve will be discontinuous. At point G it will 'jump' to point S and then will be as shown by the curve labelled MC^1.

Our monopolist now finds himself in a position to place an additional quantity Qq on the market by setting the value of his stamps so as to reduce price by Pp. By so doing, he gains additional revenue $QEBq$ while incurring expenses $QSHq$, of which $GSHL$ represent 'stamp costs'. Clearly, it would be advantageous to this firm to introduce stamps of this nature.

However, it is doubtful that any firm would be able to 'segregate' between old and new 'custom' for any period of time. It is probable that stamps would have to be given on some 'old' purchases either because of the impossibility of distinguishing between 'old' and 'new', because of the monopolist's desire to keep 'good will', or for some other reason. The exact opposite of the above case, where none of the old 'custom' received stamps, would be a situation in which stamps were given and saved on all purchases. If we assume this, then MR would continue to be the marginal revenue curve, the marginal cost curve would be altered over its entire length in a manner similar to the MC^1 segment of the previous example, and as a result the monopolist would not desire to install a stamp plan for discriminatory possibilities alone.

Certainly, these two extremes set the limits. It is probable that some of the old 'custom' would receive and save stamps, for, as we have seen above, the monopolist would find it impossible to give stamps on only 'new' purchases. It is also probable that some customers would consider stamps not worth the trouble and would not desire to save them. Since marginal revenue is defined as the change in total revenue divided by the change in quantity, then, as long as not all customers save stamps, the relevant marginal revenue curve for that portion of the demand curve which represents 'stamp-savers' will fall between point G and point H. The intersection of this latter marginal revenue curve and the marginal cost curve, adjusted to compensate for the stamp plan, would determine the optimum rate of discount for stamps.

Several important limitations of the above model should be noted. First, our analysis does not indicate whether or not the introduction of stamps causes the original price to change. Under different assumptions about the 'structural makeup' of the demand curve, the monopolist could 'separate his markets' in such a manner that the usual discrimination model would apply, and it would become advantageous for the listed price to be increased. However, in the real world the discriminatory aspect alone may be of secondary importance in influencing any movement in listed prices.

Second, the vast majority of the firms that use trading stamps purchase their stamps from an independent stamp company. Since the stamp companies usually specify the relationship between stamp issue and sales as, for example, one stamp for each ten cents of purchase, then the rate of discount may not be a variable subject to the control of the firm. Instead, the value of the stamp would be determined by the stamp company and would be identical with the optimum rate of discount of the firm only by coincidence.

Third, it may be argued that, since retailing is highly competitive, the demand curve facing the firm may be approximately horizontal. Discrimintory possibilities do not, of course, exist insofar as this is true. However, a little reflection will lead to the inevitable conclusion that trading stamps could not exist under conditions usually listed as necessary for perfect competition. Thus stamps are compatible with only a type of market formation in which the demand curve facing the firm is negatively inclined over some portion.

Stamps and prices

Most empirical studies argue that trading stamps have no effect upon prices. The purpose of this section is to examine this position theoretically and point out that it may be misleading.

Let us consider the example represented in Figure 2. Let the demand curve facing this firm before the introduction of stamps be represented by the line labelled D, the marginal revenue curve by the line labelled MR, and the marginal cost curve by the line labelled MC. The firm would place OQ on the market at price OP.

Now let us assume that the firm successfully instals a stamp plan.[5] We shall further assume that this plan makes a net addition to costs so that

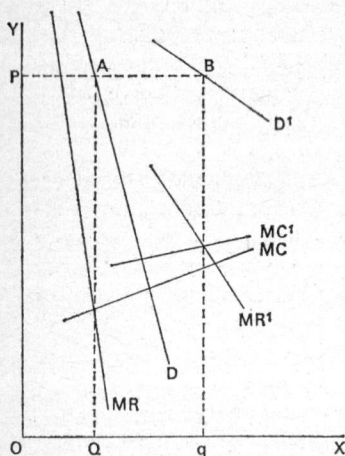

Figure 2

5. For this portion of our analysis we assume that stamps are used only for purposes of volume generation.

the marginal cost curve shifts to MC^1. The new demand and marginal revenue curves are represented by D^1 and MR^1, respectively. In its new situation the firm will place Oq on the market, but the price will remain the same. We can conclude without further analysis that it is possible for a monopolist to use trading stamps profitably without increasing his prices. However, this is only one of three possible results. Our conclusion followed because of an exact relationship between the new and the old demand curves. If we were to change the slope of our new demand curve, it would become evident that the monopolist could raise or lower prices or allow them to remain the same after the introduction of trading stamps.[6]

Let us leave our considerations of the individual firm and try to determine the effects of stamps upon the price level. Assume an economy operating at full employment in which resources and technology are considered as fixed. We shall also take the money supply and the velocity of money as given. In other words, there is to be no change in the total value of the goods and services produced in the period which we are considering.

Let us assume that all retail firms are operating under conditions which are compatible with trading stamps and that all factors of production are competitively priced. There will be in existence a determinate level of prices. We shall assume that there are no stamp plans in operation in the economy.

Now let us assume that a type of stamp plan is introduced under which only goods are used for redemption purposes. Let us also assume that every retail firm adopts a stamp plan. Under our assumptions aggregate demand could not change, although demand facing individual firms could vary. It would appear at first that the mere installation of stamps could not change the price level. However, if the stamp plans operate, then some goods are distributed free. With no additional quantity of goods being produced, it seems probable that retail prices will rise enough to cover the costs of producing and distributing the goods issued under the stamp plans. In other words, although aggregate demand itself will not have shifted, its 'direction' will have shifted in that consumers will now be demanding some goods through the purchase of other goods. Insofar as the total quantity of goods sold through direct retail outlets will have diminished, prices will have risen accordingly.

6. Assuming increasing marginal costs, it should be noted that, for prices to remain the same or be lowered, the negative slope of the new demand curve D^1 must be less than that of the old demand curve D. While we cannot theoretically determine the exact relationship of the old curve to the new, some rather speculative arguments tend to indicate that stamps do act to increase the slope of the demand curve. For example, insofar as stamps cause consumers to return to a store without 'shopping around' and comparing prices, competition is lessened and the slope of the new demand curve may be increased. In such a case, prices rise.

The results of this discussion are rather simple. If we took the total quantity of merchandise and the total quantity of money spent for this merchandise in both the period before and after the introduction of stamps, and we compared these figures, then we would find that they were identical. Thus it stands to reason that actual prices would not have changed, although measured prices, prices actually observed in the market place (which excludes the 'free' stamp goods), would have risen. The payment arrangements would have caused a divergence between actual and measured prices, for some goods would be purchased by the means of other goods.

It may be argued that our conclusion is based upon the assumption that all redemptions are in the form of goods. Let us drop this assumption and adopt the alternative assumption that all redemptions are made in cash.

If redemptions are made in the manner assumed, then each redemption would amount to a return of purchasing power to the economy that would not have otherwise been present; we would have a double use of some money in the period under consideration. The price level would be driven up until the new level of prices became higher than the old level by the exact amount of the discount allowed through stamp redemptions. In other words, if we assume a given level of prices before the introduction of stamps and consider the cash redemption as a discount, since the redemption aspect allows money to be used twice, then the measured level of prices would rise. However, a true measure of the price level would reflect this redemption. This actual measure would be the listed price minus the discount via trading stamps. The true level of prices would be the same as was the price level before the introduction of stamps, although the measured level of prices, since it would not reflect the discount, would have increased.

If our conclusion is valid, then we should be able to drop our assumption that all firms install a stamp plan and find that there would be an increase in measured prices if only a few firms adopt stamps. It is obvious that, if the introduction of a stamp plan caused the firm to increase its prices, this increase would contribute to an increase in the measured price level. However, our analysis indicated that the introduction of stamps does not necessarily cause a firm to increase its prices. A further examination of this case is necessary if our conclusion is to hold.

Since under our assumptions aggregate demand cannot change, a shift in any one demand curve in our system must cause a corresponding opposite shift in some other demand curves somewhere in our system. Let us assume once again that we have an economy that is free of trading stamps. Let us further assume that only one firm in this economy adopts trading stamps and that the shift in its demand curve is such that its price does not change. Thus the question that we have to answer is whether there will be an increase in the measured price level. For purposes of simplicity, let us make the highly restrictive and unrealistic assumption that the shift to the right of the demand curve of the firm which adopted stamps causes only one other demand curve in our system to change. We shall assume also that quantity measurements of both firms are identical.

In our Figure 2 let our first firm be represented by demand curve D, marginal revenue curve MR, and marginal cost curve MC. Let demand curve D^1, marginal revenue MR^1 and marginal cost curve MC^1 represent our second firm. Thus our first firm places quantity OQ on the market at price OP and has a total revenue of $OQAP$. Our second firm places quantity Oq on the market at price OP and has a total revenue of $OqBP$. Now let us assume that our first firm adopts trading stamps and that its curves shift so that they are identical with the curves of the second firm; in other words, D^1, MR^1 and MC^1. This firm now places Oq on the market at price OP.

The reaction on the second firm is not completely clear. Its demand curve must shift to the left, but it may or may not be identical with that of the first firm D.[7] The gain in revenue by the first firm must be identical to the loss in revenue by the second firm, which is left with the total revenue of $OQAP$. However, if goods are used for stamp redemption, then the loss of output by the second firm will be greater than the gain in output by the first firm. Therefore, while the first firm has an output of Oq in its new position, the second firm has an output which is smaller than OQ, for some resources will have been withdrawn to go into the production of goods for redemption purposes. Since the firm must have the revenue of $OQAP$ and the output cannot be as great as OQ, then the shift in the second firm's demand curve must have been of such a nature that the price which it sets will be greater than OP.

If we dropped the assumption that redemptions are made in goods and adopted the alternative that redemptions are made in cash, our conclusion would not be altered. The adoption of stamps will cause a rise in the measured price level, although this rise does not have to be reflected by the firm concerned. The adoption of the stamp plan will set in motion forces which will cause a rise somewhere else in the system instead.

Conclusion

The purpose of this discussion has been that of applying the tools of theoretical economics to the institution of trading stamps. Our analysis has

7. Under the assumptions of this section aggregate demand, both in real and in money terms, cannot vary. These assumptions do not mean, however, that individual demand curves remain stationary. Individual demand curves may move in any manner, the only restriction being that the movements are such that the aggregate demand remains fixed. Since for the case at hand we allow only two of the 'firm' demand curves to shift, the quantity of money received jointly by the two firms is a constant. For a discussion of the 'realism' of such assumptions see Friedman (1949) reprinted in Friedman (1953, pp. 47–99).

indicated that the individual firm may find it advantageous to use stamps because of their two related but conceptually separable properties. First, firms may use stamps as a discriminatory device and, by taking advantage of the fact that all individuals do not desire to save stamps, increase their revenue. Second, since the obvious purpose of trading stamps is to influence the individual's choice of stores, a firm may employ stamps to shift the demand curve which it faces. In this respect trading stamps are similar to advertising and other forms of premium promotion. Firms operating under institutional rigidities as implicit or explicit cartel agreements, resale-price-maintenance laws, or nationally advertised prices use stamps as a price-cutting mechanism.

Probably the most debated aspect of trading stamps is their influence on prices. We have shown that any firm which installs a trading stamp plan theoretically may raise, lower or keep its prices at the same level. However, as far as the price level is concerned, our analysis, which was based upon assumptions designed to isolate the effects of trading stamps from other forces in our economy, indicated that stamps cause a rise in measured prices, although their effect upon the 'true' price level would reflect the stamp discount, and this level would remain unaffected.

References

BEEM, E. R. (1957), 'Who profits from trading stamps?' *Harvard bus. Rev.*, vol. 35, pp. 123–36.

CAMPBELL, P. (1956), 'Summary transcript of representative state conference on store trading stamps' (mimeographed).

Department of Agriculture (1957), 'Trading stamps and the consumer's food bill', *Marketing Research Report*, no. 169.

FRIEDMAN, M. (1949), 'The Marshallian demand curve', *J. polit Econ.*, vol. 57, pp. 463–95.

FRIEDMAN, M. (1953), *Essays in Positive Economics*, Chicago University Press.

HARING, A., and YODER, W. O. (1956), 'Boom in trading stamps', *bus. Horizons*, pp. 36–43.

KLASS, B. (1956), *Motivation and the Retail Food Business*, California Grocers' Association.

SIMON, S. I. (1957), 'The accounting for trading stamps', *accounting Rev.*, vol. 32, pp. 398–402.

STROTZ, R. H. (1958), 'On being fooled by figures: the case of trading stamps', *J. Bus.*, vol. 31, pp. 304–10.

VREDENBURG, H. L. (1956a), 'Trading-stamp stampede', *Nation*, vol. 183, pp. 287–9.

VREDENBURG, H. L. (1956b), *Trading Stamps*, University Bureau of Business Research, Bloomington, Illinois.

23 P. T. Bauer

Traders in West Africa

P. T. Bauer, *West African Trade*, Cambridge University Press, 1954, sections 1–6 of chapter 2, pp. 22–31.

1 Number and diversity of intermediaries in West Africa

The remarkable number of traders selling imported merchandise, frequently in very small quantities, is a conspicuous feature of the West African economies. A large number of intermediaries is also to be found in the handling of produce, though here they are not quite so numerous and conspicuous. It is often said by administrators that in the southern parts of Nigeria and the Gold Coast everybody is engaged in trade, and this is scarcely an exaggeration.

The large numbers of intermediaries and the diversity of conditions in which they operate result in great differences in individual status and volume of trading. The large European merchant firms stand in a class by themselves with trading turnovers of several million pounds a year. They act as import and export merchants and are also engaged in a variety of other activities which, in the case of the largest firms, include the operation of industrial and transport enterprises, shipping lines, timber concessions and estates. Much the largest is the United Africa Company, which, together with its subsidiaries and associates, conducts a business in West Africa and elsewhere totalling between £200 and £300 million annually. There are African traders with annual turnovers amounting to several hundred thousand pounds. They often operate in streets in which children sell a few empty bottles or cigarettes. Similar contrasts can be found in produce buying.

The number and variety of intermediaries have been much criticized by official and unofficial observers. They are condemned as wasteful and are said to be responsible for wide distributive margins both in the sale of merchandise and the purchase of produce. These criticisms rest on a misunderstanding. The system is a logical adaptation to certain fundamental factors in the West African economies which will persist for many years to come. So far from being wasteful, it is highly economic in saving and salvaging those resources which are particularly scarce in West Africa (above all, real capital) by using the resources which are largely redundant and for which there is very little demand; and thus it is productive by any rational economic criteria.

2 The task of bulking and of breaking bulk in produce buying and in the selling of merchandise

West African agricultural exports are produced by tens of thousands of Africans operating on a very small scale and often widely dispersed. They almost entirely lack suitable storage facilities, and they have no, or only very small, cash reserves. Accordingly they produce on a small scale and have to sell on an even smaller scale. The large number and the long line of intermediaries in the purchase of export produce essentially derive from the economies to be obtained from bulking very large numbers of small parcels. If each of five farmers situated twenty miles from the nearest village or town himself marketed his own very small weekly output, this would require five return journeys of forty miles each. If, however, one middleman (who may in fact be one of the farmers acting for the others) intervenes and carries the produce to the market, the number of journeys is reduced by four-fifths, saving scarce and valuable capital (in the form of animal or lorry transport) as well as labour. This last economy may also be important, since, in spite of the general surplus of labour, the harvesting of produce has to be accomplished within a given short period so that at times the farmer cannot afford to leave his holding. The same principle applies at the next stage; if each small middleman carried his purchases direct to the large markets the number of journeys would be greater than if another intermediary stepped in and carried the purchases of several traders; and so on all along the line.[1] In produce marketing the first link in the chain may be the purchase, hundreds of miles from Kano, of a few pounds of groundnuts, which after several stages of bulking arrive there as part of a wagon or lorry load of several tons.

The task of bulking cannot be avoided. So long as there is competitive entry into trade the producer is not affected whether the performer of the service of bulking and transport is remunerated by salary or by the profits of trade. If the farmers formed themselves into a cooperative society these services would be undertaken by the servants of the cooperative society, whose time and effort would still have to be paid for.

The arrangements for the purchasing of palm produce in Nigeria illustrate

1. Although the wastefulness of the long chain of intermediaries is a constant theme of critics of produce marketing in backward countries, and is usually combined with proposals for a reduction in the number of links in the distributive chain, the proposals have not yet been carried to their logical conclusion. It has not yet been suggested that each groundnut producer, for instance, should deal direct with the crushing mills in England.

the economies of bulking small quantities and the saving to be obtained by leaving the task to independent traders. In eastern Nigeria it is quite usual to see African traders sitting just outside the produce-buying stations of the European firms (or even inside their compounds); they buy produce from smaller traders, who bring in palm oil and palm kernels in small quantities, and after cleaning and blending re-sell these to the firms. It pays the firms not to buy direct from the small traders but to allow dealers to carry out the bulking and blending of small parcels, as their margins of profit are less than would be the cost of supervising and maintaining a staff of salaried employees engaged in the same work. From this example it should also be obvious that the number of links in the distributive chain could nominally be reduced by simple changes in terminology or in financial arrangements without in any way saving labour or capital; the reverse would actually happen.

The same principles apply in the sale of imported merchandise. The intermediaries break bulk and economize resources at all stages between the first seller and the final buyer. Imported merchandise arrives in very large consignments and needs to be distributed over large areas to the final consumer who, in West Africa, has to buy in extremely small quantities because of his poverty. In the absence of intermediaries the consumers would have to buy in wholesale quantities, and they might have neither the financial resources nor the storage facilities to do so. The intermediary intervenes, breaks bulk and makes the commodity available in small quantities.

The activities of intermediaries thus enable consumers to enjoy commodities which would otherwise be outside their reach.[2] They also save working capital by bringing about a more effective geographical distribu-

2. This was clearly set out by Adam Smith: 'Unless a capital was employed in breaking and dividing certain portions either of the rude or manufactured produce, into such small parcels as suit the occasional demands of those who want them, every man would be obliged to purchase a greater quantity of the goods he wanted, than his immediate occasions required. If there was no such trade as a butcher, for example, every man would be obliged to purchase a whole ox or a whole sheep at a time. This would generally be inconvenient to the rich, and much more so to the poor. If a poor workman was obliged to purchase a month's or six months' provisions at a time, a great part of the stock which he employs as a capital in the instruments of his trade, or in the furniture of his shop, and which yields him a revenue, he would be forced to place in that part of his stock which is reserved for immediate consumption, and which yields him no revenue. Nothing can be more convenient for such a person than to be able to purchase his subsistence from day to day, or even from hour to hour, as he wants it. He is thereby enabled to employ almost his whole stock as a capital. He is thus enabled to furnish work to a greater value, and the profit which he makes by it in this way, much more than compensates the additional price which the profit of the retailer imposes upon the goods' (1776, book 2, chapter 5).

tion of merchandise stocks than would be the case if consumers (or small retailers) had to deal directly with the importing firms. Their operations result in a faster turnover of total stocks and therefore in a more intensive utilization of both the foreign and African-owned working capital sustaining the local economy. They also assist the importing firms by maintaining contact with consumers and petty traders and ascertaining their requirements; their knowledge of local conditions equips them for these tasks. Thus their labour and activities replace both capital and salaried personnel and expensive European supervision. They reduce the cost of imported merchandise to the consumer and serve to bring it within the reach of wider sections of the population.

The organization of retail selling in Ibadan (and elsewhere) exemplifies the services rendered by petty traders both to suppliers and to consumers. Here there is no convenient central market, and it is usual to see petty traders sitting with their wares at the entrances to the stores of the European merchant firms. The petty traders sell largely the same commodities as the stores, but in much smaller quantities. It does not pay the European-owned stores to deal in these smaller quantities on the terms on which the petty traders are prepared to handle this business. On the other hand, consumers find it preferable to deal with the petty traders rather than to buy in less convenient quantities from the adjacent stores.[3]

The low level of capital affects the situation in various ways. The lack of telephones increases the difficulty of maintaining contact with customers and discovering their wants. The poor state of transport enhances the difficulty of maintaining contact with customers and increases the capital required for a given rate of consumption. Moreover, as most of the intermediaries have very little capital they can each handle only comparatively small quantities. This greatly increases the required number of intermediaries both horizontally and vertically: at each stage more middlemen are required, and the number of successive stages is increased as some of the final purchases take place in extremely small units, which may be a single drop of perfume, half a cigarette or a small bundle of ten matches. The number of different stages in the process of breaking bulk and of finding

3. Another reason for this system of trading was also present during the war, and may have been present to a very limited extent in recent years since the war. The breaking of bulk made it easier to evade price-control regulations, which generally did not apply and certainly could not be enforced in respect of very small quantities. The profits of evasion, which accrued largely to the petty traders, nevertheless also served to benefit the suppliers and their executives, partly through conditional sales, and partly by enabling them to strengthen the position of some of their customers and also their own hold over them. However, this aspect did not account for the prevalence of this method of trading, which was practised before the war and which in 1949–50 was not confined to the very few remaining price-controlled commodities in short supply.

customers will be readily appreciated when it is remembered that these commodities are imported in consignments of scores or hundreds of cases.

The extensive trade in empty containers such as kerosene, cigarette and soup tins, flour, salt, sugar and cement bags and beer bottles presents a revealing example of the operation of these forces. Some types of container are turned into various household articles or other commodities. Cigarette and soup tins become small oil lamps, and salt bags are made into shirts or tunics. But more usually the containers are used again in the storage and movement of goods. Those who seek out, purchase, carry and distribute second-hand containers maintain the stock of capital. They prevent the destruction of the containers, usually improve their condition, distribute them to where they can best be used, and so extend their usefulness, the intensity of their use, and their effective life. The activities of the traders represent a substitution of labour for capital. Most of the entrepreneurs in the container trade are women or children. The substitution is economic so long as six or eight hours of their time are less valuable (in view of the lack of desirable alternatives) than the small profit to be made from the sales of a few empty containers. So far from the system being wasteful it is highly economic in substituting superabundant for scarce resources; within the limits of available technical skill nothing is wasted in West Africa.

3 The rationale of the multiplicity of traders

The large numbers of intermediaries and links in the chain of distribution accords with expectations; and it is the result of basic underlying circumstances.

There is an extensive demand for the services of intermediaries both in the marketing of agricultural produce, whether for export or for local consumption, and in the distribution of imported merchandise. There are many people available to perform these services at a low supply price in terms of daily earnings. Few other profitable channels of employment exist, because of the relative scarcity of suitable land, technical skill and, above all, capital; and not much skill or experience is required for the simpler trading operations. Moreover, women and children are generally unoccupied because, in the towns at any rate, there are few household duties and few schools; they are thus available to act as intermediaries even for very low earnings.

The intermediaries are productive as they conserve real resources, especially capital, substituting for it semi-skilled and unskilled labour which is abundant, stimulate production, and provide employment. Their trading methods are economic in that they use resources which are redundant, and economize in the use of capital and supervisory staff for which there is a keen demand and for which there are more valuable alternative uses.

These considerations dispose of the belief that the value of agricultural or manufacturing output could be increased by compulsory reduction in the number of traders. Such measures would only serve to add to the numbers of redundant unemployed or under-employed unskilled Africans (especially women and children), and to aggravate the low level of capital and the lack of employment opportunities. The volume of production would not be increased, since the resources set free would be of the type already redundant, while the enforced adoption of uneconomic trading methods would absorb resources (notably capital) in distribution which would otherwise be available for use in agriculture and industry.

Thus it is clear that the large numbers of traders, and more especially the large number of stages in the distributive process, are not simply redundant. If the traders were superfluous, and their services unnecessary, the customers would by-pass them to save the price of their services, that is, the profit margin of the intermediaries.

The criticisms which neglect these considerations possibly derive from a confusion between technical and economic efficiency. It is true that marketing arrangements in West Africa are primitive technically when compared with those in industrialized societies. But, given the vastly different economic features of West Africa, any attempt to force marketing arrangements more closely into line with those in other societies is certain to waste resources. A set of arrangements which are economically efficient in one society will not be economically efficient in another in which the availability of resources is different. The criticisms may also partly stem from a widespread and influential desire for tidy and controllable economic arrangements; those who share this desire regard the existing unorganized and *seemingly* chaotic arrangements as irrational.

4 Inadequacy of a familiar economic generalization

The existence of numerous intermediaries and traders in West Africa conflicts with the widely held generalization in economics that a large proportion of the population engaged in the distributive trade and other service industries is associated with a high standard of living and that this proportion tends to increase with economic progress. The generalization is based on the following reasoning. Agriculture supplies the primary necessities of life, and at an early stage of development it necessarily dominates economic activity. Resources are available for manufacturing industry or trade only when a surplus has emerged over primary necessities. In particular, labour can be spared for trade only when agricultural production is more than sufficient to satisfy food requirements; with economic progress resources can be increasingly diverted into secondary and tertiary activity. This general reasoning is said to be corroborated by the available occupational statistics of many countries; those of under-developed countries purport to show that almost their entire population is engaged in agriculture.

It is clear from West African experience that the empirical generalization is invalid, since trade is a very large proportion of total activity, though this fact is obscured in the official statistics. The analytical reasoning is defective *inter alia* because it does not recognize sufficiently that certain distributive tasks are essential in the early development of an exchange economy, and that in such circumstances they tend to be expensive in terms of available resources. It also neglects the possibility of mass substitution of labour for capital in the performance of these distributive tasks.[4]

There is at least a possibility that the proportion of people engaged in trade in West Africa may actually decline with economic progress. But it is incorrect to suppose that progress could be accelerated by compulsory limitation of the number of traders; so long as trade is productive and so long as no more productive alternative employments are available for those engaged in trade, it would be wasteful to attempt to reduce their numbers.

5 Static and dynamic productivity of trade

In West Africa as elsewhere it is often believed, especially in official circles, that trade is in an important sense less productive than agriculture or industry. Even when it is conceded that some trading activity is necessary, it is frequently suggested that trading takes up too many resources, especially labour, with a consequential avoidable loss to the community. Examination of the West African economies and analysis of the role of trade do not bear out these views.

Trade is productive in what may be termed a static as well as a dynamic sense. Statically, trade conduces to the most economic deployment of available resources. In under-developed economies such as West Africa this is a difficult task, as capital (notably transport equipment and storage capacity) is scarce, distances are great, communications poor, and individual requirements and supplies are small in quantity and dispersed geographically.

Trade is also productive dynamically, that is, it promotes the growth of resources. It does so in several directions, all of which are of special importance in under-developed economies. It widens markets and thus promotes specialization and increases production, both of export crops and

4. The relation between economic progress and occupational distribution is considered at greater length in Bauer and Yamey (1951).

of produce for local consumption. It serves to bring new commodities to the notice and within the reach of actual or potential producers of cash crops, making it worth their while to produce for sale, and, at the same time, providing a market for these products. This process encourages production and the extension of capacity, more especially the extension of the acreage under cash crops. Consumers of local produce have access to larger volumes of supplies from more numerous sources, and this tends to reduce the cost of living and the severity of price fluctuations.

The accumulation of capital and its productive employment are stimulated. The larger volume of production is likely to improve the real return on capital. It also creates a surplus for accumulation. Trade also brings into prominence and influence a type of trader–entrepreneur accustomed to the ways of an exchange economy, notably the habitual and systematic use of money. These trader–entrepreneurs are more likely to accumulate savings and place them in productive employment than are other sections of the population. The services of alien traders are likely to be of particular value, because they usually possess some special managerial or technical skills, and are generally more industrious and frugal than the people among whom they work.

So ingrained is the view that trade is unproductive that no pride is taken either by the government or by the population in the development of several large centres of trade which have grown up in the last few decades under the protection of law and order. Onitsha on the Niger is a very large entrepôt market, probably the largest in West Africa. There, as elsewhere in southern Nigeria, probably the entire population is engaged in trade on at least a part-time basis; in its two large markets alone there are probably more than 6000 traders, including petty traders. In Aba the number of traders in the central market is probably of the order of 7000 or 8000. These towns are in areas which forty or fifty years ago were very backward and almost savage. A very large volume of trade passes through these centres; and this has provided inducements to many producers in the Eastern Provinces to expand the production of palm oil and palm kernels. The process has been accomplished solely by the successful establishment of law and order without any other direct intervention on the part of the administration.

6 Trader-entrepreneurs in West Africa

The rapacious and unproductive middleman in primary producing countries is often unfavourably contrasted with the allegedly more deserving farmer. This contrast is misleading. It neglects the fact that as long as entry is free the middleman is unlikely to secure an excessive income since this would quickly attract competitors. Perhaps more important, the dichotomy is a false one. More often than not the real distinction is not between the producer and the middleman, but between unenterprising, indolent, unambitious and perhaps thriftless individuals, and others more venturesome, energetic, resourceful and frugal. The small-scale produce buyer or village trader is quite often the farmer who thinks the effort worthwhile to collect and market his neighbours' produce or to cater for their simple requirements. These intermediaries are generally members or former members of the agricultural community (or are at least closely connected with it), who have improved their position through their effort, enterprise and thrift.

I have discussed their careers with many successful African traders in different parts of Nigeria and the Gold Coast. The general impression I formed was always the same: exceptional effort, foresight, resourcefulness, thrift and ability to perceive economic opportunity. A Hausa trader, who now operates on a large scale, when a child walked with his mother from northern Nigeria to the Gold Coast, where he spent some years peddling from the Northern Territories to Accra. After saving some money he engaged in the cattle trade and exported cattle from the Gold Coast to Lagos. He returned to Nigeria in 1910, and was in the north when the railway was extended to Kano. He realized that this revolutionized the prospects of the groundnut industry, for he had seen the influence of the railway on the development of the cocoa industry in the Gold Coast. He decided to set up as a groundnut buyer with an organization of sub-buyers through which he reached producers over large parts of northern Nigeria. He provided his intermediaries with cotton piece goods partly as a means for immediate purchase of groundnuts, but also to serve as inducement goods for the cultivation of groundnuts for sale. His organization has played a valuable part in the spread of the industry. Another prominent Hausa trader gave me an account of his early trading experience, and it was a remarkable story of endurance and patience, peddling and trading over enormous areas of West Africa from the French Cameroons to Sierra Leone and the French Sudan, much of it on foot.

In the Ibo country thrift, resourcefulness and foresight were the principal themes. I met in Onitsha three African ladies who have been in partnership as traders for twenty-five years. Two of them had been at school together and had attended YWCA sewing classes. In their spare time they sewed, sold cloth, saved their earnings and with their savings bought palm kernels which they sold to a European firm. Subsequently they bought merchandise, mainly textiles, from the same firm, thus trading both in produce and in merchandise. Later they withdrew from produce buying and began to deal exclusively in imported merchandise. Today their annual turnover exceeds £100,000. Several Ibo traders told me how they began trading with a few shillings or even a few pence derived from the sale of agricultural or jungle produce. They generally turned to petty trading in imported merchandise and gradually increased their capital; at the same time they slightly enlarged their still very small scale of operations. They then proceeded to rent part of a stall in Onitsha market. At the next stage they invested in a journey to Port Harcourt, Sapele, or Warri, or even Lagos, where they bought suitable merchandise, sometimes on credit, returned with it to Onitsha, and gradually increased the size and perhaps the range of their activities. With the improvement in communications between Lagos and Onitsha the more enterprising of them were able at times to turn over their capital twice a week. In practically all cases they were members of farming families.

In Lagos I met the managing proprietor of a large firm of bicycle traders, who started life as a bicycle repairer and built up his business from his savings. Another large-scale African trader who is now at the head of a substantial trading enterprise, which includes a small manufacturing subsidiary, started as a petty trader twenty years ago, reinvested most of his profits and was a man of considerable substance already by 1939. Another prominent African business man, who started his career as a trader, now controls a transport enterprise with over thirty lorries.[5]

5. The rise of these African trader–entrepreneurs is likely to promote development in the widest sense: 'The habits besides, of order, economy, and attention, to which mercantile business naturally forms a merchant, render him much fitter to execute, with profit and success, any project of improvement' (Smith, 1776, book 3, chapter 4). The importance of this in West Africa is obvious.

References

BAUER, P. T., and YAMEY, B. S. (1951), 'Economic progress and occupational distribution', *Econ. J.*, vol. 61, pp. 741–55.
SMITH, A. (1776), *Wealth of Nations*.

Further Reading

General

D. Alexander, *Retailing in England during the Industrial Revolution*, Athlone Press, 1970.

H. Barger, *Distribution's Place in the American Economy since 1867*, Princeton University Press, 1955.

K. D. George, *Productivity in Distribution*, University of Cambridge, Department of Applied Economics, Occasional Papers no. 8, 1966.

K. D. George and P. V. Hills, *Productivity and Capital Expenditure in Retailing*, University of Cambridge, Department of Applied Economics, Occasional Papers no. 16, 1968.

M. Hall, J. Knapp and C. Winsten, *Distribution in Great Britain and North America*, Oxford University Press, 1961.

B. R. Holdren, *The Structure of a Retail Market and the Market Behaviour of Retail Units*, Prentice-Hall, 1960.

S. C. Hollander, *Multinational Retailing*, Michigan State University, International Business and Economic Studies, 1970.

J. B. Jefferys, *Retail Trading in Britain 1850–1950*, Cambridge University Press, 1954.

W. G. McClelland, *Costs and Competition in Retailing*, Macmillan, 1966.

D. Schwartzman, *The Decline of Service in Retail Trade: An Analysis of the Growth of Sales per Man-hour, 1923–63*, Washington State University, 1971.

P. Scott, *Geography and Retailing*, Hutchinson, 1970.

Part One **Retail Prices and Pricing Policies**

W. J. Baumol, R. E. Quandt and H. T. Shapiro, 'Oligopoly theory and retail food pricing', *Journal of Business*, vol. 37, 1964, pp. 346–63.

D. H. Briggs and R. L. Smyth, 'Economies of scale and grocery prices in Western Australia', *Economic Record*, vol. 41, 1965, pp. 248–53.

R. Cassady, Jnr, 'The New York department store price war of 1951: a microeconomic analysis', *The Journal of Marketing*, vol. 22, 1957, pp. 3–11.

N. F. Dufty, 'Retail price behaviour', *Economic Record*, vol. 39, 1963, pp. 222–30.

A. F. Jung, 'Price variations on automatic washing machines in Chicago Illinois, among different types of retail outlets – 1955 versus 1958.' *Journal of Business*, vol. 22, 1959, pp. 133–40.

D. Metcalf and C. Greenhalgh, 'Price behaviour in a retail grocery submarket', *British Journal of Marketing*, vol. 1, 1968, pp. 243–51.

K. D. Naden and G. A. Jackson, 'Prices as indicative of competition among retail food stores', *Journal of Farm Economics*, vol. 35, 1953, pp. 236–48.

Part Two Competition and Concentration

C. Fulop, *Competition for Consumers*, Allen & Unwin, 1964.

F. G. Pennance and B. S. Yamey, 'Competition in the retail grocery trade: 1850–1939', *Economica*, n.s., vol. 22, 1955, pp. 303–17.

J. Simmons, *The Changing Pattern of Retail Location*, University of Chicago, Department of Geography Research Paper 92, 1964.

Part Three Costs, Margins and Efficiency

J. Dean and R. W. James, 'The long-run behaviour of costs in a chain of shoe stores: a statistical analysis', *Studies in Business Administration*, vol. 12, 1942.

M. Hall and C. Winsten, 'The pattern of variation in retail margins', *Oxford University Bulletin of Economics and Statistics*, vol. 25, 1963, pp. 283–92.

W. G. McClelland, 'Sales per person and size in retailing: some fallacies', *Journal of Industrial Economics*, vol. 6, 1958, pp. 221–29.

W. G. McClelland, 'Economics of the supermarket', *Economic Journal*, vol. 74, 1966, pp. 132–57.

A. Plant and R. F. Fowler, 'The analysis of costs of retail distribution', *Economica*, n.s., vol. 6, 1939, pp. 121–55.

S. Pollard and J. D. Hughes, 'Costs in retail distribution in Great Britain, 1950–57', *Oxford Economic Papers*, n.s. vol. 13, 1961, pp. 166–83.

R. P. R. Tilley and R. Hicks, 'Economies of scale in supermarkets', *Journal of Industrial Economics*, vol. 19, 1970, pp. 1–5.

K. A. Tucker, 'Economies of scale in retailing: a note', *Journal of Industrial Economics*, vol. 20, 1972, pp. 291–94.

Part Four Characteristics of Retail Operations

R. W. Bacon, 'An approach to the theory of consumer shopping behaviour', *Urban Studies*, vol. 8, 1971, pp. 55–64.

N. J. Gruen and C. Gruen 'A behavioural approach to determining optimum location for the retail firm', *Land Economics*, vol. 43, 1967, pp. 329–27.

D. L. Huff, 'A probabilistic analysis of shopping centre trade areas', *Land Economics*. vol. 39, 1963, pp. 81–90.

K. Lancaster, 'A new approach to consumer theory', *Journal of Political Economy*, vol. 74, 1966, pp. 132–57.

Part Five **Other Aspects**

A. G. Dewey, *Peasant Marketing in Java*, Glencoe Press, 1962.

L. V. Hirsch, *Marketing in an Under-Developed Economy: The North Indian Sugar Industry*, Prentice-Hall, 1961.

NEDO, *The Future Pattern of Shopping*, Distributive Trades EDC, HMSO, 1971.

W. B. Reddaway, *Effects of the Selective Employment Tax: First Report: The Distributive Trades*, HMSO, 1970.

B. S. Yamey (ed.), *Resale Price Maintenance*, Weidenfeld & Nicolson, 1966.

Acknowledgements

For permission to reproduce the readings in this volume acknowledgement is made to the following:

1 University of Toronto Press
2 Macmillan Co. London
3 University of Toronto Press
4 Basil Blackwell Publisher
5 University of Chicago Press
6 Yale University Press
7 *Economica*
8 *Economica*
9 The Clarendon Press
10 *Farm Economist*
11 Macmillan Co. London and Macmillan Co. Inc
12 University of Chicago Press
13 University of Chicago Press
14 Basil Blackwell Publisher
15 The Clarendon Press
16 The Clarendon Press
17 University of Chicago Press
18 *Land Economics*
19 *Management Science*
20 Basil Blackwell Publisher
21 *Economica*
22 University of Chicago Press

Author Index

Subject Index

Penguin Modern Economics Readings

Economics of Industrial Structure
Edited by Basil S. Yamey

Industries and firms differ from one another in various structural characteristics which influence their economic performance. This volume of Readings attempts to 'explain' these differences by identifying the major forces which shape industrial structure and the circumstances in which changes occur. Many of the articles have public policy implications, while others discuss various aspects of business policy and strategy.

Part One considers factors determining size of firms such as the economies of scale, uncertainty and the problems of organizational control. Part Two examines the conditions affecting entry of new firms into industries. A detailed analysis of industrial concentration is contained in Part Three, while Parts Four and Five deal respectively with vertical integration and diversification.

Health Economics

Edited by Michael H. Cooper and Anthony J. Culyer

How much should a country spend on health services? How should its expenditure be financed? Is health expenditure an investment or is it consumption? What is the output of health-care institutions? What is the demand for health and what determines that demand? What contribution does better health make to the growth of GNP and the quality of life?

This book of Readings attempts an economic analysis of these questions. Part One contains some of the major theoretical contributions in the field, including Kenneth Arrow's classic examination of the US health-care system in relation to a hypothetically ideal market. Empirical questions such as the measurement of the contribution of health services to national output are presented in Part Two, while Part Three analyses the hospitals, with regard to costs and the maximization of utility. The last part examines the important problem of bringing concern for human lives into the decision-making process.

Money and Banking

Edited by A. A. Walters

The great economic debate between the Keynesians and the Monetarists continues. The key questions are: What is the role of money? How does the supply of money affect real output, prices, interest rates, investment and savings in the economy? Does money matter?

This book of Readings discusses these crucial questions. Part One contains an essay written 220 years ago by David Hume in which he identifies problems of monetary adjustment which are still discussed. Milton Friedman supplies the modern version of the quantity theory of money. The foundations of the Keynesian and monetary models are provided in Part Two, which also contains an examination of the empirical evidence on the demand for money in the US and the UK. Kaldor and Friedman debate the monetary mechanism in Part Three. The last Part looks at the actual methods banks use to control money supply through credit creation and bank deposits.

New Economic History

Edited by Peter Temin

The new economic history differs from the old by being rooted in classical economics (which derived generalizations from abstract propositions) rather than historical economics (which generated laws of economic behaviour from historical cases).

This book of Readings is an introduction to economic history as a form of applied neo-classical economics. Most of the articles present models of the United States in the nineteenth century and are concerned with questions of economic growth. The measurement of economic growth as well as its causes in the nineteenth century are discussed in detail in Parts One to Four. Parts Five and Six study economic institutions and their effect on the rest of the economy (e.g. Conrad and Meyer's seminal work on slavery). Assessments of government policies of economic growth are provided throughout the Readings.

International Investment

Edited by John F. Dunning

This volume gives the reader access to the main stream of research and writing on international investment since the Second World War. The emphasis is largely on direct investment, that is investment undertaken by companies in foreign ventures in which they have a controlling and managing interest.

Part One traces the growth of international capital movements from the beginning of the nineteenth century to the present day. The two main issues in the theory of foreign investment are discussed in Part Two: the effect of international capital movements on the economic welfare of importing or exporting countries and the determinants of foreign investments. Part Three analyses portfolio investment and the growth of new forms of international securities, while Part Four is devoted to the impact of foreign investment on industrial organization. Parts Five and Six deal in turn with the relationship between trade, balance of payments and foreign investment and then the latter's effect on economic development. The book ends with Harry Johnson's cogent analysis of the welfare implications of the international corporation.